Praise for Keith O'Brien's

PARADISE FALLS

"Paced like a thriller, [*Paradise Falls* is] a remarkable story of perseverance against impossible odds." —*Chicago Review of Books*

"Nearly two decades before environmental activist Erin Brockovich made headlines in California, a group of mothers on the other side of the country launched an epic battle to save their neighborhood in the shadow of Niagara Falls. Exhaustively reported and expertly told, *Paradise Falls* is the definitive, captivating account of the women who, against all odds, exposed the deadly secret of Love Canal. Keith O'Brien's latest is narrative nonfiction at its finest."

—Abbott Kahler, bestselling author of *The Ghosts of Eden Park*

"How does an environmental disaster become an inspiring tale of homemakers turned heroes? Start with Keith O'Brien, a gifted writer who expertly blends emotion and gumshoe reporting to tell the story of ordinary people who fought to save their families. *Paradise Falls* is a masterwork of narrative nonfiction."

—Mitchell Zuckoff, *New York Times* bestselling author of *Fall and Rise* and *13 Hours*

"Meticulously researched . . . gripping. . . . This authoritative book deserves a wide audience and should provoke reflection on just how much we have progressed in the forty-five years since the Love Canal disaster." —*Library Journal* (starred review)

"Riveting. . . . The text blisters with details. . . . *Paradise Falls* is a narrative resplendent with ordinary people who stood up against overwhelming odds. . . . O'Brien has accomplished an outstanding work of investigative journalism." —*Booklist* (starred review)

"Deeply reported, masterly. . . . A story [O'Brien brings] to life for a new generation. [*Paradise Falls* is] a marker we can use to measure how far we've come . . . in terms of environmental responsibility, and how far we still have to go." —*Publishers Weekly*

"Deeply researched. . . . In this work of investigative reporting, O'Brien narrates a tale of corporate malfeasance and inaction, governmental response (or lack thereof), and, above all, inspiring citizen activism in the face of harrowing circumstances. . . . A thorough retelling of an environmental tragedy and a renewed call for corporate accountability." —*Kirkus Reviews*

KEITH O'BRIEN

PARADISE FALLS

Keith O'Brien has written for *The New York Times*, *Politico*, and *The Boston Globe*. A longtime contributor to National Public Radio, he has appeared on *All Things Considered*, *Morning Edition*, and *This American Life*, among other programs. He lives in New Hampshire. Follow him on Twitter @KeithOB.

keithob.com

BOOKS BY KEITH O'BRIEN

Fly Girls: How Five Daring Women Defied All Odds and Made Aviation History

Outside Shot: Big Dreams, Hard Times, and One County's Quest for Basketball Greatness

PARADISE FALLS

PARADISE FALLS

A Deadly Secret, a Cover-Up, and the Women Who Forged the Modern Environmental Movement

KEITH O'BRIEN

VINTAGE BOOKS
A Division of Penguin Random House LLC
New York

FIRST VINTAGE BOOKS EDITION 2023

The Library of Congress has cataloged the
Pantheon edition as follows:
Name: O'Brien, Keith, [date] author.
Title: Paradise falls : the true story of an environmental catastrophe / Keith O'Brien.
Description: First edition. | New York : Pantheon Books, 2022. |
Includes bibliographical references and index.
Identifiers: LCCN 2021038250 (print) | LCCN 2021038251 (ebook)
Subjects: LCSH: Love Canal Chemical Waste Landfill (Niagara Falls, N.Y.)—History. | Chemical plants—Waste disposal—Environmental aspects—New York (State)—Niagara Falls. | Hazardous waste sites—New York (State)—Niagara Falls. | Pollution—Physiological effect—New York (State)—Niagara Falls. | Hazardous waste site remediation—New York (State)—Niagara Falls—Citizen participation.
Classification: LCC TD181.N72 N5136 2022 (print) |
LCC TD181.N72 (ebook) | DDC 363.738/40974799—dc23
LC record available at https://lccn.loc.gov/2021038250
LC ebook record available at https://lccn.loc.gov/2021038251

Vintage Books Trade Paperback ISBN: 978-0-593-31209-4
eBook ISBN: 978-0-593-31844-7

Maps on pages xiii and xv by Mapping Specialists Ltd.
Author photograph © Erik Jacobs/JacobsPhotographic
Book design by Michael Collica

vintagebooks.com

Printed in the United States of America
10 9 8 7 6 5 4 3 2 1

For the Pandemic Homeschool Kids

Anya, Finley, Freja, Graham, Hadley, Reid,

and my two favorites,

Cormac and Cal

Betwixt the Lake Ontario and Erie, there is a vast and prodigious Cadence of Water which falls down . . . This wonderful Downfall is compounded of two great Cross-streams of Water, and two Falls, with an isle sloping along the middle of it. The Waters which fall from this vast height, do foam and boil after the most hideous manner imaginable, making an outrageous Noise, more terrible than that of Thunder; for when the Wind blows from off the South, their dismal roaring may be heard above fifteen Leagues off.

—Father Louis Hennepin, a Catholic missionary and explorer, upon visiting Niagara Falls in 1679

CONTENTS

Lake Ontario
Niagara River
NEW YORK
Niagara Falls, NY
Niagara Falls
Love Canal
Grand Island
CANADA
Niagara River
Buffalo, NY
Lake Erie

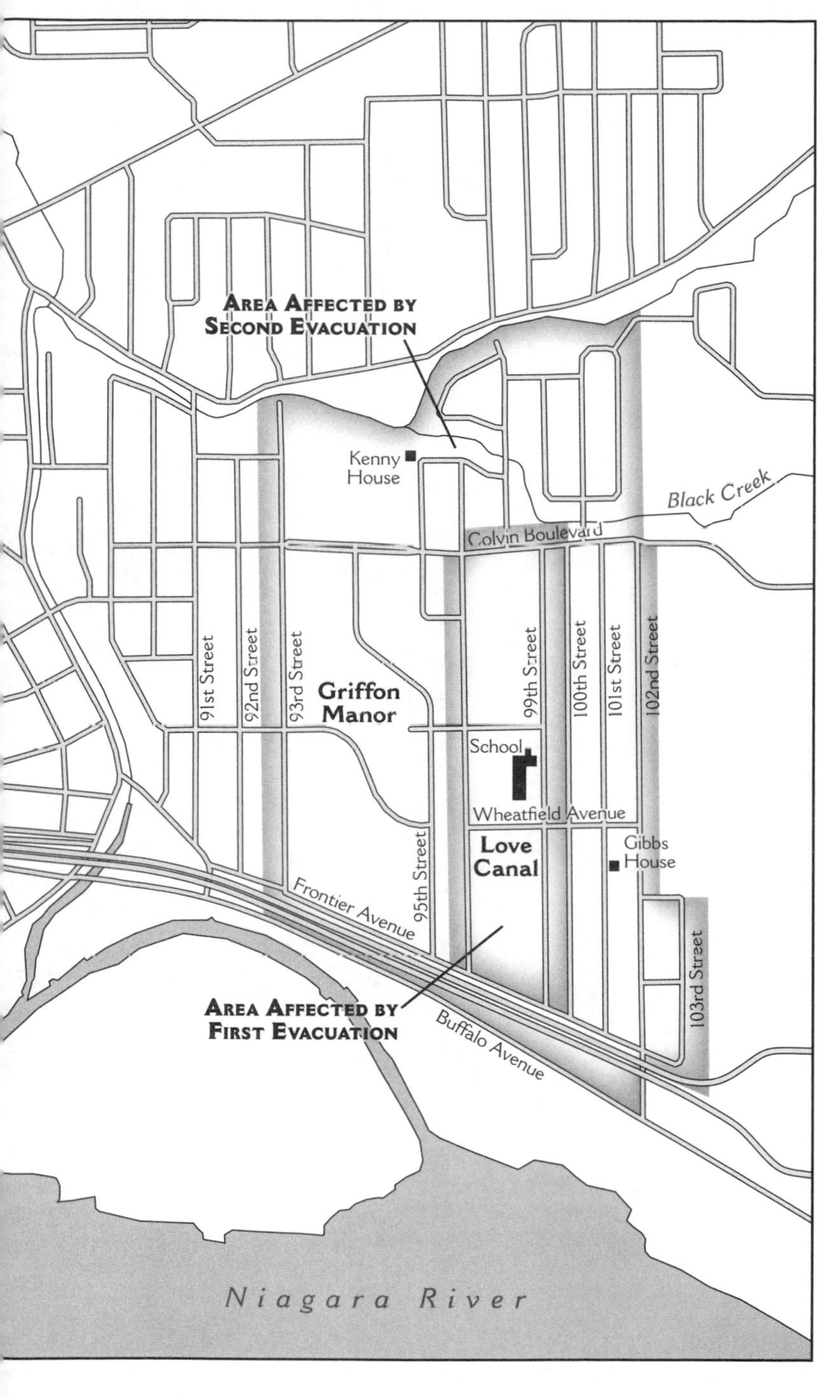
AREA AFFECTED BY
SECOND EVACUATION
Kenny House
Black Creek
Colvin Boulevard
91st Street
92nd Street
93rd Street
Griffon Manor
99th Street
100th Street
101st Street
102nd Street
School
Wheatfield Avenue
Love Canal
Gibbs House
95th Street
Frontier Avenue
103rd Street
AREA AFFECTED BY
FIRST EVACUATION
Buffalo Avenue
Niagara River

AUTHOR'S NOTE

This story is a work of nonfiction, built with the help of one hundred and thirty hours of interviews and thousands of primary-source documents never before utilized, including nearly a thousand pages obtained with a Freedom of Information request filed with the state of New York and hundreds of other important documents unearthed from boxes that had been kept in people's attics, basements, storage units, and file cabinets for decades. It takes no license with facts, characters, scenes, or chronologies. If something appears in quotation marks here, it means it is verified—taken directly from a memo, letter, journal, legal deposition, testimony, case filing, memoir, or press account—or, in rare instances, confirmed by reliable sources who took part in the conversation. Every effort has been made to portray the events as they occurred, to depict emotions as they were felt at the time, and to record them as accurately as possible—for history.

PARADISE FALLS

INTRODUCTION

MAY 14, 1972

It was a Sunday afternoon, almost summer in Niagara Falls, and the children from the little bungalows on the east side of town scampered outside to play.

The parents, mostly factory workers and housewives, didn't follow them. No adults were going to lord over the kids with rules and warnings that afternoon, because everyone knew the LaSalle neighborhood was safe and everyone knew where the kids were going. To the playground, they called it—a rectangular expanse of open land around the elementary school between Ninety-Seventh and Ninety-Ninth Streets in the heart of the neighborhood.

There were some play structures there—a swing set, a slide, and a baseball diamond, too—but mostly the grounds were wild: nearly sixteen acres of grassland, growing in clumps, untended and untamed. Parents sometimes wondered why no one had developed the property, dropped in among the tidy rows of single-story starter homes. It seemed as if someone should have built a real park there years ago. But the children asked no questions because, for them, the land was perfect. The vacant lot to end all lots. A place filled with possibility, and maybe even magic. The older boys, straddling their dirt bikes in tight shorts and white tube socks, told fantastic tales of rocks at the playground that burst into flames, that spontaneously combusted. They said they had seen it with their own eyes.

Debbie Gallo—eleven years old, with dark hair and hazel eyes—wasn't sure what to believe about the fire rocks. Her father was a welder, a son of Italian immigrants, and a Korean War veteran who walked with a limp from the shrapnel that had carved up one of his knees. The Gallos felt fortunate just to own a home in the neighborhood, and Debbie felt lucky that it was this one, on Ninety-Seventh Street. Her little one-story house, white with olive-green shutters, looked right out over the school and the empty land. She could be on the playground almost before the front door slammed behind her, skipping across the street to the open lot. On weekdays, it meant that she didn't have to walk far to get to her fifth-grade class at the school. On weekends, it meant that her front yard seemed to stretch on like the sea—forever—with friends floating everywhere, coming and going on roller skates and bicycles. This Sunday was one of those days, so Debbie laced up her shoes and headed outside.

It was warm and windy; a spring storm was coming. But Debbie and her girlfriends paid the weather—and the boys around them—no mind. While the boys churned up dust at the playground with their bicycles, clattering here and there on narrow paths carved into the high grass, the girls set about creating something pretty: sidewalk art. At their feet, they began gathering chunks of rock to use as chalk. The rocks were soft and white—"the whitest white I'd ever seen," Debbie would say later—and best of all they were easy for the girls to find amid the topsoil. Debbie took one in each hand, ran them between her fingers, and then got down on her knees to draw on the concrete.

Later, she couldn't remember how much time elapsed before her eyes began to burn. Had she been playing with the rocks for five minutes or fifteen seconds? She wasn't sure. All she knew was that rubbing her eyes only made them worse. As she pulled her hands away, the pain came on like a wave, hot and searing. Her eyes burned as if from the inside. And then she was screaming, and she was running, stumbling across the playground, trying to find her way back to her house on Ninety-Seventh Street through a haze of tears and gauzy darkness. It wasn't just the pain that worried Debbie, at this point. It was the panic growing inside her, panic over a realization that was hard to explain to her mother back at the house.

Debbie Gallo couldn't open her eyes. She couldn't see.

For one brief and scary moment, she was blind.

That night at the hospital—a short walk from the iconic waterfalls, the tourist hotels lined up along the river gorge downtown, the young newlyweds walking hand in hand in a place still clinging to its reputation as the Honeymoon Capital of the World, and the souvenir vendors selling T-shirts, tchotchkes, and picture-perfect postcards from Niagara Falls—doctors flushed out Debbie's eyes, pronounced her okay, and sent her home. The next morning, she went to school as usual.

But problems continued at the playground that Monday. Two boys, both third graders, also experienced burning around their eyes and went to see the school nurse. Someone reported the issue to the city fire department, and around 2:30 that afternoon a fire official placed a phone call—not to the school, but to a chemical plant along the Niagara River just east of the tourist district. He wanted to speak to the safety supervisor at Hooker Chemical, the largest employer and industrial taxpayer in town with a sprawling, 135-acre campus on Buffalo Avenue.

Within fifteen minutes, the head custodian for the Niagara Falls Board of Education was waiting in a car outside Hooker's main gate. The safety supervisor hopped in, and together the pair drove straight for the school, where, working efficiently, they conducted a series of interviews: with the principal, the school nurse, and Debbie Gallo, too. Hooker's safety expert then walked outside to the playground to inspect the grounds for himself.

The rains had moved in the night before, washing away Debbie's chalk art and filling the playground with puddles. But it didn't take long to find the evidence the children had reported. The safety supervisor spotted the rocks near the bicycle racks along the southern wall of the school, collected a sample, and brought it inside to the nurse—just to confirm. The nurse had not only treated the two boys that morning. By chance, she had cared for Debbie the night before in the emergency room. And when presented with the white rocks, this mushy material—whatever it was—the nurse noted that it smelled just like Debbie when she had been scared and blind and crying.

Hooker's man returned to the plant that afternoon and typed up a one-page report about what had happened that day. Across the top of the page, in large, block letters, the report was stamped "CONFIDENTIAL," though the safety supervisor made sure to send a copy to the company's insurance department—just in case. After all, it wasn't the first time Hooker had received phone calls about problems at the playground between Ninety-Seventh and Ninety-Ninth Streets, and it wouldn't be the last. Just two days later, a city health official asked Hooker's safety supervisor to return to investigate a different problem. A metal drum had surfaced this time, belching what could only be described as "rust-colored material."

For residents, these events were the latest in a litany of curious plights and odd problems. In recent years, people had reported chemical stenches in their basements; floating clouds of acidic fumes that made it hard to breathe; gas leaks that stopped traffic for hours outside the Hooker plant on the river; manhole covers that popped and blew on Buffalo Avenue, hurtling into parked cars like cast-iron Frisbees; and, yes, even rocks that could spontaneously ignite. Several years earlier, in 1966, a city official had confirmed the occurrence, warning that any child who found such a rock should not take it home, but rather submerge it in water or bury it.

The official offered this warning at the time because he understood what he was dealing with, and without question Hooker did, too. The safety supervisor believed he knew exactly what had burned little Debbie Gallo. In his report, he called it benzene hexachloride, BHC—a potent and malodorous poison exceptionally effective at killing boll weevils, spittlebugs, and other pests. It was so exceptional, in fact, that some food manufacturers refused to buy crops from farmers who used BHC in their insecticides. They thought it left an odd flavor in the food itself.

But that week in May 1972, Hooker's safety supervisor revealed little about what he knew. He couldn't say what was in the metal drum when pressed by city officials for an answer; he'd have to get back to them. And he also denied any knowledge of rocks that could burst into flames. He did, however, dutifully inform other important Hooker men about his visits to the playground that week. On Wednesday, three days after Debbie's trip to the emergency room and just hours after the discussions about the metal drum, a Hooker lawyer called a top city health official and denied any liability.

The health official on the phone found the call to be notable, because he hadn't mentioned anything about Hooker Chemical being responsible for the incidents. He just wanted to understand what Hooker knew about what was in the ground, he said, to determine if it might be harmful to people, to the kids. Yet despite the interest, the site visits, and the phone calls that week, officials in Niagara Falls kept their silence, and the residents in the neighborhood heard almost nothing about what had happened.

The incident—which had involved the city health department, the city fire department, the city board of education, the school principal, the school nurse, the hospital, children from three families, and multiple people in at least three departments at Hooker Chemical—did what incidents in the city tended to do.

It disappeared, rushing away like water over the falls.

By the end of the 1970s, that changed. Secrets, long kept in Niagara Falls, began bubbling to the surface on the east side of town, seeping into people's homes, newspaper stories, national headlines, and finally the American consciousness at large. Soon the entire country would know what had happened in this previously unremarkable suburban neighborhood until the name of the neighborhood itself became shorthand for a disaster. No one called it LaSalle anymore. Instead, people knew it as Love Canal—the name of an old, forgotten waterway buried beneath the heart of the neighborhood, a waterway systematically filled with tons of chemical waste, and then erased, as if it had never been there at all.

For decades, almost everyone ignored the problem: health officials and business leaders, the city's power brokers, and even the local press. They said little, or nothing, about the contents in the ground on the east side of town while the people living in the neighborhood, the Gallos and about a thousand other families, went about their lives, unaware of the hazards lurking just beneath their feet, their homes, the school, and the playground where their kids liked to gather. The people in power chose silence, until silence wasn't possible anymore and this issue, long buried, suddenly had the attention of *The New York Times,* all three national television networks, the governor of New York, a future vice president, and the White House, too. The president himself was calling.

The decisions made in this little window of time between 1977 and 1980 would change history, spark unprecedented federal action, launch landmark legislation, transform U.S. environmental policy forever, alter the way people thought about their own backyards, and upend the lives of thousands of people living in western New York. But none of it would have happened without a band of ordinary mothers from the neighborhood in Niagara Falls who refused to stay silent, who would not be belittled, who were willing to go to jail to save their children, and who were unafraid—even in the face of the multimillionaires running Hooker Chemical.

Working-class, just like much of the city itself, these women were neither trained nor prepared for this moment, and as a result they made mistakes along the way. They were, some officials suggested, just housewives, a term that was intended to put the women in their place and remind them that they didn't know what they were doing. But the women wore the moniker, sometimes literally, as a badge of honor.

It was true: they didn't know what they were doing. But they were about to realize that the men in power—the elected officials and corporate executives—didn't know, either. And as mothers, the women quickly discovered they had certain qualities that made them more threatening than they could have ever imagined. They knew who they were and what they wanted. They wanted to protect their children. They wanted to leave their homes on the east side of town. They wanted to walk away from the little neighborhood there—the best place they had ever lived, their corner of paradise.

At all costs, they wanted to escape Niagara Falls.

PART I

DECEMBER 1976
—
DECEMBER 1977

1

LOIS

Lois Gibbs was a sucker for Christmas decorations. Ceramic angels, miniature Santas, music boxes wired to play holiday tunes, and festive homemade crafts of every possible variety—Gibbs had it all, and each December she would lug these treasures out of storage, dust them off, and turn her small, three-bedroom home on the east side of Niagara Falls into a palace. "A Christmas palace," she called it.

Christmas that year, in 1976, was no different. After Thanksgiving, Gibbs went to work, decking her modest halls, putting up a tree, tacking lights around every window inside, and hanging the family stockings—stockings that Gibbs had sewn herself. It wasn't for her or her husband, Harry; he didn't seem to care how Lois decorated the house, as long as she had dinner on the table when he got home from his shift at the Goodyear tire factory. Gibbs did it for her children. Her son, Michael, was four years old that Christmas, and her daughter, Missy, was eighteen months, a toddler in all her glory. These were the wonder years, and Gibbs wanted to make them as enchanting as possible at Christmastime, even if the family didn't have money to buy expensive gifts or a chimney in the little house for Santa. The stockings could go by the window, and there were other ways to make the holiday special.

That fall, just before the first frost, the family planted a small fir tree in the front yard. Harry dug the hole. Lois placed the tree inside it, and then she gave her son a job. Michael would be in charge of watering the tree, she said, because he and the tree were growing up together now. Both needed to be healthy and strong.

The boy took his charge seriously, tending to the little evergreen with a watering can throughout the fall. By Christmas, it was sturdy enough to be decorated, too. Gibbs and the children hung a few ornaments on its branches, and few things brought Lois more joy that holiday than standing at the window over her kitchen sink and watching the tiny tree swaying in the snow outside.

It was more than just a tree in the yard. It was an investment, really—the first tree Lois and Harry had ever planted in front of their home at 535 101st Street.

That she had made it—that she had survived to this point—was, to Gibbs, something of a miracle. She had grown up ten miles away on Grand Island, a chunk of land dropped into the cold waters of the Niagara River rushing to the north. The island was, by most measures, a nice place to live. It was between Buffalo and Niagara Falls, but it was also carved away from the world, surrounded, as it was, by water. From the shores of the island, Lois could skip rocks at Canada, and in the summer her family flocked to swim in a crescent-shaped lagoon where they were protected from the river currents threatening to sweep swimmers away.

This danger wasn't an abstract threat. On clear days, from the northern tip of the island, residents could see the frothy mist from the iconic waterfalls, rising like a cloud just a few miles downriver, and any child growing up in the area in the 1950s and 1960s knew the stories of people who had died going over the edge in a roaring rush of water. All too many went by choice, jumping in front of crowds of horrified tourists on the esplanade downtown. But what really worried locals were the stories of freak accidents, stories of people just like them who were boating, swimming, admiring the view, or playing with friends in the river just above the falls and then were suddenly swept toward the brink by the currents.

The incidents happened in Niagara Falls with such regularity that the Maid of the Mist sightseeing boats, just below the falls, had an unofficial purpose that never made the travel brochures: the boats fished out bodies and whatever else they could find. A woman's white sneaker. A life jacket. A wallet. A paddle. But children like Lois Gibbs, growing up in the area, didn't think about any of that. Instead, if they thought about it at all, they fixated on a story of heroic pluck: a seven-year-old boy who had survived going over the falls in July 1960.

Kids knew the impossible tale of Roger Woodward, a carpenter's son from a local trailer park, as surely as they knew their own: how the small boat Roger was traveling in that day on the river had stalled, hit a rock, and capsized; how he, his teenage sister, and a forty-year-old family friend, James Honeycutt, had floated toward the 165-foot Horseshoe Falls on the Canadian side, riding the upper rapids and then the long, flat green stretch of water before the drop; how two tourists on the riverbank, acting quickly, had saved Roger's sister just twenty-five feet from the edge but had missed both Honeycutt and Roger; and how Roger had gone over the crest, watching the tourists fall away from him as he tumbled into the roar and the spray.

Honeycutt's body wouldn't turn up for days, and when it did, it was nearly half a mile downstream. But the Maid of the Mist spotted Roger just moments after he surfaced beneath the falls, dazed and scared but uninjured, *alive,* and asking just one question as deckhands pulled him to safety.

"How is my sister?" he said.

Lois was nine that summer, two years older than Roger, but like him in many ways. She had learned to swim in the river, wondering if she, too, might be lucky enough to come out unharmed. She wasn't worried about the water exactly; Lois loved swimming at the beach on Grand Island. She was concerned about what waited for her back on land: namely, her drunken father and his unpredictable, beer-fueled rages. They had grown worse after he lost his job at the Lackawanna steel plant and her youngest brother, Timmy, died in a car accident.

Her brother's death was devastating to Lois and her other four siblings. Timmy spoke with a stutter, and Lois would always remember how her father had taunted him for it, parroting the stutter back at the boy: *"W-w-what did you say?"* But in truth, the family had struggled long before the accident. Lois's parents couldn't afford to heat their little house in winter or buy new clothes for the kids before school started in the fall. At night, Lois and her sisters shivered themselves to sleep in the attic bedroom they shared, and by day they lived in hand-me-down clothes that, by middle school, made them easy targets for bullies. A home economics teacher once had Lois's older sister, Kathy, stand up in front of her class to show everyone how *not* to dress. Here, the teacher said, eyeing Kathy in her ill-fitting, mismatched blouse and skirt, was a perfect example of an improper young lady.

Quietly, the girls plotted their escape. But for Lois, the options were especially limited. She was introverted, quiet, and self-conscious about her appearance. She worried about her own mismatched clothes, her weight, or her overall look—intense, with black hair and piercing blue eyes. Also, she was a poor student. By high school, Lois was more likely to skip class to work as a cashier at the local market than she was to show up for math or English. She needed the money, she figured, more than she needed an education. Lois wanted her paychecks to buy swatches of fabric with which she sewed her own dresses, curtains, and quilts.

Sometimes, in the bedroom in the attic, she would run a hair dryer under the bedspread that she had made and then bury herself beneath it—in part to stay warm inside the freezing house and in part to go unnoticed. If her father didn't know she was there, she couldn't be a target for his anger. Like Roger Woodward, Lois was going over the edge every single day, only to survive it, surfacing after high school in the arms of Harry Gibbs.

He was a simple man, Harry, bespectacled and plainly dressed, with grease under his fingernails from tinkering with cars. But Harry was also everything Lois's father was not: kind, and generous, and gainfully employed—first as a mechanic and later as a chemical operator making tires at the Goodyear factory in Niagara Falls. Lois married him—and got pregnant with Michael—all before her twenty-first birthday, and with Harry's job at the factory they were soon able to buy the house on 101st Street in the LaSalle neighborhood east of town.

The Gibbs home was just two blocks away from the 99th Street School and the playground in the heart of the neighborhood, and Lois felt lucky to have it—so lucky that she tolerated everything else: the chemical smells that sometimes wafted through the neighborhood; the sticky residue that she'd find on Harry's car when he worked the night shift at the factory; and even the smell that clung to Harry's body sometimes after his shift was over. In bed, Harry would leave his own residue, a yellowish stain that Lois struggled to wash out of the sheets. But in a town filled with chemical plants, dotting the landscape up and down the river, this was normal. There was even a saying in Niagara Falls anytime people smelled chemicals in the air.

They'd say it was the smell of money.

2

LUELLA

Across the neighborhood—just north of the school and the playground, about a mile away, at an elbow turn on Ninety-Sixth Street—Luella Kenny felt lucky, too.

Her house there was located in a modified cul-de-sac, with a large backyard for a little redbrick house in the city. It stretched out for about half an acre, with a tidy grove of trees and wide stream at the back end of the property. Kenny loved the view of the yard from her kitchen windows; it was why she and her husband, Norman, had bought the house in the first place. But lately—if she was being honest with herself—Luella hadn't had the time to enjoy it. With three boys under the age of ten, school lunches to pack, dinners to make, Norman's heart problems to look after, two choirs to sing in on the weekends, and a demanding job as a cancer researcher in Buffalo, Kenny, it seemed, was always hustling. She was a working mother, going full tilt down the streets of the neighborhood behind the wheel of her gold Volkswagen Beetle.

With the holidays approaching in 1976, life was even busier than usual. Luella and Norman didn't just have decorations to hang and presents to buy; they juggled two worlds: one Polish and the other Italian. Christmas Eve would be celebrated the Polish way and spent at Norman's mother's house, eating fish, sauerkraut pierogi, and mushroom soup. Then the Kennys would return home to Ninety-Sixth Street and get their boys off to bed so that Luella could get to work preparing to host her side of the family the following day. This time it would be an Italian Christmas, filled with pasta, beef, cookies, cakes, red wine, and loud conversations, often led by Luella herself. To this celebration, she would invite anyone who didn't have a place to go, turning the table in their small house into a veritable banquet hall. But either way, no matter where they were, Norman would inevitably break out in song, singing Christmas carols in his beloved Polish tongue while sitting at the family's piano and beckoning for Luella to join him.

She could hardly speak her husband's language; Luella knew maybe a dozen words in Polish. But the Italian girl, born on Seventeenth Street in Niagara Falls, had learned to sing her husband's ancestral songs, in part to win his heart and in part to prove a point.

Luella Norma Mary Puccetti Kenny could sing—or do—almost anything.

From a young age, Luella had known she wasn't like the other girls in her working-class neighborhood. Luella wasn't content to be a teacher or a nurse—the only options that seemed available to a girl like her. She enjoyed science, wanted to go to college, and wouldn't let anyone push her around. When she felt that the nuns were insulting her by forcing her to copy entire chapters out of her textbook in ninth grade—a mindless task that, for Luella, wasn't at all like learning—she refused to do the work, staging her own one-girl revolt from her desk in Sister Fides's class. After school that day, there was a meeting to discuss this seditious behavior, and it wasn't long before Sister Fides was facing the wrath of Luella's mother—a turnabout that Luella quite enjoyed. The nuns had learned a lesson of their own: you didn't mess with Luella, a girl born of immigrants and grit.

Her father, Giuseppe, had come to America by ship at the age of sixteen, leaving his native Italy with just $25 in his pocket. He somehow found his way to Buffalo, where he was lucky to get a job, while Luella's mother, Jennie, was fortunate just to survive. Her first husband died after an accident at a chemical plant on the river, leaving his young widow with bills to pay. She held her husband's funeral in the small living room of their home, and the eulogies were hardly over when she began devising ways to get by without him. She rented rooms in the house, scrubbed floors, and cleaned bathrooms, and in 1936 she married Giuseppe. By then, he was working as a machinist for some of the biggest chemical plants in town, including Hooker Chemical, and he had changed his name to Joseph, to fit in with the rest of the crew. But to their daughter, born in 1937, one year after their marriage, they gave a name that, if not traditionally Italian, certainly made her stand out.

Luella went to college—just as she had planned—attending Niagara University and majoring in the natural sciences. She was a rare woman sitting among men, and upon graduation in 1958 she continued to distinguish herself. Over the objections of a human resource officer who didn't want to hire a woman, Luella caught on as a researcher studying new chemotherapy drugs at a state research institute affiliated with the University at Buffalo—a place called Roswell Park.

Around the labs there, word soon got around that the new hire, the Puccetti girl, was driving in from Niagara Falls every day, was willing to carpool, and had room in her Mercury sedan for one more. One day, Norman Kenny, a fellow researcher at Roswell Park, asked if he could have the last seat, and Luella said that would be fine. She and Norman lived just a mile apart. The only problem, Luella explained, would be Mondays and Fridays. Her car was already full then—on account of a handful of nuns whom Luella drove into the city. On those days, she explained, Norman would have to take the bus.

Norman wasn't banished to public transportation for very long. Luella found him to be handsome, wearing fashionable clothes and horn-rimmed glasses, and they quickly learned that they had one important thing in common: they both loved to sing. Luella was in her church choir and Norman was part of a Polish group, and soon each was singing with the other on the weekends. Luella loved Norman's tenor voice and the way he serenaded her. There was one song, in particular, that Norman liked to sing to Luella. It was a Polish polka about a man squandering his life—the hours, the days, the years.

Luella didn't understand the words in Polish. But the way Norman sang it, she felt the song's meaning in her bones.

They didn't have much time.

Luella and Norman got married in June 1964 at the church just behind the school where Luella had once defied Sister Fides. The church was in the Italian part of town and attended almost exclusively by Italians—a concession, to be sure, for Norman's family, who attended church at St. Stanislaus, the Polish parish about a mile away. But the reception, held at an Italian restaurant, featured a Polish orchestra, Polish dancing, and even Polish food, bringing five hundred Italians and Poles together, the way weddings often did in Niagara Falls. The young couple quickly had three boys—Christopher, Stephen, and the youngest, Jon Allen—and they were all thrilled when they found the home on Ninety-Sixth Street east of town, a home they could afford.

The house there was small, with three bedrooms; Stephen and Jon Allen would have to share a room across the hall from their parents. But the home was set back from the road in the modified cul-de-sac where Ninety-Sixth Street made a hard turn, and the real selling point was the sprawling yard with the stream out back—Black Creek. In summer, when the water was running, the Kenny boys would splash and play in it. In winter, when it froze over, they would go sledding off the banks, careening down onto the ice. No matter the season, Luella liked to watch her boys playing from the window over her kitchen sink, their little bodies casting long shadows in the twilight before dinner.

In moments like these, Luella Kenny could hardly believe her good fortune. It was as if all her dreams had come true, all her Catholic school prayers had been answered. But not long after Christmas 1976, her youngest son, Jon Allen, always sensitive and thinking of others, began to grow anxious. The five-year-old boy—with dark eyes and dark hair, just like Luella—knew his mother was about to turn forty, and he begged her not to have a birthday that year. He didn't want her to get sick and die.

Luella smiled at her little boy. She was almost forty now—it was true. She wore round glasses, and if people looked close enough they would see that strands of her dark hair were beginning to fade to silver. But the Puccetti blood ran strong with her. Her immigrant father had lived into his seventies, and her mother was still living downtown. Luella wasn't going anywhere. Like any good parent, she told Jon Allen not to worry.

—

The weather was brutal at Christmas 1976—even by Niagara Falls standards. By the holiday, the area had already recorded nearly five feet of snow, and residents had endured the coldest December in nearly two decades. Winds howled off Lake Ontario. Temperatures plummeted into the single digits at night. The first ice bridge of the season formed across the Niagara River gorge a full week before New Year's Eve. Snow piled up in drifts, and then it got worse.

The day after Christmas, a cold front spun across the northern plains, packing thirty-mile-per-hour winds and a blinding squall that buried parts of western New York under another foot of snow. The first week of January 1977, forecasters called for snow every day. The following Monday, a ferocious blizzard slammed into the city, dumping yet another foot of snow on Niagara Falls. Local weather stations reported temperature readings of minus eleven, minus twelve, and minus seventeen, and then it hit: the Blizzard of 1977, a once-in-a-lifetime storm that stranded thousands of people, crippled the city for days, whipped up the snowpack already on the ground into towering drifts deep enough to bury entire houses, hammered the region with still more snow, and then froze everything in place, encrusting the world under a thick layer of ice.

On the east side of Niagara Falls, it took months for all the snow to melt. Day after day and week after week, the season's record snows—almost seventeen feet in all—seeped into the ground, dripping away until the dreadful winter was but a memory and spring thankfully took hold. But by May 1, 1977, people living closest to the playground between Ninety-Seventh and Ninety-Ninth Streets had a different problem. Families were reporting pungent odors in their basements.

It was a new scent, this odor, and yet one that was totally familiar. Mothers there had been smelling it in the breeze—and on their husbands' clothes after their factory shifts—for years. It was the sickly sweet, unmistakable smell of chemicals, and it seemed to be coming from underground.

3

ENERGETIC, EFFECTIVE, EXPERIENCED—LAFALCE!

The telephone rang at Bonnie Casper's desk in Washington, D.C., sometime near the end of June 1977, and the man on the other end of the line introduced himself as Joseph McDougall. McDougall was a newly hired microbiologist working for the city of Niagara Falls, and he wanted to inform Casper that he was coming to Washington, along with a consultant, on the last day of the month to testify at an obscure hearing at the Environmental Protection Agency. McDougall didn't know Casper, and Casper didn't know him or the consultant with whom he was traveling. But McDougall had been told that Casper was the sort of person in Washington who could help a small-time official like him, and he was hoping she would agree to meet him and the consultant for lunch on their visit to the nation's capital. McDougall needed help and federal funding—maybe a lot of it—yet there was something in it for Casper, too. She was going to want to hear what he had to say. Also, the consultant was buying.

Casper agreed to the meeting with McDougall, hung up the phone, and didn't think anything about it. As an aide to Congressman John LaFalce—the man representing New York's Thirty-Sixth Congressional District—Casper was always meeting with someone from the suburbs north of Buffalo, the rural communities on Lake Ontario, LaFalce's hometown of Tonawanda, or Niagara Falls itself, the biggest city in his district. It was her job to keep local officials happy and make sure they thought highly of the congressman, and she did it well. But there was possibly another reason why she didn't take special note of McDougall's call. It had been a stressful year.

At home—in her apartment near the Capitol—Casper's marriage

was falling apart. She was thirty, newly separated from her husband, and careening toward divorce. Meanwhile, she was giving everything to her job, in part because she loved it and in part because she felt as if she had no other choice. LaFalce (pronounced La-FALSE) had won his seat two years earlier riding a wave of anti-Nixon, post-Watergate sentiment to Washington. But reelection the previous fall had been trickier. Casper's boss had run with three strikes against him.

For starters, the thirty-seven-year-old former lawyer was unmarried—always a political handicap, but especially challenging in the 1970s, when politicians in places like Niagara Falls were expected to show they held traditional values. Without a wife on his arm to smile and warm up the crowd, LaFalce had to appear at events on his own, wearing his political uniform: a suit, a tie, and thick horn-rimmed glasses that made him look like Clark Kent, only shorter, stockier, and without the hidden red cape. Indeed, LaFalce looked so much like Superman's bumbling alter ego that staffers around the office called him Clark Kent behind his back.

His second problem was experience, or a lack thereof. He might have been the incumbent, but at that time he was still a first-termer with a thin political résumé after two years on the House banking and small business committees—committees that rarely made headlines. And finally, most difficult to overcome, LaFalce was a Democrat—the first liberal congressman to carry Niagara Falls since the Taft administration. The idea that he might replicate that feat in 1976 had left him worried enough that he refused to buy a home in Washington throughout his first term. He'd rent, and he knew he'd have to outwork his Republican opponent in his reelection campaign by employing the strategy that had gotten him elected in the first place: "Meet the maximum number of people in the minimum amount of time."

Casper—short and petite, at just five feet three—didn't seem like the kind of person who could push LaFalce over the top. She was from Wilkes-Barre, Pennsylvania, not Niagara Falls. Her previous jobs had included teaching English in Ecuador and writing for an alternative newspaper in Vermont, and even now, as an aide to the congressman, she had no political clout. Casper didn't even have her own working typewriter. In LaFalce's fourth-floor office across the street from the Capitol, she and another aide took turns sharing the one machine that had self-correcting tape, making typos easy to fix.

Still, Casper, a student of politics, was thrilled to be there. While other girls had grown up reading Nancy Drew mysteries—or, later, *Cosmopolitan*—Casper tore through Theodore White's groundbreaking nonfiction books about presidential campaigns, *The Making of the President,* published throughout the 1960s and into the 1970s. She attended college at George Washington University less than a mile from the White House. She covered the 1968 Democratic National Convention in Chicago for a radio station back home. She wore a black armband at graduation in 1970 to honor the students gunned down at Kent State that spring—to the horror of her far less radical parents. She marched against the war in Vietnam, and she was generally pretty sure that she was going to change the world.

LaFalce was all for that—as long as he was able to carry the blue-collar vote in Niagara County in 1976. And so, in the final month of the campaign that season, he summoned everyone he could to Niagara Falls, including Casper. It was her job to drive him where he needed to go, hand out campaign flyers, record the names of everyone he met on small note cards, and then get him out of the room as quickly as possible, hustling him off to the next event with apologies, while the candidate himself shook hands all the way out the door.

"Energetic . . . Effective . . . Experienced!" his signs said. *"LAFALCE."*

Casper was a natural at all of it. A tireless worker and a talker, she made sure LaFalce was outside the chemical plants on the river between five and nine every morning to catch the overnight shift workers going home. Then, between five and midnight every night, she got him to the bingo halls, the grocery store parking lots, and the bowling alleys. LaFalce took pride in knowing the schedule of every bowling league in the district, and he wanted to hit them all—even if that meant diving into a drunken crowd on Halloween, with Casper at his side.

In the end, the election wasn't even close. LaFalce won two-thirds of the vote that November, returned to Washington in 1977 confident enough to buy a condo on Fourth and O Streets, and even earned a subcommittee chairmanship in the new Congress. He was *presiding*—a second-term, no-joke, owns-his-own-condo congressman *presiding* in Washington on the House subcommittee for small business development. "Gentlemen," he said that spring in the hearing rooms of the Rayburn House Office Building, "the subcommittee will come to order."

The only things that hadn't changed were the issues he was handling. They were either unobjectionable and boring (LaFalce wanted companies to hire more elderly workers) or difficult to understand (LaFalce wanted to hold hearings on liability insurance). The Blizzard of 1977 helped give him the visibility he needed. Reporters followed LaFalce as he toured houses in the district buried in eighteen-foot snowdrifts. And there was one other issue getting headlines back in Niagara Falls in the spring of that year that put LaFalce in the news. State officials had banned fishing in Lake Ontario while they investigated the mysterious presence of a potent poison in the lake and, also, the Niagara River.

The poison, called Mirex, was well known down south. Farmers there had used it for years to kill the pest that they loathed the most: the fire ant. They sprinkled Mirex by the teaspoon onto teeming mounds of ants. They spread it like fertilizer in their fields, three to five pounds per acre, or they watched low-flying vintage World War II aircraft—B-17s and B-25s—drop Mirex pellets from the sky. The concoction—an alluring mix of corncob grits, soybean oil, and poison—fell like rain across the South until it got into everything: the water, the crawfish, the crabs, the shrimp, and even the people. But the insecticide had no business being within seven hundred miles of Niagara Falls—except maybe one: Hooker Chemical, the large employer and community leader in the heart of John LaFalce's district.

As recently as 1975, Hooker had made Mirex, processed it, ground it into a powder at the factory along the river in Niagara Falls, and sold it by the ton. The insecticide was now leaching into the river, officials said, straight out of Hooker's outfall pipes—almost a pound of Mirex every day—a residual but troubling amount that LaFalce was investigating in the spring of 1977.

Perhaps that was why Joseph McDougall was calling Bonnie Casper in June of that year. As a microbiologist, McDougall oversaw the city's new wastewater treatment laboratory. It was his job to analyze the wastewater discharges coming from Hooker and the other large chemical plants lined up along the river. In the city of Niagara Falls, McDougall would have understood the situation better than almost anyone.

Perhaps he was coming to Washington to discuss the Mirex problem.

It was a beautiful day for a lunch in the nation's capital, when McDougall arrived in late June, flying in with the consultant—an environmental engineer named Richard Leonard. Blue skies stretched across the city, and interns gathered outside to take their lunches lounging in the sun. But by late morning, McDougall and Leonard were in a sour mood, moving with a sense of urgency and even desperation.

The two men could speak at length about water quality, the soils of western New York, or the public health dangers posed by, say, copper smelting. Yet they were lost amid federal bureaucracy, and they had completely misjudged the purpose of the EPA hearing they had flown in to attend that morning. The agents running the hearing didn't want to hear about specific problems from a specific place—like Niagara Falls. They were there to take general testimony regarding proposed grant regulations to a new law—whatever that meant—and they dismissed McDougall, even though he was the first official to approach the microphone and speak.

At lunch with Casper near the Capitol, McDougall and Leonard were intent not to be rejected again, and they got straight to the point. They weren't there to discuss Mirex, fire ants, insecticides, or problems with the water in Niagara Falls, although there were many. They had a different issue, they explained, involving Hooker Chemical, and this one was potentially more dangerous than Mirex and bigger than anyone knew.

They had reports of rusted chemical drums surfacing and rupturing on the east side of town, and they believed that other drums were buried in the ground. Lots of them, probably—with contents unknown. Hooker either couldn't or wouldn't say what was there. McDougall and others were still trying to find out. In the meantime, the most important information was this: the old chemical dump was now a school and a playground—in the middle of a residential neighborhood—and preliminary testing there had indicated the presence of toxic compounds.

"We have a real problem," McDougall said that day in Washington. "A severe health and economic problem."

But he was getting ahead of himself. McDougall needed to stop and go back. Casper wasn't from Niagara Falls. She didn't know the history, the land, or the particulars of this rectangular parcel where the children liked to play. He needed to ask her a question.

Had she ever heard of a place called Love Canal?

4

A MODEL CITY

William T. Love first laid eyes on the pristine farmland east of the falls in the spring of 1892, and the bearded prospector with grand visions and a shady past immediately pronounced it good.

Love said he'd been traveling around the country for six years seeking a spot like this one. Said his travels had brought him far and wide, from the wilds of Oklahoma to the new industrial cities springing up across the North. Now, on the river just outside Niagara Falls, he had found it: the ideal location for his utopian town.

He was calling it Model City.

Love's plan was very exciting. The city, he said, would be unequaled in beauty. As such, there would be no tenement housing, no streets strewn with trash, and no saloons. Instead, there would be schools, parks with pavilions, wide boulevards laid out in an organized grid, decorative water fountains at every major intersection, and nice homes for every family because, in Model City, everyone would own a home. Everyone would have a job.

Love—then thirty-six years old, with eyes like weathered pennies—had done his research. He knew the region had a nearly inexhaustible supply of building materials: sand, clay, lumber, and limestone. He knew that nearly two million people lived within a hundred miles of the falls. He knew that these people could easily reach Model City by railroad, and he also knew that the city's products could just as easily reach the world—on the railroad lines out of Buffalo, twenty miles away. But the key to Love's entire plan was water. He wanted to build a canal that would divert the Niagara River, just east of the falls in a rural hamlet called LaSalle, and channel it several miles north to the edge of a natural escarpment. From there, the flow of the water in the canal would rush down, connecting with the river north of the great waterfall and allowing Love to generate a seemingly endless supply of electricity.

Locals knew it was possible, and geologists agreed that it could create "the greatest water power on earth." Indeed, they had been talking about a canal like this one for years. Love was just going to finally make it happen with his usual flair and bombast.

"We are going to succeed," he vowed.

There was just one reason why no one had ever dug the eleven-mile canal in question: the work was backbreaking and expensive. Even under the best conditions, it might take crews two years to dig out the canal at a cost of $2.5 million.* That was a lot of money in the 1890s, and it was an almost impossible sum to give to a big-talking promoter like Love who had effectively shown up in New York just yesterday. The truth was, lawmakers in Albany, who needed to approve the Model City proposal, knew almost nothing about him.

Still, they voted in favor of his proposal. William T. Love—a man with no discernible past—was entitled to build his city, and dig his canal, and divert as much water from Niagara Falls as he needed. By almost sheer accident, in a matter of months, Love had become one of the most powerful people in the entire state of New York.

Two large steam shovels were among the first purchases that Love made, and the sight of them rumbling across the earth in LaSalle inspired people. To celebrate, they attended banquets and balls, gave speeches and toasts, and gathered in large numbers to mark each sign of progress: the first road going in, the first railroad stop in town, and the first day excavating the canal. The channel was going to be eighty feet wide at the top and forty feet wide at the bottom and filled with enough water to swallow a three-story building—a marvel of modern infrastructure that was worthy of cheering and even a song, set to the tune of "Yankee Doodle Dandy":

* In today's money, the construction of the canal would have cost roughly $70 million.

They're building now a great big ditch
Through dirt and rock so gritty
They say 'twill make all very rich
Who live in Model City.

But what they didn't know about Love would have filled the ditch itself. He was said to be a mighty town builder from the West and credited with settling Guthrie, Oklahoma, in the epic land run of 1889, when some fifteen thousand people moved into that community in a single day. Yet Love was likely in Guthrie as a speculator himself. He doesn't seem to have built anything there, and, whatever happened in Guthrie, Love didn't stick around. Within five days of the land run, he was back in the dusty frontier outpost he called home, a town called Huron on a wild prairie soon to be known as South Dakota.

Love was also said to be an important railroad man, and he was once. Sort of. In the 1880s, he bought and ran the small streetcar line in Huron. But he had sold it—and everything else he owned there—years earlier to move to Tennessee and build a different town. "One of the greatest enterprises ever organized in the South," the newspapers called it at the time. Only that never happened, either. The great town in Tennessee never materialized, and Love moved on yet again, leaving local reporters to come to only one conclusion: "Love has had a very checkered career in this line." And predictably, perhaps, it ended the exact same way in New York.

By the mid-1890s, the singing had stopped in Model City, and the construction had ended, too. The national economy had tanked. Landowners refused to sell to Love, and the steam shovels had long fallen silent, rusting in the snow on the riverbanks in LaSalle. The only visitors to Model City now were curious reporters and bill collectors, looking for Love to pay off his debts, of which there were many. And to get his attention, the sheriff finally had to resort to drastic measures against a previously celebrated man. The sheriff seized Love's steam shovels and placed liens on the machinery in July 1896. "Mr. Love might pay the amount covered by them," the sheriff advised, "and thereby save me from selling the property."

But it was like negotiating with a shadow. By then, Love was nowhere to be found. He was sailing to London. He was on his way to Paris. He was headed to western Ontario with a band of new investors in search of gold. He was on the move again, abandoning Model City and its partially built canal right where it stood on the river east of Niagara Falls.

"The big ditch at LaSalle," one witness said in late 1896, "is full of water."

Water that was going nowhere until Hooker Chemical expressed an interest.

The company was a fixture in Niagara Falls, deeply entrenched in the city and connected in all the places that mattered most. Hooker men—and they were always men—often descended from true Yankee blood, graduated from Ivy League schools, ran the local community chest, entertained at the Niagara Falls Country Club, sailed on Saturdays out of the Youngstown Yacht Club, and attended Presbyterian services in the suburbs the next morning with their wives and children.

In this way, the executives were a reflection of the company's namesake, Elon Hooker, who had founded the chemical outfit on the shores of the Niagara River in 1905, arriving almost as soon as William T. Love disappeared, with everything Love had lacked: money and connections. Hooker was a direct descendant of a religious dissident who had sailed to the New World from England in 1633 and started a colony of his own: Connecticut. That sort of rarefied Puritan lineage opened doors for Hooker that remained closed for most, and his chiseled good looks, Cornell University education, and friendship with Teddy Roosevelt didn't hurt, either.

But it was Elon Hooker's business sense, more than anything, that helped the man build a chemical empire in Niagara Falls and earned him a nickname: the "Poison Gas King" of America. Long before most, Hooker understood that chemicals were the future. They would help make almost everything we used in daily life, and he wanted to make sure he, Elon Hooker, would be there to give the people what they needed: sodium sulfide for shoe leather, monochlorotoluene for motor lubricants, aluminum chloride for high-octane gasoline, and thionyl chloride—for America and its allies during World War I. The volatile chemical agent—and Hooker product—was used to make mustard gas.

By his death in 1938, Hooker had made a fortune from it all at the factory along the river in Niagara Falls. He was worth more than $600,000,* and his company was still growing, making others rich, too. Hooker men were now manufacturing a hundred different chemicals a year, and with another war looming on the horizon, they were prepared to make them even faster, ready to create what they were calling an "Arsenal for Democracy." There were only two problems. The chemicals were often known irritants that could be fatal, cause nausea and vomiting, or burn employees' skin, eyes, and lungs through spillage, steam, or other mishaps. And the company was manufacturing these products so quickly executives needed a place to store the excess, the waste, the chemical residues.

Hooker needed a proper dump.

In 1941, the new Hooker man in charge—a Dartmouth graduate and a descendant of a signer of the Declaration of Independence—set his sights on buying Love's abandoned canal just a few miles upriver. The big trench looked almost the way it did when Love had skipped town nearly fifty years earlier in the mid-1890s. It was about half a mile long, a hundred feet wide, hemmed off from the river itself by a thick earthen dam, sliced up by a number of dikes that helped form deep pools of impounded water, surrounded by fifteen-foot dirt walls left over from the excavation itself, and just sort of sitting there. A local power company owned the land, but it was unused, and by the spring of 1942 the two parties had worked out an agreement for Hooker to utilize the land "as a waste disposal area."

For roughly the next decade, Hooker trucks routinely made the short drive up the river to deliver drums to the old canal, drums filled with all sorts of material. Highly reactive acids—which, at some concentrations, could cause breathing problems and nerve

* In today's money, Hooker would have left the equivalent of more than $10 million to his wife and four daughters.

damage—went there. Potent pesticides, like benzene hexachloride, did, too. Even residues of thionyl chloride—the foundation for Hooker's famous poison gases, clear or pale yellow, with a sharp, irritating odor—ended up in the canal. "A mixture of all kinds of things," as one Hooker executive said later. "Who knows what?"

Employees sometimes stood at the edge of the hole in the ground and marveled at the sight down below: drums piled on top of drums, on their ends and on their sides. A mess. But the company claimed it was taking the necessary precautions. During the day, Hooker posted a guard at the canal—just in case a fire broke out. He stood at the ready, with a fire hose attached to a city water source, while other employees arrived in trucks that dumped the fifty-five-gallon drums into the ground. They buried them anywhere from six to thirty feet beneath the surface. They dammed off the canal to try to prevent the seepage of chemicals. They erected an eight-foot barbed-wire fence around some portions of the dump to keep out trespassers, and they established a system for disposing of one element in particular: the thionyl chloride.

This particular chemical was known to react violently with water. If left enclosed in the drum, it could explode or catch fire as water inevitably trickled in over time. To avoid that, the Hooker employees delivering the thionyl chloride punctured the drums before dropping them in the water, watching them smoke and bubble and hoping that the wind was blowing away from them. It was an arduous task, given the volume. During peak production years in the 1940s, Hooker employees might come in on a Monday to find three hundred drums filled with thionyl chloride waste—lined up and ready to go to the canal. But at least the workers got a little recognition every now and then. On one memorable occasion, Hooker men from the corporate office came out to watch, serving the laborers coffee and doughnuts while the drums disappeared into the ground.

In 1946, one Hooker lawyer began to worry. At times, the lawyer noted, the surface of the water in the old canal shimmered with a sheen of oil, dotted with globs of congealed residue. He didn't need to be a scientist to know that such a place could cause damage—"serious damage," he called it—and he urged executives at the company to consider that they were exposing people to potential dangers and exposing themselves to liability.

"I feel very strongly that if this water is contaminated as a result of our dumping chemical residues," the lawyer said, "we are running a real hazard."

He was concerned about people who still swam in the canal, unaware of what Hooker was doing, and he was worried, too, about children. They showed up from time to time, wearing swimsuits or just poking around, drawn to the curious landscape. Yet the dumping continued into the early 1950s, creating its problems and also an opportunity. Hooker still owned the dump in March 1952 when the city's superintendent of schools called to make the company an offer. He wanted to build a large school in LaSalle, to accommodate the families moving east, out of town, and he wanted to buy the property that Hooker used as a landfill.

Executives initially declined. The company was now publicly traded, with two thousand employees, $36 million in annual sales, shareholders to consider, and an even brighter future ahead. In the late 1960s, the corporate behemoth Occidental Petroleum would buy the company, making Hooker a profitable subsidiary of one of America's largest petrochemical companies.

More important, the land wasn't suitable for a school.

"It's not like a city garbage dump," one executive said. "These are chemicals and some of them last a long time . . . No way."

But over the course of the spring of 1952, Hooker executives began to come around on the idea—at least, in part, for one reason. "The Love Canal property," one executive said, "is rapidly becoming a liability because of housing projects in the near vicinity." And by the following year, 1953, Hooker agreed to sell the land to the board of education for a dollar. There was just one caveat: the company wouldn't be liable for any future damages that the chemicals might cause. The two parties acknowledged that the land had been filled "in whole or in part" with "waste products," and if these products were ever to cause injury or death, "no claim, suit, action, or demand of any nature whatsoever" could be made against Hooker. Company executives wrote it into the deed—signed April 28, 1953—and then walked away.

They were out of the Love Canal business. It was the city's problem now.

5

WE SHOULD AT LEAST VISIT THE PLACE

The first time that the city's microbiologist Joseph McDougall heard this story—the story of Love's canal—he was sitting in a closed-door meeting with other city officials, and he was struck by several things. First, at the mere mention of the issue, a representative for the board of education left the room; he didn't want to discuss the problem, because the schools didn't have money to deal with it. Second, a city attorney questioned whether Niagara Falls was even liable for the problems on the east side of town—apparently unaware of the Love Canal deed signed in 1953 or hoping to shift the blame back to the board of education. And finally, McDougall thought of his own life, his childhood in western New York in the 1940s, and a memory that he had never totally understood until now. As a boy, he had played in the canal. He had swum in the water.

McDougall—tall and slender, with a shock of auburn hair—had been raised on a farm northeast of Niagara Falls and just south of that mythical place called Model City. There were no wide boulevards laid out in an organized grid and no decorative water fountains at major intersections. There were hardly any intersections at all, and there was definitely no town. Model City was just a name on a map, left over from a bygone time.

But near his home, McDougall had swum, played, and caught frogs in a pond that appeared to be man-made. It was surrounded by strangely tall and lumpy walls—the kinds of walls that steam shovels might leave behind, especially if they suddenly just stopped one day and never returned. Now it all made sense to him. As McDougall listened to the men around him speak, he realized that his own childhood playground had been part of William T. Love's abandoned dream. He had swum in the northern end of the canal, in a short channel that Hooker Chemical had never owned—a channel not connected with the waterway in LaSalle.

In this way, McDougall had been fortunate. But it was hard to feel that way now as he related the whole Love Canal story to Bonnie Casper over lunch in Washington and begged her to help him find $400,000 so the city could study the problem and better understand what was in the ground. He asked her to come to Niagara Falls and see it for herself.

"I invite both you and Mr. LaFalce to meet with representatives of the city," McDougall said, "and to personally tour the Love Canal landfill site."

Back at LaFalce's office that afternoon, Casper sat down at her desk, slipped a sheet of paper into her typewriter, and began to bang away at the keys, writing up a report to brief the congressman about everything she had learned from McDougall and the consultant Richard Leonard over lunch.

"According to these gentlemen," she wrote, "there is a terrible problem in N.F. in the LaSalle area . . . an old dump site, about 30 years old, which was Hooker's, where material was buried in drums . . . The drums have corroded, and surfaced, and just to touch the ground one can get a chemical burn . . . It is also within a school playground."

Casper told LaFalce he should consider seeing Love Canal for himself during the August recess and until then he needed to push for funding from the EPA to help cover the $400,000 the city needed to further investigate the matter. On the latter front, anyway, LaFalce went straight to work. He sent a letter the very next day to Doug Costle, the EPA's newly appointed director, asking for answers and money. For weeks, LaFalce got no reply, and Casper didn't fare any better, despite the long hours she began dedicating to the issue. She had lengthy conversations with people she knew at the EPA's regional office in New York City, and she spent entire weekends in Washington reading every piece of environmental legislation she could find, in search of a clause she could exploit to get the city the money it needed. Still, Casper came up with nothing. By the recess that August, it was pretty clear to both Casper and LaFalce that no one was interested in volunteering a big chunk of money to learn what was buried in an old canal in a neighborhood that few ever visited—and no one had ever heard of—several miles from the tourist district in Niagara Falls. LaFalce himself even seemed to lose interest in visiting the site. For the entire month of August, he failed to schedule a tour, planning to put it off until September or maybe even later in the fall.

But Casper refused to let it go. Throughout the summer of 1977, she kept talking to the EPA, looking for funding, and reminding LaFalce that it was important for him to visit the neighborhood. "When you have a chance," she prodded him, gently questioning his hesitancy to go out there. "Do you still want to wait until September?"

Meanwhile, in Niagara Falls, McDougall got angry. On the Thursday before Labor Day weekend—a full month after Congress had gone home for the summer recess and just a few days before LaFalce was to return to Washington—McDougall left a message for the congressman with one of the young staffers in LaFalce's Niagara Falls office. McDougall was tired of waiting, and he wanted LaFalce to come to the neighborhood now—over the holiday weekend.

Becky Muscoreil, a thirty-year-old staffer and former librarian, delivered the message to LaFalce. Still, the congressman wouldn't budge. A visit, LaFalce said, would probably have to wait for November, and at that point McDougall lost his patience. He told Muscoreil, now stuck in the middle between the two men, that there was no point in the congressman's visiting the canal if he was going to wait that long. Didn't LaFalce understand the situation?

"It is imperative and urgent," McDougall said, "that he come immediately."

By the time LaFalce received the second message, he had already returned to Washington—still another reason for McDougall to be frustrated. *"McDougall upset,"* Casper wrote in the margins of the note that Muscoreil faxed to the Capitol, and Casper could certainly understand why. McDougall had come to Washington to get help. He hadn't gotten anywhere at the EPA hearing, and here he was again, shouting into the void. But Casper could also appreciate why LaFalce might be hesitant to make a visit. No one—not even McDougall—knew how big the problem really was. If the chemicals weren't in the school or the houses on the east side of town, maybe it didn't warrant a visit from the congressman. LaFalce could let local officials handle it. On the other hand, if the situation was as bad as McDougall feared, that could pose a different challenge for LaFalce. He didn't have a solution. He hadn't secured a single dollar in funding to study the site, despite two months of trying, and Casper, being honest with her boss, wasn't confident they were going to find funding anytime soon. "I'm not sure," she admitted to LaFalce, "how we can get the money for them."

But in Casper's opinion, none of that mattered. He needed to go out there, she told him. He needed to visit the site as soon as he could—perhaps on a Saturday when he was back in the district. The sooner the better. And to make sure LaFalce understood she was serious, Casper underlined her conclusion in a memo to him the week he returned to Washington in early September. "I think this is an issue that we could do something about," she told LaFalce. "We should at least visit the place with appropriate officials to let them know that we are trying."

For what it was worth, Muscoreil agreed with Casper. She was getting calls not just from McDougall now, but from residents. A chorus of complaints was building, and Muscoreil decided it was time for her to intervene, too. That Friday evening, when LaFalce returned to the district, she walked into his office above the post office in Niagara Falls. LaFalce was sitting with Rich Lee, his top aide on the ground in the city. The two men were talking about his schedule for the next day and about to leave for the night. But Muscoreil wouldn't let LaFalce go until he agreed to add one more item to his weekend itinerary.

He needed to visit the neighborhood the next day.

"I'm getting so many calls on it," Muscoreil said. "You've got to see it."

6

KIDS SHOULD BE WARNED

The following morning—eighty years after William T. Love abandoned his canal, thirty-five years after Hooker Chemical started using it as a dump, five years after Debbie Gallo rubbed chemicals into her eyes there, two and a half months after McDougall's visit to Washington, four days after Casper's underlined memo, and less than twenty-four hours after Muscoreil burst into his office—John LaFalce prepared to visit the LaSalle neighborhood in Niagara Falls.

The plan was to meet McDougall, walk the playground on top of the old canal, see the problem for himself, and visit a couple of homes on the south end of the parcel, closest to the river. McDougall had arranged it, and Rich Lee would drive him out there, navigating the streets of the city in LaFalce's boxy, four-door sedan, a Chevrolet Impala.

Lee had known LaFalce since the early 1970s—since before he was even elected to Congress—and he had the utmost confidence in his boss. LaFalce might not have been a backslapper on the campaign trail, and he might have moved slower than McDougall had hoped in recent months, but when he was clicked in, as he was now, he was a great listener, substantive, with a natural affinity for working-class people because they reminded him of himself.

Before he became the first in his family to graduate from high school, the first to go to college and law school, and the first Italian American lawyer ever hired at the prominent Buffalo law firm that gave him his first job, LaFalce was just a son of immigrants and laborers. His father drove a truck at a cereal factory, moving pallets of flour, while his mother worked the second shift at a bakery, mass-producing cakes and pies. Both had given everything to help make sure John, their firstborn son, would have a better life than they did—his mother, perhaps, most of all. One night, while working at the bakery, she lost the tips of her fingers on her right hand when the machine she was operating malfunctioned. Even all these years later, LaFalce could remember the feeling of dizziness he had as a boy as he studied his mother's gnarled fingers for the first time, seeing they were just stumps now and realizing there was nothing he or anyone else could do to change that.

Pulling up next to the playground in LaSalle and stepping out of the car to greet McDougall, LaFalce was overwhelmed by a similar feeling of dread. The chemical stench burned inside his nose, and it was even worse in the little homes that he visited—homes looking out onto what McDougall described as the old canal. The owners had been complaining about problems for years: black sludge seeping through their basement walls, gaseous clouds in their yards strong enough to dislodge aboveground pools, chemical drums surfacing just beyond second base on the baseball diamond where the kids played games, and a litany of health problems—rashes, headaches, fatigue, irregular heartbeats, and children born with birth defects. But since the snowmelt, it had only gotten worse. At their home on Ninety-Ninth Street, Karen and Timothy Schroeder gave LaFalce a tour of their backyard—if you could even call it a yard anymore. The land had become a puddle of chemicals, spreading to the margins, killing the trees, and eating away at the fence posts on the back side of the property, and Karen Schroeder was pretty sure she knew whom to blame for it.

She had lived on the street since she was a girl and could remember the playground before it was filled in, back when it still looked a little like a canal and people called it the "Hooker dump." She had distinct memories of trucks discarding material into the pits there and could even recall one occasion when the workers showed up at her house, frightened and looking for help. They had been burned by the splashing chemicals they were trying to bury.

Schroeder's mother sprayed down the men with a garden hose that day while they waited for help to arrive. But the hose wasn't strong enough to put out the fires that broke out at the dump every once in a while—when the chemical drums cracked open, and the contents inside spontaneously ignited, and the few people who lived there at the time had to call the fire department to report that the land was burning. One night, in 1949, it took firefighters four hours to knock down the flames. Another time, in 1961, the fumes from a fire at the dump stripped the paint off nearby houses, giving residents further reason to complain.

Such things were "disagreeable problems," the city's air pollution director conceded at that time. But it wasn't a reason to criticize the chemical industry as a whole, he added. Companies only put materials in the ground, he explained, when the items in question would prove even more harmful if they ended up in city sewers or the river. It almost sounded as if he were saying that Hooker Chemical was helping the residents by burying the toxins—an explanation that had been hard to sell to the Schroeder family over the years and was hard for LaFalce and his aide Rich Lee to accept now as they stood there in the family's troubled yard.

Casper had been right; McDougall had been, too. The problem was potentially enormous.

LaFalce didn't even know where to start.

The congressman and his aide got back into the car and pulled away in silence. But Lee drove only a couple of blocks, just far enough to get out of sight from the Schroeders, before making a right turn, easing the Chevy Impala to the curb, throwing it into park, and reaching around into the backseat for what he called "the Manual"—a small, bound book with every possible phone number the congressman might need. Both men agreed that what they had seen was shocking enough that LaFalce needed to start making phone calls and writing letters right away: to the state, to the feds, to the press, and to the president at Hooker Chemical—John S. Coey II.

Coey was a classic Hooker man in almost every way. He was educated at Amherst College and MIT and was one of the last connections to the golden age of Elon Hooker himself. He had been hired at the company in 1937, one year before Hooker's death, and he had climbed the corporate ladder in Niagara Falls for forty years. Now in his mid-sixties, Coey was no longer the varsity athlete he had been at Amherst, playing left end on the football team and leading the basketball squad in scoring. But he was still a towering specimen, with a lanky frame, a long, taut face, owlish glasses, and friends across the city of Niagara Falls. In a letter to him, after visiting the old canal, LaFalce addressed Coey in a casual manner that suggested a history between the two men. He called him Jack.

"As you may know," LaFalce wrote to Coey, "I toured the Love Canal site in Niagara Falls with representatives of the city and residents of the area." What he had seen there—and smelled there—was distressing, LaFalce explained. But his tone was friendly. He wasn't writing to accuse Hooker of anything. LaFalce just wanted to establish "certain facts" so that he could help the city make a plan, and he asked Coey several questions: What chemicals were buried at the site? Where were they buried, and at what depth? And, finally, what might happen to these compounds after twenty or thirty years, "in terms of chemical reactions," LaFalce said, "should they escape from the drums"?

"The citizens who live in the area are suffering each and every day," LaFalce told Coey. "It is imperative that we act as quickly as possible on this issue and I, therefore, am hopeful that you will furnish me with a full report as expeditiously as possible."

Coey didn't reply to LaFalce right away. Instead, Bonnie Casper heard from Hooker's vice president of corporate affairs, its public relations chief, Charles Cain—another company man with nearly four decades on the job, a membership at the Youngstown Yacht Club, and deep ties in the community. Cain wanted Casper to know that they were on it. Coey had received LaFalce's letter. He would be getting back in touch soon, and Cain would love to meet with the congressman to discuss the matter in person.

"I would like to sit down with him some Friday," Cain said.

Yet when Casper offered Cain a chance to schedule an appointment with LaFalce, he didn't take it. Actual answers were slow to come too, while the problems in the neighborhood mounted throughout the fall.

Instead of snow, this time the rains came down. Drenching downpours toppled precipitation records that had stood since the 1870s, washed out the apple harvest, shut down the New York State Thruway at times, and flooded basements, especially on the east side of town. To keep up with the water, sump pumps worked overtime in the homes on Ninety-Seventh and Ninety-Ninth Streets, and the city installed extra pumps in the sewers in at least three locations. Still, there was no way to prevent the water from seeping into the ground around the school and no way to stop the playground from becoming a sea of mud—a lesson that Casper learned the hard way.

On her first trip to the site that fall, Casper walked the old landfill with Eric Outwater, a sympathetic if powerless EPA agent out of the New York City office and a friend. It was cold that day, and each of them made the same mistake: they showed up in the clothes they would typically wear to a hearing in Washington. Casper wore gray wool pants, with wide cuffs at the ankle and high-legged leather, zip-up boots to match, and Outwater, who had graduated from East Coast prep schools and came from money, wore his usual: Gucci loafers.

Right away, both realized the folly of their choices. They couldn't avoid the mud, and their footwear never recovered. The soles on Outwater's Guccis peeled off, and Casper had to throw out both her boots and her pants. The leather around the soles of her boots began flaking off by the time she returned to Washington just a couple of days later, and her dry cleaner near the Capitol could never get the brown stains out of the cuffs of her gray wool slacks. With each subsequent cleaning, the cuffs, mysteriously, got browner.

Meanwhile, back in Niagara Falls, McDougall's consultant, Richard Leonard, had different problems. He had been working at the site so often that summer and fall that he couldn't get the chemical smell out of his car—an issue that was obvious to anyone who stepped inside the vehicle, particularly Leonard's wife. She was worried that the odor could harm them or their two young daughters, and quietly Leonard was worried, too. Not about the stench inside the car, exactly; for him, that was just a nuisance. He was concerned about what was in the ground in the LaSalle neighborhood and how they could ever identify the extent of the problem, given the danger—"the extreme danger," he told Casper in a phone conversation that fall.

Leonard had experienced it for himself while working one day at the site. He was standing in right field on the baseball diamond just north of the school and using a handheld auger to probe about three feet into the earth when it happened: the auger punctured a drum buried in the ground.

Leonard pulled out and stepped back. He could hear the drum hissing beneath him, and he could smell the gas, and for a moment he worried that the ground beneath him might explode or catch fire. It was a crazy thought for anyone to have, much less an engineer. But because he didn't know what was inside the drums, Leonard didn't know what might happen if he accidentally unleashed the contents of them, and, therefore, he couldn't guarantee his safety or the safety of the children playing on the baseball diamond at that very moment.

He told the kids to get out of there, and then informed the school principal, McDougall, and Casper about what had happened as quickly as he could. On the phone, Leonard sounded panicked, a little scared. He was worried about all the things he didn't know. As he told Casper, "Barrels could blow up in your face, if punctured." And yet, despite his concerns, despite LaFalce's visit, despite Casper's best efforts and the growing number of meetings in both Niagara Falls and Albany with EPA agents, state environmental officers, McDougall, Leonard, and others, news of the leaking chemicals remained one of the best kept secrets in town.

City officials suggested the problem—as alarming as it might be—was isolated, consuming Karen Schroeder's backyard maybe, and possibly her neighbors' yards, too, and maybe several others at the southern tip of the old canal, but not the entire neighborhood, not all one thousand homes and apartments, and not the school, either. The city's superintendent of schools declared the Ninety-Ninth Street facility to be completely safe for the young children attending classes there. The school opened on schedule in September 1977, the same week that LaFalce visited the neighborhood, and it was going to stay open all year, as usual. Officials advised parents to ask their kids not to walk across the playground during wet weather or dig into the ground—especially not in places where a black oily goo was now bubbling up. "The material can be quite odorous and very discomforting," said George Amery, a relatively new health official for the city who had thirty years of experience working for big chemical companies. "Kids should be warned to stay away from it by all means." But it didn't pose much danger, Amery said, an assessment confirmed by the headlines in the *Niagara Gazette.* "Seepage Health Threat Slight," the *Gazette* reported in 1977.

It was regarded as so slight, in fact, that many people in the neighborhood—including Lois Gibbs and Luella Kenny—didn't even hear about it. Kenny and her three children lived on Ninety-Sixth Street, north of the old canal and nearly a mile away from Karen Schroeder's house, and Gibbs and her two kids were a couple blocks east. There was no black film oozing to the surface in their yards, no seepage, no odors, no buried drums, and seemingly no reason to worry.

In early September that year, Lois and Luella sent their children to school with the usual fanfare. Clothes were laid out the night before, lunches were packed, photos were taken, milestones were marked, and then the children marched off with their backpacks loaded down with the fresh promise of new school supplies.

At the Kenny house, Luella couldn't believe how much her three boys had grown. Christopher was starting sixth grade—fully a middle school kid now—with a wild mop of light brown hair; Stephen, quiet and serious, was going into fourth; and Jon Allen, the baby, was a first grader that fall, thrilled to be with his brothers, as always. They attended Sacred Heart Villa, a small Catholic school about ten miles away, and Jon Allen quickly proved himself to be a good student there, a fine reader for his age, if sometimes a little too precocious for his own good. At Christmas Eve Mass that December, in the school gymnasium, Jon Allen managed to slip into the Communion line undetected and receive the wafer, the body of Christ, from the priest—more than a year before he'd make his First Communion—unbeknownst to his parents or the nuns who ran the school, who noticed the indiscretion too late. But no one could stay angry at Jon Allen, especially when he shrugged and smiled.

Lois's son, Michael, was cloaked in a similar blanket of innocence in the fall of 1977. He was a year younger than Jon Allen, just five—brown-haired, freckle-faced, and about to take a big step in his young life. Michael Gibbs was enrolling in kindergarten at the 99th Street School. On the first day that September, Lois strapped Missy into her stroller, walked Michael to school, turned for home, and then celebrated. She had put in the work. She had made this happen. While her husband, Harry, had been punching his time card at the Goodyear factory, Lois had been watching *Sesame Street* with Michael, teaching him his ABCs, putting him down for his naps, soothing him when he had bad dreams, and teaching the boy to look both ways before crossing the street. He was ready for this.

Still, somehow, Gibbs had missed something—something important. She didn't see the little stories in the newspaper that spring and summer about the problems that Karen Schroeder and other homeowners were having on Ninety-Ninth Street. She didn't hear about LaFalce's visit to the neighborhood just a few days after Michael started kindergarten, and she had no idea that his school had been built on top of an old canal filled with chemical drums. Caught up in the tornado of parenting, Gibbs had missed it all, and something else, too.

That fall, at the school, teachers began to wonder why basic worksheets were challenging for Michael and soon realized he had trouble distinguishing certain colors. Lois's son appeared to be color-blind—and she was still processing the news that December when life threw her yet another unexpected problem. Over a meal at a fast-food restaurant, Michael began to twitch and struggle. Thinking he was choking on a bite of hamburger, Gibbs stuck her finger in his mouth. But there was no food to dislodge, no hamburger there.

Michael was having a seizure.

Gibbs had no idea what to do, so she did the only thing she could: she held him. The convulsions might have lasted a minute or maybe just seconds. Later, she wouldn't be able to recall. All she knew for sure was that when it was over, the boy vomited, went limp, and fell asleep, exhausted. At home, Gibbs laid Michael down on the couch and then took him to the doctor the next day, filled with questions.

"There's no history of epilepsy in either my family or my husband's," she said. "So why should Michael develop it?"

The doctor didn't know. Sometimes these things just happened, he explained to Gibbs. He was going to prescribe the boy some medication, and then they would follow him, hoping to see improvement. In the meantime, Lois needed to explain what was happening to her son in a way that he could understand. She opted to tell Michael that he suffered from "spells"—little moments when he would black out and lose time.

Michael listened to his mother and said he understood. The situation, of course, was much harder on Lois, who increasingly found herself worried, chain-smoking cigarettes in the kitchen. The other mothers in the neighborhood didn't want Michael coming over for playdates anymore. They weren't comfortable with the idea that the boy might have a seizure, one of his spells, on their watch and that they might have to handle it alone. But Lois put on a brave face for Christmas in December 1977. She decorated her little house on 101st Street as usual and did what parents often do: she pretended as if everything were fine.

It was the last normal holiday that she and the other residents would have for years.

PART II

JANUARY
—
OCTOBER 1978

7

CONTAINERS OF DUBIOUS CONDITION

Michael Brown had been thinking a lot lately about ghosts. Not metaphorical ghosts, regrets or demons from his past. He was thinking about actual ghosts—unseen forces, the supernatural, that which could not be explained.

It was—for a hard-charging, Mustang-driving, cigarette-smoking newsman—an unusual interest, and it was especially odd given Brown's ordinary background. He had been born and raised in Niagara Falls, the son of an accountant and a teacher—rational, middle class Catholics. But by his teenage years, Brown had strayed. He refused to attend church with his parents and listen to some priest discuss the mysteries of faith. He wanted to solve these mysteries for himself, and in his first job out of college in 1974, as a reporter for the *Sun-Bulletin* in Binghamton, New York, Brown would have that chance. A local high school teacher had made the controversial decision to teach his students how to communicate with the dead and how to predict the future. The town was furious, and Brown was all in. This was a story he could tell.

Brown was just twenty-three at the time, and he had a bit of Tom Wolfe in him. Like the celebrated author of *The Electric Kool-Aid Acid Test* and, soon, *The Right Stuff*, Brown wanted to immerse himself in his subjects, and he went deep with the allegedly clairvoyant teacher. His stories created a stir both in Binghamton and across the state, briefly making the teacher notorious and Brown a media star. He managed to land a book deal—a significant achievement that convinced Brown he should quit his job and go home to Niagara Falls to write. But the publisher was small. The advance he received barely covered his expenses in the end. His book on the supernatural was no best seller, and soon Brown was faced with the reality that he was just an underemployed writer living with his parents. In 1977, he was lucky to catch on at the *Niagara Gazette,* where he got paid about $150 a week to work a beat that typically went to the youngest, least experienced reporter on the staff. Brown was assigned to cover the rural communities outside the city.

Brown spent his days and nights driving his flashy red Mustang to meetings—boring, endless meetings of the local village council or small-town recreation commission in places most people would never visit. He filed stories about the largest snowdrift in Lockport and listened to residents in Youngstown debate—seemingly forever—whether to remove a single tree on Main Street. Sometimes, at these meetings, he fell asleep—it was hard not to—and he was fighting a similar urge one night in 1977 at a public hearing in the town of Porter.

Porter was twenty minutes north of Niagara Falls, and the issue that night involved a company called Chem-Trol Pollution Services. The plant loomed like a fortress in town, and everyone knew what happened there: the company stored chemical waste in six large craters—five hundred feet around and twenty-five feet deep—legal, sanctioned, and lined with industrial-grade plastic. The problem was, Chem-Trol wanted a seventh pit.

The locals revolted. They were tired of what one official described as Chem-Trol's history of incompetence and ineptitude. "Witness," the official said, "repeated spills, cracked liners, atrocious housekeeping and a lack of professionalism." The small town was ready to fight. People showed up for a series of public hearings on the matter—hearings so contentious that John LaFalce started attending them. Brown was there covering the story one night when a woman stepped to the microphone, trembling with anger.

She didn't live in town, the woman said. She had just come to the meeting to deliver a warning. If Porter wasn't careful, she explained, the community would end up like her neighborhood in Niagara Falls, a neighborhood riddled with health problems and odd occurrences, a neighborhood built on an old dump that she called Love Canal. The words themselves were strange, and the woman's behavior was, too. As she spoke, she began to cry, and that's when Brown sat up and took notice. He jotted the words down in his notebook—"Love Canal"—and made a mental note to himself.

He should check that out.

Bonnie Casper stood in the shadows at the Chem-Trol meetings, taking notes for LaFalce and collecting comments from constituents on little cards. People wanted Casper to know they were worried about the Chem-Trol craters, the discharge, the "green acidy gook" that was leaking into a nearby creek from the property, and the smell of it all. "I have been awakened every night by this miserable stink," one woman complained to Casper. "It actually burns your nose."

By January 1978, Casper had compiled these complaints and other documents into a file that was nearly six inches thick and growing by the day. Reporters like Michael Brown were all over the story. And this attention, the press attention, forced Casper to dedicate huge chunks of time to the issue. She wrote speeches for LaFalce about Chem-Trol, briefed him on the public hearings back in Porter, prepped him to attend at least one of those hearings in person, and took meetings with state officials and EPA administrators in New York.

But quietly, most officials—Casper, perhaps, most of all—knew they were dealing with potentially a much larger problem in western New York that, for now, wasn't attracting any crowds or much attention from the local press. While everyone around Niagara Falls knew about the Chem-Trol issue and seemed to have an opinion on it, almost no one was aware of what was happening in the LaSalle neighborhood—in that place called Love Canal.

Casper and LaFalce were still seeking $400,000 to help McDougall, Leonard, and the city investigate the canal site. Nominally, at least, they had some support from the newspaper. In a short editorial, the *Gazette* called the matter so urgent that Niagara Falls should consider fronting the full cost itself, even though the city was nearly broke. But Casper was beginning to suspect that $400,000 wasn't going to come close to solving the canal problem—in part because, by early 1978, Casper knew more than most. She knew what EPA agents were saying behind closed doors.

—

At LaFalce's direction, the EPA had sent an engineer from its Rochester office to visit the site in the fall of 1977 and conduct an official survey—the first of its kind, really. The engineer in question, Lawrence Moriarty, was in his sixties, with gray eyes, a slender frame, decades of experience, and a hobby that said everything about his personality: the man collected stamps. He seemed to be prone to neither panic nor hyperbole, and that made his final report about his visit all the more notable.

In walking the old canal, Moriarty said he saw rusted drums lying on the ground like beached whales; giant potholes in places where the buried drums were subsiding; cesspools of water oozing into backyards on Ninety-Ninth Street; basement sump pumps tainted with a black substance—a black "tarring oil substance"—and a stench that stayed with him. "The odors penetrate your clothing," Moriarty reported, "and adhere to your footwear." For days afterward, he could still smell the chemicals in the sweater he had worn on his trip to Niagara Falls.

It was just one visit, obviously, and Moriarty made clear in his report that he didn't understand enough to come to any conclusions. Among other things, he didn't know the history of the land itself—"the how or the why of the canal," he said. But what he had seen was far more troubling than what Casper and LaFalce had found on their visits. The situation seemed to be getting worse in the neighborhood, not better, and Moriarty knew enough, after just one day, to declare a few things for certain.

"Unknown chemicals in containers of dubious condition permeate the landfill in unknown numbers and locations," he reported. These containers created "unhealthy and hazardous conditions" both at the landfill and in parts of the neighborhood, and there was, he believed, no easy way to mitigate those conditions, leaving governmental agencies with two difficult choices. They could opt for a quick fix, some sort of superficial remediation, and the problem would probably just pop up again, or they could do what was likely needed—they could go, as Moriarty said, "full out"—and take on an expensive project that would surely require the involvement of the city, the state, and the federal government. That sort of long-range cleanup program might cost more than a million dollars, Moriarty figured, and that was only if they decided to do it on the cheap—a decision that Moriarty did not recommend. On the contrary, he believed someone needed to start taking drastic actions.

"Serious thought should be given to the purchases of some or all of the homes affected," he concluded, "resulting in the homes being torn down and the basements filled in."

The report crossed Casper's desk weeks later in the middle of the Chem-Trol crisis, and it was alarming to her for all the obvious reasons. Until then, no one had said anything about buying up houses or filling in basements. Yet Moriarty's recommendation wasn't the only reason for concern. At Hooker, the company's longtime public relations man, Charles Cain, seemed to be trying to diminish the scope of the problem as best he could. According to Moriarty's report, Cain could not say how much Hooker had buried in the canal, but he wanted Moriarty to know that Hooker had produced a "limited" amount of chemicals during the 1940s and 1950s, nothing exotic, and whatever was in the landfill was likely "bottom residue" or "sludge" left over from these limited processes. Meanwhile, the city manager seemed to question why the EPA needed to get involved in the situation at all. In a meeting with Moriarty at the convention center on the day of Moriarty's visit, the city manager said he didn't want too many actors getting involved—especially not at that particular moment in time. Niagara Falls was hoping to persuade Hooker Chemical to build a new company headquarters downtown.

Casper was facing down all of these problems in early 1978 when preliminary tests came back at the state lab in Albany, showing worrisome concentrations of chemicals around the old canal and inside at least fourteen homes.

The chemicals were hard to tease out—there were so many of them—but the elements found in the groundwater included polychlorinated biphenyls, known as PCBs, hexachlorobenzene, and something called C56, a building block of pesticides and flame retardants. The good news was the ground was frozen—in the bitter throes of yet another Niagara Falls winter—and whatever contaminants existed in the ground were probably frozen, too. "Sealed within ice for the most part," one internal report suggested. The bad news was that many of the chemicals were potentially carcinogenic. The ground would thaw soon enough, and the cold weather wasn't doing anything to dilute the chemicals that investigators were finding inside homes on Ninety-Seventh and Ninety-Ninth Streets, the homes built right on the old canal.

Chlorotoluene—known to cause tremors in mice and weight loss in rabbits—was in people's living rooms. Trichlorobenzene—known to cause liver cancer in rats—was there, too. As families ate dinner, washed the dishes, played board games around the dining room table, or read to their children at bedtime, they were breathing in chemicals—as many as forty-two different halogenated compounds. They were being exposed to low concentrations of toxic fumes all the time, and in some places the concentrations weren't that low. In many basements, officials would record levels of chemical vapors that exceeded modern-day standards—established for factory workers—by dozens or hundreds of times. "There is growing evidence," scientific experts quietly concluded, "that a wide range of chemical compounds dumped in this industrial landfill might pose a substantial health hazard to the New York State residents living in this area."

Many of these reports in Albany and Washington were stamped "CONFIDENTIAL," and they stayed that way—for now. Residents like Lois Gibbs and Luella Kenny had no idea, and at times, Casper was also left in the dark. The test results didn't make it to her desk in Washington at first. But by March 1978, Casper knew enough to know that she had been right to have been worried about the problem from the moment she met with McDougall the previous summer, and certainly from the day she had visited the old canal site. Around LaFalce's office, people started whispering that Hooker was in trouble. The state, the EPA, or the residents would surely be suing the company soon.

"I think if I lived there," said one of Casper's co-workers, "I'd be in court right now."

And yet Casper still wasn't making any progress finding the $400,000 the city wanted or having any luck convincing officials in Washington that the situation required immediate attention. At the end of March, she decided it was finally time to press her case someplace else. She planned to fly to New York City, to visit the EPA's regional headquarters just off Broadway on the edge of Tribeca, and spend a day speaking with the top regional administrators, not her friend Eric Outwater, but his bosses.

From the start that day, Casper's meeting felt doomed. One top administrator began by asking what two wishes he could grant Casper—an offer that sounded condescending and arrogant all at once. Still, she had a ready answer. She said that she wanted the EPA to clean up the canal in Niagara Falls and send someone to monitor the other problem bubbling up in LaFalce's district: the toxic Chem-Trol lagoons.

The administrator looked at the young congressional aide sitting across from him and explained that he understood her concerns—especially about the Hooker landfill. He was well aware of the potential health hazards that the canal posed to people living in the neighborhood on the east side of Niagara Falls. But he couldn't grant Casper's wishes. The EPA was already spending about $20,000 on testing and monitoring at the canal, he explained. If LaFalce and Casper wanted more money than that, they'd need to go to Congress and submit a supplemental appropriation bill or go to state officials. It was New York's problem to solve. State officials had the lead; the feds were just there for support. The only thing the administrator would agree to do was meet with LaFalce—sometime later that spring.

"I am sure he will be a totally different person with you," Casper told the congressman after returning to Washington.

But LaFalce's meeting with the EPA administrator in early April didn't go much better. The congressman got no promises and no money, and Casper couldn't help but feel that they were failing their constituents and wasting time. Spring was coming to Niagara Falls. An entire year had passed since the snowmelt of 1977, and almost nothing had changed.

8

A SEA OF RED TAPE

The young reporter, Michael Brown, couldn't shake the memory of the woman crying at the Chem-Trol hearing—or the place that she had mentioned that night, Love Canal—and he decided to do something about it. He started by digging around at the *Niagara Gazette.*

The *Gazette* building was on Niagara Street downtown, just a few blocks from the crowds of tourists boarding the Maid of the Mist sightseeing boats, and aside from the haze of cigarette smoke inside, it was a beautiful place to work. The building had a grand staircase in the foyer, curling around to the newsroom on the second floor; a bank of windows looking out onto the newspaper's iconic sign with its vertical lettering—"GAZETTE"—stretching toward the sidewalk; a row of desks along the windows, where Brown and other reporters sat; and a library in back filled with old articles clipped from the paper and organized alphabetically in metal file cabinets.

In the library, Brown read whatever stories he could find on Love Canal. Then he started asking questions in the newsroom. But no one seemed that concerned about what was happening in the neighborhood, and Brown was almost ready to let it go when a chance encounter changed everything. He found himself in an elevator in Buffalo one day with one of Richard Leonard's colleagues—Roland Pilié, another consultant working on the canal problem. Pilié was from New Orleans, tall and handsome, and inside the elevator, trapped in a small, enclosed space with Brown, he couldn't help himself. He started talking. Like Leonard, Pilié admitted, he was spooked, more worried every day about what might be buried in LaSalle.

"Every time I go out there," Pilié told Brown, "I'm more amazed than before."

It was just incredible, what he was seeing. That was the word Pilié used—"incredible." Pilié wasn't speaking bureaucratic nonsense or engineering jargon—he was conversational—and Brown, a savvy reporter, didn't miss his opportunity to ask Pilié the most important question as they rode together in the elevator. Was there a chance, Brown asked, that the chemicals in the ground could harm the people living in the neighborhood?

Pilié just shrugged.

"Someone's going to have to dig there and take a good look," he told Brown. "If you don't, your children—or your children's children—are going to run into problems."

Brown knew a good quotation when he heard one, and this one was journalism gold. But he really didn't get a chance to run with it until early 1978, when editors at the *Gazette* called Brown in from the hinterlands, promoted him out of the small towns of Porter and Lewiston, and handed him the best beat of his young career: Brown was assigned to cover Niagara Falls. He was on the city desk now, in the mix, and on the front page, with a regular byline, a column, and an accompanying headshot that portrayed him as the newest, toughest reporter in town. In his photo, Brown wore a collared shirt, a wide tie, and a trendy 1970s look, complete with a mustache and sideburns. But perhaps the most notable thing about the photo accompanying Brown's column was his eyes. Every morning, he greeted readers of the *Gazette* with an ice-cold, on-the-record glare. He might have been half broke and still living with his parents downtown. Yet Brown was ready for this moment. He was ready to make his mark.

In the late winter of 1978—while Casper was working every possible angle in Washington and New York City—Brown published a column intended to expose everybody involved in Niagara Falls: the city, Hooker, the state, and the EPA. "Red Tape Stalls Dump Solution," the headline said, and the first paragraph of the story was particularly devastating. "Whether they admit it or not," Brown wrote in the opening lines of the column, "government officials are in the throes of a full-fledged environmental crisis. And there's no solution in sight."

He went on to tell readers everything he knew: how Hooker had dumped "God knows how many harmful substances" into the ground in LaSalle; how local health officials were "underplaying" the dangers by saying that everything was fine; how people in power in Albany and Washington had known about the problem for at least a year, possibly longer; and how they had been slow to take any action to address the problem, assess the danger, or even inform residents of the situation.

"In a month or so," Brown wrote, "the city will be hauling four truckloads of clay to fill in about 50 potholes out that way, but that's mainly to stop pedestrians from falling in a mini-crater." What the city really needed, he explained, was a long-term solution to a long-festering problem that should have been cleaned up years, maybe decades, ago—well before Brown had been hired at the *Gazette* and well before he had learned about the crisis. But to Brown, there seemed to be no sense of urgency. "Instead," he wrote, "local officials are wading through the legendary sea of red tape, trying to find a government agency at a state or federal level to help out."

The whole thing was, to Brown, a symbol of failure, and he was especially hard on the EPA in his column. "Why the EPA has taken so long to put on its Superman suit is beyond me," he wrote. But if anyone got a pass in Brown's first take on the subject, it was Hooker Chemical. The company had cultivated cozy relationships over the years with the local press. Anytime Hooker promoted an executive—or hired a new one—the announcement would invariably end up in the newspapers, written as if it were copied straight out of a press release. And Brown couldn't help but wonder if his own bosses were too chummy with the Hooker men he was now covering. He noted that his publisher, Susan Clark, would greet Charles Cain, Hooker's public relations man, with a warm embrace, and on at least one occasion Brown spotted the pair having a meal together in a local restaurant.

Still, his column was a start, and good news for Casper. At LaFalce's local headquarters above the post office near the waterfalls, congressional aides clipped the piece out of the newspaper and faxed a copy of it to Casper in Washington straightaway. She would be excited to learn that the new hotshot columnist in Niagara Falls seemed to be on her side. But there was even better news coming, the biggest break yet.

Dr. David Axelrod—a rising star in Albany, one of the top scientists for the state of New York, and the director of the state laboratory—was coming to town. He was tired of reading reports about William T. Love's old canal and the chemical drums that Hooker had dumped in it.

He needed to see the place for himself.

9

CERTAIN DEFINITIVE ACTION

David Axelrod's desk at the state laboratory in Albany was, on any given day, a towering mound of memos, studies, and scientific reports. The documents piled up around him, covering seemingly every surface and usually the floor, too. But Axelrod paid the mess no mind. He was lost in his work. He oversaw hundreds of employees at the lab. He ran testing on everything from lead poisoning to water pollution, and for it all he was quickly winning the respect of New York politicians on both sides of the aisle. Some lawmakers even called Axelrod for personal medical advice. He was not just a civil servant but an Ivy League graduate and medical doctor.

Axelrod, for his part, was happy to weigh in, confident in what he knew and who he was. In high school, in a small town in western Massachusetts, he'd been president of his senior class, valedictorian, editor in chief of the school magazine, and a champion orator—twice. Upon graduation, he had batted away offers from Yale, Princeton, Dartmouth, Brown, and MIT, before choosing Harvard for both undergraduate and medical school. And yet, despite his obvious brilliance—everyone called him brilliant—Axelrod was modest. The forty-three-year-old doctor never forgot that he was the son of an Orthodox rabbi who ran a kosher deli and a tiny synagogue on a dead-end road in the Berkshires. Axelrod had grown up learning how to tend to a congregation by watching his father go to work there. Now, in Albany, the son had a congregation, too. It was just a bit larger, and none of its current members—the lawmakers or fellow scientists—cared how Axelrod organized the paperwork in his office. As they all knew, it didn't matter. Despite the mess, he could locate any report he needed and quote from it in granular detail, if necessary. The man had read seemingly everything.

Even Axelrod's boss—Dr. Bob Whalen, New York's health commissioner, the state's top-ranking medical officer—was known to defer to him. Whalen, gray-haired and slightly overweight, with rectangular glasses the size of a Cadillac windshield, was a decade older than Axelrod and far superior in title. But Axelrod was unquestionably the future. Powerful staffers inside the governor's office were already grooming him to take Whalen's job. Axelrod also seemed well suited to tackle the Love Canal issue because he was familiar with Hooker, its dumping practices, and the lengths to which it would go in order to evade sanctions.

For almost two years, Axelrod had attempted to hold the company responsible for dumping Mirex—the fire ant poison and longtime Hooker product—into the waters of western New York. He spent more than $200,000 of taxpayer money to run tests in his lab confirming its presence in Lake Ontario. He pushed for a controversial fishing ban that kept anglers off the lake throughout 1977 and into 1978, and he believed he had the high ground: scientific evidence. But Hooker hired its own doctor, ran its own Mirex studies, presented different results, wasted Axelrod's time with endless meetings—"a purposeful effort to further delay," he called it—and then the company got personal. In a phone call late one evening in early 1978, Hooker's president, Jack Coey, accused Axelrod of being emotionally unstable, made a veiled threat suggesting the fight had only just begun, and ended the conversation by slamming down the phone.

Axelrod reported the phone call and this behavior—this "unprofessional behavior," he called it—to Commissioner Whalen the next day, surely believing that his boss would support him. Both doctors had long been convinced that the Mirex in the lake posed a chronic health problem to New Yorkers. But just days after Coey slammed down the phone, the governor of New York himself got involved. Hugh Carey—an Irish Democrat from Brooklyn, square-jawed and handsome, but hard to read, aloof—sent a top aide to monitor the latest meeting in Albany between the Hooker men, their hired scientist, Axelrod, and his team.

Carey, a fifty-eight-year-old widower with national political ambitions, was staring down a difficult reelection campaign in 1978. He was going to need every vote he could get if he wanted to win the Democratic primary that fall and have a chance at remaining governor, much less running for president one day, and he had publicly made it clear that he was pro-business. He supported Hooker Chemical, and he wanted New Yorkers fishing again—Mirex or not. It wasn't long after Carey's aide reported back from the Mirex meeting that the state totally reversed course. On the last day of March 1978, New York reopened the fishing grounds in Lake Ontario—despite Axelrod's concerns, his hard work in the lab, his long fight against Hooker, and his agreed-upon brilliance.

It was a bitter lesson in sheer political power: science didn't always prevail once elected officials—and major corporations—started getting involved. And it was one that had to be fresh in Axelrod's mind as he and Whalen flew to Niagara Falls to visit the old Hooker landfill in the LaSalle neighborhood that April. The pair of doctors touched down in the city less than two weeks after the state lifted the fishing ban, effectively surrendering to Hooker.

But Axelrod was also a pragmatist, and if he dwelled on the loss, he didn't show it. He recognized that every environmental decision had political and economic implications. He knew that leaders like Governor Carey had to consider those factors when making a decision, and he was ready to assess the next crisis with his eyes wide open.

Axelrod was ready to see this place called Love Canal.

It was trench-coat weather, cold and gray, the day Whalen and Axelrod arrived in Niagara Falls in April 1978. A hard wind howled off the river and whipped across the landscape outside the 99th Street School. Temperatures were projected to dip to almost freezing overnight, and snow—more godforsaken snow—was in the forecast for the city. It was as if spring were never coming, and few understood that better than the man who met Axelrod and Whalen on the ground that day: the county health commissioner, Dr. Francis J. Clifford.

Like Hooker Chemical itself, Clifford was a bit of a local institution. A dentist's son, born and raised just outside Niagara Falls, he had earned the nickname Doc as a boy and then gone on to prove the moniker was merited by getting his medical degree in 1942 and putting it to good use. Clifford served as a doctor with the Eighty-Third Infantry during World War II and returned to run a medical practice in his hometown for two decades before being named county health commissioner in the early 1970s. He had handled outbreaks of the measles and the mumps, chicken pox and swine flu, and he could certainly handle this canal situation, whatever it was, dismissing the seriousness of the problem throughout the spring of 1978.

Clifford questioned the benzene readings that the EPA was finding in the air. "I look at the EPA's record," he said, "and notice they have to err on the right side." He cast doubts on whether any of the chemicals in the canal could cause cancer. "There's a high rate of cancer among my friends," he said. "It doesn't mean anything." And Clifford enjoyed reminding Michael Brown—who was still living with his parents while writing alarmist stories about dangerous chemicals—that he wasn't a doctor or a scientist. Brown didn't have the slightest idea what he was talking about. "When are you going to go back to being a reporter?" Clifford asked Brown at one point.

But as they walked the site that day, Axelrod and Whalen seemed to take a different view of the issue. They noted the exposed chemical drums, cresting out of the ground; the pools of discolored water gathering in the yards on the edge of the old canal; the school right in the middle of it all, a building where some four hundred children, including Lois Gibbs's son, Michael, continued to attend classes that spring as if nothing were wrong; and the generally troubled state of the land—"the deplorable conditions," Whalen said—both inside and outside the homes built along the old landfill.

Back in Albany a few days later, the toxicology committee for the state Department of Health—a committee consisting of nine state doctors—sat in a room examining the mysterious contents of two glass jars that came back from Niagara Falls. One jar contained foul water collected from a sump pump in a tainted basement abutting the old canal. The other was filled with solid waste scooped from the earth itself. The doctors passed the jars around the table, eyeing and smelling the contents, and then one of them asked a question—a question that Casper had been asking for months.

How much longer were they going to keep testing the neighborhood, he said, before they did something about it?

Three days later, for the first time in six months, Governor Hugh Carey flew across the state to Buffalo for a long day of meetings, press interviews, voter outreach, glad-handing, and one important event in Niagara Falls. The governor was going to visit Hooker Chemical.

Carey seemed to pop in at the plant on the river whenever he traveled to western New York, currying favor with Jack Coey, Charles Cain, and the company's three thousand employees. He would put in an appearance, shake some hands, and give executives a photo op with the governor for the company newsletter or the next day's paper. But this visit in late April 1978 was even more special than most. Carey was there to give a speech on the factory grounds, and despite a cold rain, a large and distinguished crowd gathered outside to hear it.

The governor wanted to remind people that he was focused on improving the economy of New York and celebrate Hooker's many contributions to that economy, including the latest. Carey praised the company's plans to build a new $65 million facility that could process solid waste into energy right there on the river. He declared it "a very bright day for the state of New York," and finally he stood over a ceremonial shovel on a patch of artificial turf that the company had rolled out to make sure the governor, the mayor of Niagara Falls, Coey, and Coey's bosses—top executives from Hooker's parent company, Occidental Petroleum, who had flown in from Houston and Los Angeles for the day—wouldn't get their shoes muddy.

Then, after the speeches and the photos, they all retired for the evening to a local art gallery for a black-tie dinner. Armand Hammer, Occidental Petroleum's seventy-nine-year-old chief executive and multimillionaire capitalist, was showcasing his personal art collection in Buffalo, and he had invited the local elite—the Hooker men, their wives, and Governor Carey—to be among the first to see it. The collection included works by Degas, van Gogh, and Rodin, but the most treasured piece was a Rembrandt—a portrait of a woman estimated to be worth at least $3.5 million that Hammer had personally delivered to the city that morning.

While Carey spoke at the factory, Hammer flew in by private jet, escorted his Rembrandt to the gallery in a motorcade flanked by motorcycle police, quickly flew to Washington for a private meeting with President Jimmy Carter at the White House—one of two meetings Hammer would have with Carter that spring alone—and then returned to Buffalo to mingle with Governor Carey that night in his tuxedo amid the beautiful paintings.

"All in all," said one reporter, "it was a triumphant day for Carey."

And without question, it was a good day for Armand Hammer, too. At the event that night, the petrochemical executive held court with his wife, opining about Rembrandt, the craft of painting, art in general, art collection specifically, and his personal philosophy that a man should only collect that which he wants. Perhaps more important, Hammer didn't have to answer a single question that day about the problems seeping out of the ground in Niagara Falls.

The most powerful Hooker man of all—Armand Hammer—hopped back on his private jet and got out of town just in time.

The following week—five days after the black-tie party at the art gallery—state health commissioner Bob Whalen finally issued a decision on the canal matter. In a tersely worded letter, he informed Dr. Francis Clifford in Niagara Falls that he was exercising his legal authority and directing Clifford to take action—"certain definitive action," Whalen said—in order to keep the public safe. There was no getting around it, Whalen believed. The canal wasn't just a nuisance; it was dangerous.

"In view of the ready access to the site and the exposed and visible pesticides and other toxic chemicals on its surface, the site unquestionably represents an extremely serious threat to the health and welfare of all those using it, living near it, or exposed to the conditions emanating from it," Whalen told Clifford. "Most particularly, the conditions on the site represent an intolerable and totally unacceptable danger to children accustomed to using the site either as a shortcut, or as a playground, both officially or unofficially."

Whalen was calling on Clifford to remove all visible chemicals, vent all contaminated homes, limit access to the land with some sort of fence, find a long-term solution, and work with the state Department of Health to conduct a massive epidemiological study—surveying thousands of people in the neighborhood—to identify the extent of the health problems.

It took less than forty-eight hours for the directive to leak to Brown, and when it did, the story of Love Canal—buried for decades—finally made major front-page news in Niagara Falls. It was above the fold and below the fold, too. Editors even chose to place the headline for the story above the *Niagara Gazette* banner itself. "State Orders Love Canal Site Cleanup," it said at the very top of the page. The only question now was this: Could officials even do it?

"Is it feasible to reduce the hazard?" Axelrod asked in an internal memo after his visit to the canal. "What are the options?"

Axelrod wasn't sure, at least in part because he couldn't say what was in the canal. Hooker Chemical still hadn't released details, leaving officials to guess for now at the exact ingredients in the toxic stew beneath the surface. And having just fought Hooker for months on the Mirex issue, Axelrod seemed keenly aware that he might not be getting much help from the executives at the factory on Buffalo Avenue. It would be up to state and federal scientists, he said, to estimate the hazards in the neighborhood as best they could. Then, in the middle of an election year, the policy makers, administrators, and Governor Carey himself would have to decide how much risk they were willing to accept.

"Safety, after all," Axelrod said, "is a political judgment, not a toxicological one, nor one of absolute certainty."

10

THIS IS OUR ANSWER

The newspaper landed with a thud outside Lois Gibbs's home on 101st Street on the last Friday in April 1978.

All that winter and spring, Gibbs had been worried about her son, Michael, anxiously awaiting his next seizure and wondering whether she would be there to soothe him when it happened or if the boy would be in his kindergarten classroom and have to explain that he'd had another spell to his teacher and classmates.

Now, unfolding the pages of the *Niagara Gazette* in late April, Gibbs felt as if she might have stumbled onto an important clue—maybe everything. The news about the old chemical dump between Ninety-Seventh and Ninety-Ninth Streets—right under Michael's school, in the heart of the neighborhood—was everywhere. The *Gazette* filled the paper with stories about the old landfill. The Buffalo newspapers were devoting pages of coverage, too. Local television networks were airing pieces on the six o'clock news, and pretty soon the national networks came sniffing around, starting with *The Today Show* on NBC, but not ending there. The rumor was that ABC News was coming to town, and *60 Minutes* was also considering the story—a notion that worried officials enough that EPA administrators asked field agents to see if Casper knew whether it was true. Casper had no idea. But unlike the others, she wasn't nervous. She welcomed the coverage, invited it even—Michael Brown's coverage most of all.

As usual, he was going deep, dedicating himself to the story full time. He interviewed the families who were living right on the old canal: the Gazys and the Wheelers, the Voorheeses and the Schroeders. He wrote about the smells in their basements, how their children developed asthma, and their mounting concerns that the two problems might be connected. He reported on the time that the city came out to Karen Schroeder's house on Ninety-Ninth Street and pumped seventeen thousand gallons of fetid water out of her backyard, only to watch the water reappear in the yard. "In two days," Schroeder told Brown. And he documented all the other problems the families had faced over the years: the terrible acne on their feet, hands, necks, and faces—rashes typically only seen in factory workers; the neighbors who had died of cancer; and the family dogs, German shepherds and cocker spaniels, that had lost their fur in clumps, and then died, too, all too young. "State to Study Love Canal Ills," read the headline above one story that Michael Brown wrote that spring. "Vapors from Love Canal Pose 'Serious Threat,'" read another.

Gibbs read Brown's stories in her kitchen, with her children at her feet, unsure about what it all meant for her family or where to turn for answers. While her husband, Harry, worked all day at the Goodyear plant—or slept all day after working the night shift—Lois was effectively alone, running a babysitting service out of her house. She had at least three kids under the age of six in her care every day: Michael, after lunchtime, when kindergarten ended for the day; her daughter, Missy; and her nephew Erik, the only son of her sister Kathy, who lived in the countryside east of Niagara Falls. Lois obviously couldn't talk about Brown's newspaper articles with the kids, and Harry, like many factory workers in the neighborhood, didn't seem all that concerned that there might be chemicals in the ground two blocks away. At the Goodyear plant, he worked with chemicals every day. But she knew someone who might be able to help her make sense of what she was reading: her sister's husband—and Erik's father—Wayne Hadley.

Hadley was in his late thirties and a Kansan by birth, with Osage bloodlines on his mother's side, a laconic manner of speaking, and a devastating knack for brutal honesty. He was also the only real scientist Lois knew. Hadley studied fish for a living as an assistant professor of biology at the University at Buffalo. One evening that spring, while dropping her nephew Erik off at his home, Gibbs approached Hadley in his backyard garden to tell him what she had been reading in the *Gazette.* The stories, she said, reported that there were chemicals in the ground in her neighborhood that could cause anemia, cancer, respiratory distress, cardiac issues, and problems with the central nervous system, including potentially seizures. As they stood among Hadley's tomato seedlings and pea plants just beginning to sprout from the ground, Gibbs wanted Hadley's opinion.

"Do you think this could be making Michael sick?" she asked.

Yes, Hadley told her. Maybe.

It was certainly possible. He needed to know more. She started bringing him Brown's stories, clipped from the *Gazette,* and Hadley started giving Gibbs advice. He suggested that if she was really concerned, if she really wanted to know more, she shouldn't talk to him. She should go straight to the source. She should go talk to Michael Brown.

Gibbs was resistant to the idea. She wasn't the sort of person who talked to reporters; she didn't even like to speak up in front of the other young mothers at the PTA meetings at the school. In her mind, she was still the girl from Grand Island: a poor student, from a poor family, wearing mismatched clothes. She worried that Brown would think she was a hysterical mother. But she was more worried about what was happening to her son—panicked about it even—and knew that her brother-in-law was right. She needed to do something.

Not long after talking to Hadley about the chemicals, Gibbs called the *Gazette,* asked for Brown in the newsroom, and made an appointment to come in and see him. The day of the meeting, she had her mother come over to watch the kids and got dressed in her Sunday best. She wore a skirt and high heels, put on makeup, and pulled her long, dark hair back and off her face to look as professional as possible, and then she drove downtown to the *Gazette* building on Niagara Street, desperate to be taken seriously and horribly nervous.

In the newsroom, Brown didn't notice anything in particular about Lois. To him, she was another concerned parent asking questions, and he was happy to help her, happy that people were starting to pay attention to what he was writing. He led her to a seat next to his desk by the windows looking over the street, and as she settled into her chair amid the smoking reporters and ringing telephones, Gibbs felt her nerves wash away. Brown was instantly impressive to her: he was smart and busy, knowledgeable and to the point, but also young like her—a year younger than Gibbs, actually—and disarming. He made her feel comfortable. If she wanted to know about Love Canal, she had come to the right place. How could he help?

Brown answered her questions and sent her home with a copy of the consultant's report that Richard Leonard had completed in the late summer of 1977. It was another thing that Gibbs had never heard of, and if she was being honest, it was hard for her to understand what she found in the report. Details about "east to west movement of contaminated leachate" and findings made by "infrared spectroscopy" escaped her. But as she read Leonard's conclusions that afternoon and evening and into the night—long after Harry had fallen sleep—Gibbs understood enough to feel validated. It certainly seemed possible to her that Michael's seizures could be connected to whatever was in the ground. Scientists hired by the city had found "viscous sludge" near the school, oil-like liquids leaking from busted drums, and high concentrations of unknown chemicals that Leonard's report classified as clearly PCBs, polychlorinated biphenyls, compounds known to be dangerous to both humans and animals.

It was like stumbling upon a key to a secret room; Gibbs didn't want to lose it. The next day, she drove to the little business center near the Tops Friendly supermarket in Niagara Falls, photocopied the thirty-two-page document, and then brought the fresh copy over to her brother-in-law's house for Wayne Hadley to read, handing it to him with a certainty that she hadn't felt in a long time.

"I think this is our answer," she told him.

11

A FULL AND FRANK DISCUSSION

Bonnie Casper needed to get to Albany. Bob Whalen was still health commissioner in New York, the state's top doctor, and it was time, Whalen informed LaFalce in early May 1978, for a discussion—"a full and frank discussion," he said—about what was happening in Niagara Falls.

Whalen was calling a meeting and inviting everyone in the know to attend: David Axelrod, of course; Eric Outwater from the EPA; Francis Clifford from the Niagara County board of health; the state's top environmental officer, Peter Berle; the Department of Health's public relations expert, Marvin Nailor; half a dozen state legislators and legislative aides who needed to be briefed on the matter; and Casper—if she could make it.

Casper would be there—there was no question about it—and she intended to be prepared for the meeting, too. At her desk in Washington, she typed up a list of every question she wanted the state to answer and then organized them thematically into four categories: long-term responsibility, short-term responsibility, health hazards, and environmental impacts. Who would do the monitoring? Who would do the cleanup work? Who was going to pay for it all? How big was the problem—geographically speaking? Where did it start, and where did it end? And how much were residents—LaFalce's constituents—going to suffer while officials in Albany wrestled with these questions?

"How long," Casper wrote in her notes, "can the people live in these surroundings before suffering physical ailments from the hazardous materials present?"

It was a question that others were beginning to ask, too. Just two days before Casper's trip to Albany, LaFalce's office received a letter from a young mother on Ninety-Seventh Street. Like Gibbs, Judy Freiermuth had read about the old canal in the *Gazette,* and she was worried. She and her husband, Harold, had purchased their house in 1974, when they were barely twenty years old. "And I knew nothing about the Love Canal or the Hooker dump site," she told LaFalce. All she knew was that they were happy, happy to have a home, and fully invested in it. The Freiermuths had used their life savings for a down payment and then made a series of improvements to the home, putting in a new driveway and building a fence around the yard, among other things. Now they were unable to sell, convinced that they would never get their money out of the house, and frightened about what they were reading in the paper. "We would like to move because we have a small boy—but can't," the Freiermuths told LaFalce. "I hope you can do something for me and the rest of the people on this block."

At the same moment, the worrisome news about the long-forgotten chemical landfill was beginning to spread for the first time among people living just west of the Freiermuths, people on the downtown side of the canal who rented apartments and townhomes in a public housing development called Griffon Manor. The development was no redbrick high-rise, and it was decidedly not a "project." City housing officials rejected that denigrating term. Instead, they liked to call Griffon Manor a "non-project," a showcase of visionary public housing where planners had thought of seemingly everything.

During construction, they arranged the apartments and townhomes in clusters, with plenty of green space to separate them, on roads shaped like horseshoe crescents. They built the units large enough to accommodate big families, with four and five bedrooms. They carefully placed these larger units throughout the development, so as not to overwhelm any one area with too many children. And then, in a proud moment for a city with the typical history of segregating people and making life hard for Black families, housing officials made sure that Griffon Manor was integrated. At times in the 1960s, a majority of the residents were white, and though the demographics had changed by the late 1970s, the development remained one of the most diverse places in Niagara Falls. Sixty percent of residents were Black, 40 percent were white, and life there was almost always harmonious. As city officials liked to boast, Griffon Manor was "a part of the LaSalle neighborhood" in every conceivable way.

As a result, the development's three hundred families had noted their own set of curious problems over the years. A steady rain could cause widespread flooding in Griffon Manor. Water rushed into basements or pooled outside. At one point in the 1950s, residents complained that it rained so hard a lake had sprung up—three blocks long and four feet deep in places—and the children who had lived in Griffon Manor the longest spoke in whispers of other secrets. Many had seen rocks that could catch fire. When they skipped them on the floodwaters, the kids said, these rocks would light up like Fourth of July sparklers. And other children remembered playing at a mythical place, a towering mound of dirt near the school that had been bulldozed years earlier to make room for more homes and more families. For reasons that escaped them at the time, the children called the mound "Canal Hill."

Now, with the revelations in the *Gazette,* it was all beginning to make sense. Both homeowners and residents at Griffon Manor wanted answers, and in Albany, Casper planned to speak for them. She'd be their champion. She'd change the world, as she had planned on doing when she first came to Washington. Or, more specifically, she'd help families living near the old canal escape their own homes. She was pushing for a bailout plan, and LaFalce was, too. Some governmental entity was going to have to buy people out of their homes, the congressman argued, just as the EPA agent Lawrence Moriarty had predicted way back in the fall of 1977. Maybe lots of homes, LaFalce believed—again, just as Moriarty had predicted—and maybe the people renting units in Griffon Manor, too.

The only question was, who would pay?

"WHO WILL BE LIABLE FOR THE COSTS?" Casper wrote in all caps.

On the second Thursday in May, Bonnie Casper flew from Washington to Albany for Whalen's meeting, her questions in hand. She reported to room 1432 at the Department of Health building, on the new Empire State Plaza a short walk from Governor Carey's office, and then she took her seat at the conference table: the only woman among thirteen men. The meeting wouldn't go according to plan.

Whalen started by giving everyone a brief history of the canal and sharing a report on the recent test results. The state identified at least eighty-two different chemical compounds in the ground there, he told the group. Eleven of these compounds were suspected carcinogens. One of them was a known human carcinogen. And there was some stunning data about exposure rates, too. According to Whalen, people at some locations along the old canal could exceed acceptable federal standards for exposure to certain chemicals in a matter of minutes. But the state had yet to inform people in tainted homes on Ninety-Seventh and Ninety-Ninth Streets, Whalen admitted, because he wasn't sure what to say to them. He didn't even know, he said, if residents wanted the state's help.

Whalen claimed that some people didn't want state officials in their basements, running tests. He also didn't want to alarm anyone by sharing inflammatory information about dangerous chemicals that were hard to understand and more commonplace than people knew. As Clifford pointed out, chiming in from across the table, there were dozens of chemical landfills in Niagara Falls—thirty-eight of them in all, actually, including three others owned by Hooker. Love Canal was just one of them.

State lawmakers and legislative aides, absorbing these details for the first time, didn't ask many questions right away. And the other officials at the table—from both the EPA and state agencies—stayed silent, too, at first. They were wary of challenging Whalen and Clifford in mixed company. But Casper jumped all over them as soon as she got the chance.

First, she asked Clifford for a map of these thirty-seven other chemical landfills. When he said he couldn't help her—"I only have one copy," he claimed—someone else at the table pointed out that there was a Xerox machine in the next room. Photocopies of the map were soon handed out to everyone at the table. And studying the map, they soon realized one thing: none of these other dumps were in the middle of a neighborhood, and none were under a school.

That seemed to make Love Canal a special sort of hazard, Casper said, and she argued that it was ridiculous for Whalen to suggest that residents didn't want help. People just didn't know whom to trust, she explained in the meeting. State officials had said it might cost $600 for families to vent the chemical fumes out of their basements. Who wanted to spend that kind of money, Casper said, on homes that were now potentially worth nothing? Also, what were they waiting for? Health officials needed to tell people everything they knew, as soon as possible, the sooner the better, she said.

Whalen seemed to grow impatient under Casper's questioning. He was a medical doctor and the health commissioner for the state of New York, and she was . . . *who exactly*? A young congressional staffer who had visited the canal site one time? But others at the table came to Casper's defense. If the test results were accurate, said Peter Berle, the state's top environmental officer, some of these homes were, indeed, now worth nothing. That alone made Love Canal a hazard—an imminent hazard—for all of the residents, Berle argued. And because the story was already in the newspaper, and people already knew there were harmful chemicals in the ground there, Outwater said he agreed with Casper. They needed to inform people of everything they knew. They could call the information "preliminary results," Berle said, trying to soften the blow. Say that they'd know more in a month or so. Limit the hysteria. But he was also with Casper: residents needed to know details—right away.

The meeting ended after two hours—Whalen had somewhere else to be—with seemingly little accomplished. As she left the room that day, Casper wasn't sure what state officials would do next. She didn't know how or if they would approach residents and she knew she had failed to answer the most important question of all, the issue that everyone was discussing behind closed doors but few were discussing in public—the question about who would pay for relocations and, possibly, entire homes. Even Casper's biggest allies in the room that day, Outwater and Berle, didn't know how to handle that situation and didn't want to ask lawmakers for money. Not yet.

Still, Casper found the meeting to be valuable.

"Because the Health Dept. was made aware of the fact that if they want to hold onto the 'lead' in this matter, they have to start doing something," she informed LaFalce in a memo after returning to Washington. "They will not be able to do what they want in any sort of vacuum," she added. "Others will be looking over their shoulder."

Four days later, back in Niagara Falls, Clifford issued a public notice:

> A MEETING OF ALL THOSE PERSONS INTERESTED IN THE PRESENT STATUS OF THE AREA SURROUNDING THE CLOSED LANDFILL SITE, POPULARLY KNOWN AS THE LOVE CANAL, WILL BE HELD ON FRIDAY, MAY 19, 1978, AT 7:30 O'CLOCK IN THE EVENING, AT THE 99TH STREET SCHOOL, LASALLE.

Casper had achieved what she wanted: a full and official airing of the facts—with all the appropriate parties. Clifford was going to be there, leading the meeting. Whalen and Axelrod were sending one of their top scientists to join him. Casper made sure Outwater would attend, representing the EPA, and then she persuaded LaFalce to send her to Niagara Falls, representing his office—the first time she would ever speak for the congressman in front of a crowd of people or a group of reporters, including Michael Brown. He would be there that Friday night, too. But as Casper made plans to fly north that week, she got a worrisome phone call about a different gathering that wasn't on her schedule. A secretary in the city manager's office told her there was going to be a "preliminary meeting" held that Friday morning in the new county office building.

Casper had no idea what the secretary was talking about. There had been no prior discussions of a "preliminary meeting." She was confused about it until a different secretary—in Clifford's office—leveled with her on the phone the day before her flight. The preliminary meeting, the secretary said, was for the "interested parties."

Casper paused and asked the obvious follow-up question.

"Who," she said, "are the interested parties?"

"Hooker, the city, and the board of education," the secretary explained.

Casper hung up the phone, realizing perhaps for the first time the depths of the problem she was facing. It was as if everyone in Niagara Falls—the alleged enforcers of the rules and the people charged with breaking the rules, the city officials who bought the land and the corporate giants who poisoned the land—wanted to make sure they were reading from the same script at the Friday night meeting with the working-class residents of the neighborhood, and Casper didn't like it.

"Either I am missing something," she told LaFalce, "or I know too much."

At the meeting that Friday night, Casper saw no reason to feel any differently. Clifford minimized the problem, suggesting to residents that the dangers were slight or unknown and that, frankly, the residents were lucky because the "interested parties"—Hooker, the city, and the board of education—cared about them. The crowd vocally rejected that notion, and at least one official on the dais at the meeting rejected it, too. Stephen Kim, a state scientist representing Whalen and Axelrod that night, explained to the crowd of about a hundred people looking on that the Department of Health believed there was a "clear and present hazard" associated with potential long-term exposure to chemicals in the old canal; otherwise, state officials wouldn't be there, testing the site and considering a full-scale evacuation of homes.

The mere mention of the possibility of an evacuation changed the tenor of the entire meeting, and also Brown's plans for his story the next day. There was real news to break here, front-page news, and he needed to get back to the *Gazette* to file it. But neither Kim nor anyone else at the meeting could answer residents' questions about when they might know if an evacuation was necessary, how this "clear and present hazard" might harm their families, or what they should do in the meantime. Should they keep their kids inside? Off the playground and out of their yards, even? All Kim could say was yes, probably, they should proceed with caution. Could they eat the vegetables from their gardens? Again, yes, maybe, probably. And if the dangers were so significant, why were they still there, anyway? Why hadn't local, state, or federal officials relocated them months ago?

"Aren't there emergency funds to move people?" one resident asked.

Casper explained that she was working on it and hoped to find funding soon. But her answer—like many of the answers that night—was unsatisfactory, and Casper knew it. They had called a meeting to tell the people what they knew, and in doing so, they had raised more questions than they could answer. People were infuriated, especially at Clifford.

The county health commissioner suggested, at points, that the problem was the residents' to solve. He couldn't do anything about their home values; that was something they would have to figure out, Clifford said. And he even warned them not to create an uproar because that sort of behavior, inflammatory behavior, could lead to bigger problems. If people got too angry, he said, someone might plant a bomb in the old canal and blow it up—a warning that struck everyone as bizarre. "From a public relations viewpoint," one internal memo in Albany declared after the fact, "it was not a very successful meeting."

As the people spilled out of the school and into the night, Casper wondered how she would explain the disastrous evening to LaFalce. She headed to a local bar to get a drink, while Brown hustled back to the *Gazette* to type up his story. The headline, to him, was obvious: "Love Canal Residents' Evacuation Mulled."

The story hit the next morning. It was a Saturday, the weekend, and a beautiful one at that. Spring had finally come to Niagara Falls. But Brown was back at his desk in the newsroom that day, chasing Clifford, Whalen, and any other official who would go on the record about what they knew for a big follow-up piece he was writing for Sunday. Marvin Nailor, Whalen and Axelrod's public relations man at the Department of Health, was frustrated. Nailor not only had to interrupt his Saturday to take Brown's calls; he felt as if Brown were jumping to conclusions that scientists hadn't come to yet. Just because there were carcinogens in the ground didn't mean people were getting cancer, Nailor told Brown that day. And even if people were getting cancer, Clifford added, it might not be because of the canal. "If we find a high rate of cancer there," Clifford told Brown, "that wouldn't shake me up."

It sounded a lot like Damage Control 101: deny, deflect, and dismiss. But the two state officials were potentially right about at least one thing. The health problems at the canal might not have anything to do with cancer at all. People in the neighborhood—mothers and fathers, grandparents and children—could be getting sick in other ways, ways that no one had considered yet. As Clifford told Brown that day, "We don't even know what we're looking for."

12

THE BOY AT THE CONCERT

In hindsight, Luella Kenny probably should have been concerned by the end of May 1978. Her house on Ninety-Sixth Street was only a tenth of a mile from the northern edge of the old canal. But authorities seemed convinced that the chemical contamination was greatest on the southern end of the neighborhood—near Karen Schroeder's house on Ninety-Ninth Street, almost a mile away. Also, the Kenny boys attended Catholic school. Luella didn't have to worry about them sitting in class in the 99th Street School on top of the old Hooker dump. She could pretend that everything was fine, and she did—at least until the night of the concert in early June.

Her youngest son, Jon Allen, had been a great student all year in his first-grade class at Sacred Heart Villa. A good listener, a strong reader, and a sweet child overall, the boy deserved to be rewarded for his hard work at school, Luella believed, and as his mother she knew the best way to do it: she'd take the whole family to see Jon Allen's favorite singer, the folk-pop-country sensation Debby Boone. Boone was on tour that summer and scheduled to appear at the Melody Fair dome in nearby North Tonawanda at the end of the month.

Jon Allen's older brothers, Christopher and Stephen, were not thrilled. At that time, the Bee Gees were strutting up the charts with "Stayin' Alive." John Travolta and Olivia Newton-John were turning "You're the One That I Want" into radio gold, and the irreverent music from the movie *Grease* was about to become the soundtrack of the summer. Debby Boone, by comparison, was a square—squeaky clean, not hip, not disco, not cool. More important, perhaps, the older Kenny boys were tired of hearing Boone's No. 1 hit ballad,

"You Light Up My Life," which even Boone had to admit had been overplayed on radio stations to the point that her friends threatened to break the record over her head.

Jon Allen, who was still just six years old, didn't feel that way at all. If the song came on while the family was driving around inside Luella's gold Volkswagen Beetle, everyone stayed quiet while the boy listened and sang along. If the song did not come on the radio, he'd demand that they search for it, spinning the tuner up and down the dial. And if they couldn't find it, if the song wasn't playing anywhere, Jon Allen would just sing it himself a cappella with childlike innocence—"You light up my life . . . You give me hope to carry on"—while his big brothers groaned in the backseat.

But as school let out for the summer, Jon Allen wasn't feeling like himself. On the morning of June 6, he woke up with swelling around his face and eyes. Luella figured it was allergies and monitored him, as any working mother might. The kids were out of school for the year, and her summer juggling act had begun. She had to race between her responsibilities at the lab she worked in at Roswell Park and her responsibilities at home—the kids. But when Jon Allen's face was still puffy two days later, Luella took him to the pediatrician's office in the basement of a brick building downtown, not far from the tourists lined up to see the waterfalls. She and Jon Allen saw the practice's young allergy specialist that day, and he prescribed the boy Benadryl, an antihistamine, agreeing with Luella's initial thought. It was just allergies, the doctor said. Just that time of year.

For the next two weeks, however, Jon Allen didn't get better. His symptoms waxed and waned, and then they grew much worse. By the time Debby Boone arrived in town for her gig at the Melody Fair, Luella's youngest son wasn't just swollen around his face and eyes. He was fatigued, sluggish, and complaining of stomach pain. Upon inspection, his abdomen almost looked distended, as if his whole body were puffing out, raging against itself. Luella took him back to the pediatrician on June 26, a Monday, and this time she demanded a different diagnosis. Clearly, Jon Allen—a previously healthy child with no history of allergies—was suffering from a problem that the pediatrician hadn't detected. But the allergy specialist claimed that the boy's distended abdomen was just the result of Jon Allen swallowing too much air. The diagnosis stood. And though it sounded crazy to Luella—who had ever heard of a child swallowing air?—she drove home rationalizing it in her mind. One of her older sons had developed allergies when he was around this age. Not terrible swelling like this, but hay fever, itchy eyes. Maybe Jon Allen's body was just changing, and she didn't need to be alarmed. Either way, they were sticking to the plan. Despite Luella's concerns, they all piled into Norman's brown Chevy station wagon that Friday night and drove to the festival grounds for the Debby Boone concert.

The whole Kenny family—Luella and Norman, Jon Allen and his brothers, and both of their grandmothers—were there. The stage was outdoors, under a tent, and the weather was perfect. The heat of the summer day had burned off by showtime. Cool air was moving in. It was going to be a beautiful night in western New York—the exact sort of evening that Luella had envisioned for her family when she had purchased tickets for the show. Debby Boone took the stage and the crowd cheered.

But Jon Allen didn't applaud. He didn't even look up. He was so sick that his eyes were almost swollen shut. He struggled to breathe and couldn't even find it in him to smile when Boone finally got around to his favorite song. While the crowd sang along with Boone during "You Light Up My Life," Jon Allen just sat there, exhausted and sick. Luella couldn't believe what she had done: she had listened to doctors who didn't know her son and dragged the boy to a concert he never should have attended.

Somehow, they made it to the end of the show. But Jon Allen didn't have the strength to walk to the car. Luella carried him across the festival grounds in the dark, cradling his swollen little body against hers amid the happy crowd of concertgoers.

She shot a worried glance at Norman. Something was wrong. Something was wrong with Jon Allen.

13

PLAN C

By the time Luella Kenny carried Jon Allen home from the concert—swollen and tired, at the end of June 1978—Lois Gibbs had decided she was done waiting for someone to save her family from whatever was in the old Hooker dump. She was calling the superintendent of schools, Dr. Robert Utter, and she was making a request. Gibbs wanted Utter to move her son, Michael, out of the 99th Street School and place him somewhere else in the fall.

This seemed, to Gibbs, like a reasonable ask. She had met with Michael Brown in the newsroom at the *Gazette.* She had read the consultants' report that he had given her. She knew in broad terms what had been buried in the ground in her neighborhood, and she knew what was happening in her own house. Michael was still having seizures—seizures that had begun only after he started attending the 99th Street School—and the boy was slated to return to that school in the fall as a first grader. To Gibbs, that was unacceptable, and she hoped Utter would agree.

Utter had been on the job for just six months. Having come from Plattsburgh, New York—a small town, near the Vermont and Canadian borders, almost four hundred miles away—he didn't know the first thing about Elon Hooker, his chemical company, or the odd complaints that had sent Hooker men out to Michael's school in the past. What Utter did know, however, was that the city schools were struggling. In order to make up for budget shortfalls that spring, he was considering laying off teachers, furloughing librarians, cutting music programs in half, and eliminating kindergarten altogether. He also had fourteen thousand students under his watch, and he couldn't start moving kids around just because a parent called with a complaint. That would create chaos. Parents across the city would be calling Utter every day. And, anyway, if Gibbs believed what she was reading in the newspaper, if that was truly important to her, hadn't she read the other stories, too? Utter's predecessor, Henry Kalfas—a man so popular in Niagara Falls that they'd already named a school after him—had publicly declared the 99th Street School perfectly safe months earlier. Utter was denying her request. Michael would stay right where he was.

Lois was furious, and she was lost. She had tried an approach that had seemed rational to her, and she had come up short, leaving her with a dwindling set of options if she wanted to move Michael to a different school by the fall. On Harry's salary at the Goodyear factory, she couldn't afford to send him to private school. And yet there was also no way Lois was going to send her son back to a school built atop a sea of rusting chemical drums. One night around his kitchen table in the countryside outside Niagara Falls, Lois's brother-in-law suggested that maybe there was a third option—a Plan C. Gibbs could gather information from others and prepare for a fight, Wayne Hadley told her. She could knock on the doors of her neighbors. Find out if other families were sick, too, and gather signatures to shut down the school.

Public officials might not listen to her, Hadley explained, if it was just her all alone. They weren't going to fear one mother with a sick child. But it would be hard for school officials to ignore the complaints of dozens of residents. All Gibbs needed to do was to go find them.

Gibbs listened to Hadley's idea, imagining the awkwardness of it all: her, a stay-at-home mother, showing up unannounced on people's stoops and porches, pretending to be an expert about toxic chemicals she'd only just learned about in the paper, revealing personal details of her son's medical condition, and then asking prying questions about her neighbors' lives.

"I can't do it," Gibbs said.

Hadley looked at her from across the table.

"You have to," he said.

—

In the waning days of June and early days of July 1978, Lois Gibbs loaded up her daughter, Missy, in a small wagon, placed Michael in charge of pulling it, gave her nephew Erik a tricycle to ride, and set off with her motley little crew, rolling down 101st Street and practicing the opening lines of her newly crafted sales pitch—her "set speech," Gibbs called it.

Hi, my name is Lois Gibbs, she began. *I live on 101st Street and my son goes to the 99th Street School. And after reading all of these reports in the newspaper, I feel like the school is really unsafe . . . So . . . would you be willing to sign my petition to shut down the school?*

She had a pen and a clipboard and some paperwork about the chemicals in the ground. She was ready, or as ready as she would ever be.

Gibbs started by knocking on the doors of people she knew, the parents of her kids' friends mostly, and no one rejected her, laughed, or slammed doors in her face. On the contrary, they agreed with Gibbs. They were worried, too. They told her about their kids who were struggling with asthma or their wives who had suffered miscarriages. One family told Gibbs that their daughter—still just a little girl—had arthritis. Could that be connected to the canal? Gibbs shrugged. That's what she was trying to find out, she told people, and folks nodded, grim-faced, taking the clipboard and signing their names to the petition.

On Ninety-Seventh Street, Gibbs met Debbie Cerrillo, a woman with thick, round glasses, three children under the age of eight, and enough problems to keep Gibbs sitting in Cerrillo's kitchen for more than an hour. Cerrillo had grown up on Grand Island just like Gibbs, but she'd lived on Ninety-Seventh Street since 1971, and she wanted Lois to know all about her issues there: the five miscarriages she'd had; her "female problems," she called them, including odd menstrual cycles; her son's persistent bloody noses; her daughter's skin problems; the shallow pond in the backyard, shimmering black on the surface; the foul odors, especially after it rained; and the short life of their family dog, Casey. The dog, an Irish setter, had died of bone cancer. Cerrillo didn't need convincing. She signed the petition and agreed to knock on doors, too. If Gibbs wanted it, Cerrillo would help.

On One Hundredth Street, Gibbs met Liz Retton, a young

woman living in a yellow ranch with her husband, Paul. Liz was a nurse's aide, and Paul was a laborer in a factory, not far from Hooker Chemical. The couple had bought their house the day before their wedding in August 1976, and Liz had slept there the night before the nuptials with her wedding gown—a white prom dress—hanging in the closet. She didn't want to spend good money on a fancy dress that she would wear only once. But she devoted herself to making her house a home. For a wedding present, Liz's parents bought the young couple a new oven for the kitchen—painted harvest gold. Her in-laws gave them a harvest gold refrigerator to match. Liz and Paul spent their own money to buy an orange-plaid living room set from a local furniture outlet. And in the weeks before their first child was born in January 1978, Liz hung blue and pink wallpaper in the nursery. The baby was a girl, as it turned out, and Liz was happy. She was sure she was never going to move away. Now Gibbs was standing in Retton's doorway, with her children on the street behind her, telling her about the problems in the neighborhood, and Retton couldn't believe what she was hearing. All of it was news to her, and she immediately worried over how it might affect her daughter, who was just six months old. Of course, she would sign Gibbs's petition. Liz Retton was angry.

One door up the street, Patti Grenzy saw Gibbs coming, and she was wary of whatever she was selling. Grenzy, a young mother of two girls under the age of three, didn't need any distractions. She was just trying to get through her afternoon list—the things that needed to get done before her husband, Ernie, came home from work. She was folding laundry on her front stoop while her girls played in a sandbox in the yard. But Grenzy couldn't help but listen when Gibbs started talking about the landfill in the neighborhood. Grenzy had lived within a few blocks of the old canal for most of her life and had never thought anything of it. Now, like every other parent Gibbs talked to, Grenzy was connecting the dots in her mind. Her daughters had suffered from sores in their mouths and struggled with breathing problems from the moment the family bought the house two years earlier. Grenzy worried about that and about one other thing: "I'm pregnant," she told Gibbs.

Grenzy signed the petition that day like everyone else. And by nightfall, when her husband, Ernie, got home from work, she told him everything about the slender woman with the dark hair who stopped by that day with her clipboard and her list of chemicals. Patti was worried.

But as she watched Gibbs walk away that afternoon—up the block and around the corner, heading west for 101st Street with her children rolling along behind her on wagons and tricycles—Grenzy couldn't help but think that the woman was a little crazy. City officials would never close the school.

"Good luck, lady," Grenzy thought, and went back to folding her laundry.

14

PRESUMED NEPHROTIC SYNDROME

Luella Kenny refused to delay any longer. The morning after the Debby Boone concert at the Melody Fair, she coaxed Jon Allen back into her Volkswagen Beetle and marched him into the pediatrician's office once again. The boy's hands and feet were so swollen by then that he could barely put on his shoes to make the trip downtown. This was no allergy—Luella knew that now—and she called the doctor's office in advance to make sure they understood that, too. She wasn't coming back in for a different antihistamine prescription or to have the allergy specialist hold her hand again and tell her everything was okay; she was coming for a different diagnosis. In particular, she wanted someone to examine Jon Allen's kidneys.

It was a Saturday, July 1, the weekend. The office was sleepy, staffed by a skeleton crew, and it wasn't long before Jon Allen was sitting in a small examination room with his mother. The door opened and in walked a different doctor—Maria Crea, the practice's lone female physician and the one whom Luella liked best.

Crea was middle-aged and had trained at Johns Hopkins Medical School in the 1950s, when many men, including her male classmates, considered it unusual—radical, even—for a woman to attempt to become a doctor. She was bold and fearless, a pioneer in her field, and she was listening to Luella. Crea recognized right away—from the looks of Jon Allen and his chart—that something besides an allergy had to be causing the swelling.

Until June of that year, Jon Allen's visits to the doctor had been due to typical problems—namely, the hard knocks of boyhood. At age three, he'd fallen off his bike outside his house on a cold winter evening and cut himself above his right eye. A few months later, he'd fallen again while playing, slicing open his left knee. And he was back one more time at age four for stitches after yet another tumble. In a house with two older brothers, such things were to be expected. Jon Allen was just trying to keep up with the boys, and doctors saw no reason to be concerned. "No allergies," they wrote in the boy's chart again and again. "Up to date on shots."

Crea ordered a urine test on the spot. Staffers at the pediatrician's office tested the urine with a colored dipstick—a simple but reliable test—and the results, coming back within minutes, were hardly surprising to Crea given the boy's symptoms. The dipstick noted high levels of protein in Jon Allen's urine. On a scale of one to four—with four being the worst—his urine scored a troubling three. The condition, called proteinuria, suggested that Jon Allen's kidneys weren't functioning properly. Instead of doing their job—filtering toxins out of the blood and converting this waste into urine—the boy's kidneys were also filtering out proteins, the molecules essential to a healthy body, and Jon Allen's symptoms were classic.

Proteinuria was the cause of the swelling around his eyes, and in his hands and feet. It was also why his abdomen looked distended, why he felt so tired, and why he was struggling to even breathe. It was the answer Luella had been seeking for weeks—only it wasn't good news, Crea informed her. High levels of protein in the urine are often a sign of nephrotic syndrome—a perplexing and often chronic form of kidney disease. Jon Allen wasn't going home that day to watch Saturday morning cartoons with his brothers or rest in his bedroom. Crea was sending him straight to the hospital.

Luella drove across town to Mount St. Mary's, feeling purposeful, and also a bit vindicated about it all. She'd been right. But it was hardly a consolation. She was worried about time lost, frustrated that the male pediatrician and the young allergy specialist hadn't conducted a urine test three weeks earlier, and furious that she hadn't trusted her motherly instincts in the first place. As a result, they had wasted nearly an entire month dithering around with Benadryl—for allergies Jon Allen didn't have—when something much more serious was happening to her boy.

Luella glanced at him in the rearview mirror, quiet in the backseat, too sick to ask his mother to look for Debby Boone songs on the radio, and too young to understand the implications of what was happening. The Fourth of July was coming up that week, and Norman and Luella had planned to throw a backyard cookout, as they did every year, with friends and extended family, Polish and Italian sausage, cheesecakes decorated red, white, and blue with raspberries, frosting, and blueberries, and the children playing with sparklers, their faces aglow, in the dark. But they'd have to cancel now.

Luella checked Jon Allen in at Mount St. Mary's at noon that Saturday, and Norman soon joined them there, bringing items from home. The hospital was perched on a hill, near the river, just north of the city, and from the window in Jon Allen's fourth-floor room, the Kennys had a magnificent view of Niagara Falls spreading out before them—a view not all that different from the one that William T. Love himself had enjoyed nearly a century earlier. Luella, Norman, and Jon Allen could look up the river toward the iconic waterfalls and out across the plains of Canada. But Jon Allen didn't have the energy to stand at the window for long. Instead, he passed the afternoon in bed, watching television, while the doctors moved in, taking their notes.

"Patient is a 6-year-old white male."

"Admission diagnosis: presumed nephrotic syndrome."

"Stomach, puffy—eyes and cheeks, puffy—feet, puffy—unable to wear shoes."

For the next couple of days—while doctors awaited further tests that would confirm that Jon Allen did, indeed, have nephrotic syndrome—the swelling remained the same or grew worse, until the skin on his legs became taut and shiny, his right eye almost swelled shut, and he ballooned into a different boy. In the span of just forty-eight hours in the hospital, Jon Allen gained three pounds—a staggering amount of weight on his three-foot-eleven frame in such a short period of time. Luella was distressed.

But doctors assured her that Jon Allen would get through it. Once the diagnosis was confirmed, they prescribed steroids—fifty milligrams of prednisone a day. The medication would help his kidneys hold on to protein and reabsorb it back into his bloodstream, instead of allowing it to leak into his urine. In turn, his body would stop swelling, and doctors would have a chance to assess the problem. The small blood vessels in Jon Allen's kidneys clearly weren't working properly. However, that didn't mean that Luella's son was going into kidney failure or would suffer from lifelong kidney problems. With treatment, it was possible that the condition would resolve as quickly as it had started. Or, doctors said, they might be able to manage the problem with medication and a low-sodium diet, staving off serious kidney damage until Jon Allen went into long-term remission, perhaps by adolescence. Many children did, doctors informed Luella and Norman. For now, they just needed to get him feeling better. The steroids would help with that, and a few comforts from home would help, too.

Norman brought in a deck of cards, coloring books, and Jon Allen's favorite stuffed animal, a soft brown dog that the boy named Scuppity. The dog went everywhere with Jon Allen and helped make him a favorite with the nurses at Mount St. Mary's. They loved checking in on him—and Scuppity—and they gave his parents permission to sleep in the room overnight, if necessary. The term "visiting hours" clearly didn't apply to the Kennys. Family members—Luella, Norman, one of Jon Allen's grandmothers, or his brothers, Christopher and Stephen—were there with him every day. And soon, the steroids began to work. By the afternoon of July 4, Jon Allen felt well enough to sit up in bed and play cards with his parents—war, go fish, and rummy, a grown-up game that one of his grandmothers had taught him. That night, he stood in the window with his mother, watching the Fourth of July fireworks explode in the distance. By the end of the week, the swelling was coming down, and his weight was, too, and by the start of his second week in the hospital, Jon Allen was beginning to look and feel more like himself. He ordered milkshakes, walked the halls with Scuppity, visited the hospital playroom with his parents, and smiled more often than before—developments that doctors noted in the boy's chart.

July 12: "Cheerful."

July 13: "Low salt diet taken well."

July 14: "Parents here—playing quietly."

But doctors had no intention of discharging Jon Allen until they saw a marked improvement in his labs. They checked his urine daily, watching for the protein levels to fall. They eventually did, and around the third week of July doctors began tapering Jon Allen off the prednisone.

The boy wasn't exactly a picture of perfect health. Off the steroids, he complained of headaches. He vomited once, and doctors noted a new loose, rattling cough. But his chest sounded clear. The headaches faded. His protein levels were normal—the most important barometer of his health—and on the morning of July 25, nearly four weeks after Dr. Crea had sent Jon Allen to the hospital, Luella finally got the news she had been waiting to hear.

If she was willing to test Jon Allen's urine at home every day—and bring him to the renal clinic at Children's Hospital in Buffalo for routine checkups—doctors at Mount St. Mary's would release him. After spending almost the entire month of July in the hospital, Jon Allen was going home to reclaim, he hoped, what was left of his summer. He packed up his things with his mother, said goodbye to all the nurses on the fourth floor, rode down the elevator with Scuppity in his arms, and then walked outside into the warm sunlight of a perfect midsummer morning.

15

THE TRUE BELIEVER

That same day, Lois Gibbs was in her kitchen, preparing to write a letter. She had overcome her fears of being rejected. She had put herself out there. She had knocked on the doors of dozens of homes in her neighborhood, and she had gathered, by her count, 161 signatures from people who supported shutting down the 99th Street School—at least until health officials could assure them that it was safe. Now Gibbs needed to deliver those signatures. Make them count. It was time to get political. She was planning to write to Congressman John LaFalce.

It had been, for Gibbs, a difficult month. Despite her successful efforts finding people in the neighborhood who felt the way she did, she had also managed to discover plenty of residents who disagreed with her point of view, who didn't like her out there on the streets stirring up trouble and, frankly, didn't much care for her, either.

One woman slammed the door in her face—as Gibbs had originally feared would happen. "Why are you doing this?" she snapped at Gibbs. "Look at what you're doing to property values." Another resident, a large man with a graying hairline, told Gibbs that he was sympathetic to her cause. He wanted to sign her petition and fight, too. But he had worked for Hooker Chemical and didn't want to jeopardize his retirement pension by speaking out against his own employer. And others just whispered about her—this woman, Lois Gibbs, appearing on their porches like a shadow. According to the rumors on the street, she was in it for herself, and perhaps had something to gain. Maybe she was just doing it for publicity, or maybe Gibbs had already sold her house.

The rumors, of course, were false, but the criticism—at least in part—was true: Gibbs was, indeed, doing this for publicity, and as far as she was concerned, she was failing. By the end of July, more people in the neighborhood had learned about the old canal in their midst, and state health officials had held a second meeting in which they admitted they were concerned about folks living on what they described as the "periphery" of the landfill—positive steps, by any measure. But by the state's definition, the "periphery" didn't include the three hundred families living in the nearby public housing development Griffon Manor. It didn't include the Kennys' house on Ninety-Sixth Street, and it didn't include Gibbs's small blue bungalow on 101st. Local officials also had no intention of shutting down the 99th Street School, even though they had advised parents to maybe keep their children away from the playground—if at all possible.

It made no sense to Gibbs. She wanted to know how the school could be safe while the playground was potentially dangerous, and she finally mustered the courage to ask that question in public.

"You are their mother," one official told her that summer at a meeting at the 99th Street School. "You can limit the time they play on the canal."

It was almost laughable to her. Clearly, the health officials didn't have children or didn't understand how hard it was to keep a ten-year-old, say, from riding his or her bicycle over to the baseball diamond or the swing set—places where the kids had gathered for years. But the answer she received was emblematic of a bigger problem in Gibbs's opinion. Government officials were denying responsibility—not taking it. They were running for cover, starting with the group that had bought the land from Hooker Chemical in the first place and built the school on top of it: the school district. At the end of June, an attorney for the city schools publicly announced that the board of education wasn't obligated to clean up anything around the 99th Street School. As far as he was concerned, it wasn't the board's problem. "The board didn't put any chemicals there," the attorney told the reporter Michael Brown, personally absolving school officials of any liability. "And even if it did, it doesn't have the financial capability to do anything about it."

Signatures on a petition were fine, but Gibbs needed help, and once again her brother-in-law, Wayne Hadley, was there to provide it. First, he introduced her to Richard Lippes, a young attorney who waged legal fights for hippie draft dodgers, wronged prison inmates, and other lost causes. Lippes wasn't exactly big time; the thirty-three-year-old lawyer, with wide ties and long sideburns, didn't even have a secretary in his one-man office in downtown Buffalo. But he drove an Audi, and he had bona fide environmental credentials. Lippes represented the Niagara chapter of the Sierra Club, one of the nation's oldest and most prominent environmental advocacy groups. Hadley then discussed the situation with his colleagues around campus at the University at Buffalo, hoping a credentialed expert, perhaps even a Roswell Park researcher, would agree to assist Lois and the residents of the neighborhood.

Only one volunteered. Her name was Beverly Paigen.

Paigen was what colleagues liked to call a "true believer." She was an established scientist with magna cum laude honors, a doctorate degree in biology, dozens of published journal articles to her name, and a curriculum vitae strong enough to earn her appointments on local, state, and federal panels charged with tackling the new hot issue of the day: pollution. But like a growing number of scientists in the 1970s, Paigen (pronounced PAY-gen) didn't shy away from politics when the facts led her there. She believed objective evidence clearly showed that people—corporate executives, industry leaders, everyday consumers, and humanity as a whole—were slowly destroying the environment. And emboldened by this evidence, Paigen was willing to stand with her feet firmly planted in two different worlds. She could be a scientist, she thought, and she could be an environmentalist, too.

The word itself, "environmentalist," was relatively new—at least when applied to conservation. Until the 1960s, it was typically used as a sociological term at the heart of the nature-versus-nurture debate. An environmentalist believed that children were a product of their home lives, their educations, and their family dynamics—their environments—while a hereditarian believed that children were almost exclusively a product of their inherited traits, their DNA, their genes.

But the word began to take on new meaning in 1962, when the

biologist and nature writer Rachel Carson prepared to publish her fourth book—a project she had titled *Silent Spring*. Carson was no obscure author at the time. She had spent the 1940s and 1950s documenting ocean life in a trilogy of books that made marine science accessible to the masses and sold millions of copies. Her 1951 book, *The Sea Around Us,* was her biggest success to date. It stayed on best-seller lists for eighty-six weeks, was translated into thirty different languages, allowed Carson to quit her government job at the U.S. Fish and Wildlife Service and devote herself to writing full time, and made her an intellectual star. As *The New York Times* noted in 1952, "Only once or twice in a generation does the world get a physical scientist with literary genius." Carson was that writer; she was that kind of big. "A publishing phenomenon," the *Times* called her, "as rare as a total solar eclipse." Then *Silent Spring* came out in the fall of 1962, stunning readers and turning Carson into a legend.

The book laid bare the toxins all around us in a modern industrial world: pesticides and insecticides; legal poisons, like Hooker's ill-fated fire ant bait Mirex; and DDT, a colorless, tasteless compound incredibly effective at killing pests. Carson argued that these chemicals were getting into everything—the soil, the water, the crops, the food supply, the birds, the insects, the fish in the sea, and human bodies, children—and she predicted that if society didn't act now, these "poisonous and biologically potent chemicals" would forever taint the earth. "It's ironic to think," Carson said, "that man may determine his own future by something so trivial as his choice of insect spray."

The $300 million pesticide industry, horrified by the contents of the book, cranked up its PR machine to attack Carson two months before *Silent Spring* even came out. Industry lobbyists dismissed the book as one-sided, while chemical executives personally insulted Carson. She wasn't a real scientist, one executive publicly declared. She was just another "fanatic defender of the cult of the balance of nature," he said. At least a few conservative politicians agreed. In 1965—three years after the book came out and one year after Carson's death, too young, at age fifty-six, from complications of breast cancer—a House subcommittee, chaired by a pro-segregation Mississippi Democrat, released a report calling *Silent Spring* unscientific propaganda intent on creating hysteria and purposely ignoring "the immensely useful role played by pesticides in the U.S. economy."

Such critics, however, were increasingly out of step with the changing times and the new movement that *Silent Spring* had helped spawn. By the end of the 1960s, politicians on both the left and the right risked defeat at the polls by ignoring voters concerned about the environment. In April 1970, roughly one out of every ten Americans—an estimated twenty million people—participated in the first Earth Day celebration, and two years later the U.S. government finally banned the insecticide at the heart of Carson's book. Farmers could no longer use DDT to kill caterpillars, beetles, or armyworms in their fields.

But environmentalists were hardly claiming victory. Despite *Silent Spring*'s lasting impact, the wheels of change were slow to turn throughout the 1960s and 1970s. Environmental leaders often lacked the transcendent moments they needed to mobilize people. Aside from Carson's book—or, say, the polluted Cuyahoga River catching fire in Cleveland in 1969—ordinary Americans could ignore the obvious problems in the world and tune out these new "environmentalists." In some circles, the word itself became a pejorative, a term synonymous with tree-hugging liberals or tie-dyed peaceniks, people so intent on saving redwoods, streams, or the American bald eagle that they would surely destroy the economy.

"I call them cultists," one labor leader complained in 1977.

In western New York, Beverly Paigen had heard the insults over the years; she knew what some people thought. But like Rachel Carson herself, Paigen didn't care. On the contrary, she became a Carson disciple, crafting both her career and her image with Carson in mind.

Paigen worked with the lawyer Richard Lippes at the local chapter of the Sierra Club. She organized Buffalo's first Earth Day. She publicly tangled with corporate polluters in the city. She gained a measure of local fame in the 1970s by publishing an annual "dirty dozen" list—a list documenting the worst air polluters in the region. And when the polluters on the list complained, Paigen defended her positions with science, with facts, almost daring the companies to come after her. "The list we published was accurate," she'd say. "The figures—and the list—were checked."

She was almost forty in the summer of 1978. But by any objective measure, the fight for Paigen had begun decades earlier as a girl growing up in a rural village west of Chicago. Her parents were fundamentalist Dutch Christians who believed young Beverly had to know God's grace, yet needn't bother with education after high school. She would marry young, as they did, have children, and the Lord would take care of the rest.

Finding a man, however, was going to be hard, Beverly guessed. Her father was a second-generation garbage collector with a big white truck and a fastidious streak that compelled the entire family to work on weekends. Beverly would have to wash the truck with him until it shone and then sit quietly in the passenger seat as he drove her to church and school. *There goes Beverly Vander Molen,* the other kids would say, *the garbageman's daughter.*

To overcome that reputation, Beverly put her intellect on display for all to see. At Wheaton Academy, a strict religious high school near her home, she wrote for the school newspaper, helped run the yearbook, sat on student council, organized intramural sports for girls—the only athletics permitted for the female students at the time—and excelled at the thing that mattered most at Wheaton: Beverly became a Bible whiz kid. At a school where students were urged to "yield to the Holy Spirit," biblical knowledge gave Beverly a currency that made her rich. She memorized large chunks of the New Testament verbatim. She led the school's Bible Quiz Team to second place in the West Suburban League "Youth for Christ" competition. And she impressed religious leaders so much that they invited Beverly to attend adult Bible study classes on Sundays at Wheaton College nearby. It was there, sitting in a circle with a dozen well-educated adults, that she learned it was okay to question the Bible—despite what she had been taught. It was okay even to reject some teachings out of hand. It was important for a person to think for oneself.

This was a lesson she rarely discussed later—and certainly not with her parents—but it was one that changed her life. Suddenly Beverly felt as if she had permission to question everything: her teachers, their lessons, and her future. At her graduation at Wheaton Academy in 1956, she took the stage in a gleaming white cap and gown, addressed the crowd as valedictorian—no one was smarter than Beverly Vander Molen—smiled one last time in a group photo with her classmates, and then never looked back. She attended college against her parents' wishes, majored in biology, got married, and left Illinois for good in 1960. Beverly's husband had been accepted into medical school in Buffalo, and the young couple had crafted a plan to make things work. He would become a doctor, while Beverly got a job and paid the bills, and then she would enroll in medical school after he was finished, and he would, in turn, help pay for her training.

But life didn't work out that way. Beverly gave birth to her first child, David, in 1966 and the couple soon divorced. Medical school was off the table for Beverly. She'd have to settle for a doctorate in biology from the University at Buffalo, a degree that, initially anyway, netted her nothing. As a highly educated female scientist in the late 1960s, Beverly couldn't find a job. In one interview, a prospective employer asked what she was doing for birth control. In another, an employer declined to hire her because she was divorced with a child, and thus a woman of questionable integrity—an opinion that Beverly's own parents shared about her. They had disapproved of nearly every decision she had made since standing on the stage as high school valedictorian in 1956, and they were about to disapprove of her next decision, too. In 1970, Beverly married a prominent cancer researcher at Roswell Park. Ken Paigen was Jewish, was a full decade older than Beverly, had three teenage children from a previous marriage, and was Beverly's postdoctoral supervisor—in other words, her boss.

"Ours is a truly modern household," she explained to folks who inquired about her marriage in the 1970s. The Paigens moved into a modest brick home in Buffalo, had one child together, a daughter, to round out their family, and spent their weekends at a cabin in the woods in western New York. Yet it was a love of science, more than anything, that Ken and Beverly had in common, and unlike others in her life Ken supported Beverly: when she took on the steel plants, when the local chapter for the National Organization for Women named her Buffalo Woman of the Year, and when she finally joined

Ken at Roswell Park in 1974 after a series of low-paying jobs elsewhere. Ken and Beverly could now drive to work together, if they wanted, parting ways in the corridor to go to their respective offices.

But most days, Beverly drove alone because she liked to get in early. She wasn't just the new hire—or the woman on staff, one of just a few, with her short brown hair, mod, oval eyeglasses, and signature laugh, a loud joyful cackle, that could be heard through the walls. She was the department head's wife. Beverly knew she was going to have to prove herself again and again, and she quickly set her mind to doing that. By the summer of 1978, she had raised more than half a million dollars in grant money to support her research, and she had earned praise from top administrators at Roswell Park. They liked that she was a visible presence, out in public giving talks about how elements in the environment could cause cancer. "It is important," one administrator told her, "that the institute's visibility and contribution in this area is maintained." And they also seemed to appreciate that she was different from most academics.

"Academic scientists tend not to get involved," Beverly told a reporter at one point in the 1970s. "They see themselves as distant, objective people, seeking truths."

Beverly, if anything, was the opposite. She was seeking truths, and she was absolutely involved. She wasn't interested in just publishing her work in medical journals. "Which, of course," she said, "most people don't read." She wanted her findings to reach real people. She wanted to connect science to daily life, and when she learned about the situation at the old Hooker landfill in Niagara Falls, she got that chance. The chance of a lifetime, really. This wasn't just a subject that Paigen could understand and help decipher for others. These were people like her. She was a mother, too, and she knew how it felt to worry about a child.

That spring, her eleven-year-old son, David, had spent weeks in the hospital, struggling with a host of painful and mysterious symptoms ultimately diagnosed as Crohn's disease. Beverly didn't need to imagine what parents were going through in Niagara Falls, wondering about the chemicals in the ground. She got it, and she told Lois's brother-in-law, Wayne, that she was on the case.

That July, Beverly Paigen started running her own soil tests in the neighborhood.

—

Gibbs had everything she could possibly need now. She had an attorney affiliated with the Sierra Club, a female scientist with street savvy, a petition with 161 names on it, and a plan. She heard that state officials were going to hold a big meeting about Love Canal in Albany on August 2. Maybe she would go and personally deliver her petition there. But first, everyone agreed, Gibbs needed to start introducing herself to people in power: state legislators, senators, and congressmen, including the man representing her district, John LaFalce. And so, on a Tuesday in late July 1978, the same day that doctors were discharging Jon Allen Kenny from the hospital and Luella Kenny was driving him home, Gibbs sat down at her kitchen table and started writing letters.

"I am a homeowner in the City of Niagara Falls near the Love Canal," Gibbs wrote to LaFalce. She wanted LaFalce to know that she was disturbed that officials were holding important meetings in Albany, three hundred miles away from Niagara Falls. "Many homeowners in this area would like to attend," she explained, "but financially cannot afford to travel that distance." She begged LaFalce to ensure that future meetings were held closer to home, and then she signed the letter.

"Cordially yours, Lois Marie Gibbs."

She wasn't just a mother anymore. She claimed to be representing lots of people, and according to Gibbs the group even had a name. She wrote it at the bottom of the letter, just beneath her signature.

"Love Canal Homeowners Committee," it said.

16

WHITEWASH

Gibbs's letter reached Bonnie Casper's desk on the last Thursday of July, six days before the meeting in Albany was to be held. The note was, on the face of it, not much different from others that Casper had already received that summer from different homeowners in the neighborhood. It was handwritten on stationery decorated with wildflowers and peppered, at times, with exclamation points. "The meeting concerns our health, property, and future!" Gibbs wrote. But the organization mentioned at the bottom of the letter caught Casper's eye. She had never heard of this group, this "Love Canal Homeowners Committee."

Casper filed the letter away; someone in the office would need to write back to Gibbs. But it was hardly her top priority. Casper herself was struggling to get answers that month and feeling at times as if health officials were intentionally withholding information from her, too. Casper no longer trusted the county health commissioner, Dr. Francis Clifford—"Carcinogenic Clifford," she called him behind his back. His comments at the first public meeting at the 99th Street School in late May—including his odd statements about not wanting residents to create an uproar for fear that someone might blow up the canal—made it clear to Casper that Clifford didn't care. And she was pretty sure that other local officials were in Clifford's camp. As she informed LaFalce in a memo, "The County, City, Bd. of Ed. and Hooker are all going to stick together to minimize the situation and whitewash it if necessary."

To make sure that didn't happen, Casper tried to stay on top of health officials in Albany and EPA administrators in New York City. But the story was moving fast and changing, seemingly, all the time. At first, the Department of Health said it would launch its comprehensive epidemiological study in the neighborhood on September 1. Then, under pressure, it began gathering data at the end of June, running a battery of blood tests and asking people medical questions door to door. Health officials intended to limit the tests and questions to those living on Ninety-Seventh and Ninety-Ninth Streets—folks with homes right on the old canal. However, under pressure yet again, they offered to test anyone living in the vicinity of the canal—a decision that stoked panic throughout the neighborhood, because residents on surrounding blocks had been told for weeks that they were unaffected. The halls of the 99th Street School—typically quiet in summer—swelled with hundreds of people, Black and white, residents of Griffon Manor and homeowners, waiting in long lines in the stifling heat to fill out twenty-two-page questionnaires and have their blood drawn for tests.

But doctors working for Bob Whalen and David Axelrod said it might be years before they fully understood the chronic effects of living near the canal. "I'm not God," one doctor told residents. "I can't say what will happen." Doctors also couldn't say whether Gibbs was right to be concerned about sending her son to the 99th Street School. In public, they repeated the oft-stated party line: the school was safe. But behind closed doors in Albany, some admitted they were troubled. After heavy rains, one state doctor said, water would gather in puddles outside the school, and vapors from these puddles might seep right into the classrooms through exterior air vents. The only way to guarantee the safety of the school, the doctor concluded, was to haul in more topsoil, improve drainage, and eliminate the standing water altogether.

Experts, however, said they were against adding any more topsoil to the site. The city tried that approach for years, and all it had managed to do was turn the land into a small, rounded hill—of sorts—pushing water runoff into the yards of the people who lived around the old canal. "The net result," one high-ranking health official told Whalen, "is that when it rains, soil and chemicals are dumped into their lawns." And based upon his preliminary observations, this official believed the chemicals might be causing health problems. "There appears to be an unusually high incidence of chemical burns among pets (particularly dogs), and children in this area," he told Whalen privately. "There appears to be an unusually high incidence of miscarriages . . . There appears to be an unusually high frequency of allergies, acne, and respiratory complaints among residents . . . There appears to be an unusually high frequency of certain malignancies."

Casper had to be honest with LaFalce: she wasn't sure whom to believe anymore. State and local officials were sending conflicting messages, while Hooker men continued to say almost nothing—except that they had tried their best in the 1950s. "Twenty-five years ago, many companies and governments weren't aware of the hazards of the products that we eat, breathe, and use," one vice president said in a rare public statement that summer. Then a new piece of information surfaced that further complicated the situation. A man approached the city manager in Niagara Falls with a story.

This man said he had worked as an engineer driving bulldozers and steam shovels for the city in the 1940s. He had witnessed the dumping in the canal, and he wanted the city to know that it wasn't just Hooker fouling the land. He alleged that other companies—and the U.S. Army—had done the same. He claimed he'd personally seen the military unloading waste there. "They came in with special drums," he said. Drums that were smaller, shaped almost like beer kegs. "I think there were sixteen—sixteen or eighteen drums all told."

The tipster's name was Frank Ventry. He was sixty-seven, the son of Italian immigrants on Nineteenth Street, about five miles downriver from the canal, and a veteran who had served in the army during World War II. Presumably, he knew what military trucks looked like, and his story was so detailed, so specific right down to the keg-shaped drums, that it was impossible to ignore. He could recount fires that sparked in the old canal and cave-ins along its edges. He could say which way the water flowed in the ragged channel back in the 1940s and 1950s, and what would happen if the Niagara River ran high or if there was a strong westerly wind. The water would rise, he said, and the canal would flood—problems that continued to happen even after Hooker filled the canal. That's why water sometimes pooled on the surface or spread like a lake toward Griffon Manor, Ventry said. And he argued that the seepage was still happening today. People just couldn't see it. The problem was buried underground, he believed, beneath the topsoil and clay and chemical drums left there by Hooker, and maybe the military too. "You see, they had a factory downtown—the Army did," Ventry explained. "And they emptied that factory out, and all the waste and material that they had, they put in that canal." Ventry could even identify the exact location of the alleged military drums on a map, if asked.

"Right here," he said, pointing.

Both LaFalce and Axelrod demanded answers from the U.S. Department of Defense as soon as they learned about the existence of Frank Ventry. "Immediate and thorough action," LaFalce said. "Prove these allegations either true or false." Then, perhaps just to make sure the feds would listen, Axelrod leaked the news to Michael Brown at the *Gazette,* knowing exactly what Brown would do with it. Brown splashed Ventry's story all over the front page that summer, exacerbating fears in the neighborhood and launching an entirely different investigation. The U.S. Army was sending a team of people to Niagara Falls to conduct nearly forty interviews related to Ventry's allegations.

It would be August, almost the end of the summer, before anyone had answers. In a twenty-five-page report that month, the army concluded it had not been involved in dumping chemicals in the neighborhood—"no evidence of direct Army involvement at the Love Canal site," the report said. Apparently, Frank Ventry was mistaken. But even with the report, the army questions wouldn't go away. They would linger like a cloud over the neighborhood, forcing Casper to recognize, even before the report came out, that her boss, John LaFalce, might be dealing with this problem for years. In a lengthy memo that July, she and LaFalce's congressional counsel, George Randels, outlined the potential benefits and the obvious risks at stake. The subject heading on the memo was "Love Canal—an Overview."

"We believe you are perceived, by both the affected residents and the general public, as a prudent, responsible champion of the people," Casper and Randels told LaFalce. But that perception could easily change. As a result, they said, LaFalce needed to preserve and enhance his image by helping the residents near the canal while not jeopardizing his relationships with the agencies involved. In short, LaFalce needed to push for action but be cautious about what he said and to whom. "This obviously requires careful treading at some points," they wrote.

For starters, Casper and Randels said, LaFalce needed to be wary of every government official in Niagara Falls, in particular those working for the city. They came across as defensive, secretive, and aligned with Hooker. "While the City and its leaders, to say nothing of the City Manager, are important clients of ours in a vast array of other circumstances," Casper and Randels wrote, "we think that with respect to the L.C. they are a potential adversary and should be treated very carefully."

LaFalce also needed to be wary of state officials—namely Governor Hugh Carey, the state health commissioner, Bob Whalen, and Whalen's successor-in-waiting at the Department of Health, David Axelrod. "Axelrod has become de facto coordinator in Albany—if not elsewhere," the memo correctly perceived. But Casper wasn't sure if Axelrod was committed to solving the Love Canal problem, and LaFalce clearly couldn't rely on EPA administrators, either. "They have been unwilling or unable to come up with assistance in terms of dollars," the memo said, "except to pay for the testing and contracting out that they have already done. We are disappointed in this, and we do believe that they could do more than they have to date."

LaFalce needed to keep working with top EPA administrators through proper channels, while Casper worked her backdoor angles with her friend Eric Outwater and others at the agency's regional office in New York City. There was, however, one other avenue available to the congressman. LaFalce could start funneling off-the-record tips and background information to the media.

"Our views on this are ambivalent," Casper and Randels told LaFalce. "On the one hand, we see this as an opportunity for your image to be spread more widely—and in a very positive vein." LaFalce would no longer be the bumbling Clark Kent under this scenario. He'd be Superman, saving the day in Niagara Falls. "On the other hand, we realize that increased media attention will also spur increased demands for a solution—demands that may not be realistic in terms of timing, funding, etc." Still, it was something to consider, "SHOULD WE WANT TO PURSUE SUCH A COURSE," Casper and Randels informed LaFalce in all capital letters.

Casper knew how she felt about it, anyway. Since early June, she had been working with Michael Brown at the *Gazette.* When she knew of a development, Casper called him—sometimes right away. And in return, Brown shared details with Casper that others didn't have—like the fact that he was on the cusp of selling an article about Love Canal to a major American magazine, *The Atlantic.* By talking to him, Casper had a conduit to the neighborhood, a way to know what people were thinking and feeling on the ground in Niagara Falls. But not everyone appreciated what the *Gazette* was doing. State officials complained to Casper about the newspaper, and Hooker executives complained, too—until they finally decided to do something about it. At the end of July 1978, they called the *Gazette*'s publisher, Susan Clark, to ask for a meeting.

Hooker wanted a word with Michael Brown.

17

THE WITCHES' END OF FAIRYLAND

On the first day of August 1978, Brown left his desk at the *Gazette,* climbed into his red Mustang, and pointed the nose of the car south, following the river—past the factories spewing their sulfuric acid mist into the sky, into the malodorous cloud of vapors rising above the city, and onto the sprawling, 135-acre campus at Hooker Chemical, where Elon Hooker had once stood fifty years earlier surveying his growing empire.

The land there was hemmed in by Buffalo Avenue and a "scenic" parkway following the river to downtown Niagara Falls. But with factories lined up on the chemical strip like steaming brick soldiers—Carborundum, Union Carbide, Goodyear, Olin, DuPont, Goodrich, and Hooker—the term "scenic" was a bit of a stretch. By day, the air along Buffalo Avenue smelled of rubber, acid, gunpowder, and pesticides dancing together amid the smokestacks and forming totally new scents—like Bug Spray on Leather, a reporter once noted, Chlorine Fruit Smoothie, or, a local favorite, Firecracker Smog in a Sewer. At this time of year—August—the smells were especially offensive in the heat of the day. And by night, the strip almost glowed, with fires and flares, spotlights, and the sad glimmer of a seedy topless bar, Kach's Korner, where factory men liked to unwind after their long shifts over the chemical vats. There was a reason why *The New York Times* would describe this part of town as "the witches' end of fairyland." It was dark, and alien, and *alive.*

Brown walked through the doors at Hooker and was ushered into a luxurious boardroom with his publisher, Susan Clark, and three Hooker men: a company physician; Hooker's public relations chief,

Charles Cain; and the new ranking executive in the city, Bruce Davis. Davis was replacing Jack Coey, who after four decades of service was being promoted to company headquarters in Houston. Though he was new to the company and new to town, Davis was cut from the familiar Hooker mold. He was a Cornell man. Had played football there. In his home, he kept a photo of himself barreling down the field, a pulling tackle ready to knock someone down, and there was no question that Davis had the power to do it—even now at age fifty. He was six feet four and at least 220 pounds. A classic Hooker hire, perhaps, in every way except one. Bruce Davis didn't live in Niagara Falls. He flew in every Monday from suburban New Jersey and returned home almost every Friday night. In a long corporate career, Davis was just passing through.

Everyone greeted one another—handshakes all around. Cain gave Brown's publisher, Susan Clark, a hug, and then he sat down at the head of the table to begin the meeting in proper fashion: with the airing of grievances.

Hooker disagreed with Brown's language—Cain thought Brown used the terms "toxic" and "carcinogenic" too often in his articles about the canal—and the company quibbled with Brown's conclusions, too. Hooker's doctor didn't feel it was accurate for him to report that residents were in danger, when, according to the company's data, they weren't. The men argued that Hooker was a responsible corporate citizen that had used the best available technology when dumping in the canal in the 1940s and then sealing it off in the 1950s before selling it to the school district for a dollar. And finally, they emphasized that no matter what Brown wrote, no matter what he said, Hooker would outlast the *Gazette.* Hooker had three thousand local employees and decades of goodwill built up in the city. It would prevail.

"Let me just say this," Cain told Brown in the boardroom. "We did a little survey, and we found Hooker is more popular in town than the *Niagara Gazette.*"

Cain wasn't just insulting him and the paper. He was reminding Brown of the order of things—the local hierarchy, long established, that few knew better than Cain. He had been working at Hooker since 1940, a full decade before Brown was even born.

Brown looked at Cain and fired back.

"Well," he said, "we did a little checking, too, and we found the most popular business in town is neither Hooker nor the *Gazette*."

It was the little place down the street, Brown explained. The topless bar that was popular with the Hooker rank and file.

Maybe Cain had heard of it.

"Kach's Korner," Brown quipped.

The meeting dragged on for roughly three hours. But leaving the Hooker campus around dusk that evening, Brown didn't feel as if they had accomplished much. If anything, he had more questions now than he did before the meeting had started. "Did Hooker really believe they weren't in trouble?" he wrote later. "Did those at the meeting honestly believe, despite their expertise in chemistry and biology, that their waste material was not toxic?"

Brown drove his Mustang across the city in the coming darkness, heading home on streets he'd known all his life, but feeling for the first time that he was living in a foreign place and realizing that everything was about to get stranger still. He had information that Hooker wasn't discussing, information that almost no one else knew. After more than a year of waiting, months of quiet closed-door meetings with Bonnie Casper pushing for action, and a handful of increasingly contentious public hearings at the 99th Street School on the canal matter, Whalen, Axelrod, and authorities in Albany were about to make an announcement that would change everything. Brown was reporting that state officials weren't holding a meeting in Albany the next day—Wednesday, August 2. They were going to be handing down a declaration of sorts. People were going to be evacuated from homes near the canal.

"Tomorrow," a source told Brown, "there should be some very explicit statements."

The county health commissioner, Francis Clifford, laughed at the absurdity of the notion, when he first read it in the *Gazette.* Clearly, Brown was misinformed; his source must have gotten it wrong. But by the time people started arriving in Albany the next morning, *The New York Times* and the Buffalo newspapers had confirmed what Brown had first written. It was front-page news. People would be leaving—or encouraged to leave—the neighborhood around the old canal in Niagara Falls. The big question now was, who?

In Albany, state health officials prepared for a massive crowd, securing a large auditorium for Whalen to make his announcement. They had heard about Lois Gibbs's petition, and they were worried that the 161 residents who signed it might show up that day. Authorities, however, failed to understand the constituents in question. As Gibbs had explained to LaFalce, people in her neighborhood couldn't afford to take a day off work and drive to Albany on a Wednesday morning—much less buy an airplane ticket and fly there. Only 26 people attended the meeting, and only a handful of those lived in the neighborhood around the canal.

But if Whalen looked out across the auditorium that day and believed that the empty seats in the room reflected a lack of interest, then he was going to be sorely mistaken. Lois Gibbs drove all the way from Niagara Falls in the family's Oldsmobile Cutlass with her husband, Harry, and their neighbor on Ninety-Seventh Street Debbie Cerrillo. Michael Brown was there, taking notes, and Bonnie Casper was there, too. She chose to sit with Outwater and others from the EPA, but she just as easily could have sat with Karen Schroeder from Ninety-Ninth Street, whose house LaFalce had visited the previous September, or Joseph McDougall, who had first alerted Casper to the canal problem over lunch in Washington fourteen months earlier—both of whom were also in the room. A few Hooker men were in the audience, and David Axelrod brought roughly a dozen people to represent the Department of Health—a veritable wall of state scientists and medical doctors assembled to support Bob Whalen.

These experts, Whalen informed the crowd, had been reviewing the facts for months at his direction. They had visited the canal site, identifying more than eighty different chemical compounds at the location. They had conducted tests and determined that at least seven of these compounds were known to cause cancer in animals and one of them—benzene—was known to cause cancer in humans. They had met, just three days earlier, in a large conference room at LaGuardia International Airport in New York City to discuss everything they knew—namely, increased rates of miscarriages in the neighborhood and other "unusual occurrences" of allergic and neurological diseases in the area—and they had reached some conclusions that Whalen now wished to share with the public.

"I do hereby find, conclude, recommend, and order—as follows," Whalen told the crowd.

That pregnant women living on Ninety-Seventh and Ninety-Ninth Streets and the northern border of the canal, Colvin Boulevard, temporarily move from their homes as soon as possible . . . That families with children under the age of two on these particular streets also arrange to move from their homes—again, as soon as possible . . . That people on these streets avoid their basements, especially for sleeping, and refrain from eating out of their gardens, too, due to the elevated levels of chemicals in the air and in the ground . . . That residents in the general vicinity of those streets—people like Lois Gibbs—work with officials to identify any other hazards still unknown . . . And that the city of Niagara Falls delay the opening of the elementary school on the site—the 99th Street School—that fall in order to prevent children from being exposed to chemicals while authorities pursued, what Whalen called, "corrective construction activities."

Gibbs couldn't believe what she was hearing. The land was poisoned enough that after years of doing nothing, the state was urging vulnerable populations to leave. But where were they supposed to go? How would they get there? And what were the rest of them supposed to do? "If the dump will hurt pregnant women and children under two, what, for God's sake, is it going to do to the rest of us?" Gibbs asked. But she couldn't get a reply that satisfied her. For people like Gibbs on 101st Street, or Luella Kenny just north of the old canal, there were no definitive answers. The state was still conducting its epidemiological survey—the comprehensive and exhaustive look at the neighborhood that had begun in June and would ultimately include, by the time it was over, thousands of medical surveys and blood tests. Residents needed to be patient and wait for the science to come in.

Gibbs had a different idea. In the auditorium, she started to scream.

"You're murdering us!" she wailed.

Michael Brown looked at Gibbs from across the room and thought she was overdoing it. He was fixated on the 97 families currently living right on the old canal—230 adults and 134 children—people who had potentially been living amid toxins for years and still didn't have clear answers. If anyone was justified to shout "murder," it was them, Brown thought.

But Gibbs believed what she was saying. While Brown hurried off to write his story, and Casper found a telephone to call LaFalce, and the Hooker men traveled back to Niagara Falls in style—likely by plane or helicopter—Gibbs drove home in silence in her Oldsmobile, riding a wave of anger down the New York State Thruway. For hundreds of miles, the only sound in the car was the scratchy recording she had made of Whalen's speech on a handheld tape recorder.

Fast-forward. Rewind.

Fast-forward. Rewind.

Gibbs couldn't stop listening to it, and she was so furious she could barely think straight. But at least she wasn't alone. News had spread quickly back home. When Gibbs pulled in to Niagara Falls that evening, she found that residents in the neighborhood had taken to the streets, yelling, giving interviews to national news reporters, burning their mortgage statements in a bucket in one homeowner's yard, and blocking a road near the school in a spontaneous display of indignant rage.

To Gibbs, the crowd looked like a mob. Roughly two hundred people stood in the intersection of Ninety-Ninth Street and Wheatfield Avenue, people who just hours earlier would never have considered making such a scene, people who just that morning would never have burned a mortgage statement in a bucket. Now they were taking turns standing on a box and shouting into a microphone that someone had procured. One man declared they should stop paying taxes, and people cheered. Another man shouted that they shouldn't move their children anywhere until the state agreed to buy their homes and move them all, and everyone cheered again.

"There's a big ugly monster with long arms living in the canal between 97th and 99th streets," the man said, "and it's reaching out to pull us all in."

Gibbs stepped out of her car, listened to the speeches, and waded into the crowd.

"Oh, God," one local official thought. "What is going to happen?"

She had found the microphone. Lois Gibbs was ready to speak.

18

IF ANYONE SHOULD COMPLAIN

The last thing that Barbara Blum needed was a mob gathering in the streets of Niagara Falls to protest a chemical landfill in their neighborhood—another crisis. At EPA headquarters in Washington, Blum already had plenty of those.

Tainted water in Tennessee. Cancer clusters in New Jersey. Giant chemical slicks floating down the Ohio River—seventy-five miles long—and the volatile political elements that came with almost every problem: leftist outrage and corporate subterfuge. Since being appointed deputy administrator of the agency in the spring of 1977, the No. 2 in charge at the EPA, Blum had publicly wrestled with all of it, facing down one problem after another until the pattern, for her, became familiar—crisis, crisis management, repeat. Whenever disaster struck, there was Barbara Blum standing in the klieg lights of the television cameras: the public face of an agency that could never win.

Blum was perfectly suited for the EPA job because she wasn't the typical bureaucrat. She wasn't a lawyer, scientist, or policy wonk; she was a housewife turned environmental activist from suburban Georgia and a mother of four children between the ages of ten and sixteen who had pushed her way into the old boys' club in Washington by impressing one man most of all: President Jimmy Carter.

As governor of Georgia in the early 1970s, Carter had seen Blum's work firsthand: how she helped save the Chattahoochee River in her own backyard; how she became a lobbying force in Atlanta; and how she turned heads in the state capitol building with a powerful combination of grit, savvy, youth, and beauty. Reporters, in particular, loved to mention Blum's appearance whenever they wrote about her, remarking upon her "sensuous" figure or comparing her to "a Phi Beta Kappa beauty contestant."

The sexist comments spoke to the challenges that Blum faced, and comments, sometimes, were the least of her problems. She had to develop the skill of inching away from male politicians who got a little too handsy, too fresh. "She moves carefully away and keeps on with whatever she is talking about," a fellow lobbyist noted at the time, with a touch of awe. "A man never feels that he has been put in his place."

But all the attention also helped get her noticed, which wasn't so terrible. Carter didn't go canoeing with just any lobbyist when he was governor, but he did with Blum to help boost awareness of environmental issues. In turn, she hosted a fundraiser for Carter at her house on the Chattahoochee and campaigned for him across the country when he ran for president in 1976. When Carter won—an improbable victory for a previously little-known southern governor—Blum claimed her spoils. At age thirty-seven, she was leaving her children behind with her husband in suburban Atlanta to commute to Washington every week and serve the president at the place where she wanted to be most of all: the EPA.

The idea of dedicating a single federal agency to protecting the environment was still fairly new at the time, and the credit, at least in part, went to one of the most reviled politicians of the decade: President Richard Nixon.

In his very first act of the 1970s, Nixon stood outside his home in California and announced that it was long past time for the country to make clean air and water a right for every American. "We are determined," Nixon said that day, "that the decade of the '70s will be known as the time when this country regained a productive harmony between man and nature." A brief period of enlightenment ensued. Republicans and Democrats, lunch-pail midwesterners and coastal elites, all supported the cause. The new agency, with its $1 billion budget, easily won House and Senate approval, and a series of sweeping environmental victories followed. The federal government banned dangerous pesticides like DDT, phased out leaded gasoline, passed the Clean Water Act, reduced smog levels in America's largest cities, and revived dying ecosystems. As a result, beaches that had long been closed to swimmers reopened, and salmon returned to lakes and rivers where they had not been seen for years.

But the EPA was hardly perfect, and its missteps made it an easy target for criticism—from the left and the right. Liberals railed against the agency's inability to stop major corporations from polluting, while conservatives complained that the EPA was destroying the economy with harsh restrictions that hobbled big business. By the mid-1970s, the latter argument was finally gaining traction as unemployment rates reached levels not seen since the Great Depression and double-digit inflation drove up prices on everything from coffee to college tuition. Economic doom was no longer an abstract fear. People everywhere were worried, and corporate executives were quick to blame the nation's economic problems on overzealous regulation and the government's largest regulatory agency in particular: the EPA.

Everyone was in favor of a better environment, a cleaner earth, they argued. But the EPA, with its nine thousand employees, was going too far, corporate leaders often said, undercutting the four pillars of the American economy at the time—steel, coal, cars, and chemicals—with too many cumbersome rules. One executive at U.S. Steel argued that EPA regulations had poisoned "the lifeblood of America's economic strength." Another at the National Coal Association blamed environmental activists for paralyzing the energy industry. And chemical lobbyists across America bemoaned the nation's declining pesticide production. Thanks to Rachel Carson, *Silent Spring,* and, most of all, the EPA, manufacturers that had once produced as many as seven hundred new pesticides each year were now producing just a couple dozen new compounds at most, lobbyists argued. If that trend continued unchecked, farms would be overrun by weeds, insects, and fungi, they predicted. Harvests would fail, and food shortages would follow. Even Nixon, the man who helped create the EPA, would come to criticize his signature achievement. He'd complain that the agency had "run amok."

If anything, the opposite was true, and Carter knew it. When he moved into the White House in early 1977, the EPA had neither the staff nor the budget to police America's greatest polluters or enforce the flurry of new laws that Congress had passed in the early part of the decade. To solve these problems, Carter beefed up the EPA's staff, hired new agents, and brought in progressive leaders like Blum, who came to Washington vowing to go after bad actors and eager to convince all Americans that environmentalism was more than just an "esoteric upper-class movement." "The people most affected by pollution," Blum said during her confirmation hearings before Congress, "are the ones who least understand it."

But by the spring of 1978, just as the secrets buried at Love Canal were beginning to seep to the surface in Niagara Falls, the agency was caught in a familiar vise—trapped between an idealistic vision of what it wanted to become and the political reality of the moment. As the economy worsened by the day, and inflation rose to the point that Congress declared it America's No. 1 domestic threat, Carter aides recognized that the president's reelection chances for 1980 were already in peril, if he didn't stop the economic bleeding. Carter appointed a new special counsel—Robert Strauss, a Texas millionaire and former Democratic national chairman—to tackle the inflation problem, and within days Strauss said he had identified three places where he believed governmental cost cutting could help everyday Americans. He wanted to target labor contracts, fight wage increases at the U.S. Postal Service, and curb regulations being pursued by the EPA. As Strauss told EPA administrators directly, it was time for them to join the "inflation fight."

Strauss's public proclamation, singling out the EPA, came during a visit to Pittsburgh, within hours of a closed-door meeting that Strauss had with a handful of steel industry executives. But the president apparently agreed with his new inflation guru. That spring, Carter directed all federal agencies, including the EPA, to cut, trim, and scale back regulations that might limit economic growth. At the EPA, it was Barbara Blum's job, of course, to explain this directive to the public, and that summer she returned to Congress to testify that she was personally analyzing every EPA regulation in order to find the cheapest approach to saving the environment. "The lowest cost means," she said, "of reaching environmental goals."

In the meantime, top administrators informed field agents to avoid "parallel investigations," whenever possible. Federal agents didn't need to get involved in a situation if state officials were already investigating. Blum believed it was possible to be both frugal and aggressive. Yet some agents weren't so sure—including, perhaps most notably, the manager of the EPA's hazardous waste program, Hugh Kaufman.

Kaufman was ostensibly charged with monitoring fifty-seven million metric tons of hazardous waste every year, including thirty-five million tons generated by the chemical industry alone—a veritable mountain of toxic sludge and slurry. Yet according to a whistleblower's complaint from the summer of 1978, Kaufman claimed he had no budget, one employee on staff, almost no way to regulate the transport, storage, and disposal of such waste with corporate lobbyists and lawyers fighting him every step of the way, and no power to contend with the likes of Armand Hammer, Occidental, or Hooker—well-financed parties leaving a trail of problems not just in Niagara Falls but across the country at that very moment.

In early 1978, Hammer flew to Florida to celebrate a new twenty-year, $20 billion deal between Occidental and the Soviet Union. Under the historic agreement, the Soviets would supply Hammer with thousands of tons of ammonia, which Occidental would then use to manufacture fertilizer at its plant in north Florida, before turning around to ship the final product back to the Soviet Union and to other destinations, too. "It's the largest commercial transaction ever consummated between a private business and a government," Hammer boasted as the first Russian tanker, loaded down with ammonia, docked in Tampa. And most exciting, Hammer said, this wasn't just about money but about a more noble ideal: global harmony. At a time of frosty relations between the Americans and the Soviets, Hammer suggested that his business dealings with the communist nation, including the ammonia contract and an offer he made to build Moscow's first eighteen-hole golf course, might be beneficial for all. "Where there is understanding and reason," Hammer said that summer, "there will be peace."

But Florida environmental officials were hardly cheering. The state was about to seek $8 million in damages from Occidental for allegedly emitting nearly ten times the allowable levels of pollutants from its north Florida fertilizer plant and covering it up by submitting doctored reports—an apparent violation that the state had failed to catch because, essentially, the company had been self-reporting its pollution totals. Florida didn't have enough regulatory agents to monitor Occidental, and escaping oversight, the company had engaged in what one state official described as "the most serious and deliberate violation of environmental laws" that he had ever seen.

While executives in Florida declined to comment to reporters and Occidental itself pleaded no contest in court, the company faced a host of different problems at a Hooker plant twenty-five hundred miles away in Northern California. Male employees there had gone sterile and hired a lawyer who attributed their problem to a product that Hooker produced at the site: a toxic compound designed to kill microscopic roundworms. Perhaps just as troubling, the company's environmental coordinator on-site believed more lawyers might be calling soon. By his count, the California plant was dumping tons of pesticides into a pond not five hundred feet from the drinking wells of their nearest neighbors, and these wells were now tainted. "If anyone should complain," the environmental coordinator informed his superiors, "we could be the party named in an action."

Finally, there was the problem unfolding that year in Montague, Michigan—a small town where Hooker had a chemical plant employing twelve hundred people. The narrative there had all the familiar themes. A pristine lake in Montague had become contaminated over time with Hooker waste—drums of C56, Mirex, and other volatile chemicals dumped into the ground near the shores of the water—and the company was fighting the local newspaper over its coverage of the issue. Darwin Bennett, the publisher of Montague's small-town weekly, *The White Laker Observer,* said Hooker's response when he began writing stories about the toxic lake went something like this. "First, shocked innocence and denials of guilt," Bennett wrote in the *Observer* at the time. "Then the pointing of fingers at other parties it feels are responsible for its predicament. Then anger and attempts to strike out at all who disagree with them, and, finally, efforts at reprisal."

Bennett began to feel threatened. Under pressure not to cover the Hooker pollution story anymore, he even began to fear for his life, and he publicly admitted something to his readers just a few months after he printed his first story on the problem: the tactics of the Hooker men were working.

"We dare not oppose their wishes," Bennett wrote in a public apology, "for what chance would a small country weekly have against one of the nation's most powerful and wealthy industrial firms?"

He had come to a decision—a decision that would haunt any true journalist, Bennett included. From now on, he told his readers, the *Observer* wouldn't be publishing articles about the Hooker situation in Montague. Instead, the newspaper would feature a blank space where those stories should have been.

"I'm ashamed to admit," he said, "that this newspaper has been intimidated."

Barbara Blum didn't scare so easily. But the old Hooker landfill in Niagara Falls was about to expose the limitations of Blum, Carter, the White House, and the EPA in ways that previous environmental calamities had not. It wasn't just because of Bob Whalen's stunning health order or his evacuation recommendations handed down in Albany in early August 1978. And it also wasn't just because people were burning their mortgage statements in the street that night—or that the whole thing had made the national news, the front page of *The New York Times*. It was because of a numbers problem, really—another secret that almost nobody knew.

"There are probably thousands of Love Canals," one EPA agent said.

Thousands of long-abandoned dumps created long before the agency even existed. Thousands of old landfills that no entity had immediate and obvious authority to handle and remediate. And for each of them, there would be a question—a question that Blum's agents were asking themselves at that very moment.

"Who's going to pay to clean this thing up?"

Blum didn't know, and White House staffers didn't, either. But a reckoning was coming, driven by anger, fear, and, most of all, that woman in Niagara Falls standing amid the crowd in the street with the microphone in her hand on a hot night in early August 1978. She wasn't all that different from Barbara Blum, but she was about to become one of the agency's loudest critics.

"Hi," the woman said. "Everyone knows me. I'm Lois Gibbs."

19

A LONG, STRANGE DREAM

Gibbs was nervous speaking to the people in the street the night she arrived home from the meeting in Albany. The microphone shrieked with feedback. She stumbled over her words, and her brother-in-law's in-the-moment coaching didn't exactly help put her at ease. Standing at the back of the crowd, Wayne Hadley raised a finger in the air every time Gibbs stuttered or filled the silence with "okay." As in, "I'd like to talk to you, okay?"

It was a verbal tic that Hadley was helping her eradicate. If Gibbs was going to be a spokesperson in this cause, she was going to have to learn to speak. And it was clear to the people around her, anyway—Richard Lippes, the attorney; Beverly Paigen, the scientist; and Hadley, of course—that Gibbs was indeed going to be a spokesperson. They were grooming her for the job, knowing that it was important for a grassroots movement to have a face, a central point person for reporters to call and cameras to photograph. Lippes, in particular, thought Gibbs was perfect for the job. She was young, bright, a mother, a homeowner with a stake in the outcome, and, like Blum, photogenic—attractive, Lippes noted. The cameras would love Gibbs, and already, as if sensing her importance, state officials started turning to her for help in managing people in the neighborhood. The day of the street protest, officials asked Gibbs if she'd spread the word that Whalen would be visiting Niagara Falls the following night and holding a meeting at the 99th Street School to answer any questions people might have.

"I'll make sure," Gibbs said, "there is standing room only."

Gibbs created a hand-drawn flyer—"Meeting: Thursday, 7 p.m. . . . Update & Discussion of Situation"—and then passed photocopies of it around the neighborhood. On the flyer, she changed the name of the organization, calling it the Love Canal Homeowners Association—not committee—and she noted that Lippes would be there that night, too. The residents would have a chance to hear from both him and Beverly Paigen. But it probably wasn't necessary for Gibbs to do all that work to draw a crowd. Everyone had heard the news about Whalen's announcement, and roughly five hundred people packed the school auditorium that night to see him, sitting shoulder to shoulder in the stifling summer heat. The meeting went poorly right from the start.

Whalen couldn't even finish his preamble before people started screaming. They didn't want to hear him reread his announcement from the day before. "We've already heard your order," one person cried out, interrupting the health commissioner. They wanted to know what it meant, peppering him with angry questions shouted over the din of the restless crowd.

"My wife is eight months pregnant. What are you going to do for my baby?"

"How do you determine if a child should stay?"

"Do I let my 3-year-old stay?"

"Where do you draw the line?"

The people were furious that top political leaders were absent that night: the governor, the mayor, executives from Hooker, and the entire city council. They were frustrated to learn that roughly half of these officials were on vacation. It was easy for residents to imagine these alleged leaders sitting poolside somewhere while they were trapped there, in the auditorium, breathing the hot chemical air. And when a representative from the governor's office tried to explain that Hugh Carey was actually working hard at that very moment, that he was back in Albany trying to hammer out legislation to help the people in the neighborhood, the crowd interrupted him, chanting.

"Right now . . ."

"Right now . . ."

The crowd was so angry, at times, that officials didn't think they could continue the meeting, and they asked Gibbs if she could maybe talk some sense to her neighbors. Gibbs stood up, looked out over the crowd, and, as usual, said the first thing that came to her mind—unedited and unfiltered, but, at least in this case, without an annoying "okay?" tagged onto the end of her sentence.

"I suggest that you sit quietly and listen to the questions and listen to the answers," Gibbs told the people, "and then boo the hell out of them."

The crowd cheered. But not everyone. People booed Gibbs, too.

"You don't represent me," one resident shouted. "No one does."

There were plenty of reasons for them to be upset. For starters, Whalen's announcement was meaningless to most of them. He had recommended evacuation to families with pregnant mothers and children under the age of two living in homes right on the old canal. But in a neighborhood with roughly a thousand families, only two dozen were being encouraged to relocate—and "encouraged" was the key word. Because it was only a recommendation, Whalen didn't offer to finance the relocations or find new homes for the displaced residents. People were on their own.

With nowhere to go, some started moving out, anyway. Almost overnight, people sent their children to live with grandparents across town, packed up their belongings, boarded up their homes, or just abandoned them altogether, vowing not to pay their mortgages anymore. "If this means I'll lose my house, they can have it," said one homeowner on Ninety-Seventh Street. He was willing to sacrifice the $4,000 he had built up in equity—and face any other consequence—just to get his two kids out of there right away. "I think jail is safer than this house—believe me."

By the first weekend after Whalen's announcement, nearly fifteen families were already gone. They found temporary homes at a nearby military base and in empty downtown hotels, where hesitant managers checked them in, worried about who would pay the bills and what the tourists might think about the people from Love Canal who came with signs saying, "Wanted: Safe Home for Two Toddlers." At the city's Convention and Visitors Bureau, officials assured tourists that Love Canal was miles away, if asked. Yet it wasn't far enough to dissuade the curious from driving out to see it.

The tourists might have come to see the waterfalls, and ride the Maid of the Mist out into the spray, and cross over into Canada, and send postcards home—"Greetings from Niagara Falls." But they could also make time to visit the city's newest attraction—the poisoned neighborhood—to ogle the sad people in their worthless, little houses. "I'm thinking about putting a toll booth up at the end of the street," one homeowner joked. Her new pastime was to sit outside and watch the cars with the out-of-state license plates roll by: up Ninety-Seventh Street, down Ninety-Ninth, past the school that officials were now closing—at least for the year—and past the fire hall where residents who could not afford to leave were meeting again that Friday night.

The fire hall meeting was set to happen just forty-eight hours after Whalen's initial announcement in Albany and only twenty-four hours after the unruly gathering at the 99th Street School. It was going to be the third straight night of shouting, and chanting, and crying in the summer heat, and already Gibbs was exhausted. She was working on three hours of sleep and shirking all of her typical duties. Her house was an embarrassing mess. Her kids were parked in front of the television, and her husband, Harry, was fending for himself at mealtime. Lois couldn't prepare proper dinners. She was drafting statements with her brother-in-law's help and giving interviews to reporters in her kitchen. Lois Gibbs was following the path that Wayne Hadley had laid out for her. She was formally running for president of the new homeowners' association—a loose, somewhat disorganized, and increasingly contentious group of people who really had only one thing in common: they had made the unfortunate decision to buy an affordable home on the cusp of the old Hooker landfill.

"Why am I here?" Gibbs thought, walking into the fire hall election that Friday night. "Why am I doing this?"

She felt like a fraud—an impostor living inside a dream. "A long, strange dream," she called it. She was also keenly aware that some people didn't like her. Worried about their property values—or their jobs at Hooker Chemical—they wished that Lois Gibbs would stay quiet and stay home, or, as one person had shouted at the meeting in the school, stop pretending that she represented anyone. But Gibbs must have been good at hiding her fears and masking her insecurities. Watching her in the neighborhood that week, Michael Brown got the sense that Gibbs really wanted to be president, that she was campaigning for the position. He saw it in the way she handled herself in the neighborhood. She was no longer the timid housewife who had sat at his desk at the *Gazette* weeks earlier, asking him questions about what he knew. Gibbs appeared, to Brown, like a woman who was politically astute, despite her lack of education, and knowledgeable about the canal situation, despite having never heard of it until recently.

The people in the fire hall that Friday night, apparently, saw the same thing. In the crowded room, hot and angry all over again, the residents cast their votes for Lois Gibbs: aged twenty-seven, mother of two, a high school graduate, president.

20

MANY ABUSIVE PHONE CALLS

Gibbs barely got a chance to address the crowd inside the fire hall when John LaFalce arrived, walked into the room, and took the microphone out of her hand. He had some exciting news to announce.

After nearly fourteen months of searching, he said, his office had finally helped secure $4 million in federal funding to clean up the site. The crowd cheered, giving him a standing ovation. LaFalce was coming through for them, and the timing was perfect. By announcing the news at the fire hall that night, he would make it into the next day's papers. LaFalce would make headlines while also currying favor with the residents, a stroke of political genius that the people wouldn't soon forget.

"He's super," people said about LaFalce.

"Dealt with us from the beginning."

"He called me. We had personal calls."

"That's LaFalce."

In Albany, Governor Hugh Carey's aides took note and advised that the governor follow what one described as the "LaFalce line." Go to Niagara Falls. Meet with the residents. Express his concerns—the governor needed to be concerned—and then vow to help while stopping short of committing to buying up homes, a financial obligation that the state of New York was hoping to avoid. If it purchased one street full of houses, the people on the next street might want out, too, and as the residents themselves had asked, "Where do you draw the line?"

It was an issue that was suddenly important for Carey, and not just because of Whalen's announcement or LaFalce's grand gestures, but because of the broader politics of the moment. There was about a month to go before the Democratic primary in the governor's race, and Carey found himself in an unusual situation. For the first time in his political life, he was in danger of losing, locked in a battle with his own lieutenant governor, Mary Anne Krupsak, a former ally and running mate whom Carey had managed to alienate and offend. According to the latest polls, Carey was only two percentage points ahead of Krupsak—a virtual dead heat—and there was more bad news. One poll indicated that Krupsak—the forty-six-year-old pride of Schenectady and the daughter of first-generation Polish Americans—had a better chance than Carey at defeating the Republican nominee in November, should she make it to the general election. Perhaps most problematic, Krupsak was also outflanking him with voters in Niagara Falls. She had visited the city the day of the meeting at the fire hall and was making Love Canal a central campaign issue, believing that it exposed all of Carey's well-known shortcomings: his lack of interest, his inability to engage, and his general indifference to the problems facing ordinary New Yorkers.

On the campaign trail that August, Krupsak accurately noted that state agencies had been aware of problems in the neighborhood since 1977—and done nothing to alert residents—and had known of the potential health hazards since the spring. And, again, they had done nothing. The governor, she said, didn't even weigh in on the issue until it hit the newspapers, and still he hadn't visited the site—all of which she considered an outrage.

But Krupsak didn't have to do much to portray Carey as being out of touch. The governor was doing the work for her. A few days earlier, he mistakenly referred to the area as "Love Creek," apparently unaware of the proper name.

That needed to change—right away, if possible.

Aides were sending Carey to Niagara Falls.

Beverly Paigen watched LaFalce from across the fire hall that night, sweating in the heat like everyone else and waiting for her turn to speak.

On a Friday evening like this one in late summer, she could have been home in Buffalo, some twenty miles away, with her husband,

Ken, and their children. Unlike the residents of the neighborhood, Paigen had no mortgage to lose and no children in danger. And unlike LaFalce, she had nothing to gain by speaking to the crowd, no votes to win. But ever since Hadley had alerted Paigen to the problems around the old canal, she couldn't stop thinking about them.

Over the last few days, she had collected soil samples from thirty-one different locations near the old landfill and at certain places along the river, where the canal would have connected with the main channel of water decades earlier. She brought them back to her lab at Roswell Park, dried the samples, ground them into a fine dust using a mortar and pestle, and exposed them to bacteria—salmonella. The experiment, called the Ames test, was a scientifically proven way to determine if elements were mutagenic—able to damage human cells, causing cancer and birth defects. If the salmonella cells changed after exposure to the sample, the scientist would know there was a problem.

In her tests, Paigen quickly eliminated about two-thirds of the samples as normal or unknown. Then she ran into problems. Five came back mutagenic, and five others killed the salmonella cells, leaving Paigen to hypothesize that the samples themselves had been "very toxic." But there were other problems, too—odd circumstances that gave Paigen further reason for worry. In one case, the sample in question was almost entirely white powder, making it impossible to prepare for the testing process. Several other samples also broke down, possibly because the chemicals were volatile, Paigen speculated, and she had to cut testing short after her lab technicians came to her with what she considered valid complaints. "The laboratory smelled like the Love Canal area," she noted in a report, "and the two technicians had the taste of these chemicals in their mouths after going home from work."

Based on these findings, Paigen believed that most of the chemicals in the ground were mutagenic, and she thought there was evidence of that in the neighborhood, too. Among twenty-four recent births there, Paigen counted four children with defects. A small sample size, to be sure. But at this rate, an expectant mother living near the canal was up to eight times more likely to give birth to a child with congenital problems than the average American mom. And even babies born healthy around the canal weren't in the clear,

Paigen believed. Indeed, the problems for them were just beginning, because, as Paigen pointed out, the chemicals weren't contained to the soil. They were floating in the dust, on the wind, in the homes around the canal, and being tracked inside on the soles of little feet.

At the meeting that Friday night, when she finally stood up to talk, Paigen wasn't looking to excite anybody or inflame the situation. She was just hoping to provide people with some sound, rational, medical advice, and she started by talking about health risks in general. She explained that everyone in the room faced risks in their lives. If they adhered to a healthy diet, they could imagine their risks decreasing, like mercury dropping in a thermometer. But if they smoked a pack of cigarettes a day, the risks went up and the mercury did, too. If they worked in a chemical plant, breathing fumes all day, they could imagine the mercury rising a little more. And, yes, Paigen told them, sadly, there was a certain amount of risk associated with living in the neighborhood and going home at night to sleep in their own beds. How much risk? Paigen couldn't say. But it was enough that she believed the state should consider evacuating more people.

"If it were my home and my family," Paigen told residents. "I wouldn't feel comfortable."

She needed to be honest with them.

"I don't think the neighborhood is safe."

Paigen and Gibbs walked home together in the dark that night, heading back to Gibbs's house, along with Wayne Hadley and a small group of others.

It was nearly midnight when they left the fire hall, another long day in a seemingly endless week. But running on adrenaline and panic over her new responsibilities as president, Gibbs had no intention of going to sleep, much to her husband Harry's dismay. She wanted to stay up and strategize in the kitchen with Paigen and her brother-in-law about tomorrow, and the next day, and the day after that. She had much to learn, and she was concerned that if she didn't, people would realize the truth about her: that she didn't know what she was doing.

As Gibbs carried on, talking about her worries, Paigen was hardly paying attention. She was fixated on something else: the smell of the air in the night, and how the odors changed, depending on where they were in the neighborhood, as they walked down Frontier Avenue and up 101st Street toward Gibbs's house, heading home. Every time they went past a manhole, Paigen noticed, the chemical odors were stronger.

Gibbs didn't understand why Paigen kept talking about manholes. As Gibbs saw it, they needed to be discussing other things—like the telegram they needed to send to President Carter the next day. They needed a strategy to pressure top politicians to show up for meetings. But Paigen kept turning to the sewers, pausing and sniffing the air. "I felt," Paigen said later, "like I was breathing poison." Poison that could not be contained, Paigen knew, by the fence that state officials were starting to erect around the southern portion of the old canal or the imaginary lines they were drawing on the map. Poison that, Paigen believed, was migrating underground.

"It's moving," she said.

The next morning, while Paigen pondered how she might prove that hypothesis, reporters were seeking her out. It was a Saturday, but the big news in Love Canal scrambled everybody's schedule. President Carter was sending his federal disaster chief to Niagara Falls on an early morning flight to assess the situation. LaFalce was going to meet the disaster chief at the canal site for a tour. State health officials were phoning Gibbs at her house, inviting her to join the two men, and she was going. She would be there. Gibbs hustled out the door in the best clothes she could find in her closet on short notice. Harry—or Lois's mother—would have to watch the kids again. And reporters, like Michael Brown, were working overtime, fanning out across the city, touring toxic basements, following Gibbs and LaFalce around the neighborhood, and calling Beverly Paigen at her house.

One of them, a reporter for the Buffalo *Courier-Express,* had obtained a document that he thought might interest Paigen: an official list of the eighty-two chemicals that the state had identified—so far—in the neighborhood. He was hoping to interview her about them, and Paigen happily went on the record, discussing each chemical one by one.

Paigen explained how toluene caused liver damage, how benzene was linked to leukemia, and how trichloroethylene was a known neurotoxin, causing problems in humans since 1915. She explained how at least eleven of the eighty-two chemicals on the list had been proven to cause cancer in animals; how symptoms of exposure to these chemicals could include everything from birth defects to headaches, cancer to depression; and how children—"the very young," Paigen said—would be especially at risk. Finally, she explained how no one could accurately predict what would happen if all of these compounds were stirred up together in a single place and left to percolate for decades in the ground. "You would have to be a walking encyclopedia," Paigen told the reporter, "to recognize all of those chemicals."

The story ran on the front page of the *Courier-Express* that Sunday, and Paigen didn't think twice about it. She was busy at home that weekend, packing the car and preparing to leave for a family vacation at a cabin near the ocean on Mount Desert Island in Maine. She also knew that nothing she told the *Courier-Express* would come as a surprise to her bosses at Roswell Park. Just a few days earlier, she had given them a formal report on her preliminary Love Canal soil findings.

But Roswell Park was a state institute, funded by taxpayer dollars, under the umbrella of Whalen and Axelrod's Department of Health. Paigen's bosses ultimately reported to Albany, and Albany had questions about this employee, Beverly Paigen, who was showing up at the fire hall in the neighborhood, giving advice, suggesting that people should be afraid, and talking to the papers. Even before the *Courier-Express* quoted her that Sunday, Whalen wanted to know more about her, and the director at Roswell Park—its top doctor, Gerald Murphy—was forced to respond. Murphy sent Whalen's public relations man, Marvin Nailor, a file of newspaper clippings on Paigen. He confirmed that she had been conducting research—"appropriate environmental cancer research," Murphy said—in the neighborhood that summer, and he indicated that Paigen hadn't tried to hide her involvement. On the contrary, it was right there in the departmental reports that anyone in Albany could have read, had they cared to look.

Then Murphy—a urologist with a reputation for running Roswell Park with dictatorial zeal—asked Whalen for direction.

"I'd like to know," he said, "if you wish me to pursue this matter at a local level any further."

By that Sunday, Murphy had his answer, and it was urgent enough that he couldn't wait until Monday morning to meet with other top administrators at Roswell Park and discuss the situation. He started typing up memos that day, spending his weekend informing his colleagues that they might have a Beverly Paigen problem.

"Dr. Whalen feels that some of her statements are not backed up by data," Murphy told his fellow administrators Edwin Mirand and David Pressman. Then, in a tone far different from the one he had used when discussing Paigen just two days earlier, Murphy demanded answers in order to satisfy Albany and also a more detailed report about what Paigen had gathered at Love Canal. "To my knowledge," Murphy said, "it has never been presented, gathered, or recorded at Roswell Park." If that was the case, he argued, there was a problem. "A serious breach of scientific credibility," Murphy called it.

Mirand and Pressman got right on it. Mirand was one of the nation's most respected cancer researchers, a pioneer in the field, and Pressman had authored papers with the likes of Linus Pauling, the two-time Nobel Prize winner and iconic American chemist. They would get Murphy the answers he wanted as quickly as possible, tracking down Paigen on vacation if necessary. She had hardly arrived in Maine on Tuesday, when the phone began to ring in the cabin near the ocean. Pressman was on the line, demanding information.

Paigen, caught off guard and unprepared, tried to explain to him that she didn't have her data with her and that it would be hard to get at that particular moment. Because she was on vacation, others in her lab had taken the week off, too. The request, she said, would probably need to wait until she got back in ten days or so. Pressman refused to accept that answer. He also declined to say what had precipitated his request or why it was so important. When Paigen asked him about it, he mentioned nothing about the story in the newspaper or Whalen's interest in Albany. Instead, he told her it was none of her business. Her job was to comply with the request within twenty-four hours—a deadline that Paigen promptly missed.

Back at Roswell Park in Buffalo, Murphy grew increasingly frustrated and began blaming Paigen for things she had not done. First, he accused Paigen of releasing her data to the newspaper, when, in fact, it was the other way around. The reporter had called her—to share his information with her. She had only helped him understand it. Then Murphy ignored the fact that Paigen was nine hundred miles from her lab—at a cabin in Maine on vacation with her family—and twisted her excuse around to suggest to Mirand and Pressman that maybe she was fabricating information. "I am shocked to hear from you," Murphy said, "that Dr. Paigen has no way of documenting her data."

Again, he asked them to look into the matter—immediately. And again, the phone continued to ring in Maine. All week.

"Many abusive phone calls," Paigen noted.

But why? She had no idea.

21

MOMMY'S GOING TO STAY

The doctors had given Luella Kenny specific instructions when they sent Jon Allen home from the hospital at the end of July. She was to check the protein levels in her son's urine every day, using the easy dipstick test that Jon Allen's pediatrician had used to detect the problem in the first place. She was to keep the boy on a strict, low-sodium diet, and she was to report to the renal clinic at Children's Hospital in Buffalo for Jon Allen's first post-hospitalization checkup in one week—on Wednesday, August 2.

Driving home from the hospital the day he was discharged, Luella felt good about the plan. Jon Allen wasn't cured. As a scientist herself, Luella recognized that. He was still swollen in the face, puffy around the eyes. In recent days, he had complained of both headaches and a cough. And despite the beautiful summer weather, he was hardly going to be bounding outside to play anytime soon. After nearly one month in the hospital, with doctors and nurses checking on his vital signs at all hours of the day and night, Jon Allen was tired. As soon as they pulled in to the driveway of their home on Ninety-Sixth Street and walked in the front door, he curled up on the couch with his stuffed dog, Scuppity, in his arms. He wanted to rest.

Still, Luella and Norman Kenny had every reason to be optimistic. Jon Allen might have been a little tired, but he had been off steroids for days and his protein levels remained normal. The boy, who had needed to be carried home from the Debby Boone concert at the end of June, was now walking out of the hospital on his own and smiling at the nurses. The Kennys believed doctors when they said that Jon Allen would likely outgrow this problem. And at the first checkup appointment at Children's Hospital on August 2, Jon Allen got more good news: He could break his low-sodium diet that night and have his favorite meal for dinner. He could eat pizza.

Luella drove him home and called his grandmothers. They were all coming to dinner, a celebratory meal. On the night when nearby homeowners burned their mortgage statements in the street and Lois Gibbs waded into the crowd seeking out the shrieking microphone—"Okay?"—the Kennys were going out. They piled into Norman's station wagon, backed out of their driveway, turned right out of their neighborhood, skirted past the northern corner of the old canal, and crossed over Black Creek, bound for the Pizza Hut at the corner of Seventy-Eighth and Niagara Falls Boulevard, a couple of miles away.

Luella and Norman were well aware of the news coming out of Albany, if not the angry mob gathering with Gibbs near the school. Everyone in the neighborhood, from Griffon Manor to 103rd Street, was talking about Whalen's announcement and what it meant for them. But like any parents with a sick child, they didn't have space in their lives for abstract fears about unknown chemicals in the ground or the capacity to think about how Whalen's announcement might affect the value of their home. They were already dealing with a crisis while trying to hold down their jobs and continuing to be functioning parents to their other sons, Christopher and Stephen, who had their own sets of needs and problems.

Whatever revolution Lois Gibbs was planning on the other side of the canal would have to wait for another night, or perhaps another week. This moment was reserved for Jon Allen, greasy-fingered and smiling over a table full of pizza. This moment was about reclaiming a little piece of normalcy in a summer of trouble. For the first time in a long time, the Kennys were a family, doing what families do. They were having dinner at a Pizza Hut on a Wednesday evening.

Luella went to sleep that night down the hall from her children, holding on to the memory of the dinner they shared as if it were a charm that could ward off evil spirits. It didn't work. By August 11, Jon Allen's protein counts were climbing again, inching up after nearly three weeks of healthy readings. On a scale of zero to four—

with four being the worst—Jon Allen was now considered a two. Luella called Children's Hospital and told doctors what she was seeing. But for now, they saw no reason to bring him in. The boy was scheduled for a forty-eight-hour stay at the hospital later that month for some clinical tests and a rigorous round of high-dose steroids. Doctors told the Kennys to continue to monitor his protein counts and report any spikes, but otherwise they should plan to stick to the schedule.

Luella agreed to do that, and then Jon Allen's body began to swell again. He became so distended around his abdomen that soon he was no longer able to buckle his pants. In order to go out, Luella had to make him wear suspenders. It was the only way to keep his corduroys or jeans from falling down over his rounded belly. Meanwhile, Jon Allen was increasingly exhausted, lethargic, uninterested in his usual activities, and by the time he reported to the hospital on August 21, a very sick boy once again.

"Today," doctors noted at check-in, "he is a four."

Jon Allen was as ill as he had ever been back in June. He was right back where he had started, and he knew it wasn't going well.

"Mommy's going to stay," Luella told him as they settled in on the fourth floor of the hospital. Their room, 419B, had two beds, and Luella had received permission in advance to sleep there for their stay. She wanted Jon Allen to know that she wasn't going anywhere. He was going to be okay. The doctors were there to take care of him, she said, and the steroids were going to help him feel better again.

She was right, at least, about the steroids. After just two days in the hospital, Jon Allen was back home, pumped full of prednisone and rallying once again. He was going to be healthy enough to start second grade with the rest of his class at Sacred Heart Villa at the end of the month, and he was looking forward to his seventh birthday on September 19. Luella was planning two parties—one for family and one for friends.

But the hard summer—in and out of the hospital, swollen and sick—had stolen a bit of innocence from Jon Allen. The boy wasn't sure what to believe anymore, a change noted by everyone during his stay at Children's Hospital in August. As nurses moved in to draw blood and take his vitals before yet another round of incessant tests, he looked different.

"Patient very upset and nervous," they noted in his chart.

"Irritable and crying."

"Color pale."

Jon Allen was afraid.

22

GIVE MY REGARDS TO BROADWAY

Governor Carey flew into Niagara Falls the week after Whalen's announcement—five days late and two hours behind his scheduled arrival. A public meeting that was supposed to start at eight o'clock that Monday night at the 99th Street School was now going to start around ten, upsetting residents, who had arrived early for the meeting, and frustrating reporters, who were going to struggle to meet their deadlines because of the delay.

At least the reporters already knew what they were writing. Under pressure from LaFalce, Barbara Blum at the EPA, the federal disaster chief who had toured the neighborhood with Gibbs over the weekend, and Governor Carey, desperate to win votes, beat Krupsak in the upcoming primary, and end the crisis in Niagara Falls, President Carter had decided to take unprecedented federal action that Monday. For the first time in U.S. history, a president was ordering a federal emergency not because of a blizzard, a hurricane, a tornado, a forest fire, or a flood but because of an unnatural disaster, a man-made catastrophe: a chemical dump buried in the heart of a neighborhood.

The president's order, handed down that Monday afternoon before Carey's plane landed in Niagara Falls, empowered federal officials to spend taxpayer money to "save lives, protect property, public health, and safety, or avert the threat of a disaster." More pointedly, for residents, it made people in the neighborhood eligible for federal financial assistance—the financial assistance that LaFalce had promised was coming. But just who would get help—and how—wasn't exactly clear to anyone. Even LaFalce wasn't sure, and he was slated to take the stage that night at the school with Carey—under some very specific instructions. Carey's aides informed LaFalce that under no circumstances should he, or Carey, or anyone else promise to buy anyone's home around the canal.

LaFalce understood what was expected of him—whether he agreed with it or not. Carey, on the other hand, either did not understand or changed his mind, in a bid to win some popular appeal to improve his ratings, once he faced the fury of the crowd. Shortly after arriving in Niagara Falls, Carey met privately with Gibbs and a few other homeowners in a room inside the school. Then he took the stage and began making promises.

Mortgage payments? Carey said people in contaminated homes wouldn't have to make them. Selling houses? Carey announced that everyone living on a contaminated property would have that option. And getting out? Carey made it sound as if that were a possibility for everyone, too. In fact, they should just go, he said, abandoning their houses now, with everything still inside, if they wanted.

"Leave it behind," he told the crowd, as they cheered him, roaring.

Surely, the state would have to draw a line somewhere. But Carey, mired in a heated primary against his own lieutenant governor, wasn't going to get into the details now and risk getting booed by two hundred angry voters. He kept making promises instead, and the people loved him for it.

They bathed Carey in applause. The residents living close to the canal believed that the state would buy their homes, and the residents living farther out—people like Gibbs—believed that if they could prove their homes were contaminated, or that they had health problems as a result of chemical exposure, the state would buy them out, too. Everyone was pleased—except for Carey's aides, watching the governor's performance.

"Oh, my God," one of them muttered.

Gibbs overheard the comment and was confused. She didn't understand why one of Carey's top staffers would be upset about his comments. But LaFalce understood. He knew what was coming next. Someone was going to have to walk back the promises and clean up Carey's mess. Even Carey himself understood that he had altered the script in a way that was going to have ramifications. When the meeting ended, the governor turned to one of his staffers and informed him that he was going to have to stay in Niagara

Falls and set up an office inside the school while the governor jetted home to prepare for an even bigger meeting the next day: the president was coming.

Carter was flying to New York City in just fourteen hours on Air Force One for a celebration in lower Manhattan, signing legislation that guaranteed $1.65 billion in loans to help save the great and troubled city from bankruptcy. In doing so, Carter was fulfilling a campaign promise. In 1975, President Gerald Ford, Carter's predecessor, had vowed to deny federal bailout aid to the floundering metropolis, prompting the famous *New York Daily News* headline "Ford to City: Drop Dead." A year later, in a surprisingly bitter fight to defeat Ford in New York, Carter made the headline a centerpiece of his campaign against Ford in the city, and he wanted to return now to demonstrate to New Yorkers that Jimmy Carter was a man of his word.

The event that Tuesday in August 1978 was the sort of festivity that a struggling president like Carter desperately needed. It was both extravagant and huge, starting with the president's entourage itself. He boarded Air Force One at Andrews Air Force Base in Maryland that afternoon with the First Lady, the entire congressional delegation for New York City, both U.S. senators for the state of New York, seven Secret Service agents, five White House staffers, his personal doctor and photographer, and ten members of the White House press corps, including reporters for *The New York Times,* the Associated Press, and CBS, and perhaps most important of all Carter was traveling with his confidant and special assistant for intergovernmental affairs, Jack Watson.

Watson, like Barbara Blum, was part of what the press liked to call Carter's "Georgia Mafia." He had known the president since his days as governor down south. But the young, charismatic Atlanta attorney—with a Harvard law degree and the touch of a southern gentleman—had earned his spot in the White House, smart and handsome, and in the know. It was Watson who had suggested the day before that Carter order a federal emergency in Niagara Falls. It was Watson who had helped arrange that day's event in New York City, and it was Watson who was preparing Carter before the trip for whatever Governor Hugh Carey might throw at him after they landed at JFK.

The two men—Carter and Carey—were hardly close. Carey had been slow to endorse Carter in 1976, a fact that neither Carter nor Watson had forgotten. And when Carey finally did give Carter his support, it was without enthusiasm. Carey casually mentioned the endorsement at the tail end of a press conference about another matter, like a postscript, an afterthought, and the endorsement arrived when the outcome was already clear: Carter was going to be the Democratic nominee. Carey was intentionally late to the party. But the chill between the two men was over more than just a political slight. Carter and Carey were just different. The governor was more liberal—on many issues. The president was more genial—almost always. They had almost nothing in common—except power—and they were about to spend the entire day together.

Air Force One landed at JFK around mid-afternoon, and Carter climbed aboard a Marine helicopter for a short flight into the city, where Carey was waiting for him with a gift. He presented Carter with an "I ❤ NY" button for the lapel of his suit jacket. Carter happily pinned it on, and the two men rode downtown together in the presidential motorcade, through a grid of skyscrapers and into a sea of humanity, people cheering Carter and even singing: "Give my regards to Broadway! Remember me to Herald Square!"

The scenes from the afternoon gala didn't exactly play well in Niagara Falls. Angry residents there wondered why the governor and the president were busy glad-handing a crowd in New York City—and attending a Broadway show together that night—instead of coming to visit their troubled neighborhood on the east side of town. If Air Force One should be landing anywhere, they thought, it should be there. As one resident informed Carey that week, "I would greatly appreciate your meeting with President Carter in Niagara County . . . not in New York City." But at the very least, Carey, desperate to make good on the bold promises he made the night before in Niagara Falls, had been advised to discuss Love Canal with the president that day. He needed to get federal help in buying up houses, or at least get the White House involved in some way. Whatever Carey told the president that day must have worked. Late that Tuesday night, just as Carter and Carey were settling into their seats for their Broadway show, Gibbs got a phone call at her home on 101st Street. It was Carter's federal disaster chief on the phone inviting her to attend a hastily arranged gathering scheduled for the morning.

Lois Gibbs was going to Washington.

The next day, for Gibbs, was a blur of boardrooms and press conferences, flashbulbs and flights, as Bonnie Casper and John LaFalce helped usher her from meeting to meeting. By the time it was over, she nearly nodded off in a chair in LaFalce's office as Casper looked on. But at least Gibbs was returning home with some results.

In the Roosevelt Room at the White House, Jack Watson huddled with Carey's top aides and helped hammer out a robust plan to relocate not just the 97 families initially mentioned in Whalen's health order a week earlier but more than 230 families in all—anyone living on either side of Ninety-Seventh and Ninety-Ninth Streets. These families would be eligible to receive $300 per month to cover rental costs wherever they moved—as well as a onetime sum of $400 to cover moving expenses*—and officials pledged to find some way to buy their homes, too. In the span of just a week, Whalen's recommendation that certain families with pregnant mothers and young children should consider moving had exploded into a full-scale government-ordered evacuation of a residential neighborhood that was projected to cost as much as $7 million. Watson hoped that would be enough—he didn't want the federal government to be in the business of solving Hugh Carey's problems—and Carey's aides hoped it would be enough, too. That day in Washington, they tried to get assurances from Gibbs that residents would stop shouting at officials and stop protesting at meetings. But she couldn't make that promise. As Gibbs saw it, the problem still wasn't solved.

Another seven hundred families—roughly three thousand people, including Luella Kenny, everyone in Griffon Manor, and Lois Gibbs herself—were still trapped there. They were farther away from the old canal than the soon-to-be evacuated people on Ninety-Seventh and Ninety-Ninth Streets. But they were still living on the

* In today's dollars, a relocated family was receiving about $1,200 to cover rent and nearly $1,600 to move—a windfall of money for many working-class families.

canal's fringes and about to be looking out over a wasteland of abandoned starter homes dotting the landscape around a vacant school.

Gibbs boarded her flight home that evening wondering what was going to happen to her. Then, in a moment of fitting symbolism, thunderstorms grounded her flight and Gibbs was stuck on the tarmac. She wasn't going to be arriving home on time. When her plane did finally get in the air, it had to be diverted to Rochester, seventy-five miles east of its intended destination. Gibbs had no choice but to travel the rest of the way by bus, stumbling into her house long after Harry and the kids had fallen asleep. She had no one to talk to about her day, but there was a pan of freshly baked coffee cake in the kitchen, as if by some miracle, and she began to devour it, stress eating in the dark.

It was morning before Lois realized her mistake. Her sister Kathy had left the pan of goodies in the kitchen for Lois's son, Michael. He was turning six that day—a milestone that Lois hadn't just forgotten. She had managed to make it worse.

In the middle of the night, mostly broken and half-asleep, she had eaten her own son's birthday cake.

23

LET OUR PEOPLE SPEAK

On the other side of the old canal, Elene Thornton was finally paying attention to the news, and she was starting to worry about it.

Thornton was one of the longest-tenured residents of Griffon Manor. The single Black mother—almost forty years old in the summer of 1978—had lived in the housing development off and on for more than twenty years. She was well known among residents. She cut quite a figure on the paths of the development—a small woman at just four feet eleven—and she was something of a permanent fixture at Ladies' Night in the local bowling leagues. Amid the smoke and the haze at the Pine Bowl or Beverly Lanes, there was Thornton, gliding across the polished maple floors throwing strike after strike. The woman knew how to do it all: how to address the ball, how to follow through, and even how to pick up the dreaded 6-7-10 split, with the pins standing like goalposts in the far corners of the lane.

But somehow, Thornton had missed this. Like many people in the neighborhood, she had failed to recognize the urgency of the problems surfacing near the 99th Street School. She had read the stories in the newspaper all summer, pretending that the chemicals didn't affect her. Now she was starting to think that maybe she had been lying to herself. Her townhome on Ninety-Third Street was about as close to the buried chemicals as Gibbs's house on 101st, and some people in Griffon Manor lived even closer than many homeowners. It stood to reason that if Lois Gibbs was in danger—and in interviews with reporters that August, Gibbs was sure acting as if she were in danger—then Elene Thornton was, too. Everyone at Griffon Manor could be at risk.

Yet no one was inquiring about the health and safety of Thornton's family. No one was asking about the well-being of her six children, two of whom still lived in the townhome with her. No one seemed interested in the story of her late son, Gregory. The boy, Thornton's third child, had died of leukemia in the housing development almost seventeen years earlier, in 1961, before his second birthday—a tragic death that took on different meaning now. And no one was inviting Thornton—or anyone else from Griffon Manor—to go to Washington, to meet privately with Governor Carey at the school, or give interviews to the press. The renters in the neighborhood—both Black and white—felt as if they were being ignored. They were invisible, and they wanted to be seen, be heard.

"They forget us low-income people—they think we're trash," complained Dorothy Atkinson, a white mother in her late forties living in Court 10 at Griffon Manor. Atkinson had never graduated from high school, didn't have a job, and was living off welfare—$285 a month. But she refused to be treated like a second-class citizen. "We're people, too," she told others at the time. "We've got kids—and we worry."

Atkinson was concerned about the chemical odors in her apartment. She believed they were wafting up through her pipes and out of her sink. Sometimes, to beat back the smell, she would pour bleach down the drain, fighting chemicals with chemicals—a choice that was potentially not helping. And she was especially worried about her family's long history in the neighborhood. Atkinson had lived in Griffon Manor for more than a decade and had spent several years on Ninety-Ninth Street before that—back in the 1940s when Hooker was still using the canal as a dump. She could remember the Hooker trucks rolling into the neighborhood, the small explosions that would rattle the windows of the homes after the trucks pulled away, and the fires flickering in the night. Too many fires to count. "I knew it was chemicals," Atkinson said now, in hindsight. "Because, at night, after they buried them, you'd be sitting there about five or six o'clock and you'd hear—*boom*—and you'd look out there and there'd be a fire."

Atkinson might never have graduated from high school, but she was savvy enough to know the question that was coming next. If she had known about the Hooker dump for so long, why hadn't she left? If she had known about the chemicals in the ground, why was she still there? The answer, for her, was simple: "We can't all pick up and leave." She lived in Griffon Manor because her relatives were nearby, and because it was the only place she had, and because it was affordable. Also, she didn't truly understand what Hooker had been doing out there in the 1940s and never figured it would come to this—with the state ordering 230 homeowners to leave and giving them $300 a month to get out. That wasn't just more money than Atkinson received each month in her welfare check; it was more than many of the people in Griffon Manor had. It was easy, then, to imagine that something had to be horribly wrong over there, and just like the homeowners, many residents of Griffon Manor began making mental checklists of every medical problem they'd ever had and cross-referencing them with the conditions mentioned in the newspaper articles.

Atkinson wondered if chemical fumes had caused the dizzy spells her daughter suffered while attending the 99th Street School. Shirley Woodcock, another white mother in Griffon Manor, wondered if the chemicals helped explain why her youngest daughter had been born with a hole in her heart. Throughout the development, Black mothers and grandmothers worried that the landfill might be harming their kids, too. One grandmother of eight children at Griffon Manor said she fretted about it all the time. "You're afraid," she said. "You're living in fear." And Sarah Rich, a Black mother in Court 4, understood that feeling. Rich lived in her apartment with her two kids, a nephew, a niece, and her seventy-nine-year-old mother, and it seemed as though they all had problems. Eczema, asthma, kidney infections, headaches, and dreams. Bad dreams. Lately, Rich and her children were tormented by nightmares. She'd dream that the canal had exploded, while her nephew, aged eleven, also had visions. In his dreams, "bad people" were coming. He was surrounded, he said, by "bad people."

It was a hard way to live, and Elene Thornton was hoping to put an end to it. She wanted to organize all three hundred families living in Griffon Manor, and in mid-August, just days after Gibbs returned home from Washington, Thornton brought her idea to Agnes Jones—a Black leader in the development's newly formed tenants' council. Jones was in her mid-thirties and she was an outsider in Griffon Manor. She had only moved there about a year earlier, when a fire ripped through her previous house on Frontier Avenue, three miles away, near the chemical plants on the river. She had no history in the neighborhood, no roots there. But like Thornton, Jones was a single mother, with two teenage girls to raise. And like Thornton, she was known for being fiercely independent. Agnes Jones wanted to help.

She agreed they needed to be focusing their energies on the canal. They needed to organize a group of their own and maybe even start attending the meetings that Lois Gibbs was holding. In one of her very first acts as president, Gibbs had made it clear that the homeowners' association, despite its title, intended to represent everyone living between Ninety-Third and 103rd Streets, Black Creek and the river—a chunk of land that included all of Griffon Manor. Anyone living there was welcome to attend meetings and, indeed, seemingly encouraged to do so. As Gibbs said, "It is extremely important that we work together."

But the paperwork that Gibbs's attorney Richard Lippes filed with the state that month, officially incorporating the association, mentioned nothing about renters. The wording only referenced "property owners"—an oversight that Lippes failed to catch and that Gibbs would come to regret. By late August—when Thornton, Jones, and other residents of Griffon Manor attended a homeowners' meeting for the first time—the whole collaborative, "work together" feeling had blown off like a morning fog on the river. Everyone was arguing, and it wasn't just homeowners against renters. Under stress, people were turning on each other, regardless of where they lived.

Two of the three homeowners elected to serve with Gibbs had already betrayed her, trying to start their own splinter organization. They lived on Ninety-Ninth Street and wanted to make sure that they got in line first for whatever money the government would be handing out. In their minds, Gibbs lived too far from the canal—way out on 101st Street—and therefore wasn't personally invested in helping those living in the most contaminated homes. But

Gibbs had also lost others because she was too radical, too vocal, and these factions had begun to squabble, too. In a matter of just days, neighbors stopped talking to neighbors—or even waving over the fence—if they believed the other person might be able to move before them. And as tensions grew, Gibbs was about to learn a hard lesson in leadership. Because she had been elected president of the homeowners' association, because she was being quoted in the newspaper almost every day, and because the state had even given her some office space in an old teachers' lounge inside the school to get her group started, she was part of the establishment now, too. In some people's minds, she was not all that different from Governor Carey or David Axelrod.

"Forget it," one homeowner said when asked about Gibbs.

He didn't want anything to do with her, and many homeowners felt the same about the residents in Griffon Manor.

"Why don't they just move out?" another homeowner asked in what was becoming a popular refrain.

"Welfare pays them to move," another agreed.

"If I were renting in this area," said still another, "you better believe I would have been out a long time ago."

Some homeowners worried that the residents of Griffon Manor complicated an already complex situation. State and federal authorities would never move the homeowners in the outer rings of the neighborhood, they believed, if that meant they'd also have to clear out a three-hundred-unit public housing development in a city already short of affordable places to live. For that reason, people living, say, on 102nd Street didn't want their financial fortunes tied to Elene Thornton and Agnes Jones in Griffon Manor. But Gibbs knew she was wrestling another problem: deep-seated racial prejudice.

"It's the minorities," one homeowner admitted behind closed doors.

At the meeting attended by Thornton and Jones at the end of August, all of these issues bubbled to the surface, like the buried chemicals in William T. Love's old canal, leaching through the room and poisoning the community. Wayne Hadley tried to put a stop to the bickering, and Gibbs did, too. In early September, about a week after the contentious homeowners' meeting, members of Gibbs's group went over to Griffon Manor to attend a public forum called by the state. But the 80 Griffon Manor residents in attendance that night wanted to hear from state health officials—not mothers who owned houses—and Agnes Jones let them know it. When a homeowner approached the microphone to ask a question, Jones stood up and ordered the woman away.

"This meeting," Jones snapped, "was not called for homeowners. It was called for us people—as you people call us."

She wanted the homeowners to sit quietly and listen.

"Let our people speak," Jones said.

24

THE BOY IN BED 11

The nun called Luella Kenny at work on a Friday in late September around lunchtime. Luella picked up the phone in her lab and heard the unmistakable voice of Jon Allen's second-grade teacher, Sister Denise Cona, on the other end of the line. Sister Denise was young, diminutive in size, and Sicilian by birth, a native Italian speaker who tended to sprinkle her conversations with side comments like "Thanks, God," as if he had a hand in everything, which, as Sister Denise saw it, he did. On this call, however, the thirty-eight-year-old nun got straight to the point. In her thick Sicilian accent, she explained that she was sorry to interrupt Kenny at work, but relieved to have found her. She was calling about Jon Allen.

The boy had been discharged from his two-night stay at Children's Hospital almost exactly one month earlier, and just as before he had stayed healthy at home—for a while. Taking fifteen milligrams of prednisone three times a day, Jon Allen started to look and feel like himself again. His protein levels returned to normal. His kidneys were, apparently, functioning as they should. He felt well enough to play basketball in the driveway with his father. He started school that September on time at Sacred Heart Villa with his two older brothers. Just that week, on September 19, Jon Allen had turned seven—a moment that the Kenny family had quietly marked with balloons, streamers, and cupcakes at home and planned to celebrate in full over the weekend. Jon Allen was inviting his second-grade friends to the house, and Luella had ordered a large sheet cake from a local bakery—a chocolate cake covered in white frosting and decorated with sweet, sugary rosettes. "HAPPY BIRTHDAY JON," it read.

But even as she prepared for the party, Luella was beginning to worry about her son again, noting familiar signs. At a routine checkup the week before his birthday, doctors found that his blood pressure was alarmingly high—a side effect of the medication he took. In order to bring it down, they began reducing Jon Allen's steroid dosage and planned to keep tapering it in the weeks to come. Yet this decision led immediately to the problem that Luella feared most of all. Within just two days, Jon Allen was spilling protein again. Once again, his condition was worsening—and fast.

On his birthday at least, the boy remained asymptomatic. Jon Allen said he was fine, despite his protein readings, and he looked healthy, too. There was no swelling or complaints of exhaustion. He ran and played and rode his bicycle outside on Ninety-Sixth Street, scampering in the fading light of the summer that he had mostly missed and taking advantage of the last warm days of the year, like the other kids in the neighborhood. But on Thursday—just two days after the family sang "Happy Birthday" over the cupcakes at the kitchen table—Jon Allen felt listless and tired. His body ached all over, he said, and the symptoms continued into the next day. Jon Allen woke up Friday morning with a light headache. Still, the boy was adamant that he was going to school. His birthday weekend was on the horizon. The sheet cake was already in the refrigerator in the kitchen, ready for the party, and Jon Allen was excited about all of it. He wanted to go to school and spend the day with his friends.

Luella considered her son's position, amid the typical morning chaos. Norman had already left for work. Jon Allen's older brothers were packing up their bags. Luella needed to get everybody out the door and then hustle to work herself, driving across town from the school to Roswell Park in rush-hour traffic. She had already missed so much time since June that it was hard to rationalize missing another day of work for a boy who claimed he was okay. Luella looked at Jon Allen and loaded him into her car with everybody else, bound for school.

At Sacred Heart Villa, he took his seat at his desk near the door in the front row of Sister Denise's class and felt fine—until language arts, late morning. Jon Allen had just finished reading out loud from a book in front of his class when he told Sister Denise that he didn't feel well. He wanted to find his brothers, and Sister Denise gave Jon Allen permission to go. He often liked to visit with Christopher or Stephen in the middle of the day, and because he was such a good student, such a good listener, Sister Denise liked to give him the opportunity. But this time, the boy didn't make it down the hall to the middle school classrooms. Pale and nauseated, Jon Allen turned for the bathroom and threw up all over the tiled floor.

"I'm sorry," he kept saying, when Sister Denise found him in there moments later. "I'm sorry."

She assured him it was fine, helped him wash up, led him to a cot that served as the nurse's office, and then began the process of tracking down his mother. Luella drove right over as soon as she got the phone call, careening across town, angry at herself for having sent Jon Allen to school in the first place—what kind of mother was she?—but mostly she was just worried. The rest of the day, Jon Allen felt worse and worse. When he wasn't vomiting in the bathroom at home, he was dry heaving. And when he wasn't dry heaving, he was in bed in the room that he shared with his older brother Stephen nestled under his *Star Wars* sheets and the afghan that Luella's mother had made for him, with Scuppity in his arms.

Late that night, Luella was concerned enough about him that she moved Jon Allen into her bed down the hall. It was just a gut feeling, a mother's instinct. She wanted to be able to monitor his breathing throughout the night.

Sometime around 2:30 that morning, the boy began to gurgle, moan, and shake.

Jon Allen was having a seizure.

"Norman!" Luella cried, waking her husband.

The couple examined their son in the bedroom. His eyes were open, yet he was nonresponsive. Wouldn't answer to his name. Couldn't speak. In a panic, the Kennys called a neighbor to come over and stay with their older boys while the couple hurried to the hospital in the middle of the night, carrying Jon Allen's limp body to the station wagon in the driveway. The streets of the city were silent—and the station wagon was too—as Norman drove and Luella cradled their son in the backseat. They chose Mount St.

Mary's, the closest hospital to their house and a place where doctors knew Jon Allen well. It was where he had stayed for nearly the entire month of July. Upon arriving, Jon Allen immediately had a second seizure, and doctors, including the pediatrician Luella trusted most, Dr. Maria Crea, decided it would be best to send the boy to the specialists at Children's Hospital in Buffalo, almost twenty-five miles away.

An ambulance pulled up outside the emergency room moments later to take him there. Inexplicably, the driver admitted he didn't know how to get to Children's Hospital. Luella shook her head and climbed into the front seat with the driver—she knew the way—while paramedics loaded her son onto a stretcher and placed him in the back.

It was five o'clock in the morning when doctors finally whisked him into the ICU at Children's, placed him in bed 11 in the unit, and then watched as he seized again. This time the seizure lasted for eight minutes. But Luella didn't see it. She wasn't allowed to go into the ICU. She stood in the doorway of the hospital, all alone, as the sun began to rise over the city and the doctors loomed over her son, their patient in bed 11, writing their notes. For the first time, they were taking an interest in the Kennys' address.

"Live near Love Canal," the doctors wrote in Jon Allen's chart. "Live in house."

25

TWO SIDES OF THE SQUARE

Hooker Chemical was looking to make it a great day.

That Saturday morning—while Jon Allen Kenny was in the ICU at Children's Hospital in Buffalo, falling in and out of consciousness, the corporate giant was trying to move on. Hooker hoped to get people to focus on the positive—all the great things the company had done, and continued to do, for the city of Niagara Falls.

Many people in town didn't need convincing. They knew the Hooker name, and they typically also knew someone who worked there: a friend or a family member, often their own fathers. They recognized that Hooker—as the largest industrial taxpayer in the city—helped keep the lights on in town, maintain the public parks, or make sure the snowplows were running in winter. If they had to take a side, many people chose Hooker—even some folks who were living in homes right on top of the canal where Hooker had dumped its chemical waste.

William Brennan was perhaps the starkest example of such loyalty. He was a homeowner on Ninety-Ninth Street; one of the 230 families being evacuated; a man slated to have his home purchased with the help of the state and the newly brokered federal relief money—whenever that came through; a man whose life was in chaos, at least in part due to the decisions his own company had made. And still, Brennan refused to hold Hooker accountable. "I blame the city of Niagara Falls," he said. "They gave the company permission to dump here in the first place."

The press, however, was less forgiving. Though there were several parties to blame for the current mess in Niagara Falls—the city, the board of education, the county health officials who ignored the warning signs since at least the 1960s, or the developers who built near the old canal, sometimes knowing full well that there were dangerous contents buried inside it—the press fixed its attention on Hooker Chemical itself. Reporters were calling all the time, asking tough questions and forcing the company's public relations man, Charles Cain, to roll out a new media strategy that he had crafted with the help of an outside consultant.

Cain explained to local employees around this time that the company needed to make a change. For years, he told his colleagues, Hooker had done business while considering just "two sides of the square"—what was technologically possible and what was economically beneficial. But due to an "evolution of life style and standards," Cain said, Hooker now needed to pay attention to the other two sides of the square. He described these sides as "Societal Demands" and "Political Constraints." A societal demand—say, for a weed killer, a fire ant poison, or a better toilet bowl cleaner—could, in time, become politically controversial, leading to legislation and lawsuits. To avoid such unsavory outcomes, Cain suggested that Hooker needed to realize that corporate responsibility was part of the cost of doing business, a built-in, bottom-line expense. The company also needed to take a more proactive approach to changing the narrative—or, as Cain put it, telling "the proper story."

At a corporate level, that meant setting aside more funding for Cain's public relations team. But Cain couldn't do it alone. He asked the three thousand employees in Niagara Falls to educate themselves about the company's philosophy and positions, so that if friends or family members complained about Hooker at a backyard barbecue or a Little League game, employees could speak in an informed way about the company and humanize the chemical manufacturer.

"We must make them aware of the fact that Hooker is not just smokestacks, reactors, cells, and other equipment," Cain told employees. " 'Hooker, neighbor, is the person you bowl with, go to church with, and whose kids go to the same school.' "

In other words, Cain said, Hooker was Niagara Falls.

"We should be able to say, 'I not only work here, I live here.' "

The fact that Bruce Davis—the company's ranking executive in the city—didn't actually live in town could apparently be overlooked because more than anyone else Davis was the face of Hooker in this time of crisis. Company headquarters in Houston directed any employee with questions about the canal to go see him, and it was Davis, more often than not, who sat for the television cameras and fielded the reporters' calls that August and September, telling "the proper story."

Davis pointed out that Hooker had only sold the land to the city after school officials persisted and the company revealed that it had used the site as a dump. It had then been the board of education's choice—not Hooker's—to erect a school on the landfill and the city's choice to allow developers to build a neighborhood around it. It was perhaps not surprising then, Davis continued, that the "security" of the landfill had been breached at some point, leading to the problems that newspapers were writing about now. But the press was missing the point, he argued, focusing too much on Hooker, and that was a shame, because, as Davis said, "we are sure as hell concerned about the people out there."

He wanted the folks in the neighborhood to know that Hooker was doing everything it could to help. The company was offering $280,000 for any remediation plans, even though it wasn't legally obligated to do so. It was working closely with authorities whenever possible, and it was agreeing to be open and candid about the past.

"We believe," Davis said, "we have been a responsible corporate citizen."

What Davis failed to mention was that state investigators—at that very moment—were probing three other sites in the city of Niagara Falls where the company had dumped toxic waste in recent years. One of those sites was small and near the Hooker plant downtown. The second wasn't far from Lois Gibbs's house—at 102nd Street and the river—and it was so volatile that two neighborhood boys had been injured there in 1970 as the ground began to smoke beneath the soles of their sneakers, popping, one of the boys said, "like a shotgun." And the third site—called Hyde Park, on the other side of town—was potentially the worst of them all. The Hyde Park dump was about the size of Love Canal but held as much as four times the amount of waste, including some thirty-eight thousand discarded drums, according to internal Hooker records. These drums contained everything from pesticides to "Misc. other," flame retardants to "Unknown."

Davis also typically failed to mention one other thing: that Hooker had yet to give authorities a detailed accounting of every chemical in the canal. Hooker was working on it, open and candid, considering every side of the square. But it was going to take a little longer, which maybe wasn't such a terrible thing. In one interview, Davis said he was hoping that "emotionalism" would die down and reason would finally have a chance to, once again, prevail in Niagara Falls.

26

CAN I GO HOME SOON?

The seizures for the boy in bed 11 lasted for most of the morning. Jon Allen Kenny thrashed so much, at first, on that Saturday in September 1978 that doctors at Children's Hospital in Buffalo restrained him, tying down his arms and legs. Then they inserted a plastic airway, ensuring he would be able to breathe, and injected him with a small dose of Valium to help stop the shaking.

Briefly, anyway, the measures worked, and doctors invited Luella into the ICU to see her son. To her eyes, it looked as if Jon Allen were no longer inside his own body. Even when he wasn't seizing, he didn't respond—not to verbal commands, not to painful stimuli, not to lights shined in his distant eyes. At one point, when Luella wasn't there, a doctor gently slapped the boy on the face, trying to wake him. Still nothing. Then he seized again—his eyes rolling back in his head and his face and legs twitching—as the pattern repeated itself once more. Thrashing, Valium, silence, and finally, that Saturday, a tenuous and horrible equilibrium.

Jon Allen was unresponsive at nine o'clock that morning. Unresponsive at noon and still unresponsive that evening. He was so catatonic that it was considered a sign of progress when he said "Ouch" late that night as a new intravenous line was being inserted into his arm and when he cried out for his parents—again and again. Haunting cries that drifted down the hallway in the night.

"Mommy," he screamed.

"Daddy."

"Mommy."

Jon Allen needed help.

—

Doctors tried to calm Luella as they searched for answers. They ordered a lumbar puncture to check for signs of infection, namely meningitis—a condition that could cause seizures. Five nurses had to hold Jon Allen down on the bed as one of them inserted a large needle in his spinal column. The test came back negative. No infection. No answers.

Next, the doctors ordered a raft of studies to examine Jon Allen's head. A CT scan revealed that parts of the boy's brain were slightly enlarged; he was suffering from increased intracranial pressure. But it showed no cancerous mass, no bleeding, and no obvious medical problem that could spark violent seizures in a child. With no other tests to run, doctors chose to continue to medicate Jon Allen and monitor him. They kept him on a small dose of Valium and one other sedative. They assured Luella not to be concerned when the machines in the room sounded their frightening alarms—Jon Allen's shaking body was just loosening the cords—and they urged Luella and Norman to speak with their son, even though he couldn't speak back, and tell him that Mommy and Daddy were there.

Finally, after about twenty-four hours in the hospital, Jon Allen awoke Sunday morning, looking and feeling more like himself and asking his parents questions.

"What hospital am I in?" he said. "Can I go home soon?"

He was allowed to sit up in bed unrestrained, watch television with his stuffed dog, Scuppity, in his arms, and spend the morning with his mother. But by midday the problems began again. Jon Allen reported that the walls had turned red, that there were spiderwebs everywhere, and that his mother was on the TV.

Look, he said. Look.

Luella turned to the television screen and then back at her son. He was laughing "inappropriately," nurses noted. It was time to page the doctor and send Luella away.

Jon Allen was hallucinating.

For the next two days, the odd and worrisome visions continued. Jon Allen saw yellow spots on the curtains, flies all over the room, three hands on his father's arm, and other things. He thought his hand was bleeding; it wasn't. He thought he had a loose tooth—he didn't—and he thought people were firing sugary treats and cubes of bubble gum at him from an imaginary candy store that, also, was not there.

"Look at all the candy they're shooting all over me," he said.

"I see eyes and noses on the wall."

"I see blue water and fish."

It was all so real, he reported. Just look at Scuppity.

"My dog's ear is a fish's mouth. See?"

Luella had canceled Jon Allen's weekend birthday party and moved his chocolate sheet cake to the family freezer in the basement of their house. For obvious reasons, all of that would have to wait. Luella was planning for another long hospital stay—aware of the new reality of their broken lives—and she was refusing to leave, no matter how upsetting it was to hear her little boy report seeing blood on his hands or on her face. "Mother here," the boy's chart noted again and again. "Mother here."

And then, just as quickly as the problems began, they resolved themselves. The seizures stopped; the hallucinations did, too. By Wednesday that week, his fifth day in the hospital, Jon Allen was reading storybooks in bed with Luella and walking the halls with her, smiling at the nurses, as usual, with Scuppity. His belly was still distended and his small body swollen; Jon Allen was spilling too much protein yet again. But he was active and perky—an otherwise typical seven-year-old boy trapped inside a hospital.

That Friday, based on these improvements, doctors decided to discharge Jon Allen—a choice that Luella fought. Just look at him, she told the doctors. He was still swollen, only a few days removed from his delirious visions, and pumped full of medication: sedatives for the seizures, steroids for the proteinuria, mineral supplements to treat the declining potassium in his blood, and two different drugs to control his high blood pressure. This was not a child who should be leaving the hospital, Luella argued, no matter how much he had improved since the previous weekend. She wanted Jon Allen to stay. Yet doctors overruled her, remarking upon his stable condition, and sent the Kennys home. She could always call, they said, if there were any problems, or return to the hospital if necessary.

Outside, it was a beautiful autumn day, clear and crisp. The leaves had begun to change, and the parking lot at the hospital was filled with chestnuts blown from the trees. It was the sort of thing that a parent would never notice, hurrying through the day, but Jon Allen looked upon the fallen chestnuts like treasure. On his way to the car, he stopped every few feet to pick them up, rolling them around in his swollen fingers and sliding them into his pockets. He was pleased with himself, and Luella was pleased, too. She let him linger in the parking lot, collecting his bounty. Then they climbed into the car and drove home—back to Ninety-Sixth Street on the edge of the old canal.

27

MARKED HOUSES

Jon Allen's neighborhood by then was increasingly becoming a ghost town—a troubling development for Luella and everyone else still living there. More than 150 families had fled since Carter's emergency declaration six weeks earlier, abandoning their homes in a panic and leaving them almost as they had stood—frozen in time, quiet and vacant, and already being reclaimed by the earth.

Yards were becoming overgrown. Weeds were sprouting through asphalt driveways. No one was there to rake the first fallen leaves of autumn or to stop the opportunistic thieves now rolling through the neighborhood along with the curious—the disaster tourists. To protect against the would-be burglars seeking an easy target, many people boarded up their houses, local police stepped up patrols, and the state started erecting a chain-link fence, eight feet tall and miles long, around the relocation area, walling off the tainted land from the rest of the neighborhood and protecting the state's investment—the homes it was being forced to buy.

By Friday, September 29—the day that Luella drove Jon Allen home from his latest stay in the hospital—Governor Carey's team had spent more than $5 million purchasing homes inside the relocation area. Officials were still out there, lining up appraisals, to finish the job, preparing to buy another eighty-five houses, for roughly $3 million more. But money couldn't solve everything. With 230 families seeking a new place to live, there was suddenly a housing shortage in the city. There was no place to go and no room in the hotels, either. Indeed, hotels were threatening to evict some Love Canal families who had overstayed their welcomes. At least a few had been living in hotel rooms since the second week of August, after Whalen's bombshell announcement in Albany recommending evacuation for certain families, and not surprisingly these families were coming unglued. James Starr—a homeowner on One Hundredth Street—reported that he, his wife, and their two children felt "like monkeys in a cage."

The Starrs lived on the cusp of the evacuation zone, just outside it. The government was not going to be buying their house anytime soon, despite the blistering skin rashes they suffered, their concerns about their children's health, or their view of the new fence going up outside. They were stuck there with Gibbs and others in what real estate agents were now calling "marked houses."

"People hear of a home in the 90s"—that stretch of the city between Ninety-Second and 103rd Streets—"and they don't even want to look at it," a Century 21 real estate agent bluntly admitted. Prospective buyers wanted to see something else, and agents happily obliged, knowing they weren't going to make any commissions on a Saturday afternoon trying to move a "marked house" with a view of a fence, walling off a landfill on the edge of an empty school. "Wherever they draw the line," one local real estate agent advised clients, "I wouldn't want the first house on the other side. I would pay for some distance."

The problem wasn't just the fence, or the negative publicity, or the odors, or the threat of chemicals seeping through the walls of the basement. It was also the state's imminent plan to come in with heavy-duty trucks, diggers, and workers armed with gas masks to remediate the canal site—as soon as possible. Under the plan, contractors would clear trees, brush, residential fences, aboveground swimming pools, and any garages abutting the canal. Then they would dig two long, parallel trenches on each side of the old landfill; line these trenches with roughly one and a half miles of porous tiles and clay pipes, buried up to twelve feet underground; use the trench system to collect what they called "lateral migrating contaminants"; and funnel this foul slurry into a massive holding tank at the foot of the canal, near the river.

Lois Gibbs was pretty sure this was a horrible idea, and the homeowners' lawyer, Richard Lippes, agreed. According to the contractors' own report, the installation of the trench system posed health risks to both remediation workers and residents. In digging, they could strike an air pocket filled with chemical vapors or a long-buried drum bursting with flammable liquid. There could be fires, some speculated, or perhaps an explosion—as some had long feared. Lippes was prepared to go to court to stop the work on behalf of Gibbs and the homeowners. Meanwhile, some residents were threatening to stop the remediation through other tactics: they were refusing to sell their homes, blocking the trucks and diggers from moving in.

Around the end of September, the two sides forged a truce: homeowners would sell and Gibbs's group would allow the trench digging if the state presented an appropriate safety plan. In response, the state promised to send in a convoy of buses—sixty hulking vehicles in all—costing taxpayers $7,000 a day. The buses would idle on predetermined street corners, at the ready to ferry residents to safety if something happened, if it was necessary. Resigned to the reality of the situation, Gibbs agreed to stand down. She wouldn't ask Lippes to stop the remediation at least in part because it felt like a waste of time and money. Authorities finally had a plan, and the remediation workers were coming, whether residents wanted them to or not. "There doesn't seem to be much we can do about it," Gibbs told others.

But the buses only exacerbated the nightmares—the bad dreams—that some people were having at night when they lay in bed. Residents dreamed of running for the emergency vehicles in the dark, with their children in their pajama feet, only to find that the buses were gone. The drivers had left early. The canal was on fire and they were stuck there, with no way out. And others, like Elene Thornton in Griffon Manor, refused to believe that the evacuation plan solved anything. At the end of September 1978, Thornton was still struggling to organize residents in the public housing development, and it wasn't just because of simmering tensions between homeowners and renters. Just like Gibbs, Thornton was dealing with competing factions and personal rivals. Agnes Jones—Thornton's neighbor—was trying to lead the renters, too.

Both Thornton and Jones asked state health officials to focus more on the health of people living in the public housing development. Both called for more testing. Both demanded action—"immediate action," Thornton said at the time—and both went door to door, circulating dueling petitions that had at least one positive effect: the local chapter of the NAACP took notice.

William Abrams, the chapter's president, couldn't help but be interested. He and his wife had lived in Griffon Manor for most of the 1960s, waking up every morning less than a hundred feet from the old canal and eating vegetables out of a garden they kept there. Now Abrams's wife was dead, at age forty-seven, of liver problems, and like everyone else making mental checklists of physical maladies, Abrams wondered if maybe her death was connected to the canal. "Many Black people grew vegetables on the Love Canal site," he said that fall, regretting the decision now. "So it is possible that we ate some of the chemicals blamed for causing cancer." At a minimum, he believed, authorities had lied to him and everyone else living in the development. At times in the 1960s, Abrams and others had complained about foul odors in their units—only to be told that the smells were emanating from nearby factories on the river. Griffon Manor residents had nothing to fear.

While Abrams lobbied state officials to relocate residents in the housing development, just as they were relocating homeowners—and Jones gathered signatures for her petition—Thornton tried to establish herself as a leader by hiring an attorney, a Black man named Lester Sconiers. Sconiers was in his mid-thirties, young and lean, with a small law office half a mile from Thornton's townhome and a low tolerance for interpersonal drama when litigation was on the line. Sconiers didn't care who was leading—Thornton, Jones, or Gibbs. It was immaterial to him, as long as there was a case to make in court, and there was clearly a strong legal case for everyone who had ever lived around the canal. First, at Thornton's direction, Sconiers filed an injunction to stop the proposed canal remediation in court; he was trying to block the project that the state wanted and that Lois Gibbs had chosen to allow. But when the challenge failed that fall—as Sconiers knew it would—he turned his attention to gathering personal injury claims at Griffon Manor.

In general, he believed that the renters and homeowners had different legal arguments to make with state and federal officials. The homeowners had investments—real property that they could not sell, he said—while the renters just needed to get out. In this way, he thought it best that the two groups work separately, if along parallel lines, and he had to admit that he liked Lois Gibbs. Sconiers saw Gibbs as a tree shaker, and for him that was a compliment. "Sometimes," he said, "you need someone to shake the trees."

Yet when it came to potential exposure—exposure to the chemicals buried in the ground—Sconiers knew that everyone was equal, no matter where they lived or what they looked like. He began funneling the personal injury claims he was gathering at Griffon Manor into a larger lawsuit that Richard Lippes was building—a soon-to-be $16 billion case involving nearly fourteen hundred residents, Black and white, renters and homeowners. Everyone, it seemed, had a plausible argument to make, connecting health conditions, small or large, to the landfill behind the new chain-link fence erected around the old dumping grounds to keep people safe.

On his first visit to the neighborhood around the end of September, Sconiers parked his Buick near the fence and eyed it like everyone else, almost laughing at the absurdity of it all. It was clear to him that the fence wasn't doing much to protect people. It couldn't stop any chemicals, say, in the groundwater.

"Water just moves," Sconiers said.

And it was still moving, he believed—underground.

Beverly Paigen felt the same way. From the moment she walked home from the big fire hall meeting with Gibbs in early August, smelling the pungent odors spewing from the sewer grates in the night, Paigen was convinced that the contaminants were on the move—"laterally migrating," as the contractors put it. But how? She wasn't sure.

Returning to her lab at Roswell Park in Buffalo after her family's trip to Maine, Paigen found it increasingly difficult to do any work studying the chemicals in the neighborhood. Her bosses—the doctors who reported to Whalen and Axelrod in Albany—seemed intent on controlling her and maybe even silencing her. As a new rule, Dr. David Pressman asked that Paigen report any meetings or public statements weeks in advance. "The administration," Pressman said, "must be kept informed of all your activities in this area, since inquiries do come in about your work."

Paigen was concerned about his tone, and also her job security. Late at night, inside her home in Buffalo, Beverly and her husband, Ken, had long talks after the kids went to sleep, discussing the family finances and what they would do if administrators fired Paigen, if she lost her job. They lived modestly on two salaries in public health, making far less than they would have in the private sector. It would have been a blow to the whole family to lose Beverly's income, and even though Ken was a department head, held in high esteem and long tenured at Roswell Park, he knew he would not be able to protect his wife if Pressman, Gerald Murphy, or the powers in Albany wanted her gone—yet another reason for concern.

But mostly, Beverly was just furious—a familiar feeling for her. Pressman's demand that she report all public interactions to him struck her as not just unfair and ridiculous but chauvinistic, a demand he would never have made of a man, and she knew what she had to do. As a girl, Paigen had defied her religious parents and gone to college. And as a young wife, she had defied expectations again: by joining the workforce, by divorcing her first husband to escape an unhappy marriage, and by marrying Ken—all scandals. Now she was going to defy her bosses because, Paigen believed, it was the right thing to do.

"When I make public statements," Paigen told Pressman, "I am guided by my responsibilities to the public health, to the proper role of a scientist in society, and by my loyalty to Roswell Park and its reputation."

It seemed ridiculous to her that an institution that claimed to be devoted to medical knowledge would fail to recognize these responsibilities, or would want to stop her from investigating a national health crisis just twenty minutes away from her lab. And it seemed excessive, she explained, that she should have to work under these new restrictions. "I know of no other individuals (except department heads) who must write a monthly report," Paigen told Pressman in a tersely worded memo that September. And no one else, including department heads, had to disclose their meetings and talks in advance. "In reply," she concluded, "I would like to receive a written explanation of why this request has been made."

It was nine days before Pressman got back to her. When he did, he simply explained that her areas of study were newsworthy—

"of interest," he said, "to the general public"—and he only reiterated what he had already told her: "We shall expect you to keep us informed." It was an answer that Paigen found dissatisfying, intentionally vague, and possibly threatening, leading to more anxiety about what she and Ken would do if she lost her job.

But for now, she decided to play along—sort of. If her bosses wanted a monthly report, she'd give it to them, typing it up in great detail and taking almost perverse pleasure in writing lengthy descriptions of everywhere she planned to go and speak. *September 14:* Lecture at Buffalo State College. *September 15:* Meeting to discuss handling of toxic substances. *September 28 and 29:* Meetings with EPA agents in Washington. *Oct 6:* "Women in Science" career workshop—this was important to her. And finally, several upcoming lectures that she had titled "The Chemical Industry and Environmental Cancer."

What Paigen left out was that she was still working with Lois Gibbs almost every day, and about to be communicating with Elene Thornton, too. She and Gibbs were developing a new idea that they were calling the swale theory. Over the summer, scientists at the state Department of Health had unearthed aerial photographs of the LaSalle area dating back to 1938—before anything had been built around the canal and before anything had been dumped in it, either. These photos revealed a landscape slightly different from the one most residents imagined. The canal was there, yes—a jagged valley of water, just as William T. Love had left it, about half a mile long and a hundred feet wide. But also present in the old photos was a tangled web of swales, more than a dozen of them, slicing through the canal, east to west and north to south, including one large stream that the state labeled the "major swale" that started east of 103rd Street, ran through the neighborhood, cut across the canal just north of the school, and then connected to the existing stream behind Luella Kenny's house: Black Creek.

The significance, to geologists, was obvious. The streambeds offered natural drainage. They connected with the old canal in at least half a dozen places. And even after the swales had been filled in during the 1950s—to make construction possible in the neighborhood—the small channels could have provided a conduit for migration because the swales themselves functioned as dumping sites. In the ground there, geologists found stone, rubble, trash, glass, and plastics—fill that was, by nature, more permeable and created an underground pathway into the neighborhood well beyond the governor's relocation area.

Gibbs decided to investigate. While the state conducted its epidemiological surveys, gathering data door to door, Gibbs started gathering data, too, with the swales at the top of her mind. She was no geologist, of course; she wouldn't have known the first thing about glacial outwash or alluvial materials—the makeup of the canal—or how to distinguish the two. But she knew her neighborhood, and one night that September, alone in her kitchen on 101st Street, she pulled out a street map and went to work. Gibbs placed pins in a grid around the school marking reports she had received of miscarriages, cancer, respiratory complaints, and other unusual symptoms. Then, working off the hazy recollections of a few longtime residents in the neighborhood, Gibbs penciled in a couple of swales that people had reported seeing long ago and stood back to see the results.

The rendering in the kitchen was rough at best—hand-drawn citizen science by a woman who had barely managed to make it through high school biology. But what she saw was significant enough that Gibbs decided to pick up the phone and call Beverly Paigen. There were clusters, she explained to Paigen. Clusters of pins on her map, around the old swales. If they could get the aerial pictures from 1938—if they could determine with certainty where the streams once flowed—then maybe they would have something.

Paigen listened and considered her options. In a perfect world, she would have had money, time, and a team of graduate students to help her gather this information—real scientists, working on this kind of project for months or maybe even years. But unlike the state—which had budgeted $500,000 for its neighborhood health surveys—Paigen had no funding for Love Canal research, and she figured she wouldn't be able to obtain any given the problems she was already having at work. It didn't matter, anyway: Gibbs wasn't going to wait. She wanted this information now—as soon as possible—in hopes of making a compelling case that families like hers needed to be evacuated, too.

Paigen understood that, but she was also clear: it was time to start over. They couldn't go to the state—or to the media—with a map full of "maybes" compiled over the summer while Gibbs was going door to door with her children at her feet or through personal phone calls she had received from people worried about their health. They needed to do a real survey—"a systematic phone survey," Paigen called it—documenting the problems of everyone living near a swale. That was about 116 families in all, because, as it turned out, the swales were everywhere in the neighborhood. Three cut deep into Griffon Manor. Several crossed over 101st Street and kept going, and two swales ran north—beyond Colvin Boulevard and all the way to the edge of the creeks still flowing there.

Gibbs's own home was sitting near the top of an old swale. And by Paigen and Gibbs's calculations, so was the little house in the cul-de-sac at the elbow turn on Ninety-Sixth Street, the home with the three little boys and the yard rambling toward Black Creek.

Paigen and Gibbs logged the address of the house as 1064 Ninety-Sixth Street.

Family name: *Kinney.*

Luella and Norman *Kinney*?

1950s, ’60s, and ’70s, young working-class
·s moved to the LaSalle neighborhood on the
de of Niagara Falls, drawn to its suburban feel,
w public school there, the tidy rows of affordable
homes, and modern public housing. (*Courtesy of*
iversity Archives, University at Buffalo)

Children flocked to the playground on the school grounds in the heart of the neighborhood, making it, for many families, an ideal place to grow up. (*Courtesy of Mickey H. Osterreicher*)

What most people didn’t know is that the land had once been a canal, conceived and partially built by a dubious prospector in the 1890s. William T. Love, the man with the beard standing next to the man with the shovel, believed the canal would allow him to build a “model city” on the Niagara frontier. (*Courtesy of the University Archives, University at Buffalo*)

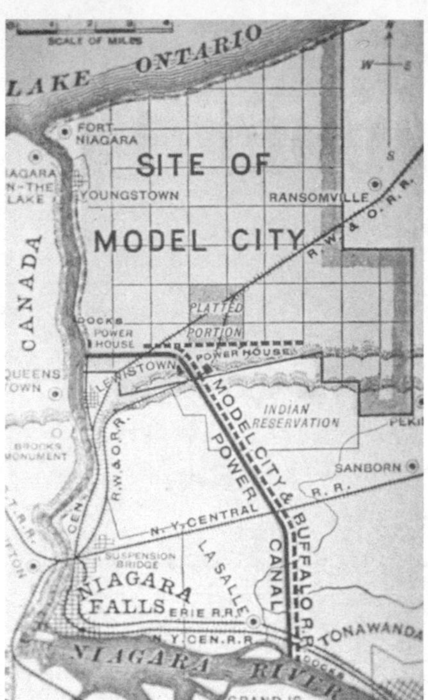

Map of Love's proposed Model City. (*Court the University Archives, University at Buffalo*)

In the 1940s—five decades after William T. Love skipped town—Hooker Chemical, the largest employer in town, with a sprawling plant on the Niagara River, acquired the abandoned canal and started using it as a dumping ground for chemical wastes and residues. (*Courtesy of Bettmann/Getty Images*)

and Norman Kenny, here with their *rom left to right*) Stephen, Jon Allen, and opher, were thrilled to move into a house alle, on Ninety-Sixth Street, shortly before len was born in 1971. (*Courtesy of Luella Collection*)

From left to right: Stephen, Christopher, and Jon Allen Kenny, Christmas 1976—one of the last normal Christmases they would ever have. (*Courtesy of Luella Kenny Collection*)

After the blizzard of 1977, chemicals began leaching from the canal, creating problems on the playground and in homes closest to the school. (*Courtesy of* The Buffalo News)

Lois Gibbs, a mother of two children on 101st Street, was among the first to raise the alarm, going door to door in the spring and summer of 1978 to inform people about what was happening. (*Courtesy of* The Buffalo News)

On the other side of the neighborhood, Jon Allen Kenny, pictured here in his first-grade school photo, began to feel sick that June, requiring weeks of hospitalization fo unexplained kidney problems. (*Courtesy o Luella Kenny Collection*)

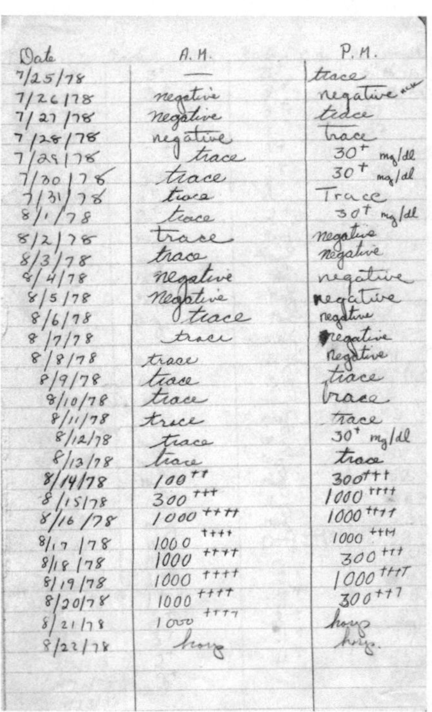

Date	A.M.	P.M.
7/25/78	—	trace
7/26/78	negative	negative
7/27/78	negative	trace
7/28/78	negative	trace
7/29/78	trace	30^{+} mg/dl
7/30/78	trace	30^{+} mg/dl
7/31/78	trace	Trace
8/1/78	trace	30^{+} mg/dl
8/2/78	trace	negative
8/3/78	trace	negative
8/4/78	negative	negative
8/5/78	Negative	negative
8/6/78	trace	negative
8/7/78	trace	negative
8/8/78	trace	Negative
8/9/78	trace	trace
8/10/78	trace	trace
8/11/78	trace	trace
8/12/78	trace	30^{+} mg/dl
8/13/78	trace	trace
8/14/78	100^{++}	300^{+++}
8/15/78	300^{+++}	1000^{++++}
8/16/78	1000^{++++}	1000^{++++}
8/17/78	1000^{++++}	1000^{++++}
8/18/78	1000^{++++}	300^{+++}
8/19/78	1000^{++++}	1000^{++++}
8/20/78	1000^{++++}	300^{+++}
8/21/78	1000^{++++}	hosp
8/22/78	hosp	hosp.

In handwritten charts, Luella tracked Jon progress, recording how much protein wa spilling into his urine. (*Courtesy of Luella Collection*)

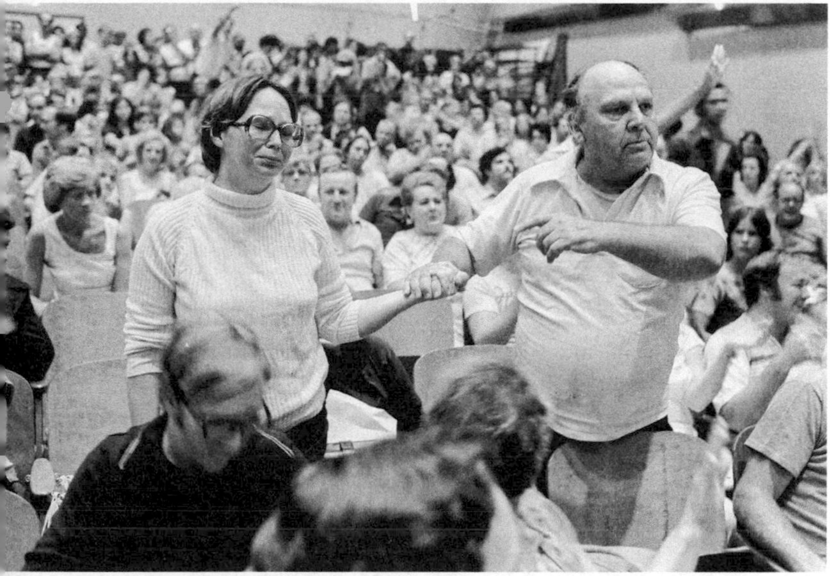

In August 1978, authorities recommended evacuating families living closest to the old canal. Then they closed the school altogether, setting off a panic in LaSalle and inciting anger among large crowds of people who came to state meetings to learn more. (*Courtesy of Mickey H. Osterreicher*)

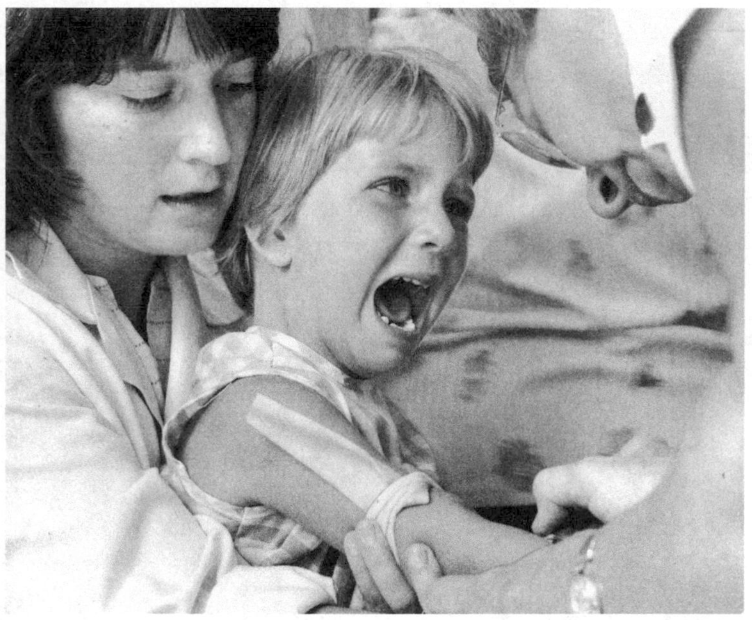

On the west side of the canal, Elene Thornton was certain that she and her family were in danger and tried to organize residents of her public housing development, Griffon Manor. (*Courtesy of Jacqueline Nix Collection*)

Elene's son, Gregory, had died of leukemia in LaSalle before his second birthday, more than fifteen years ea
(*Courtesy of Jacqueline Nix Collection*)

Federal officials, including Congressman John LaFalce, came to town to try to calm residents. (*Courtesy of the University Archives, University at Buffalo*)

e's young
onnie Casper
, *in pattern shirt*
ht pants) was
l in pushing
take the canal
ns seriously
laying out a
help people
neighborhood.
(*esy of Mickey H.*
icher)

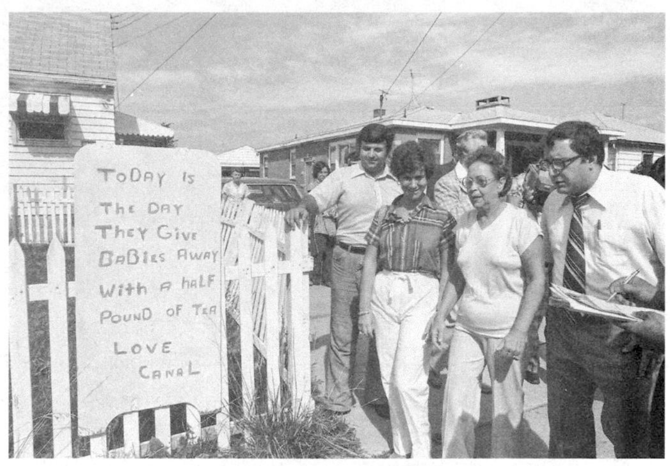

TODAY IS
THE DAY
THEY GIVE
BABIES AWAY
WITH A HALF
POUND OF TEA
LOVE
CANAL

Within days of the first evacuations in August 1978, Lois Gibbs (*far right*) gave LaFalce (*far left*) a tour of the canal, along with other federal officials sent to Niagara Falls by President Jimmy Carter to learn more about the problem. (*Courtesy of Mickey H. Osterreicher*)

began personally pressing her
the most powerful man in New
Governor Hugh Carey, a rising
cratic star who was facing a bitter
ion battle in the fall of 1978.
(*esy of the University Archives,*
sity at Buffalo)

Carey visited Niagara Falls seven times in the fall of 1978, but he stopped coming—and refused to evacuate any other families from the neighborhood—after winning reelection in November that year. (*Courtesy of* The Buffalo News)

For help, neighborhood residents turned to Beverly Pa (*right*), who moved to Buffalo as a young scientist in t 1960s and by 1978 could appreciate Gibbs's plight. Sh a mother, too. (*Courtesy of Getty Images*)

Paigen argued that the chemicals had migrated deep into the neighborhood, traveling along a series of old streambeds, or swales, that at one point had been larger than the children who had played in them. (*Courtesy of the University Archives, University at Buffalo*)

28

GOD ONLY KNOWS

On the last Friday of September—the day Jon Allen was discharged from Children's Hospital after his week of seizures and hallucinations—the entire Kenny family gathered at Luella's mother's house for dinner. The doctors had recommended a high-protein diet for Jon Allen, as a way of fortifying his little body, and Luella's mother thought she had just the thing for it: her family's famous spaghetti and meatball supper.

Jon Allen was excited for the meal and in a playful mood as Luella rang the doorbell outside her mother's home. With his pockets still bursting with the chestnuts he had gathered in the parking lot of the hospital that afternoon, he hid behind Luella's legs and instructed his mother to pretend he wasn't there. Jon Allen was gone. When his grandmother opened the door, he hid for a moment and then jumped out, surprising her. Everyone played along, smiling. Everyone was happy—at least for the night. The little boy was home again and excited to return to school, and Sister Denise's second-grade class, that Monday morning.

But Luella's smile was just a mask, and if anyone looked close enough, they would have noticed that it was fraying around the edges. Despite the doctors' decision to discharge her son and the boy's playful demeanor at his grandmother's front door that night, she knew that Jon Allen had slogged through yet another difficult day. He complained of headaches, nausea, exhaustion, and nosebleeds in the hours after leaving the hospital. He'd had two nosebleeds since coming home that morning. And the fact that he was able to goof around with his grandmother, hiding behind his mother's legs, or attend a family dinner wasn't necessarily a sign that he had recovered, but rather evidence, Luella believed, of his personal determination to be a kid again, and she knew better than anyone that it might not last—that, indeed, it likely wouldn't.

Since the start of July that year, the Kennys had endured three hospital stays, three discharges, and three reports that Jon Allen's health would improve, if he stayed on his medication—only for him to go home and end up right back in the hospital again. If this time felt different, it was only because Luella was even less certain of the future than she had been before. Doctors had sent her home from the hospital that day with five different medications for Jon Allen. A boy who had been completely healthy just a few months earlier now needed a battery of pills and capsules to get through the day. While Jon Allen was stuffing his pockets with chestnuts, Luella was carrying a veritable pharmacy in her purse. She was marking the hours by what medication her son needed to take next, and she was running headlong into other reminders that their lives had changed. The state's new fence, walling off the canal from the rest of the neighborhood, wasn't far from the Kennys' house on Ninety-Sixth Street. Even on a celebratory night like this one, they couldn't ignore the fact they were living on the doorstep of a wasteland and going to sleep that night in a house that no one in their right minds would ever want to buy.

The weekend went about as well as Luella might have expected. Jon Allen was able to get through the spaghetti dinner at his grandmother's house, sleep in his own bed under his *Star Wars* sheets that night, and spend a quiet day around the house that Saturday, taking it easy, per the orders of the doctors—and his mother. Yet when he awoke early Sunday morning, stirring in the darkness a couple hours before sunrise, Jon Allen was confused, congested, more swollen than he'd been the day before, and suffering a litany of other symptoms—new problems Luella had never seen before. He was struggling to breathe, almost panting, and so pale that his lips had turned white.

Luella considered bringing him back to the hospital right then. But Jon Allen took his medications without complaint and went back to bed feeling at least a little better. He was resting—comfortably, it seemed—and around nine o'clock that morning he rallied enough that he was able to drink a breakfast shake. Briefly, Luella let herself believe that he was going to be just fine. They were home, and he was fine, and then, within thirty minutes of drinking the shake, Jon Allen vomited.

Luella picked up the phone. She was calling the hospital again.

Outside, it was a busy weekend around the canal. LaFalce was back in town, and he'd brought others with him this time. Jacob Javits—a liberal Republican from Brooklyn and one of New York's two U.S. senators—was there to tour the site and report back to his colleagues in Washington. He held court at LaFalce's office downtown, huddling with mayors from all the nearby cities and towns worried about their inability to fight big corporations like Hooker. Then Javits walked the old landfill with a scrum of more than two dozen people, including newsmen, state officials, aides to Governor Carey, LaFalce, Gibbs, and Thornton, who, if not officially invited, was determined to crash the party.

Gibbs and Thornton were trying to connect with the senator and hoping that he might make them some promises. Thornton wanted Javits to know that folks in the housing development were being overlooked, while Gibbs tried to impress upon him that homeowners like her needed federal help in order to escape their homes. Neither woman got the answers she was seeking—Thornton least of all. "Madame, I have to go," Javits told the Black mother from Griffon Manor, seemingly blowing her off. "I cannot substitute for your local health authorities." And Gibbs hardly managed any better. Javits—who had served in the Chemical Warfare service during World War II and knew well both the promise and the danger of chemical agents—wasn't going to commit to anything. Unlike Carter's staffers and the president's top administrators at the EPA, Javits wasn't even ready to admit that dumps like Love Canal were a national problem, and he wasn't going to blame Hooker for everything, either.

Sure, the company had polluted in Niagara Falls.

"But in those days," Javits said, "who cared?"

The senator wanted to see the canal for himself.

Gibbs nodded, all smiles, and steered him toward a pool of black sludge, oozing out of the ground not far from the abandoned school and the empty houses on Ninety-Seventh and Ninety-Ninth Streets.

Be careful, Gibbs advised Javits.

"That'll eat your shoes right off, Senator."

"God only knows what that is," LaFalce agreed.

They poked at the sludge with a stick to the delight of the newspaper photographers and then went their separate ways: LaFalce and Javits returned to Washington, Thornton to Griffon Manor, and Gibbs to her house on 101st Street to prepare for what she was now calling "D-day"—the remediation, scheduled to begin in less than two weeks. Trucks, diggers, and evacuation buses were mobilizing. It seemed to Gibbs and Thornton, and many others, as if an invasion were coming, and the residents who were left behind—those living just outside the state's new fence—were told to pack a suitcase and be prepared to leave immediately if they heard an alarm sounding out of the newly installed public address system.

"Respond to public address system AT ONCE," the state informed residents in a written directive. "Shut off stove or any electrical appliance you are using . . . Hustle children outside . . . Stay together and go direct to your bus . . . Don't waste time . . . Don't wait to pack a suitcase . . . Don't take your pets with you; they are not allowed."

Finally, people were advised to stay away from their homes between the hours of 8:00 a.m. and 6:00 p.m., if possible, when the backhoes would be carving deep trenches into the old canal. Nothing was going to explode, a remediation contractor said, trying to reassure people. Crews felt comfortable with only gas masks at the ready.

But he noted, "It's going to smell."

On the phone with Jon Allen's doctors that Sunday, Luella wasn't thinking about evacuation drills. She didn't have the luxury of worrying about the world falling apart outside her front door. It was crumbling right in her living room, where Jon Allen was curled up on the couch. She explained to doctors at Children's Hospital that he was vomiting, that he couldn't even hold down a breakfast shake, and that she was scared. They all knew how this had ended the last time: Jon Allen had arrived at the ICU by ambulance in the middle of the night.

But despite the boy's recent medical history and the location of his home on Ninety-Sixth Street, not far from the canal, a location clearly documented in his medical chart, doctors resisted calling him back into the hospital. Instead, on the phone, they tweaked Jon Allen's medication and instructed Luella to continue to monitor the boy—a task she took seriously. She started taking notes on his symptoms, documenting his decline in real time that day. She recorded how he tried to eat around two o'clock; how he vomited again at around three; how he fell asleep for the night about an hour later, long before the sun went down; and how he seemed to gasp for air in his little bed as darkness crept over the neighborhood and the Kennys' house.

"Breathing heavy, labored, with moans," Luella wrote, keeping vigil in the shadows.

Jon Allen wasn't going back to school the next day, as he had hoped. He was returning to Children's Hospital, and this time Jon Allen was too sick to even protest the decision when his mother broke the news to him in the morning. Shortly after the older Kenny boys left for school, Luella helped Jon Allen get out of bed and get dressed. She affixed suspenders to help hold up his pants under his swollen belly. She helped him find Scuppity, and then they walked to the car outside, driving off together.

Out the window, Jon Allen watched the world he had known fade into the distance: the house that his parents liked to decorate at Christmastime; the basketball hoop in the driveway; the yard with the creek out back where he and his brothers liked to run and play; the cul-de-sac where he had learned to ride his bike; and all the little houses on Ninety-Sixth Street—his neighbors, his friends, his home. It slipped from view, falling away, until Luella eased the car to a stop at the end of the street. The state's new fence was in front of them, just a couple blocks away. The road to the hospital was to the right. Luella pulled out onto the quiet boulevard, skirted the edge of the canal, crossed the Niagara River, and pointed the car toward Buffalo, driving away from the falls.

At the hospital, doctors moved in to examine Jon Allen—in a ritual that had become familiar to both the mother and the child.

They didn't like what they saw. His heart was racing. His skin was mottled and pasty, and he was almost hyperventilating. In order to help him, doctors placed Jon Allen on oxygen, and for a while that day his breathing improved. But by nightfall, he was struggling again, even with the assistance of the enriched air being pumped into his lungs. There was no other way to say it. "Jon is very sick," one doctor declared on Tuesday. They were moving him back to the ICU.

Luella called Norman in a panic, summoning him to her side. She had grown accustomed to hospitals in recent months and even to the whir of life in the intensive care unit. But this visit felt different: the tone of the doctors' voices, the oxygen dome placed over Jon Allen's head, and his quickening breaths coming in rapid-fire bursts. At times, he was gasping for air more than once a second—seventy-six breaths a minute—a pace that seemed impossible to maintain and difficult for his parents to see on the few occasions when they were allowed back into the ICU to visit.

"He can't go on like this," Norman told Luella, and she agreed.

She wanted answers, but as before doctors didn't have any. She wanted to comfort Jon Allen, but she couldn't. The boy couldn't get enough air into his lungs. He was drowning within himself, and, understandably, it scared him. Several times over the course of the day he became agitated, crying, grunting, or groaning, as he struggled to breathe. Yet by nightfall that Tuesday—his second day back in the hospital—Jon Allen had rallied again, as usual. He was sitting up in bed and watching television. His breathing had slowed—at least a little. He was well enough that Luella didn't even object to the doctors' directive that she sleep apart from Jon Allen in the guest quarters reserved for the parents of children admitted to the ICU. Luella and Norman tucked Jon Allen in, said good night, told him that they loved him, and left the room. Norman was going home to Christopher and Stephen, who'd been under the supervision of relatives and neighbors all day, while Luella walked to her room in a different part of the hospital. They would meet again in the morning in the waiting room outside the ICU, hoping to learn that Jon Allen had continued to improve.

The next day dawned warm and bright—a beautiful fall morning in western New York—and Norman came early, bearing gifts. He had Jon Allen's toothbrush, which Luella had forgotten on Monday, some toys from the gift shop for their son, and eggplant parmesan sandwiches for lunch, Luella's favorite. They settled in, ready for another long day in the hospital—waiting, they thought, too long. It was ten o'clock that morning before doctors called them back to see Jon Allen, and right away they understood why.

The boy had spiraled overnight. He was disoriented, unable to speak, and laboring. Most alarming, his lips and extremities had turned a shade of blue. Luella locked eyes with her son through the transparent plastic of the oxygen tent, desperate to help him and pleading to stay. But she was not allowed. She and Norman had to go. Almost as quickly as nurses ushered the Kennys in, they hurried them out. The parents were only going to get in the way of the people who were now fighting to save Jon Allen's life.

His heart rate was falling. Nurses were paging multiple doctors, and they were rushing to his bedside, assembling in the room, looking down at the boy, and then up at the clock.

At 11:32 that morning, Jon Allen's heart stopped beating.

Luella and Norman were in the hospital cafeteria when they heard Jon Allen's doctors being paged. The couple had been wandering the halls for roughly an hour at that point, pacing and waiting, watching television in the waiting room, and pacing some more. Banished from the ICU, with no knowledge of what was happening inside, they had to keep moving to stay sane and they had just started picking at their eggplant parmesan sandwiches, when the page went out. Luella threw down her sandwich and went running, a mother barreling down the halls of the hospital, trying to get back to her son.

Behind the doors of the ICU, doctors worked on Jon Allen for eighty long minutes. They ripped away the oxygen dome, started chest compressions by hand, and intubated him, pumping air into his lungs on a doctor's mark. They started two different arterial lines and injected his body with a cocktail of medications to help get his blood flowing. Finally, about thirty minutes in, they placed electrodes around his heart and tried to shock it back into action with small jolts of electricity, and for a moment this worked. Jon Allen's heart began beating once more. But it was an artificial effect and short lived at that. There was no saving this child. Just before one o'clock that afternoon, they finally called it. The boy was unresponsive, his chest quiet, his brown eyes fixed and dilated. Time of death: 12:53 p.m.

"I want an autopsy!" Luella Kenny shouted at the doctors outside the doors of the ICU, when they finally emerged to give her and Norman the news.

"I want an autopsy!" she screamed again.

She had been calm and measured. She had been reasonable and quiet. But no more. At home that night, unable to sleep, she decided her house was dirty. Everything about it, dirty. And so Luella got down on her hands and knees and began to clean. She scrubbed the linoleum floor in her kitchen. She scrubbed the linoleum floor in the hallway, too, and then, at some point, she cleaned out her freezer. She pulled out the sheet cake that she had purchased for Jon Allen's birthday and drove it back to the hospital. Someone should eat it, she thought. The nurses, maybe. It was only later, much later, that she'd realize the almost absurd sadness of the errand. She was a mother arriving at a hospital with her dead son's birthday cake. Even if the nurses ate it, it would be without candles, or presents, or songs—or, of course, the boy himself.

Maybe Luella was just looking for a reason to get out of the house and avoid the telephone. Everyone was calling the Kennys—reporters and television producers, most of all. Lois Gibbs had personally helped make sure of that. She and other mothers in the neighborhood couldn't stop talking about what had happened to Jon Allen Kenny. Here was proof, they thought, of the danger, of the risk, of the price of living near Love Canal. The mothers, mourning for the Kennys and worried for their own children, needed reporters to tell that story.

But Luella declined to comment. She had a funeral to plan and important decisions to make in her divided household. The city's Polish undertaker would handle the arrangements, per Norman's wishes, and also host the wake that Thursday and Friday night. But the child would be buried on Saturday in the Italian cemetery amid Luella's people in a white casket filled with Jon Allen's favorite toys. Luella instructed his brothers to place the items inside, before adding one herself: Jon Allen's favorite stuffed dog, Scuppity. Then she stood back, as schoolchildren arrived by the busload to pay their final respects. The kids didn't understand what had happened to their friend and classmate, yet they knew what to do. That Saturday, the kids lined up in two columns outside the church, standing like an honor guard, and the Kenny family walked between the columns, down the path that the kids had formed, through the crowd, to the hearse waiting in the street, ready to drive to the cemetery across town.

The season's first frost was upon them. Snow was in the forecast. Winter was coming, and Luella Kenny was going dark.

PART III

OCTOBER 1978
—
DECEMBER 1979

29

WE'VE DONE EVERYTHING WE CAN

Lieutenant Governor Mary Anne Krupsak wore a special necklace on the night of the gubernatorial primary. "I Love New York," it said in small gold lettering. It seemed like a safe fashion choice for Krupsak, win or lose, and it really popped over the royal blue dress she had chosen for the occasion. But more than that, the necklace was a fitting piece of jewelry to wear on a night when Krupsak hoped to make history, toppling the aloof Hugh Carey and putting herself on the path to become the first female governor of New York.

In the final days of the campaign, Krupsak had hopscotched across the state from Oneonta to Brooklyn, Herkimer to Binghamton, making a final plea for votes with a growing sense of desperation. The polls had turned against her in August, and her renegade campaign was now fading. In the Bronx, Krupsak ran alongside a jogger—in her full dress clothes—talking policy between strides while trying to win his vote. In midtown Manhattan, she plunged into an ethnic street fair behind a small Chinese American band heralding her presence to the crowd. In Lackawanna, just south of Niagara Falls, she waded into a smoky tavern popular with unemployed steel mill workers, hoping to convince them that she—not Carey—had fought for them when they had been laid off. "I was there," Krupsak said over beers. "Where was he?" And at the sixth annual German Alps Festival in a small town on the Hudson River, Krupsak, the woman whom Carey dubbed the "Polish Eagle," proved she knew how to play to a Bavarian crowd wearing lederhosen. She stepped onstage and sang "Edelweiss"—in a measured, pitch-perfect, professionally trained soprano voice.

It was in moments like these that Krupsak believed she was going to win, no matter what the latest polls said. Internal campaign numbers showed her defeating Carey in the largest tenement houses in New York City—a good barometer of Democratic turnout—and she figured she could count on Carey to step on his own toes, tripping himself up before the finish line by just being himself. In stop after stop, Carey arrived late, sometimes three hours behind schedule, and he chucked his written remarks, ad-libbing his way through entire speeches, as he had done in front of the residents in Niagara Falls. While staffers exchanged worried glances, reporters noted that at least the old Hugh Carey was back—out in the world, alive and well, making speechwriters obsolete again. "There are reams of paper in the Capitol filled with words Carey never said," a reporter joked after one of the governor's appearances upstate. "He can't resist the extemporaneous speech." Or the extemporaneous comment—and Krupsak hoped that Carey's unscripted remarks might alienate an important voting bloc: women. In their final debate, just days before the primary, the governor had the audacity to complain that Krupsak was interrupting him and suggested that she should never have left his side.

"If you waited around," Carey told her, "you would have been governor."

But in turning on Carey, Krupsak had also poked a political bear of sorts, awakening him as if from hibernation and reminding him that he knew how to win. Indeed, Carey had never lost an election, and he didn't intend to start losing now. He had a new running mate at his side: an ambitious politician named Mario Cuomo. He had the state's Democratic machine behind him. And the promises Carey made in Love Canal—ad-libbed or not—certainly weren't hurting him. If anything, they were helping. His administration was buying up people's houses as it had vowed to do and planning ahead. The latest state budget being considered in Albany set aside $10 million for the purchase of homes in the relocation zone in Niagara Falls, with another $8 million allocated for the cleanup of the site. He even personally flew into town to hand over a check on the steps of the Niagara County Courthouse, buying the very first contaminated Love Canal house. Voters saw all of it, and in the end the election wasn't close. The people chose Carey over Krupsak by almost twenty points.

Carey was moving on to the general election in November and preparing to face his Republican opponent—a millionaire lobster wholesaler from Long Island. But Lois Gibbs was right where she had been the entire fall.

She was in her home on 101st Street, and she was angry.

Back in early August—three months and, it seemed, a lifetime ago—Gibbs had often worked in the homeowners' office inside the 99th Street School placing calls to the governor that never got through. Operators in Albany would ask her to leave a message. Or, worse, they'd put her on hold. "Oh, lady," Gibbs would tell the operator over the phone, "if I get another recording on long distance, I'll—"

Click.

Some days, she felt as if nothing happened, nothing changed, and there was nothing that she could do about it, either. Roughly seven hundred families were still living in the neighborhood around the canal. But by October at least, Gibbs had a team of women working with her: Debbie Cerrillo, the mother from Ninety-Seventh Street who had been helping Lois since July; Marie Pozniak, a mother of three children on Colvin Boulevard who was so worried about her youngest daughter, aged nine, an asthmatic, that she had sent the girl away to live with relatives; Grace McCoulf, a mother of two living across the street from the Pozniaks, who had planned on having a third child but now wasn't so sure; and Barbara Quimby, another mother, who personally believed the chemicals stretched at least as far as her home on 103rd Street, two blocks beyond Lois's house and well outside Governor Carey's relocation zone. One of Quimby's two girls, aged six, had been born with multiple, debilitating birth defects. These women were willing to do whatever Lois needed.

Pozniak, a morning person, opened the homeowners' association office at the school every day, unlocking the door and starting a pot of coffee. Quimby, loud and brash like Lois, only with flowing blond hair, usually joined Pozniak there, answering the phone until Lois herself arrived. Cerrillo, the artsy one, painted the protest signs whenever they needed them, which, lately, was all the time. McCoulf, a former bank teller, filled in the gaps, typing, fundraising, networking, and all of the women were ready to snap into action when Carey made the mistake of campaigning in western New York at the end of October.

The visit was going to be more than just your typical campaign stop. For his day in Buffalo, Carey was appearing with an entourage of marquee politicians: John LaFalce; the junior senator for the state of New York, Daniel Patrick Moynihan; at least seventy other local Democratic kingmakers; and one other figure sure to draw a crowd. President Jimmy Carter was flying in to stump for Carey.

Carey greeted the president in the shadow of Air Force One at the airport in Buffalo, and the two men stepped onstage together moments later, acknowledging the large and adoring crowd assembled before them. Despite terrible weather, a cold and steady rain, five thousand people had turned out for the rally, and even cynical reporters, beaten down by life on the road with Carey, had to agree: it was a perfect scene—"a superbly run political show," one journalist called it—that would help the governor at the polls. As one county chairman said, "It will mean votes."

Carey, however, spotted a potential problem even before he and the president shook hands. Lois Gibbs's women, and a handful of other Love Canal residents, stood in the crowd along the steel barricade at the airport, waving their handmade signs. "Chemicals-Children-Death," said one placard. "You Give Aid to Foreign Countries—Why Not Us?" said another. Marie Pozniak's fourteen-year-old daughter carried still another sign, saying, "Someone say hi to my sister. She can't live with us anymore." And Grace McCoulf's five-year-old son carried a sign, too. His said, "Will I see age 6?"

Carey had to say something.

"We've done everything we can with the Love Canal problem," he told McCoulf, walking up to her in the crowd.

"But I'm worried about my kid getting leukemia," McCoulf replied.

"Now, now—"

"Yes," she said, cutting Carey off. "I'm worried about my child. What are you going to do?"

"We've done everything we can," Carey told her. "You people are blowing this all out of proportion. You're giving the Love Canal a worse name than it already has."

It was an ugly scene, and it only devolved from there. When Carter stood up to make his prepared remarks—and praised Carey for how he had handled Love Canal—Gibbs's people interrupted the president. "Are we supposed to die?" one person shouted. And when it was Carey's turn to speak, the residents broke in again and again, intent on derailing the governor and garnering some attention.

"We're warm-hearted people in this state," Carey said, trying to quell the protest.

"Welcome to the Love Canal!" someone shouted.

"This governor's been with you day and night," Carey said.

"Baloney!" someone cried.

It got so bad that Carey finally had to address the hecklers directly from the stage. "We're doing all we can for you and your children," he said, and then he asked them to please be "good neighbors" and lower their signs so that people standing around them could see. The residents complied with the request, but only after one of them shouted at the stage one last time, loud enough for everyone to hear.

"Do one of you good neighbors want to buy my house?"

The disruptions made the newspapers and the nightly news, which had been Gibbs's goal from the start. But the day worked out for Hugh Carey, too. About a week after his appearance in Buffalo with President Carter, the embattled governor narrowly defeated his Republican challenger, winning reelection. Carey—down by twenty points in the polls in mid-July—was headed back to Albany, and he was so excited on election night in November 1978 that he immediately began making more promises in the middle of his nationally televised victory speech.

He had apparently learned nothing—except for maybe one thing. Carey was finished going to Niagara Falls for a while. After visiting the city—and Gibbs's troubled neighborhood—seven times during his reelection bid, the governor had no plans to return anytime soon, and President Carter had no plans to go at all. His campaign stop with Carey in Buffalo in late October 1978 would be the closest Carter would come to the city for the next two years.

But he wanted the residents to know that he cared.

"I'm praying for you," the president whispered to the women as he shook hands along the barricade during his stop in Buffalo that day. "For all of you."

Then, waving to the crowd, he boarded Air Force One and flew back to Washington.

30

USELESS HOUSEWIFE DATA

The morning after Election Day, Governor Carey boarded a plane for a quick victory lap across the state. Despite getting just four hours of sleep the night before, he was in high spirits, impersonating the famous sports broadcaster Howard Cosell for reporters on the plane, boasting that he knew he was going to win all along, promising to be less grouchy in his second term—"Sincerely," he said, "it's about time I changed my personality"—and then turning his thoughts to the weekend. Carey was going to the Bahamas with his girlfriend, a blond heiress to the Ford Motor empire—great fodder for all the gossip columns in New York City. But Gibbs derived no pleasure from reading the juicy stories about Carey's girlfriend or their imminent lovers' getaway. She felt betrayed by the governor as she listened to the low rumble of heavy trucks, backhoes, and diggers moving into the neighborhood.

The remediation work had started on the canal. And even though Gibbs had conceded, allowing the trucks and diggers to move in, she didn't feel good about what was happening. On the first day of operations at the site behind the fence, contractors received state-issued gas masks, learned how to use emergency breathing tanks, practiced putting on full-body protective suits that made them look like industrial age spacemen, and rehearsed what to do—and where to wash—in the event that someone got splashed with buried chemical sludge. It wasn't a drill, really. In digging the trenches, workers knew they would strike hidden contaminants, and pretty soon they did. Some days, they found significant levels of benzene and toluene, layered like a cake in the ground. Other days, their discoveries defied recognition—at least without testing—and so they logged their findings as best they could with a litany of less scientific terms: "black oily goo," "bubbling action," "oozing liquid," or, on one day that fall, "a gushing stream of leachate-water." The stream, it was noted, pooled everywhere under the weight of a backhoe, until the hulking vehicle crawled off and a second vehicle rumbled in to suck up the fetid pool like a vacuum.

The disturbed earth belched new odors into the air and forced workers to employ the safety measures they had practiced. At times, they wore their gas masks all morning, waiting for the wind to carry the stench away—out over the neighborhood and beyond. But that was hardly any comfort to the residents. There were no gas masks for them to wear, and since Jon Allen Kenny had died, it was impossible for them not to wonder what they were breathing, what was in the air. Rumors spread and arguments broke out, especially between husbands and wives, who were trapped inside their worthless homes and buckling under the stress of it all.

Lois and her husband, Harry, were arguing all the time these days—about the supper that wasn't made, the laundry that wasn't folded, the house that wasn't clean, and their marriage that wasn't the same. In quiet moments, Harry found himself longing for the past—and not just the days before Lois started gathering signatures to shut down the school but for the time before their daughter, Missy, was born, four years earlier. Lois still worked then, pulling a regular 3:00-to-11:00 shift as a nurse's aide in a home for the elderly, and their days, Harry felt, had a certain rhythm then. He'd work the night shift at the Goodyear plant and then sleep all morning while Lois watched Michael. Then she'd go to work in the afternoon after Harry got up. And finally they'd cross paths in the driveway late at night, when Lois returned home from work and Harry headed back to the Goodyear plant for yet another overnight shift.

It hardly felt like anything worth celebrating at the time; their lives were so ordinary that Harry had believed then that he and Lois were in a rut. But he wished for that kind of workaday boredom now that Lois was gone every day—and sometimes every night—toiling away at the homeowners' association office inside the school. And even when she wasn't gone, it wasn't the same. Lois would fall asleep early, exhausted from another long day. In the time it would take Harry to shut off the television in the living room and turn off the lights, Lois was out cold in bed. Or she'd be working late in the kitchen, with her maps and her reports and her experts. Harry griped that there were too many people in the house, day and night, and too many phone calls. "Not a regular household," he grumbled.

Friends pitied him—"Poor Harry," became a refrain around the neighborhood—while others, the women namely, worried about Lois. They could feel her drifting away from her husband and understood her internal conflict better than anyone. Lois wanted to fix Missy's hair, read bedtime stories to Michael, or sew new school clothes for the kids, cutting them out of store-bought fabric and threading them herself, as she used to do. But she was too busy now. With everything going on, Lois barely had time to lay out the kids' clothes in the morning or comment upon Missy's hair before bed.

"Who made you pretty today?" she'd ask. "Daddy?"

It wasn't just affecting her marriage; it was taking a physical toll on her. Amid the stress, Lois was smoking more, eating less, and losing weight. Since the summer, she'd lost more than twenty pounds off her already slender frame, making her look not just thin but frail. And yet there was no going back now. Just as Lois had drifted away from Harry, she was floating away from her former self and looking down on the person she used to be as if from thirty thousand feet, wondering how she had ever lived that way. She had changed—fundamentally—and she knew it. "Now that I've gotten into this, gotten involved," Gibbs admitted to one reporter hanging around the homeowners' office, "I'm not sure I could just go back and be a housewife."

Despite everything—her marital problems, the tension in the neighborhood, and the anxiety of being trapped in Love Canal—Lois Gibbs liked going to work. She enjoyed reporting to the homeowners' office, and she wanted to be in the fight. It wasn't just about making signs to bring to some campaign rally to humiliate Governor Carey. That fall, Gibbs was putting the women to work for Beverly Paigen, chasing the theory that they had first crafted in her kitchen: that the health problems people were experiencing followed the old swales deep into the neighborhood, clustering in the places where the water had once flowed.

Paigen's instructions had been simple if difficult to follow in practice: If housewives were going to be employed in gathering this data, they needed to be methodical in their approach. They couldn't contact one house five times and another house two times; every house had to be called the same number of times. Then, once they got somebody on the phone, they couldn't just wing it, Paigen said. They couldn't make casual conversation just because the person on the line was a friend or a neighbor. They had to work off a script. "A structured questionnaire," Paigen called it. Finally, once they were asking their questions, the women had to record exactly what the respondents said and then ask, "Were you treated by a doctor?" If they were, Paigen said—if the malady could be proven to be real—they could log it. Put it on the map.

"Go laterally, just like that stream bed," Gibbs instructed the women, pointing to one of the swales she had charted. "Take three houses up and three houses down along that stream bed, and then tell us what their statistics are."

But they weren't stopping there. Gibbs and Paigen wanted the women to canvass a huge swath of the neighborhood, whether there was an old swale nearby or not. They were calling more than five hundred houses north and west of the canal—a massive job for a handful of housewives working out of an old teachers' lounge inside a tainted school.

"We're checking for everything," Gibbs said. "Miscarriages, stillbirths, malformations, liver problems, kidney problems, epilepsy, breakdowns, nervous disorders—just about anything you could think of."

With these directions in mind, the women picked up the phone and started calling—a slow and tedious task. Some people never answered, while others hung up on them. They refused to divulge personal medical information to a bunch of women who also happened to be their neighbors. The questions, at times, were too prying. "Have you ever had a nervous breakdown?" the women asked, following Paigen's script. "Did somebody in your family ever attempt suicide?" Or they declined to participate because they didn't believe in the swale theory.

State officials were publicly—and privately—casting doubt on it. One top scientist at the state Department of Health called the theory "totally, absolutely, and emphatically incorrect," and another put it even more bluntly. He told Gibbs that her work was a waste of time and energy—"useless housewife data." Still, the women made progress.

By Election Day 1978, they had contacted 76 percent of all homes west of the canal and 54 percent of their control group north of Colvin Boulevard, nearly three hundred homes with a thousand residents. It was a pile of new information, and Paigen dove in. More than anyone, she was aware of the scientific limitations of the data they had gathered. First, Paigen knew that everyone involved was potentially biased. The women making the calls wanted to get out, and the people answering the questions likely did, too. People might intentionally exaggerate their health problems—or accidentally misreport them by failing to properly understand them—and, second, there was no way for the women to double-check or confirm. They weren't following up with each individual's doctor, and they still didn't know the exact location of the old swales. By any measure, these results had to be considered preliminary.

But even with all that in mind, Paigen found what people were reporting across the neighborhood to be significant—namely, elevated rates of kidney problems, bladder disease, epilepsy, miscarriages, stillbirths, and birth defects, clustered, it seemed, around the old swales, the former streams, floodplains, or historically swampy ground.

Gibbs had been right, Paigen believed. There was a pattern.

"Definite illnesses," Gibbs said, "following a definite pattern."

Paigen needed to tell her bosses at Roswell Park what they were finding, and around Election Day that fall she did just that. In an effort to follow the new rules that administrators had issued for her back in August, Paigen immediately filed a report explaining what she knew. "It appears likely," she wrote, "that chemicals from the Love Canal are migrating down old stream beds." Then she went one step further: she informed David Axelrod directly, and flew to Albany in early November to meet him, with the results of the homeowners' survey plotted on maps and rolled into a courier tube beneath her arm. Walking through the airport with it, she began to feel as if the tube were a pipe bomb and the contents inside volatile and dangerous.

The whole thing, Paigen thought, was about to explode.

31

CLUSTERS

Paigen boarded the plane for Albany that November with the latest scientist to join the effort: Stephen Lester, a toxicologist from Washington, D.C. Lester was the homeowners' new consultant, paid for by the state to appease the residents, and he came with Ivy League credentials just like Axelrod. Lester had attended Harvard, earning a master's degree in toxicology there. The man knew his chemicals and poisons, and he was at ease walking the canal site, now crawling with remediation workers. He was comfortable with his state-issued gas mask in hand. But from the moment Stephen Lester arrived in Niagara Falls, checking into his room at the Rodeway Inn near the canal, Gibbs couldn't get over his general lack of experience.

She had expected a gray-haired scientist in his sixties, and instead here was Lester. He was in his late twenties, just like her, thin and mustachioed, with large glasses and bushy brown hair, worn long. Gibbs thought he looked like a hippie college kid. She wasn't sure she could trust him, and Lester was equally skeptical of her. He was trying to understand the science and wary of anyone trying to sway his opinion, one way or the other, and Gibbs was always trying to sway opinions. But she wouldn't have the chance to do that with Paigen, Lester, and Axelrod at the November meeting in Albany. She wasn't even allowed to attend. State officials didn't think it appropriate to discuss sensitive medical data with a private citizen, even though the private citizen in question—Gibbs—had been the one gathering the data.

It was a beautiful morning to fly, clear and cool, the day of the meeting. The commuter plane took off in Buffalo around eight o'clock, and within an hour Paigen and Lester arrived in Albany, driving over to the Empire State Plaza and settling into a conference room at the Department of Health to see Axelrod and a handful of other notable state scientists. Only one person of import was missing, in fact—the health commissioner himself, Bob Whalen—and Paigen was about to learn why. With Carey returning for a second term, Whalen was out and the long-discussed future of the Department of Health was in. Axelrod was interviewing for the health commissioner job, and, not surprisingly, he was interviewing well.

The governor's top aides liked Axelrod—both his demeanor and his résumé. He had built a modern lab for the state; he had fought Hooker on the Mirex issue; and he had proven himself to be not only science-minded but politically astute—an asset for any governmental appointee. In the final weeks of the governor's bitter campaign that year, Axelrod, a rabbi's son, had even offered Carey advice on how to win the Jewish vote in New York City. But it was his work on Love Canal that proved to Carey's team that Axelrod was ready to replace Whalen as health commissioner.

In recent months, Axelrod's lab had been helping conduct one of the largest epidemiological studies a state health department had ever run. Just like Gibbs, Axelrod wanted to know who was sick and if the illnesses might be connected to whatever was in the ground. Indeed, it was Axelrod's scientists—not Gibbs—who had first suggested and pursued the theory that old streambeds might have compromised the canal and spread contamination. As Axelrod said that fall, correcting Gibbs, "The buried stream theory is ours."

But to date, examining the blood work and the epidemiological questionnaires, Axelrod hadn't found evidence of any clustering of health issues around old swales or anything else for that matter. Surveys were still coming in, slowly. State scientists wouldn't know for sure until the end of the year—or maybe early 1979—about the extent of health problems in the neighborhood. For now, however, they saw no reason for alarm outside the current relocation area, no need for further evacuations, and no way to prove cause and effect—which happened to be an inherent shortcoming of most epidemiological work.

Scientists can rarely say with 100 percent certainty why a mother suffered a miscarriage, why a father died young of cancer, or why a previously healthy child might suddenly begin to develop seizures, kidney problems, or leukemia. There could be countless reasons for such maladies—or none. It could be because of toxic waste in the ground or low levels of chemical vapors in the air, or it could be because of something else entirely, or nothing at all. And because the situation at Love Canal was unprecedented, and the exact threat not totally known, causation was going to be even more difficult to prove, maybe even impossible, allowing people—even scientists—to take opposite positions on the same data.

Aides for Governor Carey appreciated the fact that Axelrod understood this complexity. Axelrod recognized—as he said that spring—that safety was often a political judgment. "Not a toxicologic one, nor one of absolute certainty." He understood that the governor would have to draw a line somewhere and he had a perspective, a certain scientific worldview, that made drawing lines possible. Axelrod subscribed to what could be called the Merril Eisenbud philosophy on environmental health.

Eisenbud was an environmental scientist with impressive credentials. He had served as the first health and safety chief for the U.S. Atomic Energy Commission after World War II and was appointed the first environmental health administrator for New York City in the late 1960s, during America's great environmental awakening. He had personally helped clean up the city—one of America's dirtiest at the time—removing trash from the streets, identifying long-term waste disposal solutions, improving sewage treatment, and enhancing the quality of life for millions of New Yorkers. But Eisenbud was also an unapologetic pragmatist who believed that environmental policies had to be both politically feasible and economically viable to work in an overpopulated world. He decried what he called "alarmists."

By the late 1970s, Eisenbud had left public service to be a professor at NYU Medical Center, and he now saw these "alarmists" everywhere. He had come to reject the nation's entire approach to environmental health. He argued that billions of dollars were being spent every year, trying to reduce pollution levels by small, decimal-point margins without any clear-cut evidence that such reductions saved human lives, while ordinary public health threats, like cigarette smoking, excessive drinking, fatty foods, and poverty, hastened the deaths of millions of people every day. Eisenbud believed that humanity would be better served if authorities focused more energy on reducing these, to his eyes, solvable threats, and Axelrod happened to agree.

Axelrod wasn't just a disciple of Eisenbud's; he was Eisenbud's friend. On at least one occasion in the late 1970s, Eisenbud even asked Axelrod to proofread a draft of a major speech he was about to make on his radical approach to environmental policy, and Axelrod warmly accepted the offer, reading Eisenbud's prepared remarks and writing back with a few comments. He told Eisenbud that the speech would probably attract a good bit of attention and controversy. But Axelrod thought that was a good thing and couldn't offer meaningful edits, "since the position you take is so akin to my own." He fully agreed that society was ignoring important problems while spending too much money—"great sums of money," Axelrod said—making small, incremental gains aimed at reducing environmental hazards. "I have often compared it to attempting to go from 90 percent to 99.9 percent fidelity of sound," Axelrod told Eisenbud. "For every small increment, the economic costs are vast."

It was a point of view that mothers trying to protect their children on the edge of a toxic landfill were never going to share. The math simply didn't work out if the extra 9.9 percent in fidelity meant their son or daughter didn't have to suffer from seizures or die from a rare, inexplicable, and fast-moving illness. From their perspective, the economic costs were meaningless. But Eisenbud and Axelrod's position was a valid scientific argument, a subject worthy of discussion, and perhaps most important it proved two things about Axelrod himself. This was a man who thought deeply about science and a man who would also defend Governor Carey's positions on Love Canal even if these positions were unpopular in the neighborhood, and even if it meant going to war with Beverly Paigen.

Still, he was willing to listen to her. As Paigen flew to Albany that November, Axelrod cleared his schedule for the day and asked his top public health lieutenants to attend the meeting. Everyone gathered—respectful and collegial—as Paigen unfurled her maps and began to speak.

—

The preliminary results of the housewives' surveys, she announced, indicated three major health problems outside the governor's relocation area: kidney and bladder disease; central nervous system abnormalities, like epilepsy, mental illness, depression, and suicide; and, most alarming to Paigen, a class of problems that she called "toxicity to the very young." "Miscarriages," she said, "stillbirths, crib deaths, and birth defects."

None of this, she continued, was really unexpected, because several chemicals dumped in the canal were known to cause problems to the urinary tract and central nervous system, and every scientist knew that young children were especially at risk of chemical contamination. That was why the state had urged, in the first place, that pregnant mothers and children under the age of two leave their homes on Ninety-Seventh and Ninety-Ninth Streets.

What particularly troubled Paigen was the concentration of the problems—where they were clustered. A pregnant woman living in the neighborhood had almost a one-in-five chance of having a miscarriage, a stillbirth, a crib death, or a child born with a birth defect, according to the numbers gathered by the housewives. That was well above national averages. It also appeared that these problems followed a pattern, Paigen said. They were more frequent at the southern end of the canal or along the swales that had once sliced through the neighborhood.

As she spoke, Paigen believed that she was making a compelling scientific case. The men in the room were listening, and they seemed to be taking her concerns seriously. When they pointed out problems, it was not to dispute the sum total of her findings or to shout her down but to question her numbers or the location of a certain swale. These were flaws in her presentation that, frankly, Paigen had expected. She knew she wasn't working with all the facts. But it was a good start, she thought. The meeting ended after seven hours of discussion, and everyone agreed on a few things: swales had indeed existed, carving through the old canal; health surveys were incomplete at present; maps had to be drawn using the exact contours of the old swales before they could determine whether the streambeds were connected to a pattern of health problems; and going forward, everyone would work together—"open and direct"—to do the right thing for the residents.

Paigen and Lester flew back to Buffalo that evening in the dark, feeling good about what had been accomplished. In his daily log—filed to state officials in order to document, in effect, that he was doing his job—Lester noted that it had been a productive meeting. "Entire day spent in Albany," he wrote. "Several clusters were apparent . . . Much useful information was exchanged." He expected to spend the next several days monitoring the remediation work at the canal, meeting with geologists, overseeing the sampling of chemical sludge excavated there, and helping Paigen and Gibbs with their swale theory or with anything else they needed. But when Paigen and Lester returned to Niagara Falls, it became clear that state officials weren't going to be as "open and direct" as they had indicated. In the next morning's newspapers, Axelrod publicly criticized Paigen's data.

He called it speculative, unsupported by what the state had found to date, not scientific, and basically meaningless. He declared that Paigen had presented nothing that the state didn't already know—except for where she was wrong. In those instances, health officials had corrected her, Axelrod said, fixing her map. In further interviews, the Department of Health sought to make other corrections, too.

Health officials told reporters that seizures could be caused by high fevers or head injuries; a woman might mistake miscarriage early in an alleged pregnancy for a problem with an intrauterine device, or IUD; and mental illnesses, like depression, could be caused by all sorts of factors, especially at this particular moment, a time of great stress for the residents. "How do you separate the effect of chemicals from the psychological impact they have suffered over the last three months?" Axelrod asked, before casting doubt on Paigen's data again. "It can't support anything," he said. "It's all unverified."

Paigen and Lester couldn't believe what they were reading. It was as if they had attended a totally different meeting from the one Axelrod was describing in the newspaper, and they couldn't help but think that he had gotten on the phone with the press as soon as they had left Albany. Upon returning to Buffalo, Paigen even learned that her state-funded employer refused to cover the travel expenses for her trip to Albany. She was approved to meet with Axelrod, but not allowed to bill the trip to Roswell Park.

"It is the opinion of the administration," Paigen's bosses wrote in a short memo, "that your presence in Albany was as a public person."

Paigen was so angry about her expenses being denied that she considered going public with her concerns. She could go to the press to report her growing list of problems at Roswell Park, file a whistleblower complaint, and be a nuisance, perhaps even in a court of law. Yet she was worried that any challenge from her would only distract from the real issue—the chemicals in the canal and the people still trapped around them. And so, Paigen decided on a different approach. She'd work harder on the survey data, clean up the figures, get more documentation, find the aerial photographs so that they could plot the swales accurately, and continue working with the residents. Paigen knew they needed her help. The day of her trip to Albany had made that clear to her all over again.

While she was in a conference room with Axelrod that morning, a tanker truck working on the edge of the canal site sank into the soggy ground and tipped over to one side, spilling five hundred gallons of unknown chemical leachate onto Ninety-Seventh Street until workers could locate a small crane and right the vehicle on its wheels once again. The liquid—a mixture of rainwater and whatever was buried in the canal—puddled on the pavement where children had once played, glistening in the sun. Still, by Love Canal's standards, it was a minor problem. Trucks like this one were hauling away six thousand gallons a day, enough to fill a swimming pool, and the work quickly resumed.

After about twenty minutes, the diggers and vacuum trucks roared back to life, clawing at the tainted ground.

32

WHITE MICE

The spill on Ninety-Seventh Street that November was surely proof to Elene Thornton that she had been right from the start: the work needed to stop.

The fact that the mother from Griffon Manor had already failed to prevent the remediation in court that fall didn't seem to matter to her. She was looking for another angle, and with the remediation mishaps at the canal, Thornton finally found the opening she needed. A growing number of people—both residents of Griffon Manor and homeowners, Black and white—smelled new odors, eyed evacuation buses on the street corners, heard the steady rumble of trucks through the neighborhood, and read the stories about spills at the canal site. They decided they wanted to end the work or at least disrupt it in some significant way, and they were prepared to protest outside the governor's fence in order to make it happen.

Gibbs hated the idea of the protest—at first, anyway. For one thing, it was cold and getting colder by the day. It was not the best time of year to be standing around outside for hours with protest signs. For another thing, she and the others didn't technically want to stop anything. Gibbs's soil expert—an independent scientist working at the University at Buffalo—told her in no uncertain terms that they needed to allow the work to happen. "Do *not* try to stop the present construction," the soil expert said, pleading with her. The fact that they were finding chemicals in the ground—or even spilling some on Ninety-Seventh Street—didn't alarm him. It meant, he said, that the trench system would work; chemicals would flow away from the people through the newly installed pipes. However, if the system wasn't running by springtime, when the annual snowmelt and rains turned the canal into a swampy sea of mud, the buried contaminants would flow someplace else—possibly toward their basements—and residents would be right back where they had started. "There must be other ways to get your attention and be heard," the soil expert told Gibbs, "without endangering the necessary work."

Gibbs trusted the soil expert. But the man—an academic—had no idea what she was facing in the neighborhood. Authorities were now looking for dioxin in the canal. The highly toxic chemical—dangerous to humans even in trace amounts and fatal to small mammals in quantities as minuscule as one one-thousandth of a milligram—was perhaps the most infamous toxin in America in the late 1970s. Everyone knew it as the chemical used in Agent Orange, the herbicide that U.S. military planes had sprayed on jungles in Vietnam, clearing the dense forests of Vietcong bunkers and then poisoning everything else: fish, farmers, unborn children, and even U.S. soldiers. Many people remembered how it had sickened dozens of horses in Missouri in 1971, when ranchers sprayed dioxin at a riding stable there to keep down the dust, and most knew the cautionary tale of Seveso, Italy, a small town forced to evacuate in the summer of 1976 when a cloud of the potent chemical escaped from a local plant and fell like rain over the community, killing thousands of animals and sending children to the hospital.

People speculated that they'd find the same element in the canal, and Michael Brown, at the *Gazette,* was one of them. Brown knew that Hooker had manufactured a compound called 2,4,5-trichlorophenol from 1947 to 1972. And he knew that an unwanted by-product of 2,4,5-T was dioxin. It stood to reason that if Hooker had dumped residues from this chemical into the canal, then dioxin would be there, too. When Brown asked Hooker about it, the company responded by asking him to put his questions in writing. He did so, and then waited for days. There was no reply. Finally, on the Friday after Governor Carey was reelected, Brown got Bruce Davis on the phone, and Davis, considering every side of the square, gave Brown an answer in a cold, controlled voice. Hooker had indeed dumped 2,4,5-T in the canal, he said. Roughly two hundred tons of it.

Brown hung up the phone, slipped a piece of paper into his typewriter, and started writing another story that would make headlines across the country and incite panic in the neighborhood in new and frightful ways. According to one expert that Brown interviewed, the amount of dioxin buried in the canal could equal the total amount sprayed across Vietnam over the entire Agent Orange campaign—a staggering figure that was almost hard to imagine. And Brown wasn't finished breaking news. Within days, he also learned that the total number of chemical compounds in the canal wasn't eighty-two, as the state had announced back in August. It was more than two hundred, some of which still couldn't be identified and had to be considered "organic curiosities."

Privately, Axelrod admitted he was concerned, fixating, in particular, on the dioxin problem. It was one of the most toxic synthetic compounds ever produced, and it was almost surely in the canal. Yet when his top lieutenants returned to Niagara Falls at the end of November to hold the latest public meeting at the 99th Street School, they said they hadn't discovered any dioxin yet. "In the event that we find it," one health official promised, "we'll tell you."

In another time, two years earlier, say, before the events of recent months, the assembled crowd—about two hundred people, Black and white, union workers and stay-at-home moms—would have been inclined to believe the scientist or at least listen politely. But not anymore. Axelrod's men didn't even make it through their presentation before people started shouting at them and deriding their credentials. One of the state experts that night was a veterinarian.

"It's a cover-up!" one person shouted.

"I want out," said another.

Thanksgiving was coming, and none of them felt safe preparing a holiday meal in their kitchens. They also didn't understand why the health officials in the room kept saying that any additional evacuation order would be a political decision—Carey's decision. "It will be a cold day in hell," one person said, "when Carey runs the health department."

Nearly fifty people in the auditorium walked out in frustration, huddling in a classroom down the hall and then meeting again in the days ahead—without Lois Gibbs, at least once. In a twist that state officials would have found ironic, this newly assembled group—including both homeowners and residents of Griffon

Manor, Gibbs's neighbors and Elene Thornton—believed Lois to be too compliant, too quiet. They wanted to make a point by shutting down the remediation work.

"I've lost control of these people," Gibbs remarked.

They weren't just arguing with the officials in the auditorium. They were shouting at each other again, divided over what to do and how to do it and who should be in charge—if anyone. At one point, the arguments almost became physical when a white man referred to the residents of Griffon Manor as "you people." A Black woman lunged at him and had to be held back. But the divisions were hardly just racial. Many residents of Griffon Manor, including Thornton's rival Agnes Jones, agreed with Gibbs: they didn't want to stop the remediation work. Consensus was going to be impossible to find, and then somehow, in early December 1978, after days of arguing, they stumbled into it.

Community leaders met inside the library at the 99th Street School on the first Monday of the month. All the important players were there: Gibbs and Thornton; Jones and a dozen other residents, all homeowners. Together, they presented their demands to Axelrod and a few other state officials. The group wanted the state to agree to move dozens of residents from their homes and from Griffon Manor, due to the specific health concerns of these residents and the deteriorating conditions in the neighborhood overall. On this point, even Thornton and Jones could agree. Recent inspections at Griffon Manor had found basements seeping with water, sinks backed up with reddish ooze, basins that gurgled anytime it rained, rooms prone to flooding, and spiders and roaches, living in the damp conditions. Thornton didn't think it too much to ask that the state help a few dozen affected families find new apartments, and Gibbs made a similar case for the homeowners. Her list included fifty-three families, living outside the current relocation zone, who were reporting rashes, seizures, children with asthma, wives who were six months pregnant, elevated levels of several chemicals in the air inside their homes, and their own critter problems. Rats had now moved into the neighborhood, scavenging through piles of trash left behind by people who had fled their homes in a hurry.

"I have a 10-year-old son who hasn't gone to school in five weeks," one resident told Axelrod at the meeting in the library that night. "And last night, he crawled out of bed, went under the couch and said, 'I want to die. I don't want to live here anymore.' "

She and other residents increasingly felt as if they were test subjects. "Just white mice for more data collection."

Axelrod disagreed.

"To some extent," he said, "we're all white mice."

The arguments hadn't swayed him. The state wasn't moving anyone else, and its entrenchment on the issue helped unite people—really, for the first time. Homeowners agreed to work with renters. Renters agreed to work with homeowners. They'd stick with Lois as their representative for now—"We are still with Gibbs," one leader of the new splinter group declared—and Lois knew just what to do next. She still didn't want to shut down the remediation work; that hadn't changed. Yet if a revolt was what people wanted, she'd give it to them. She knew people were craving action, and she also knew what Governor Carey feared most of all.

"The last thing he wants," one aide explained off the record, "is to have a bunch of Love Canal folks standing in front of a bulldozer on television."

While Paigen worked the science, Gibbs began crafting a new plan.

It was time to find a bulldozer.

State officials assigned to the problem in Niagara Falls begged Gibbs not to do it, bargaining with her and others right until the last moment.

"Lois," one of them said, "what are you doing to me?"

But on the second Friday of December, Gibbs awoke in the dark and reported to the gates at the southern end of the fence at 5:30 a.m. with half a dozen other picketers to stand in the street and try to stop the trucks from coming or going. The effort wasn't successful at all. The weather was cold and wet, a miserable morning. Niagara Falls had already seen its first snowfall for the year, but what was falling from the sky on this day, the first day of picketing, was just rain, and the dreadful conditions hurt turnout. At times, there were more reporters than residents standing outside the gates. The best the protesters could do was hold up a truck for a few minutes. Workers walked right past them.

The next morning brought more of the same, only—if possible—the weather was worse. Temperatures hovered in the teens as Gibbs gathered with others in the predawn darkness. And, again, nothing happened. No arrests. No newsworthy incidents. No trucks being turned away. It was another slow day for Michael Brown at the *Gazette* and mercifully so—he was going on vacation—until his phone rang that evening.

It was Albany calling. Axelrod on the line. Brown wasn't going on vacation anymore.

"We found it," Axelrod said. "The dioxin."

Scientists had detected an unknown quantity of the chemical in a newly excavated trench in a yard on Ninety-Seventh Street, about thirty feet from the landfill itself, and Axelrod said they wanted to inform everyone right away—just as state officials had promised they would. But the discovery, Axelrod said, changed nothing. They had expected to find dioxin, and now they had.

"Now," Axelrod said, "we know the answer."

Except not really. Like everything else at Love Canal, they had enough information to be concerned, one state scientist said that Saturday, but not enough to draw actual scientific conclusions about risk—the risk that the dioxin posed to the people living there. They needed to do more testing. In the meantime, people were told to be patient, knowing that symptoms of low-level dioxin exposure might be, as the state described them, "pretty vague." The chemical might cause depression, chronic rashes, liver disease, kidney damage, and birth defects. It wasn't, however, cause for further evacuations in the neighborhood. Dioxin was buried across Niagara Falls in multiple locations, including in Hooker's other large city dump, Hyde Park, which wasn't in a densely populated residential neighborhood like Love Canal, but was on the edge of campus at Niagara University. By December, Hyde Park was making headlines too. It was known to have significant amounts of 2,4,5-T buried in the ground—sixteen times the amount that investigators expected to find at Love Canal. Indeed, they were already discovering dioxin at Hyde Park, a worrisome amount, in the mud just south of the academic halls, student center, and library—where students gathered, unaware of the dangers. To avoid all human contact with this particular compound, officials would have had to clear multiple neighborhoods on the east side of town and maybe a college campus, too.

The *Gazette* printed Brown's story about the dioxin discovery on a Sunday, and Hooker Chemical clicked into damage control. By the next day, a company toxicologist filed a report to upper management, summarizing the fast-moving situation in Niagara Falls and offering some insight on how to handle it—from a public relations point of view. Executives could explain that the dioxin levels in the city were extremely low when compared with the disaster that had occurred in Italy, and they could also remind people that dioxin could be found everywhere—in household dust, in chimney smoke. A recent Dow Chemical report on the ubiquitous nature of the compound would be particularly helpful, the toxicologist said, in "softening the impact" of the Niagara Falls problem.

Gibbs, however, was taking a different approach: she was hoping to capitalize on the news. Residents had struggled to get much attention during their first two days protesting outside the gates of the remediation site. Now everyone was calling: the newspapers, the local TV stations, Beverly Paigen, and other residents. One station wanted to send a car and bring Gibbs to the studio. Another hoped to get Paigen and put her on the news. At times, over the weekend, Gibbs's phone rang off the hook. In order to get anything done, she had to disconnect it. Yet she wasn't complaining. The dioxin news was perfectly timed for her purposes, giving Gibbs a reason for the protests that she didn't have just a few days earlier.

"Dioxin is the most toxic chemical man has made," she told residents. "Get out there and join the pickets."

Before dawn that Monday, more than four dozen people reported to the gates at the remediation site, standing in the twelve-degree temperatures in the dark, and this time they were angry. They chanted, "Dioxin's in—we want out." They shouted at workers. "Don't you know there's dioxin in there?" Gibbs said. "You'll be bringing it home to your children." By 10:00 a.m., six people had been arrested for blocking the road, and Gibbs returned the next morning, Tuesday, hoping to add her name to that list. In fact, she was almost desperate to go to jail, in order to maintain her standing and credibility. Lippes advised against it, and Paigen did, too. They didn't think it a good idea for Gibbs to get hauled downtown, charged with disorderly conduct, and locked up in a holding cell—or maybe worse. But Gibbs wasn't listening. In the dark that morning, she linked arms with Grace McCoulf, planted her feet in the road in front of a bus, and refused to budge, even as a pair of police officers moved in, shaking their heads.

"Do you want to arrest us?" McCoulf asked.

"Don't be like that, lady," one of the police officers said. "Let me explain it to you," he continued. "Your purpose is ideal. I agree with it in my own little way." But the women were putting him in a bad spot, and he really wished they would step aside.

The waiting bus inched forward and Gibbs shouted at it.

"You're going to die!" she said.

The officer had no choice. He arrested Gibbs, placed her in the back of his squad car, and drove her downtown.

Later, after Lippes secured her release, Gibbs would have a lot of explaining to do to her children. Both Michael and Missy were upset that Mommy had been arrested. Michael was even crying about it at home that night, and Gibbs had to have a long talk with him, assuring her son that she wasn't a "bad guy"—a conversation that made her feel guilty, as if she were a terrible mother.

But in the moment that morning, inside the squad car, looking out on the protesters still standing in the street through a screen of metal mesh, Gibbs felt almost relieved. The squad car was warm, and she was thankful for it. She hadn't realized how cold she was—or how tired. As soon as she was booked, fingerprinted, and led to a small cell inside the jail, Gibbs lay down on the cot that was provided for her and promptly fell asleep.

33

UNCOMFORTABLE FEELINGS

The Kennys didn't put up Christmas lights that December. Norman—who loved the holiday tradition, going overboard until every gutter of their house on Ninety-Sixth Street glowed and every tree branch in the yard sparkled—didn't have the heart for it. He couldn't even find the strength to play the piano, sing carols around the house, or attend rehearsals with his Polish choir, the things he once enjoyed most. Instead, Norman sat at the kitchen table, suspended in an amber of memories.

Mornings reminded him of taking Jon Allen to school. Nights reminded him of snuggling Jon Allen into bed with Scuppity and all his other stuffed animals. Even the simple act of coming home from work was painful for Norman. He'd park the station wagon next to the basketball hoop in the driveway in the dark, remembering the time, just before Jon Allen got sick, when his son celebrated after making five shots in a row, and then he'd walk into the house, remembering how Jon Allen used to run up and greet him at the front door squealing, "Daddy!"

Now the house was quiet, the family lost. In their grief, one of Jon Allen's brothers had stopped eating, Luella and Norman had stopped talking, and Norman often holed up alone, writing sad letters to the son who wasn't there anymore.

"Dear Jon," Norman wrote. "Daddy's little boy. I feel empty because you've left . . . Remember how I tucked you in at night with all your animals? Night, night, Jon. And then I'd wake you for school . . . Remember how busy you were with homework, getting all your words and math? Daddy remembers . . . Oh, Jon—did Daddy fail you? We trusted the doctors. They couldn't see you weren't like all the other children sick with nephrosis—if only they'd known."

Luella felt guilty, too. She and Norman were scientists. They should have been able to protect Jon Allen, she thought, and shouldn't have dismissed the possibility that living near the landfill had contributed to his medical problems. Luella began to question why they had ever moved to the neighborhood in the first place, rolling back the tape of their lives to the moment right before they purchased the house and stopping it right there. She wanted to cut, edit, and make a different choice or sell the house and move now. But, of course, neither was possible. Like Gibbs, Thornton, and more than seven hundred other families in the neighborhood, the Kennys were stuck there for Christmas in 1978. It was the worst Christmas of their lives.

The state Department of Health was allegedly investigating the cause of Jon Allen's death; the press had announced it the day of the boy's funeral. It was unusual for a seven-year-old boy to die, state officials said, and they wanted to check it out in hopes of disproving any connection to the chemicals in the ground and putting the Kennys' neighbors at ease. As one of Axelrod's colleagues put it, "We hope we can dispel some of their uncomfortable feelings."

But that was news to Luella. No one had ever contacted her about collecting Jon Allen's medical records or launching an investigation into his death. No one in Albany was apparently concerned enough about her "uncomfortable feelings" to give her the courtesy of a call. The only official she ever heard from was Congressman LaFalce, who at Bonnie Casper's urging wrote her a few days after Jon Allen's death to extend his sympathies and offer to help in any way he could. But even LaFalce couldn't have prevented what happened next. The press reports, which listed the family's full address on Ninety-Sixth Street, made a target out of the Kennys. In early December, their home—just a short walk from the abandoned houses on the northern edge of the canal—was burglarized for the first time. Jon Allen's brother Stephen, now ten, came home to find every drawer in the house ripped open, every room ransacked, and the family's belongings spilled out all over the floor. Stephen, shaking, picked up the phone and promptly called his mother at work.

The perpetrator hadn't left with much—just petty cash, loose change, small valuables. Yet it was hard not to feel violated, knowing he—or they—had been in every room in the house and had even paused to notice the little things. Someone had ripped open Luella's pincushion in her sewing basket inside her bedroom closet, perhaps thinking that it might contain hidden jewels or money.

The Kennys decided to spend the holidays with Norman's sister in Florida. They'd leave town for a week, get away to somewhere warm, and let the boys escape and enjoy a holiday with their cousins. Only the troubles followed them there, too. On New Year's Eve, Stephen was hit by a car as the two families walked to the beach before midnight. He was running ahead with his cousin, excited to catch crabs in the surf, and then, suddenly, his body was flying through the air. Luella watched in horror, knowing where they were headed next: back to the emergency room, back to the hospital. Stephen would be fine; doctors said he was fortunate to have landed in the sand on the roadside, instead of on the pavement itself. But it was almost too much for the Kennys to bear. In the hospital waiting room, Luella and Norman sat in silence, looking up at the clock ticking toward the New Year—1979.

The only solace they could find that winter was in the library. In evenings after work, during lunch breaks, and on weekends, Luella and Norman started taking turns visiting medical archives in Buffalo, trying to understand the cause and complications of nephrotic syndrome—the condition that had precipitated Jon Allen's death. They were effectively launching their own investigation in a gauzy haze of sadness and finding purpose once again deep inside the quiet stacks housed at Roswell Park and the University at Buffalo. Luella and Norman couldn't wrap their minds around what had happened to them—or their family—over the span of just a few short months. But being scientists, they could make sense of even the most arcane medical journal, and they began communicating with each other in a new way. They photocopied journal articles about nephrotic syndrome and left them in the kitchen for the other to read.

Right away, Luella and Norman wished they had visited the library sooner. In article after article, journal after journal, researchers reported finding rapidly progressing nephrotic syndrome in two particular kinds of subjects: industrial workers exposed to hydrocarbon mists and vapors, and lab rats—animals intentionally poisoned by chemicals.

Scientists first made the connection in the early 1950s. An Irish pathologist and a pair of biochemists at the University of Wisconsin induced nephrotic syndrome in rats by feeding them a grain diet mixed with a minuscule amount of chemicals—.043 percent of a compound called N,N'-Diacetylbenzidine. The element—commonly found in paints, dyes, and many chemical plant processes—could harm the rats within three to four weeks, the scientists reported in 1952 in *The American Journal of Pathology*. And the rodents' symptoms sure sounded familiar to Luella and Norman. The symptoms included severe proteinuria; extreme swelling of the face, neck, and abdomen; chronic weakness; and death.

Three times in the next twenty years scientists confirmed these findings. Again and again, rats exposed to small amounts of chemicals developed nephrotic syndrome over time. They became swollen and sick, just like Jon Allen. Then, in 1972, a pair of American doctors began investigating nephrotic syndrome in humans. They wrote detailed case studies of eight people suffering from nephrosis and found that six of the patients had extensive exposure to industrial solvents. These people were factory workers and housepainters with a history of handling fuel oils, degreasing agents, and paint thinners—not seven-year-old boys. Three years later, a top journal called *The Lancet* repeated these findings in an analysis of a much larger group of more than sixty patients. Hydrocarbon solvents were the most frequent trigger of the disease, *The Lancet* reported, and it often didn't take much exposure to spark serious problems in some people. Luella and Norman repeatedly found evidence of that in the medical literature, including one article they discovered in Sweden's leading medical journal. The article, published in 1976 and translated into English, documented the case of a healthy fifty-nine-year-old man who began exhibiting symptoms, just like Jon Allen's, after coating a floor with thirty liters of paint. Within a month, the man's body became swollen. He struggled to breathe and required a four-week hospital stay in order to stabilize again.

This patient, the Scandinavian doctors noted, improved by taking steroids—evidence that Jon Allen's doctors had chosen a proven path to recovery. But the medical journals also made clear that people suffering from nephrotic syndrome didn't always fare well. Many patients ended up on dialysis. Others, taking long-term steroids, suffered from circulation problems and potentially fatal blood clots. Children, in particular, were at risk of dying.

By the end of January 1979, Luella looked at Norman with a growing sense of dread. They had spent weeks in libraries across Buffalo. They had become fixtures at copy machines, their faces aglow in the blue light. They had compiled a stack of journal articles that would have worried any parent, and they knew what they needed to do next. They needed to start speaking out, Luella said. Go public. Talk to the reporters who kept calling. Something. If not for Jon Allen, then for Christopher and Stephen, his brothers, who were still living in the house on Ninety-Sixth Street—a house that Luella was increasingly convinced was not safe.

Norman nodded. He agreed.

"It has to be done," he said.

34

THE PAIGEN PROBLEM

The David Axelrod era at the Department of Health began officially, just after the New Year, with Carey's inauguration amid the bitter chill of another brutal winter.

As Carey stepped inside the New York State Assembly chamber to place his hand on a Bible that had been in his family for more than a century and take his oath of office, a winter storm swept across the state, packing conditions that New Yorkers hadn't seen since the Blizzard of 1977 almost exactly two years earlier.

In Albany, temperatures hovered in the single digits, forcing the soldiers performing Governor Carey's ceremonial fifteen-gun salute to shiver in the cold near the snow-covered steps of the assembly. But it was positively balmy that day in the capital compared with what Lois Gibbs, Luella Kenny, Elene Thornton, and others were facing back in Niagara Falls. The early January storm dumped more than a foot of snow across western New York that morning, shutting down the entire region. Schools and bridges closed; the New York State Thruway did, too. Residents were told to prepare for wind-chill temperatures of minus fifty and to stay off the roads, if possible. In the blinding squalls, there was little visibility.

Still, remediation work continued at the canal site uninterrupted. Bulldozers cleared new ground. Vacuum trucks worked through the night, and tankers hauled away another two thousand bathtubs' worth of chemical leachate—roughly eighty-six thousand gallons in all. For the workers, the cold weather was better than rain—tanker trucks wouldn't sink into the ground in these conditions—and Axelrod refused to let the storm change his plans either.

He was moving into Whalen's corner office on the fourteenth floor of the health tower on the Empire State Plaza, breaking in his new handpicked secretary to his relentless, around-the-clock workaholic pace, stacking piles of reports across his desk—as usual—and inviting his top staffers to join him at an event that would celebrate every employee at the Department of Health. Axelrod wanted to wish them all a happy New Year and let them know there was a new doctor in charge—arguably the most modern physician to ever serve as health commissioner in the state. Axelrod was pro-vaccine, anticigarettes, forward thinking, dedicated to improving health care for the poor, and excited for the chance to stand before his employees. "At that time," Axelrod informed his top deputies, "I will also seek their support in recommitting ourselves in 1979 to preserving and protecting the health of New York state's citizens. Governor Carey and I believe that the strength of the state, and the happiness of its residents, depend on our ability to do so."

In his first few weeks in office, however, Axelrod learned right away just how monumental a task that was going to be. On any given day as health commissioner, he faced at least half a dozen different crises involving delinquent nursing homes, sleepaway camps with poor sanitary practices, state hospitals infested with insects, rogue developers using substandard materials that endangered the lives of New Yorkers inside their own homes, and other unexpected problems. He had to become knowledgeable about the dangers of formaldehyde foam insulation and what to do about it. He had to understand why breast cancer rates were skyrocketing in New York City's poorest neighborhoods and, again, decide what to do about it. He had to address potential contaminants within his own building—the Empire State Plaza was filled with asbestos—and he had to find the time to write letters to every employee who suffered a death in the family or retired after years of service, dictating these notes, and others, to his secretary amid the mess of his office. "The formidable pile of garbage," he called it. Yet nothing dominated Axelrod's time that winter more than Love Canal. For starters, he had a Beverly Paigen problem that simply wasn't going away.

Paigen was still upset that her travel expenses to Albany the previous fall were denied, but it was hardly her only complaint at this point. Starting that November, within days of her meeting with Axelrod to discuss the swale maps, both she and her husband, Ken, began to face a series of setbacks at work.

Roswell Park denied Ken the opportunity of being a visiting lecturer at the University of California that winter—a pro forma request typically approved without much debate. Indeed, a month after Ken's application was denied, a different department head received approval to work in Israel for an entire year. Meanwhile, at the exact same time, Beverly's bosses leaked to Whalen a rough draft of a new grant that she was pursuing to study hazardous waste sites in Erie County, in Buffalo.

Paigen had only submitted the draft to her bosses at Roswell Park because she had been asked to do so. As she pointed out to them, "You have requested that I keep you informed of what I am doing." And it infuriated her to learn that Whalen—still health commissioner at the time—was reading the proposal in its unpolished, unfinished state. "It never should have left my office in that form," she said. But she figured it would be all right because so many others outside the Department of Health had supported the grant she was pursuing.

Federal officials, local politicians, and even top scientists in the state's office of toxic substances were excited about Paigen's involvement in the project. Her expertise, they all agreed, was integral to the plan. But Whalen, apparently, felt differently. In one of his last acts as commissioner, he informed Paigen's bosses that he and Axelrod had reviewed her plan and found it lacking. "The major difficulty with the proposal," Whalen told Paigen's supervisors, "is that it represents another relatively undisciplined environmental data gathering expedition."

Both she and Ken were beginning to feel like outcasts in their own building, pariahs in their own workplace. But Beverly wasn't giving up; she was digging in. As she waited for official word on her proposal that winter, Paigen continued to review the health problems that Gibbs's housewives had identified in their survey of the neighborhood. Paigen checked the data against the figures the state itself had gathered through its own epidemiological work and focused on one data point in particular: miscarriages. She was convinced that the state had miscalculated the miscarriage rate and, in doing so, was minimizing the problem—an issue that she reported to both Gibbs and Thornton that winter, just before Christmas.

For starters, Paigen informed them, the state had failed to notice that women living in the area had a lower than average miscarriage rate prior to moving to the neighborhood. They suffered miscarriages less than 9 percent of the time, she said, well lower than the national average of almost 13 percent. But while living in the neighborhood, women on Ninety-Seventh and Ninety-Ninth Streets reported a miscarriage rate of 21 percent, and women elsewhere in the neighborhood reported a rate of 16.5—notable changes that indicated to Paigen that the simple act of moving there could increase the chance of losing a child.

"Any scientist," she told Gibbs and Thornton, "would have said that there was definitely a change in the pattern of miscarriage rate before and after living on the canal."

But the state didn't say that, Paigen argued, because scientists in Albany had calculated something else wrong: the control group. For the control population, the state used a cohort of women in Montreal. These women self-reported miscarriages without confirmation from a doctor and had a miscarriage rate of almost 15 percent. That would have been fine, Paigen said, except the state was counting only doctor-confirmed miscarriages in its survey of Love Canal residents, and as she already pointed out, these women had suffered miscarriages at a much lower rate prior to moving to the neighborhood. If the state wanted an accurate picture of the problem, it should have used the Love Canal women themselves as a control group, Paigen argued, or at least compared their miscarriage data with a cohort of other doctor-confirmed cases—apples to apples, not apples to melons. "The fact that the Montreal population is not appropriate for comparison," she said, "should have been immediately apparent to a biostatistician."

Finally, she pointed out, there was one more problem. Women who have miscarriages in three or more pregnancies are very hard to find. According to the Montreal study, the chances of a woman having three miscarriages was less than half of 1 percent. Yet Gibbs's survey—which didn't include people living on Ninety-Seventh and Ninety-Ninth Streets, didn't include Luella Kenny's house or anyone else living north of Colvin Boulevard, and didn't include Griffon Manor, either—had documented seven such women living just between One Hundredth and 103rd Streets for a habitual miscarriage rate of 3.7 percent.

"This number of women with three or more miscarriages is very high, much higher than expected," Paigen told Gibbs and Thornton. "Even more striking," she added, "is that all seven of these women live along a swale."

35

RELOCATION BY IMPREGNATION

In early 1979—during the first weeks of his tenure as health commissioner—Axelrod still refused to publicly concede that the swales were significant in any way. State officials had dismissed the theory back in November, and Axelrod was standing by that decision now, declining to evacuate anyone else from the neighborhood—even when residents picketed outside a state health office in Buffalo on a visit that Axelrod made there in mid-January.

Unafraid of a confrontation—or even of the reporters following the residents that day—Axelrod invited the small crowd inside to meet with him in a conference room and then told the people that their kids were as healthy as anyone else's. "I truly believe that," he said. As he explained that day—and other times that winter in thoughtful, well-written letters sent to worried residents—he understood their concerns, and he recognized why they might believe that their various health problems might be connected to the old Hooker landfill. But he told them, "We may never be in a position to describe the specific etiology of your illnesses." The canal might have caused their medical issues or not. The chemicals might be to blame or not. "We can only make a best judgment," Axelrod explained, "on the basis of the information we have gathered." And for now that information still suggested that no one else had cause to leave the neighborhood.

Then, sometime near the end of January, the pile of epidemiological and environmental data that the state had been chasing for several months finally came in. It included information gleaned from four thousand medical questionnaires and blood samples;

four hundred phone interviews with people who had lived in the neighborhood in the past but were now scattered across thirty-one different states; and nearly a thousand tests on water, air, and soil. The medical questionnaires alone were so voluminous that a state computer had to help synthesize the findings, and the general picture was so detailed that the neighborhood instantly became one of the most studied pieces of land in America.

From aerial photographs, for example, Axelrod knew that impounded water in the old canal had very likely been displaced by the dumping, flowing away from the channel through what he called "existing surface drainage pathways"—in other words, the swales. He knew that much of Griffon Manor had once been a swamp and that at least a dozen lots between One Hundredth and 101st Streets had been, too, until developers had filled in the land decades earlier with trash-laden dirt of unknown origin. He knew that storm sewers—at three locations in the neighborhood—tested positive for four different dangerous chemicals at levels exceeding the EPA's current-day standards for human exposure. He knew that these same four chemicals had been found at even higher levels in the creeks behind Luella Kenny's house. He knew, from the medical questionnaires, that people reported 150 different kinds of maladies in the neighborhood, and he knew, from the blood tests, that residents seemed to suffer from liver problems at rates greater than a sample of twenty-six thousand people tested in nearby Rochester.

But Axelrod saw no pattern to the 150 different maladies that people reported. He found no elevated rates of cancer, say, or any other health problem. And he was comforted by the notion that once people moved away from the canal—and had their blood retested—their liver functions returned to the normal ranges. This particular data point suggested that state officials could mitigate long-term health damage by moving certain families, and they had already done that: many of the families with abnormal liver tests had gotten out months earlier. These people were already living miles away from the old canal. There was, really, just one area of concern, Axelrod believed, and on the last day of January 1979 he informed one of Governor Carey's top cabinet members about this concern in a detailed, three-page memo.

Axelrod explained that there was indeed a pattern—a pattern

of birth defects, liver abnormalities, and miscarriages potentially following the old swales, just as Paigen and Gibbs had argued the previous fall. The magnitude of the pattern appeared to be small. "Sufficiently small," Axelrod said. But officials at three federal agencies—including epidemiologists at the Centers for Disease Control—had reviewed the data at Axelrod's request and everyone agreed. "There is," Axelrod told the governor's office, "some increase in risk for some biologically adverse response in those individuals living on these historically wet areas." It was also likely, he said, that the increased risk of birth defects and miscarriages extended beyond the swales—into the neighborhood at large. "Our own conclusion," he said, "is that there is a certain risk level that we cannot accurately quantitate."

The question, for Axelrod, was, what to do about it?

"In view of the posture we have previously taken," he continued, "and the statements by the governor that families will be moved where there is a health hazard, there is the anticipation that these health effects, inconclusive as they might be, are sufficient to propel us to new actions to relocate large numbers of people."

The next question then was, which people?

"The decision as to the acceptability of a given level of risk goes beyond science," Axelrod informed the governor's office, "and is a formative political decision." Therefore, he wanted to make the governor aware of a new political problem: the residents of Griffon Manor, led by Elene Thornton and, increasingly, Agnes Jones. "The allegations by this group have been that there has been inadequate attention given to the problems of the community because of their color and social status," Axelrod said. Officials needed to be aware of that in Albany as they weighed their decision about a new evacuation—a decision that Axelrod believed they should not make in a vacuum. He concluded his memo by informing the governor's office that he was reconvening a panel of medical experts that had first met the previous summer under the former health commissioner, Bob Whalen. Axelrod was summoning them to New York City for a meeting at LaGuardia International Airport on the first Wednesday of February. He needed advice.

—

The panel of experts was a great idea—in concept. Axelrod could presumably get the best guidance from objective scientists, studying the canal crisis with clear eyes. The group even had an official name that sounded both important and innocuous at the same time. The state called it the Blue Ribbon Panel. The problem was, everything about it was cloaked in secrecy—an approach that might have worked the previous July, when almost no one was watching or even aware of Love Canal, but secrecy wasn't going to fly now with both reporters and residents asking persistent questions about the status of the long-awaited health studies.

Residents wanted to attend the Blue Ribbon Panel meeting or at least know the names of the so-called experts. But the state declined. And the mere suggestion that Axelrod had the health studies in hand but planned to discuss them in secret—with a group of experts no one knew—before he made any public announcement set off a new wave of furor. Residents refused to accept that a small handful of scientists—all men, operating behind the curtain, off the record, and in the shadows—would be helping Axelrod make a decision that would alter the lives of the three thousand people still living in the neighborhood. If there was a discussion to be had, they believed it should be had in public. One of Gibbs's neighbors even filed a Freedom of Information request in the days before the meeting, demanding answers under the law right away. But there was nothing anyone could do to stop the meeting from happening. At Axelrod's direction, the Blue Ribbon Panel gathered behind closed doors that February to consider seven options—each just as secret as the panel itself.

Option one, Axelrod explained in a memo before the meeting, was the nuclear choice. "Buy all of the remaining homes in the area." It was by far the most expensive plan, costing the state approximately $10 million. But then they'd be out. It'd be over. Authorities could remediate, without the threat of protests and pickets. Axelrod wouldn't have to deal with Gibbs or Paigen anymore. Residents would get what they want, and officials could move on—in peace.

Options two, three, four, and five were effectively Axelrod's hybrid models. Under these plans, the state would buy a certain number of homes—say, thirty houses soon to be affected by remediation work, fifty houses with pregnant mothers or young children, or every house built along an old swale, now estimated to be more than 40 percent of the neighborhood. "This would be justified," Axelrod explained, "on the basis of the most recent analysis." But it could also create problems, turning neighbors against each other in new and potentially destructive ways. Some people as far out as Ninety-Third or 103rd Street could escape their homes, if they lived on an old swale or had a toddler in the family, while others would have to stay, trapped next to their neighbors' boarded-up ranches, emptied as if by bombs falling in a random fashion from the sky.

One way to avoid that particular outcome was to pursue yet another option—option six. Under this model, Axelrod explained, the state wouldn't buy any homes, but rather offer temporary relocation to families with pregnant mothers or young children. Or, he explained, the state could choose option seven, the opposite of the nuclear choice. Under this model, the state would do nothing.

"Offer no temporary or permanent relocation for anyone."

The day after the secret, closed-door, blue-ribbon meeting in New York City, Axelrod flew directly to Niagara Falls to deliver his decision inside the auditorium at the 99th Street School. The crowd that night was one of the largest ever assembled in the neighborhood. Roughly 350 people—Black and white, residents of Griffon Manor and homeowners—turned out to hear Axelrod speak, and Gibbs had everyone whipped up into a frenzy even before he stepped to the microphone. Residents had made the usual assortment of angry signs—"Dioxin Kills," said one. But tonight, Gibbs had added another element—a creative touch to mock the state for its secret meetings discussing their lives. People wore blue ribbons on their shirts, and the ribbon on Paigen's blouse was extra special. It came with a title written right on it. "Expert on Useless Housewife Data," it said.

Axelrod looked out upon this crowd and got straight to the point, issuing a new declaration, a new health order. In it, he explained, the state had considered everything: the 250 chemicals that Hooker was known to have manufactured during the time it operated the dump in the 1940s and 1950s; the trace amounts of dioxin found in a backyard on Ninety-Seventh Street; the migration of chemicals through storm sewers and potentially old swales; the fact that this migration extended not only south, east, and west of the canal but also to the north, draining into the creeks still flowing behind Luella Kenny's house; the new data documenting a possible pattern of problems along these swales; and the somewhat stunning revelation that people evacuated from their homes on Ninety-Seventh and Ninety-Ninth Streets the previous fall were already healthier now, according to blood tests taken before and after their moves.

But the state also had to consider a series of mitigating factors, Axelrod declared. He believed the remediation efforts at the southern end of the old canal were working to limit the spread of toxins and would continue to work. In the meantime, authorities needed to conduct further studies to understand the boundaries of the contamination, the extent of the migration, and the true nature of the health problems in the neighborhood. As a result, he was taking a conservative approach.

Axelrod was going with option six. The state was going to temporarily relocate families with pregnant mothers and children under the age of two—about a hundred families in all, living both in Griffon Manor and in the homes in the tidy grid of streets east of the canal and south of Colvin Boulevard.

Nothing more.

"You're going to kill us!" one woman shouted.

"We're not people to you—we're numbers."

"We want out," others chanted. And then a boy from 102nd Street stepped up to the microphone. He was nine—too old to be considered for Axelrod's newly announced relocation order—and he had a question for the health commissioner.

"Will I grow up to be a normal man?" he asked.

The people roared, showering the boy with the loudest cheers of the night and cursing Axelrod and other state officials with disgust. They thought Axelrod's order to be both preposterous and hypocritical. What was a young woman to do, they asked, if she wanted to have a child or give birth to a second baby? Just not have a family? Proceed as planned and put the fetus at risk? Or choose a third solution: Get pregnant just to get out?

"Bravo," one bitter resident joked. "Relocation by impregnation."

But Beverly Paigen wasn't laughing, or even enjoying the irony that Axelrod seemed to have come around to partially agree with her. People were still in danger, she believed. Unborn babies most of all. "By the time a woman finds out she's pregnant and moves out," Paigen declared that night, leading the chorus of criticism, "the most critical period of fetal development will be over." The damage could already be done. If the state was truly interested in protecting the health of the fetus, Paigen alleged, Axelrod would have opted to relocate all women of childbearing age. Instead, they were stuck there—again—only with even fewer options than they had before: they now knew it to be dangerous to get pregnant in their homes and apartments.

In the days ahead, Lois Gibbs made a scene, as only she could. She drove to Albany with a small group of residents and a large rectangular box, painted to look like a coffin and wrapped in spools of blue ribbon, an ironic touch. She was making a special delivery, and she knew it would get the attention of the press. Gibbs intended to bring the large box, her cardboard casket, to Governor Carey himself. "We're going to leave it in his office," she boasted. "As a reminder of what he hasn't done for us."

As it turned out, she didn't get within 150 miles of the governor that day. Carey was in New York City on other business. But with reporters and photographers following her everywhere through the halls of the capitol, Gibbs did manage to get a meeting with some of Carey and Axelrod's top aides, and in that meeting one of the aides—a dentist by training—accidentally gave Gibbs the headlines she craved.

"The health statistics in Harlem and the South Bronx are worse than the Love Canal," he said, trying to offer some perspective. "Let's look at the South Bronx—"

"No," Gibbs said, interrupting him. "Let's look at the Love Canal."

Reporters scribbled the exchange in their notebooks, and after the comment made it into the newspapers, Axelrod moved in to clean up the mess. He wanted to assure people, including Congressman LaFalce, that the aide hadn't intended to insult anyone living in the neighborhood or minimize the problems in Niagara Falls. "What he was attempting to bring to everyone's consciousness," Axelrod explained to LaFalce, "was the fact that there are major problems in every aspect of health in the Harlem area, which presumably could be very much mitigated by the removal of those residents from their environment."

But by then, Axelrod had an even bigger public relations crisis on his hands. At the contentious meeting inside the school that February, one resident spoke up for the first time, breaking months of silence. She was both feared and respected, a perfect complement to Lois Gibbs and great fodder for the press. Her name was Luella Kenny, she announced from the microphone inside the school auditorium. She lived on Ninety-Sixth Street, and she was there to ask a few questions.

"Do you know what it's like to lose a child?" she said that night. "Do you? Because I can tell you exactly what it's like to lose a child."

36

NOW AND FOREVERMORE

Gibbs watched Kenny walk to the microphone that night, eyeing her with awe from across the auditorium. The two women had been circling each other for months now. Kenny knew everything about Gibbs after reading about her in the newspaper and watching her protests on the nightly news, and Gibbs, in turn, knew everything about Kenny. But the pair had never spoken until Kenny showed up at the meeting in February. Gibbs approached her in the hallways of the school afterward to offer her an invitation. It was time for Kenny to come in, Gibbs said. Time for her to visit the homeowners' association office, still located inside the teachers' lounge at the school. Gibbs wanted to put Kenny in touch with every reporter she knew. Have her give interviews. Sit down, tell her story. Be herself: the mother of the boy who died at Love Canal.

In a meeting later that week in the office, amid the ringing phone and the chatter of the other women, Kenny didn't need to be convinced. Under ordinary circumstances, she and Gibbs wouldn't have had much in common. Gibbs was twenty-seven, had barely graduated from high school, didn't work or attend Catholic church anymore, and smoked half a pack of cigarettes a day, while Kenny was a college graduate and a scientist working at Roswell Park. She sent her boys to Catholic school, never touched cigarettes, and felt old just sitting next to Gibbs. Luella was staring down her forty-second birthday that spring. In another time—the peaceful time before anyone knew about the canal—the two women most likely wouldn't have been friends, and their husbands wouldn't have been, either. Norman, a choirboy, was into singing; Harry, a gearhead, was into cars. The truth is, the two families probably would have never even met. But now Lois and Luella were members of a sisterhood they each wanted to escape. They shared everything.

In the office with Gibbs, Kenny agreed to start giving interviews right away—the worst possible news for both the governor and the EPA, state and federal officials. The last thing they needed was Luella Kenny sitting in front of television cameras, asking her unanswerable questions like "How many more children have to die?" or "How much more evidence do they have to see, before they realize something is wrong here?" Kenny was already formulating these questions in her mind. But as she prepared to sit down with reporters for the first time, officials failed to note the importance of the meeting between Gibbs and Kenny. They were too busy at the moment, arguing about money.

In just six months, the state had spent more than $20 million to address the landfill problem in Niagara Falls, and the situation wasn't even close to being resolved. Remediation work, already over budget, was scheduled to continue throughout the year. Axelrod's decision to move pregnant mothers and children under the age of two was going to cost New York at least another million dollars. And while that was clearly cheaper than the other options that Axelrod had considered, Gibbs's attorney, Richard Lippes, was pretty sure that the new relocation order would lead to more evacuations in time. By acknowledging there was a danger to unborn children throughout the neighborhood, but leaving young wives inside their homes and apartments, the state was suddenly on shaky legal ground, Lippes believed, and that was a terrible position to be in because Governor Carey had made it clear to subordinates in Albany that he was done. He hadn't returned to the neighborhood since winning reelection in November 1978. Love Canal had effectively dropped off his map, and he didn't want to allocate another dollar to scooping up land around it—a feeling that he finally made public near the end of February. "We are not purchasing the homes," Carey said simply.

Carey thought the federal government should take over. But the Carter administration—which was busy slashing federal budgets and reining in regulations as it eyed the president's own reelection chances in 1980—wasn't about to take on a massive public works program in Niagara Falls. In doing so, they would create a precedent. Other cities, states, and corporations would be able to lay their troubled chemical landfills on the steps of the White House and walk away.

One EPA agent suggested that city officials in Niagara Falls assume any remaining costs in the contaminated neighborhood. After all, he said, "they bought it for a dollar." And Carter's federal disaster administrator—who had visited the canal the previous summer and walked the soggy ground with Lois Gibbs—also refused to accept any further financial responsibility. "Let's be honest about it," a source admitted to reporters. "The administrator is not about to accept a proposal that would haunt them now and forevermore."

As Congress returned to Washington that winter, Bonnie Casper—now thirty and not so green anymore—hoped to be part of brokering some kind of solution. She and others in LaFalce's office had spent weeks preparing new legislation that would enable people to file claims in federal court if they were exposed to chemicals, allow victims to receive up to $50,000 in instant benefits, and improve current environmental laws by stopping companies from dumping such material in the first place. With her divorce newly finalized just before the holidays that year, Casper was able to throw herself into her work without any distractions, and LaFalce did his part, too. He made sure to get himself in front of local reporters to tout the efforts his office was making to help folks like Lois Gibbs, Luella Kenny, and Elene Thornton.

But LaFalce was at a disadvantage. His seats on the House banking and small business committees gave him almost no authority when it came to matters of the environment, and by late February it was increasingly clear that his legislation was going nowhere in the new congressional session. High-level EPA administrators were working on their own legislative plans, and the rumor on Capitol Hill was that these plans were going to be big—worth waiting for. Top administrators were involved: the agency's director, Doug Costle; his number two, President Carter's old friend from Atlanta Barbara Blum; and her colleague Tom Jorling, a former congressional counsel, with a unique combination of skills, attributes, and experience. Jorling, a thirty-eight-year-old lawyer, had friends on both sides of the aisle in the Capitol, a detailed knowledge of environmental law, and an innate understanding of how to lead. Jorling wasn't just a former high school quarterback from Cincinnati; he had helped craft the Clean Air Act of 1970.

Together, these administrators recognized that Love Canal exposed all the holes in the system. For decades, companies had dumped wastes almost wherever they wanted—unregulated and unwatched by any level of government. Now, by Jorling's count, there were an estimated thirty-two thousand forgotten landfills scattered across the country. At least six hundred of these posed an imminent threat to public health, and roughly a hundred of them, including Love Canal, had been well documented. And yet it wasn't clear, by statute, who should pay to clean them up. As one agent explained, "The one who pays is whoever gets left holding the bag."

What the government needed to address these landfills, these administrators decided, was a large fund—a superfund, some people started to call it in Washington—financed not with taxpayer dollars but with payments from corporations themselves so that a reserve of cash would always be on hand in the event of a man-made disaster like Love Canal, no matter the status of the federal budget or the politics of the president sitting in the White House. In February, as Axelrod announced the latest round of evacuations in Niagara Falls and Casper hustled through the halls of the Capitol pushing LaFalce's plans, EPA administrators huddled in Washington, hammering out the final details of their massive new proposal, and then they hit the road to sell it. Jorling flew to Kentucky to give nearly two dozen reporters and lawmakers a tour. He wanted to show them a dystopian landscape just south of Louisville known to locals as the Valley of the Drums.

The Valley of the Drums was less notorious than Love Canal, in part because it was remote; no one lived next door. But regional EPA agents had informed Jorling that the site would make for better visuals, better television, because you didn't need to dig for the problem in Kentucky; it was right there on the surface. In the dump, near Louisville, as many as 100,000 chemical drums were piled helter-skelter in various states of disrepair: dented, rusted, buckled, riddled with bullet holes, and spilling their contents into the ground. A perfect picture of American environmental dysfunction. Or, as Jorling called it, "leverage." On the trip that February, he had the junket circle the site in helicopters. Then they landed nearby and motored in by car, and everyone stepped out, crunching across a blanket of fresh snow as they walked toward the drums.

"Goddamn," one person exclaimed as they got close.

"Look at that," said another.

The drums were oozing black liquid straight into the snowy ground—a sight that filled one EPA agent with dread of almost biblical proportions.

"Yea, as I walk through the Valley of the Drums," he said, "I shall dissolve."

Jorling had his leverage—in the form of photo ops and headlines. Newspapers across the country—including, most important for political purposes, *The Washington Post*—carried the bleak story of his landfill tour, the news of the EPA's forthcoming legislation, and photos of Jorling himself, standing amid the snow-covered drums in the middle of a Kentucky winter. It was exactly what the agency needed to draw attention to its many problems—financial, toxic, and otherwise.

But Jorling also had help back in Washington that winter from a surprising source: one of the EPA's loudest critics, a young, unproven congressman just starting his second term in office. At thirty years old, he was the exact same age as Bonnie Casper and one of the youngest politicians serving in Washington. Still, his committee assignment and his political pedigree made him impossible to ignore. He sat on the oversight subcommittee of the House panel through which every environmental bill had to pass. He was a gatekeeper who mattered, handsome and ambitious, and a former senator's son who knew how to play the game. His father had served in Congress for three decades. And now that the son was following in his footsteps—and sitting in his father's old seat—the young man was ready to make some headlines of his own on an issue that increasingly mattered to him: the environment.

Albert Gore Jr. was interested in Love Canal. He wanted to question Lois Gibbs and Beverly Paigen about the health problems in Niagara Falls, and in early March they finally got an official invitation. Gore's subcommittee was bringing the two women to Washington to testify before Congress.

37

LISTEN TO THE PEOPLE WHO KNOW

Lois had become adept at giving interviews in recent months in part because she had learned that she could be herself. She could be the indignant mother from the neighborhood—imperfect, unpolished, and filled with rage—and reporters would love her for it, lapping up whatever she was serving, no matter what she said or how she said it. But testifying before Congress was a bigger challenge, and the idea of it scared her.

She worried that she'd sound stupid on her biggest stage yet, that she'd botch her prepared statement, crack under questioning before Congress, and that if she failed in such a public manner, she wouldn't just fumble the opportunity she was being given; she'd set back everyone in the neighborhood, hurting their chances to escape. "I have no idea what to write," Gibbs admitted in the days before going to Washington, "or what to talk about." Also, there was another concern: "I don't have the vocabulary or the writing ability to get it down smooth."

Paigen suggested they practice—a lot. Yet an early dress rehearsal on a Friday morning at LaFalce's office in Niagara Falls hardly inspired the two women with confidence. Paigen had created slides to present her miscarriage findings and evidence of other problems around the old swales, and Gibbs had trouble operating the projector. No matter which way she turned the slides, the images kept appearing upside down on the wall of LaFalce's office. And amid the confusion, the congressman himself seemed disinterested, or at least distracted. LaFalce had stayed out late the night before and seemed to be nursing a hangover.

The women left his office feeling frustrated, and the day only got worse from there. Upon returning to the neighborhood that morning, Gibbs and Paigen found a river of chemical sludge spilling into the street next to the canal, and this time it was not because a tanker truck had tipped over onto its side. It was just *happening*. The leachate was rolling off the canal, flowing toward the river, and draining into the storm sewers—apparently unnoticed by the workers. Gibbs immediately alerted the press. Reporters started calling state officials for comment, and one official, furious about Gibbs's decision to notify the press before contacting the state, couldn't help himself. While television trucks rolled into the neighborhood to capture footage of the leachate in the street, the man, red-faced and eyes bulging, stormed into Gibbs's office to yell at her in front of everyone.

If he was looking to intimidate her with his show of brute force, it didn't work. After the official was finished shouting, Gibbs paused for a moment, looked at him, and laughed in his face. He clearly didn't understand that she had already won this battle. At least two television stations would feature stories that night about the leachate in the street and the workers' manic efforts to divert the chemicals away from the sewers by digging a shallow hole that quickly filled with the malodorous liquid—a total mess. A bigger problem for Gibbs was the savvier play that Bruce Davis was pursuing across town inside his office at Hooker Chemical.

Davis wasn't shouting at anyone; the tall, bespectacled corporate vice president was just considering every side of the square—the Hooker Chemical way—in an effort to stem an ever-widening crisis. In recent months, lawyers, including Richard Lippes, had filed nearly $3 billion in lawsuits against Hooker and other parties associated with the dumping at the canal and the building of the school on top of it. Both the state and the federal governments were now considering coming after Hooker, too. Carey, for one, thought it the best way to recoup the $20 million the state had already spent in Niagara Falls, and it had now become widely known that the canal was just one of four Hooker dumps within the city limits. By the state's count, at least one of these other dumps, the so-called Hyde Park dump, near the campus of Niagara University, contained even more toxic waste than Love Canal, and all of this information, including previously confidential company documents, was about to come to light with Al Gore's committee sniffing around and with Gibbs and Paigen about to testify in Washington.

Hooker needed to do something, and just days before the two women flew to Washington, the company finally made its move. Davis summoned the press to the Statler Hilton hotel in Buffalo, stood before a room of reporters, looming large as always, and issued a series of denials in new and forceful language. Yes, the company had dumped chemical waste in the old canal and also at other sites in Niagara Falls. But Davis refused to classify any of these dumps as a threat to public health. He tried to shift the blame to city officials and private developers who had disturbed the canal's clay walls over the years. He argued that these officials should have heeded Hooker's warnings not to build there and deemed it unfair to judge the company based on decisions it made thirty years earlier under different circumstances and in a different time.

The press conference was hardly over when Davis launched a new public relations blitz. The day before Gibbs and Paigen flew to Washington, Hooker began taking out full-page advertisements in the local papers under a new tagline: "Listen to the People Who Know." The goal was to both defend and humanize the company by countering its critics, glossing over its alleged failures, and featuring the photos and words of actual employees who believed in Hooker, including—soon enough—Bruce Davis himself. In one ad that ran that spring, he was pictured sitting at a desk with a phone pressed to his ear and papers scattered before him, looking concerned and, apparently, working hard because he cared. He cared about the people of Niagara Falls.

"You see," the ad read, "Bruce knows that Hooker Chemical has been part of this community for almost 75 years. And he knows that Hooker is an extremely important part of the Falls. How important? Well, in the last three years alone, Hooker has invested more than 200 million dollars in Niagara Falls. 200 million. That's a solid investment."

The campaign—slick, smart, and expensive—laid bare the differences between executives at Hooker Chemical and the residents of the neighborhood. Lois, at the moment, didn't even have enough money to afford a second car. With Harry working the second shift at the Goodyear plant these days—leaving home before four o'clock in the afternoon and getting back after midnight—Lois needed to bum a ride anytime she needed to go somewhere in the evening. And the homeowners' association was struggling financially, too. That winter, Gibbs had taken to begging for money from local companies—anything to help cover the costs of postage, supplies, and travel. Anything, she said, to help keep the group solvent. A raffle, sponsored by the local Super Duper grocery store, helped bring in enough money to float Gibbs's operation for a while. But there were no focus groups to vet the presentations that she and Paigen were about to deliver to Congress. No teams of PR experts editing the speeches for tone and content. Instead, Lois and Beverly worked together in Gibbs's kitchen on 101st Street, recording their speeches on a tape recorder and playing them back for Grace McCoulf, Marie Pozniak, or other residents to hear. They would rewrite by hand and record again.

By the weekend before their testimony, Paigen felt good about what she had: great details, stunning scientific data, compelling anecdotal evidence of health problems extending all the way to 103rd Street, and, for the first time, photographs—photos depicting the notorious swales in the neighborhood. Paigen was ready to put on a show and prove to Congress what state officials still refused to concede: that she knew what she was doing.

Gibbs, however, was less confident. The committee had requested fifty typed copies of their presentations by the Monday before their arrival in Washington—a deadline that, for Gibbs, seemed impossible to meet.

"I don't know how I'll ever finish," she wrote in despair.

Stephen Lester, the young toxicologist and state-hired consultant, agreed to assist her. On the Saturday night before the deadline, he worked with Lois in her kitchen for hours, helping her practice her lines and then practice them again. Every once in a while, Harry emerged from the bedroom to check in on them or to complain that they needed to move his car out of the street. He was worried about getting a parking ticket. Still, Lois and Stephen kept working, not finishing up until three o'clock that morning.

In the dark, Lois thanked Stephen for his help. A mere five months earlier, Stephen hadn't been sure what to think of Lois, and Lois had rejected Stephen at first sight, worried about his age, his lack of experience, and his long hair. But now Lois was beginning to realize that Stephen was an ally, that she could trust him, and that, indeed, she couldn't have done this without him. She liked having his scientific expertise—to go along with Beverly's—and she needed his help that Monday with another, more specific task. Congressman Gore was coming to Niagara Falls for a visit in advance of the hearing. Lois wanted Stephen to take her car—Lois and Harry's only car—and give Gore a tour of all the Hooker dumps in town.

"Harry will have a fit," Lois said.

Still, she didn't care. With every passing day, the couple was floating further and further apart. There was no animosity between them, really. Just a deepening reality that was getting harder and harder to bridge. Harry hadn't changed—or didn't want to change—and Lois had. She had become someone new. She liked that person, and this person—this new version of Lois—was going to do whatever she wanted with the family car or anything else.

That Monday, as planned, Lester picked up Gore from the airport in Lois and Harry's beat-up Oldsmobile. While he drove the congressman around to visit the sites, Lois prepared for her trip, making sure the kids had childcare and everything else they needed for the rest of the week. Then she hustled them off to bed, practiced her testimony a few more times, packed a suitcase, and left it by the door, ready for her flight the next morning.

Lois Gibbs was going back to Washington.

38

NO JOB IS WORTH YOUR LIFE

Do you solemnly swear to tell the truth, the whole truth, and nothing but the truth, so help you God?"

Paigen and Gibbs looked up at the panel of congressmen before them, raised their hands in the air, nodded their heads, and agreed.

"I do," they said.

The previous twenty-four hours had been, for the two women, a whirlwind of events. They had flown from Buffalo to Washington, taxied into the city, and attended a series of last-minute meetings with LaFalce, Casper, congressional counsel, and other witnesses who had been called to testify about Hooker's landfills in Niagara Falls.

The witness list, in addition to Gibbs and Paigen, included a family with children suffering from health problems, the pediatrician who treated those children, two union workers from a factory near Hooker's Hyde Park landfill, and a third worker who claimed to have witnessed the company's dumping practices since the 1950s. When the day's meetings ended, Gibbs met Stephen Lester for dinner inside her hotel and then retired to her room to practice her presentation one last time. But it was hard to get anything done. One of the union workers kept interrupting her there, calling her in her room three times after dinner. He allegedly wanted to ask her questions about their testimony the next day, have her edit his remarks, or show her some archival photos that he had of the canal, though Gibbs believed she knew what he really wanted. She couldn't believe she had to deal with this problem now, too: the union worker on the line asking to come visit her in her room. She awoke the next morning with a sore neck and a raging headache, having slept wrong—or not at all—and then headed to the House building to testify with Paigen, who was running late for possibly the biggest moment of their lives.

"The subcommittee will come to order," declared the chairman, a bow-tie-wearing liberal from Texas, as he started the proceedings and then quickly turned things over to Gore, "our colleague from Tennessee."

The young congressman was an unexpected environmental crusader in at least one important way: his father, the former senator Albert Gore Sr., worked for Occidental Petroleum, running a coal subsidiary for Armand Hammer and getting paid more than $200,000 a year to do the work. After a life in public service, modeling himself as a "populist shinkicker" and fighting for civil rights and an end to the war in Vietnam—moral stands that ultimately turned Tennessee voters against him and got him voted out of office in 1970—Albert Gore Sr. was cashing in. At least he was honest about it. "Since I had been turned out to pasture," the former senator said in an interview around this time, "I decided to go graze the tall grass."

It was an irony that newspaper reporters delighted in mentioning but that the son, Al Jr., preferred not to address—especially not now, in public, at his congressional hearing focused on Occidental's other subsidiary: Hooker Chemical. Instead, Al Jr. started by explaining that he had personally visited both the Valley of the Drums and Love Canal in recent weeks and was stunned by what he had found—especially in Niagara Falls. He described how Hooker had utilized the old canal there before selling it in 1953; how the company had then moved its dumping practices across town to Hyde Park and continued dumping unabated, burying chemical drums in the ground; how authorities had found dangerous pesticides and dioxin at both sites in recent months; and how he didn't need to be a scientist to know the earth in the city was poisoned. On his visit to Niagara Falls that week, Gore reported that his eyes and throat had burned just standing near the landfills and the creeks slicing through them. In places, he testified, these creeks ran black.

"At the present time?" the chairman asked, incredulous.

Yes, Gore replied.

"There is scum on top of the water that is so thick it looks like leather."

Gore understood Hooker's argument: that it had sold the canal twenty-five years earlier; that it had, effectively, attached a warning label to the bill of sale; and that developers in recent years might have precipitated some of the chemical problems in the neighborhood by disturbing whatever was buried in the ground. But if a man had a bottle of nitroglycerin—a dangerous explosive—and gave it to another person on the street, Gore said, the man wouldn't be innocent when the bottle blew up in the other person's hands in the middle of the village square. He would be considered guilty, too, and the same legal theory applied here, Gore argued. Only this was worse. "These chemicals," he said, "are more dangerous than nitroglycerin."

Casper watched from the back of the crowded room, taking in the testimony with everybody else. She had been frustrated in recent weeks that LaFalce's environmental bills weren't getting any traction in Congress and then angry when she learned that Gore's committee had invited Gibbs and Paigen to testify before the House—without first notifying LaFalce about it, a sign of respect typically given to a fellow congressman. But the subcommittee had agreed to let LaFalce join the panel for today's discussion. He was sitting next to Gore, a part of the conversation, and begrudgingly Casper had to admit that this was the moment they had needed from the start—a full and detailed airing of the facts on a national stage.

Casper watched Gore finish his opening remarks and then settled in for the long day of testimony, with the pediatrician from Niagara Falls up first. In recent years, the doctor told the subcommittee, he hadn't just diagnosed a stunning array of respiratory problems in the troubled family that had joined him in Washington that day. He had identified what he believed to be a cluster of kids struggling to breathe and to thrive in Niagara Falls. "It pinpointed," the pediatrician said, "to an area between 56th Street and the Summit Mall, which is the LaSalle area." But because people were always moving, it was impossible, he added, to just draw lines around that part of town and leave it at that. One of his sickest patients, for example, was a boy who lived fifteen miles north in the rural community of Ransomville. The boy had leukemia—bad luck, the pediatrician thought, until he started piecing together the child's medical history. "This little boy," the pediatrician said, "lived in a basement in Love Canal for three and a half years."

The three union workers told a different story. They explained that they worked in factories on the edge of Hooker's Hyde Park landfill and on the shores of the contaminated stream flowing away from that dump, a stream called Bloody Run. One of the workers reported that this waterway flowed through a large pipe right under his factory and that noxious fumes from the pipe often wafted up through a manhole onto the factory floor. "Complaints got so bad that the company covered the manhole with plastic," the worker testified, "but this was to no avail." In time, the vapors ate away at the plastic shield, forcing the company to seal the manhole with a steel cap. It was the only way to stop the fumes, but it didn't stop the problems. The other factory worker explained that health surveys from the two plants documented birth defects, miscarriages, cancer, asthma, and acne. "Acne problems," he said, "included almost the whole shop." The third union man testified that he believed he knew what was causing it. He had worked in the factory since the late 1940s. He had watched Hooker dumping its drums just beyond his factory fence for years, and he had toiled too many days, he said, in a cloud of fumes.

"Have any of the three of you had any problems lately with this?" Gore asked.

"Monday," one of them said. "Last Monday."

"Tell us what happened on Monday," Gore probed.

The wind was coming out of the east, the men explained, pushing the Hooker stench right inside their factories until workers' eyes watered, their throats burned, and some men finally chose to abandon their posts, seeking fresh air outside.

"As Congressman Gore said," one of the factory workers testified in conclusion, "if you go out on the street with a bottle of nitroglycerin and hand it to somebody else, you would probably get arrested."

He wanted to know why that hadn't happened here, with Hooker.

"They are polluting our air. They are ruining our environment. They are killing our people. If that is not a crime, I do not know what is."

—

The night before, Gibbs had thought the union workers disorganized and a bit sketchy, especially because one of them called her in her room after dinner, trying to talk his way upstairs. But their shortcomings—whatever they were—hadn't hurt their presentation. They appeared honest, gritty, blue-collar, and tough, throwing punches at Hooker and making it clear that after years of silence they didn't care if they lost their jobs for speaking out. As one of the workers testified that day before the subcommittee, "No job is worth your life."

Beverly Paigen was making a similar calculation. With state officials watching in the back of the room, and David Axelrod slated to testify the next day, she swore to tell the truth, and nothing but the truth, and began informing Gore, LaFalce, and everyone else on the subcommittee that state health officials had it all wrong. The dangers, she said, extended for at least five blocks around the old canal. Hundreds of other families needed to be evacuated.

The swale theory was real.

"I will present information," Paigen testified, "that leads me to conclude that toxic chemicals are presently migrating through the soil along the paths of old streambeds that once crisscrossed the neighborhood."

She started by presenting her newest evidence: three photographs.

"I have here, for instance, a photograph of the Love Canal area in the early 1950s."

In this first photo, congressmen could see that the canal was dammed up and partially filled with waste and that a large stream was cutting right through it.

"Here, you see the path," Paigen said, pointing to the photo.

She then displayed a second picture that showed this particular stream in greater detail. In this image—a family photograph from 1958—two young boys were smiling for the camera, playing in the streambed, and dwarfed by its size. This was no little creek. It was almost a channel. "You can see that the streambed is at least 10 feet deep," Paigen said, "and may be as wide as 20 or more feet."

Finally, she presented the third photo—an aerial image showing all the swales that had once sliced through the area and even a few swampy lakes that had existed decades earlier. "For instance," Paigen said, "here is an old lakebed. Down here is a swamp. Here is another swamp." Her point was that water had always flowed freely through the neighborhood—before, during, and after the time that Hooker Chemical had used the land as a dump—potentially carrying contaminants well beyond the current relocation zone and potentially causing health problems blocks away from the canal. In the wet areas, in particular.

"What you are telling us, Dr. Paigen, is that the 230 families already evacuated are not the only families that are endangered by this site," Gore said. "You are recommending that 140 additional families be evacuated immediately and that another 500 families may have to be evacuated eventually on top of that."

Paigen nodded. That was correct, she said.

She then explained her medical findings: increased rates of asthma, kidney disease, nervous system disorders, birth defects, and miscarriages—all clustered around the old streambeds. For this, she had photos, too—images with colored dots showing each pattern. "I think you can immediately see that miscarriages are clustered in homes lying on streambeds or in wet areas," Paigen told the panel. But the same was true of the other maladies. "These all lie along streambeds or in very wet areas."

It was, in essence, a more detailed rendering of the same information that Paigen had previously presented to Axelrod, and that puzzled Gore. He wanted to know why state officials weren't listening to her.

"When did you present your findings to the state of New York for the first time?" Gore asked.

Paigen said she had first discussed the data with state officials by phone nearly six months earlier—early October 1978. But they had ignored her, she said, put her off, and then ultimately dismissed her after her meeting with Axelrod in Albany in November. "There were several comments made to the press over the next month," Paigen said, "that the data were unscientific, that I was looking at useless housewife data, and that the swale theory was wrong."

But after hearing her testimony on this day, Gore didn't feel that way at all. To him, her theory made sense. He welcomed her recommendations, and Paigen offered several. In addition to the families being evacuated from the wet areas—and maybe the entire neighborhood—Paigen testified that every woman of childbearing age should be evacuated; vulnerable people suffering from medical problems—any problems—should be cleared to move, too; health officials needed to also remember the people living west of the canal, in Griffon Manor, a low-lying area, long known to be swampy; authorities needed to evacuate many Griffon Manor residents as well, Paigen said; and in the meantime the federal government absolutely had to start treating Love Canal as a natural disaster. It was like the Blizzard of 1977 for these people, Paigen testified, only it was more serious and longer lasting. "Their chemicals will not melt away in springtime," she explained. Instead, they would linger in the ground and potentially inside the people themselves. If the congressmen wanted evidence of that, all they needed to consider, Paigen said, was the photograph of the two boys playing in the old swale.

They were men now, of course, these boys. Paigen had asked Gibbs's team of housewives to track them down, and they had. One was twenty-five and living with headaches, rashes, and chronic ear and throat problems. The other was thirty-one and faring much worse. As a child, he suffered from bone tumors. As a teenager, he was diagnosed with gastrointestinal bleeding. And as an adult, Paigen told Gore, he continued to struggle with a series of odd health issues: muscular tremors of the eyes and arms, inexplicable nervous disorders, and cardiac symptoms that resembled a heart attack but defied any official diagnosis.

"This is a boy," Paigen said, "that played in one of those streambeds."

Back in Niagara Falls, state officials desperately tried to track down advance copies of Paigen's and Gibbs's testimony, knowing that Axelrod might need to respond when he appeared before the subcommittee the next day. And Gibbs was upset to learn later that one of the women in her office had actually turned over the copies. But in the House building that day, Gibbs realized it didn't matter, because the men in Washington—Gore, LaFalce, the others on the subcommittee, and the reporters covering the hearing—were hanging on their every word.

In the press room, reporters complimented Paigen on her remarks. At lunch that day, LaFalce introduced her and Gibbs to everybody he could find—senators, representatives, staffers, lawyers, and aides—putting the two women from western New York on display and then basking in the glow of their new political stardom. And when it was finally Gibbs's turn to testify, following Paigen late that afternoon, the subcommittee showered her with praise. Gore thanked Gibbs for her activism and her efforts to save her community. LaFalce suggested that someone should present her with an honorary doctorate degree in biology—she had taught herself that much about science—and Gibbs soon felt her anxiety wash away. By the end of her testimony, she was even bold enough to criticize the subcommittee. She was a little upset, she said, that everyone seemed to be talking about her situation in the past tense, as if it were over.

"I just wanted to make it clear that we are not past tense," she told the panel. "We are present tense and we are just at the beginning."

Children had played on the canal the previous summer, she explained. "With halter tops, bare feet, dirt bikes, and just having a good time, raising the dust." These kids had breathed in that dust for years, and many of them, including her own children, Gibbs pointed out, were still living there, staring down another summer, the worst summer of their lives, trapped in Love Canal—unless Congress did something about it.

"I ask that you do what you can for us," she said, "and do what you must to prevent what has happened to us at Love Canal from ever happening again."

But any hope that their appearance before the subcommittee would lead to some kind of swift and immediate change—or widespread evacuation—quickly faded almost as soon as the two women had finished testifying. The next day, Axelrod explained to the subcommittee in detail why he didn't agree with Paigen's scientific data. "I do not question her ability as a biologist nor her integrity," Axelrod testified. Still, he said, she wasn't an epidemiologist. She wasn't a statistician. She hadn't gathered the survey data herself, and no one had confirmed the reports of alleged medical problems with physicians.

One of the congressmen on the committee argued that the state's own surveys were also similarly flawed at times. They, too, had been collected by others—not Axelrod—and then presented to a panel so cloaked in secrecy, the Blue Ribbon Panel, that even Congress didn't have a right to know the details. Al Gore's subcommittee was denied permission to review transcripts of the panel's meetings or learn the names of the experts who attended. But Axelrod had an explanation for that, too. Health officials, he said, were worried about threats being made on their lives. The confidentiality, while unusual, was necessary, he explained, and he believed it to be legal. He quoted from the state law that he claimed supported his position. And though the chair of the subcommittee disagreed with Axelrod's interpretation of the law—and was frankly somewhat disturbed by it—there was no changing it today. Lawyers would have to sort it out in the months ahead while residents stayed put: trapped inside their homes.

Lois's house, for one, was in total disarray by the time she returned from Washington. An embarrassing mess of dirty dishes and unfolded laundry awaited her there. She dreamed of a day when she'd be able to keep a clean house again, and yet she knew that it probably wouldn't be anytime soon. In the chaos of her life, she couldn't even keep track of her schedule anymore. The morning after Axelrod's testimony, Gibbs forgot that a reporter was coming over to her house to interview her. She answered the door in her nightgown and ended up giving the interview just like that: face unwashed and hair unbrushed, sitting in her robe in her kitchen.

"Who cares?" she thought.

The whole disheveled tableau fit perfectly with the trouble unfolding outside her front door. Residents were arguing with each other yet again. Reporters were chasing rumors that the homeowners' association was folding, or disintegrating, or both. At their regular meeting inside the school auditorium in early April, people shouted at one another, as usual, fighting over seemingly everything, and then they all stumbled outside into the night, having solved nothing, only to find more commotion across the canal on the edge of Griffon Manor.

—

The dynamic in the public housing development was changing that spring. Both Elene Thornton and Agnes Jones would soon be leaving. Thornton was moving with her children to a different public housing development across town, a place called Unity Park, while Jones was moving into a small house on Fifty-Ninth Street—almost three miles from the canal, but hardly any sort of escape. Jones's new home sat in the shadow of Hooker Chemical itself. Whatever the factory was spewing into the air every day along the river, Jones and her 15-year-old daughter, Carol, were breathing inside their house. Carol, at least, didn't live there long.

In the fall of 1979, just months after moving out of Griffon Manor, Agnes Jones stabbed her daughter in the back of the head with a kitchen knife in an outburst fueled by alcohol and rage. The girl survived the assault; with stitches, she'd be fine. But for Carol, it was just another trauma, the worst kind, and it was also a stark example of the price that the canal was exacting on people's lives. Agnes Jones never made headlines again, and Elene Thornton also quickly faded from the spotlight. She died in obscurity in 1987, unrecognized for her work at Griffon Manor. Her short obituary in the *Niagara Gazette* didn't even mention it.

In the years to come, Lois Gibbs would face criticism for not working more closely with Thornton and Jones and not uniting the homeowners and the residents of Griffon Manor under a single banner of activism—a criticism that Gibbs would, in some ways, accept. In notes she made for a book she was writing in the 1980s, she listed two key mistakes from the early days of Love Canal. Gibbs regretted that she had ever believed politicians, and she regretted labeling her organization as being one for homeowners. "Therefore," Gibbs wrote in her handwritten notes, "renters felt left out"—a missed opportunity for all. Had the two groups come together, Gibbs admitted later, they could have been a powerful political force. "But how do you know that," Gibbs asked, "when you're dealing with chaos?"

Arguments, shouting, financial stress, and fear had rippled through the neighborhood from the start. And in this moment, Gibbs and most others were just hanging on, just trying to survive—without the benefit of hindsight, the perspective to always choose the right path, or the ability to bring people together, even if they wanted to, as the neighborhood bounced from one crisis to the next, little fires everywhere. It was no wonder, then, that Thornton and Jones wanted to leave—and took the opportunity to do so as soon as they could. But their looming departures left Griffon Manor teetering on the edge of a leadership void by early April 1979, when Gibbs drifted over in the dark to check out the latest problem—the newest situation that had everyone in the neighborhood talking.

A late-winter storm had blown through two days earlier, dumping several inches of snow across the region, and then warmer weather had quickly moved in behind it, melting everything. The snow was now slush. It was running off the old landfill in crusty rivulets, and a crowd had gathered on Ninety-Seventh Street to inspect one rivulet that was obviously different. Amid the slushy runoff, an oily streak of green chemical leachate was flowing off the canal, puddling in the street, and filling the night air with a foul stench.

That was it: Lois needed a drink. She went over to Grace McCoulf's house to join a motley assortment of residents, reporters, and even one weary contractor, drinking wine well into the night inside a kitchen on the edge of a disaster. It was after three o'clock in the morning when Gibbs finally caught a ride home from another woman from the neighborhood. But instead of going straight back to Harry and the kids on 101st Street, they veered toward Griffon Manor to check out the chemical leak again.

Gibbs was tipsy, and it was late. But it was easy to find the green chemical goo.

It was flowing like a river, right down the street.

39

THE BIRD IN BLACK CREEK

Sometimes, just before nightfall, when the shadows grew long outside and she was standing before the window above her kitchen sink, Luella Kenny peered through the glass, into the backyard of her house on Ninety-Sixth Street, thinking she saw something.

Jon Allen was playing amid the trees.

He was on their little swing set. He was bouncing a ball. He was splashing in the water of the family's aboveground swimming pool, or he was running. Luella was sure she saw Jon Allen running for the stream at the back end of their property—Black Creek.

In the weeks after his death, she had convinced herself that they couldn't move away from the house, couldn't leave. Their memories were there, and the party line, from state officials at least, was that the creeks in the neighborhood were safe and the Kennys' house was, too. All the homes north of Colvin Boulevard remained outside the relocation zone, and the contaminant that people feared most of all—dioxin—hadn't migrated that far. Authorities had found no evidence of the dangerous chemical beyond the remediation trench on Ninety-Seventh Street where authorities had discovered it back in December 1978.

But Paigen's testimony about the swales had changed the way everyone north of Colvin Boulevard was thinking about their homes—Luella Kenny included. She refused to allow her sons, Christopher and Stephen, to play in the backyard anymore. They weren't allowed to slosh through the waters of Black Creek or come home caked in mud, as they had done before. And at least one of the Kennys' neighbors—a young couple with a teenage daughter, three doors down—had taken more drastic action. They abandoned their home. Just left.

They made their choice after months of discussion and many arguments. The wife wanted to go while the husband wished to stay. In the seven years they had owned the home, the couple had invested everything they had in it—renovating rooms and even putting in a swimming pool—and they knew that in leaving, they were potentially setting themselves up for financial ruin. They were still obligated to pay the mortgage and pay taxes on the house, too—a total of $3,600 in annual bills that made it almost impossible for them to live anywhere else. But their house, just like the Kennys', was located along one of the swales that carved through the neighborhood. The state had found levels of both benzene and toluene inside the house that would have been considered unacceptable for factory workers pulling an eight-hour shift—much less the daily life of a family. To limit exposure, a state official had told them to seal off their living room and shove rags beneath the doors—a recommendation that sounded absurd on its face. Sufficiently worried, they finally went to Beverly Paigen to ask for her advice: What would she do? Paigen, as usual, didn't hesitate to tell the truth.

"I recommend that you move," she said simply.

The couple, like everyone else in the neighborhood, felt as though they had been placed in a terrible position. Leave and suffer, or stay and struggle, enduring the unknown. They ultimately decided to go and tried to sell the house. But real estate agents refused to even list it. No bank would approve a mortgage without a certificate of habitability from the state, and because the state refused to grant such certificates, agents knew they wouldn't be able to close a deal. The family then tried to rent it, listing the home in the *Gazette* with an enthusiastic classified ad. "Three-bedroom house," it said. "LaSalle area. Two fireplaces, swimming pool." But when a few potential renters actually called about the ad, the couple felt compelled to disclose what they knew about the swale and the toxins, putting an end to any interest. They were stuck there with the benzene and the toluene.

"And who knows what else?" the wife said.

This couple, at least, had options. They owned a rental unit near the shores of Lake Ontario and prevailed upon their tenants there that winter to cancel their lease, freeing up a refuge for them—a shelter in this chemical storm. But Luella would have to ride it out. She watched her neighbors move, leaving behind yet another empty house, another target for vandals and thieves. Then she hunkered down, holding her memories close on Ninety-Sixth Street, as the bad news continued to crash around her like waves.

In mid-April 1979, just a few days after Gibbs and other residents gathered around the green river of chemicals flowing down the street on the edge of Griffon Manor, the state acknowledged that dioxin levels around the canal were higher than expected—twenty times higher than what the EPA would later consider safe for a residential area.

Axelrod's public relations man, Marvin Nailor, admitted to reporters that the Department of Health wasn't "entirely comfortable" with the new dioxin data. But instead of ordering more evacuations—to remove families from an area clearly tainted by one of the most toxic chemicals known to science—officials called for further testing. They wanted to know more about what was in the soil and the water, the creek behind the Kennys' house. If the stream was found to be contaminated, perhaps authorities would wall it off with a fence—a decision they had already made for Bloody Run, the polluted creek next to Hooker's Hyde Park landfill. The dioxin levels there were far too high to risk any child venturing into the water.

In the meantime, the very same week, a former Hooker employee leaked a devastating report to Michael Brown and others in the press that gave Luella still more reason for concern. The report, an internal audit from 1975, documented that Hooker executives were aware of the "troublesome" and "long-term" problems that their operation was causing in Niagara Falls; that these problems weren't just old landfills but more current missteps that regularly released mercury, chlorine, phosphorous-based gases, and carcinogenic pesticides into the air and sewers of the city; and that, sooner or later, these failures were going to hurt profits.

"I know that two out of every three people in Niagara Falls are going to think I'm a crank. They are going to definitely believe that what I'm doing is wrong, and that really hurts," said the source of the leaked report, the former Hooker employee. But he had been raised in North Tonawanda, just east of town, a good kid and former honor student there. He was worried about his community, and he felt that he had to tell everybody what he knew.

"People have got to understand that if it doesn't change soon, Niagara County will be a disaster," he explained. "A ghost. Nothing and nobody."

Gibbs didn't particularly like the former Hooker man. He was clearly excited about all the media coverage he was getting—maybe a little too excited, Gibbs thought—and he had turned his fifth-floor hotel room overlooking the Niagara River into a royal court of sorts, a place where he could live and give interviews day and night, relishing his whistleblower moment. At one point, he gave an interview while shaving in front of his bathroom mirror, with a towel wrapped around his neck. At another, he allowed photographers to snap pictures of him while he lounged in his hotel room's whirlpool bathtub. "He's a little crazy," Gibbs remarked after her own odd meeting with him inside the hotel room.

But, of course, others felt the same about her. On Easter weekend that month, people ignored Lois at a party that she attended in the neighborhood, cold to her and her family. They were upset she had even been invited because some of the people at the party had formed a new splinter group, and this one, comprising both renters and homeowners, stood in direct opposition to everything Lois was trying to achieve: They didn't want to move away at all. They wanted to stay. They were angling to get a meeting with David Axelrod, and their cries for attention weren't the only new voices shouting to be heard on the edge of the canal. Yet another faction had emerged as well.

A religious coalition—formed by activists, faith leaders, and nuns, and now operating out of the Methodist church on Colvin Boulevard—was trying to bring everybody together to work for the greater good. "Meeting . . . Tonight . . . 7:30 p.m.," their flyers said. "We welcome each and all!" Gibbs played nice and attended their meetings at the church, whenever possible. But privately, she wasn't happy about the religious group moving into the neighborhood. It gave anyone who didn't like Gibbs—and there were plenty of those people now—somewhere else to go. It highlighted the fact that the residents in the community had never really come together. And though designed to unite them all, the church organization also proved to be divisive in its own way. Some residents, Gibbs included, didn't want to be told by a collection of nuns and pastors—who didn't live in the neighborhood—what they should do or how they should feel. "I just found out if you pray it won't do you any good," Gibbs said after one meeting at the church. "They are just as sick as I am."

Right or wrong, Gibbs continued to pursue her own strategy. The day that *The New York Times* picked up the story of the former Hooker employee's leaked documents from 1975, Gibbs led a group of residents into the streets around the 99th Street School with torches. The goal: burning Governor Carey and David Axelrod in effigy. The crowd that day, Black and white, poured gasoline on two dummies dressed in clothes that Gibbs and the other women had pilfered from their husbands' closets. Then they lit the dummies on fire and stood back to watch them burn.

That night, Gibbs flipped from channel to channel inside her house, checking the television news to see which stations had covered the stunt. But she didn't linger long at home. Gibbs and Paigen had a meeting to attend across town. They were teaching families who lived around Hooker's Hyde Park landfill how to conduct their own health surveys, and the two women were also huddling, late into the night, making plans for a showdown with the two men whom Gibbs had just burned in effigy in the street. At the end of the month, Carey was making a rare visit to Niagara Falls to speak at a convention of the state teachers' union. He had agreed to bring Axelrod with him, and he had also agreed to sit down with Gibbs and Paigen for a private discussion at the Hilton hotel downtown.

"The time is still not set yet," Gibbs informed residents a few days before the governor's arrival. But she told everyone that they needed to be there, outside the hotel, ready to greet Carey.

"Let's let him know," Gibbs said, "how our lives are being jeopardized."

The night of the meeting, about a dozen people, including Luella Kenny, protested the governor's arrival at the airport, while a much larger group, five times that size, marched in the street outside the hotel where Carey was set to speak, shouting and carrying signs.

"We Voted You In, Now Get Us Out," said one sign.

"Gov. Carey Is Hazardous Waste," said another.

But Carey was prepared for the chilly reception on the ground there. In a briefing before his arrival in Niagara Falls, aides informed the governor that Gibbs had burned him and Axelrod in effigy just days earlier—if he didn't know it already—and that he should anticipate more of the same animosity on his first visit to the city since his reelection six months earlier. "Expect demonstrators and pickets while in Niagara Falls," they told him. The aides then proceeded to write for Carey the answers to nearly a dozen questions he was sure to face in his meeting with Gibbs and Paigen—if not in the streets with the angry protesters.

If people asked why Carey was allowing young women, who might become pregnant, to remain in a neighborhood where the state had determined pregnant women should not live, he should tell them he was simply following the advice of the Department of Health, which had studied the issue in depth. If they questioned what Carey was going to do about their worthless homes, he should remind them that remediation efforts would prove successful and one day make their neighborhood desirable to potential buyers once again. If they pressed Carey to learn why he wasn't doing more, he should tell them that, in fact, he had done everything he could do and, indeed, more than anyone else. "Since the beginning of the Love Canal emergency," aides wrote for Carey, dictating his answer, "the State has been on-site tending to the needs of the people of the area." Then the aides boiled it all down for the governor, making it simple.

"Bottom line of all questions," they told him, "we want to be relocated!"

"ANSWER: All persons identified by Dept. of Health testing program that are in need of relocation have been identified and offered opportunity to relocate!"

In other words, state officials weren't compromising. They had drawn their lines. And, this time, Governor Carey stayed on script. Inside the hotel that night, Axelrod and two other top state officials walked into the room first, sitting down with Gibbs and Paigen, and one of the two officials with Axelrod immediately put the women on the defensive. As part of his greeting, he asked if Gibbs had gotten pregnant yet in order to escape her house. The governor then walked in, flanked by other aides, and Gibbs proceeded to lay out her demands. She explained that residents had documented health risks throughout the neighborhood, just as they had been asked to do. She said that Paigen's scientific analysis—and Jon Allen Kenny's death—proved that the risks were real, widespread, and potentially fatal, and she restated the same request that she had been making for months. She asked the governor to relocate everyone living between Ninety-Third and 103rd Streets, both renters and homeowners.

Almost immediately, everyone began to argue. Paigen accused Axelrod of belittling her in front of Congress, and Carey quickly came to Axelrod's defense. He pointed out that Paigen's survey data was flawed because it had not been confirmed by a doctor. Gibbs was offended by that point and started arguing, too. She informed Carey that she and a handful of other women had personally gathered the surveys themselves. In attacking their validity, the governor was essentially attacking her, and he was also missing the point. The state had defined the wet areas by sharing with the homeowners the old aerial photos that depicted the swales. Residents, for the most part, didn't even know they were there, Gibbs told the governor, and therefore they couldn't have known to overreport their health problems in a pattern that miraculously fit some old photo that they had never seen.

The meeting lasted for about an hour. When the two sides finally emerged from the room afterward, Gibbs tried to put a positive spin on what they had accomplished—both for the press and for the other residents who wanted to know. But with Luella Kenny, she was more honest. She had tried, Gibbs said. She had invoked Jon Allen's name, hoping to interest the governor in their cause and to spark some kind of change. And still, she had failed. The meeting had accomplished nothing except to expose the yawning chasm between the residents and the state, Paigen and Axelrod, Gibbs and, seemingly, everyone. She drifted back into the hotel and slipped into the teachers' union convention, hoping she might be able to grab a seat in the auditorium where the governor was speaking and glare at him from the crowd. Yet she failed at that, too. Gibbs wasn't able to get any closer than the balcony and finally left, heading home, exhausted from another long day and totally defeated.

But Kenny thought Gibbs was being a little hard on herself. At least she had managed to get a meeting with Carey and Axelrod. Kenny had been trying for weeks—to no avail—and it was her son who had died. She called Axelrod and didn't hear back. She wrote and waited. "But even after a couple of reminders," Kenny told one of Axelrod's colleagues in Albany, "I haven't heard a word." She asked if this colleague could maybe prod the health commissioner into contacting her, and then, to fill the void that spring, she became more and more involved.

Kenny gave television interviews in the homeowners' association office, but also happily worked with the nuns in the Methodist church on Colvin Boulevard, attending their meetings in the basement of the church to strategize. Unlike so many others in the neighborhood, Luella didn't feel any allegiance to any of the factions that had ripped people apart since August 1978. She just wanted to get out. She was willing to work with anyone who might help make that happen, and finally in the late spring of 1979—eight months after Jon Allen's death, four months after she had first spoken out, and six weeks after Gibbs had quarreled with the governor inside the Hilton in Niagara Falls—Luella got word that Axelrod would meet with her during a regularly scheduled visit to Roswell Park in Buffalo.

The day before the meeting was scheduled to happen in early June, a scientist from the state Department of Health visited the Kennys' house, joined by Stephen Lester. The scientist was collecting soil samples in yards across the neighborhood that week, and Lester had tagged along with him to see what he might find. But the Kennys' house was of particular interest, given what had happened to Jon Allen and also because of the many complaints that Luella had made. She greeted the two men at her door, walked them to the edge of Black Creek on the back side of her property, and then left them there to do their work, turning back for her house.

Right away, Lester realized there was a problem. The creek was almost orange in places and clearly contaminated with something—

something "coming from the Love Canal most likely," Lester wrote that night. But there was another problem, too. As the state scientist knelt down to begin gathering his samples, a small songbird landed in the shallow water at the edge of the creek. Lester and the scientist watched the bird dip its beak into the water, drinking it down, and then Kenny heard the two men in the trees behind her. They were talking in excited tones, and one of them was running. The scientist was coming up through the trees, looking for Kenny. He needed her help. The songbird had toppled over and died right there in the creek.

That afternoon, at the scientist's request, Kenny placed the dead bird in the freezer inside her house and closed the door, agreeing to maintain the bird in its current state until the scientist could return later that day to collect its cold, wet body. It was, for Kenny, yet another horrifying development and further evidence that Jon Allen's death had to be connected to the canal. But in the weeks ahead, testing in Albany determined that the bird had died of a virus. In any case, the next day, the story of the animal dropping dead in the creek did nothing to sway David Axelrod's opinion of what had happened to Luella Kenny's son.

As a father himself, Axelrod would have understood Kenny's grief. But he couldn't give her the answers that she wanted. In a small room at Roswell Park, the health commissioner informed Luella that she needed to move on. She had to let her son go. There was no way for him to say—with any medical or scientific certainty—what had killed Jon Allen. Little boys got kidney disease, Axelrod said, for all kinds of reasons.

40

ALL-OUT OPPOSITION

Back in Washington, Tom Jorling was beginning to fear that the EPA's legislative plan was falling part. The EPA administrator and former high school quarterback had led the tour at the Valley of the Drums in February. He had presented compelling evidence that new and sweeping legislation was required to clean up forgotten landfills scattered across the country. He had publicly promised that such legislation was imminent—"Something must be done with these sites now," he told reporters—and he had managed to get the attention of Al Gore, John LaFalce, and a handful of others in Congress.

But inside the dark and tangled web of the federal bureaucracy, Jorling was meeting resistance at every turn to the EPA's plans to create a superfund—a reserve of money paid for primarily by the polluters themselves and there to help people living near sites like Love Canal. Some agencies didn't want to place new demands on corporations. Other agencies didn't want to cede turf to the EPA by granting the relatively new agency greater powers. And top administrators at the Office of Management and Budget were opposed to the legislative proposal almost on principle. As a knee-jerk reaction, bureaucrats at OMB resisted policies that might give the federal government new authority and, therefore, new budgetary commitments, and the authority being laid out in Jorling's proposal was especially large. The superfund in question was expected to be $1.6 billion—just for starters.

One evening late that spring, Eliot Cutler, an associate director at OMB, finally broke the bad news to Jorling and Doug Costle, the director of the EPA. Cutler happened to support the EPA's proposal, he said in a brief phone call to Costle's office. He was young, thirty-two years old, and a progressive environmental lawyer from Maine who, in his early years in Washington, had helped to write both the Clean Air and the Clean Water Acts. He knew Jorling. He knew the costs of cleaning up forgotten landfills were going to be astronomical, and he also knew that as a result the budget in question needed to be insulated from politics and appropriations, just as Jorling had drafted it. But there was no support among other agencies for the EPA's legislation, Cutler informed the two men. And there was outright resistance to it at OMB. It didn't matter what he thought or what Jorling thought, either. The superfund legislation wasn't going anywhere.

Costle hung up the phone, and Jorling stared out the window of his office, completely deflated. The two men had been preparing to make an announcement, at a press conference that week, to introduce the new legislation and practicing lines that could best sell the package—to the press, to the public, and to Congress. Now, with Cutler's phone call, all of that was on hold, suspended in federal bureaucratic limbo. Jorling rode his bicycle home that night, thinking about his next play, while Congress kept pushing and asking questions about Love Canal.

Just days after Gibbs and Paigen testified before Al Gore in the House, the Senate launched hearings of its own before a star-studded joint subcommittee featuring some of the chamber's heaviest hitters. The panel included the former presidential front-runner Edmund Muskie, from Maine; the future Democratic vice presidential nominee Lloyd Bentsen, from Texas; the young and ambitious Gary Hart, from Colorado, a future presidential front-runner in his own right; and a man with a vested interest in delivering results to voters in Niagara Falls—the junior senator from New York, Daniel Patrick Moynihan.

The senators' plan was to hold hearings in both Washington and Niagara Falls throughout the spring to make it easier for residents around Love Canal to testify. Gore's subcommittee, meanwhile, wasn't dropping the issue, either. It, too, continued to hold hearings in April, May, and June. Everyone, it seemed, wanted to hear from residents like Lois Gibbs—ordinary citizens caught in the chemical crosshairs. But senators and representatives were also interested in interrogating a new set of witnesses who might be able to reveal even more about the situation. They wanted to question former and current employees at Hooker Chemical about what they knew and when they knew it.

They heard from a newly retired employee who testified that as recently as the previous summer—July 1978—Hooker was dumping chemicals in Niagara Falls. "Up until the time I left," the former employee said, "thousands of gallons of acids and other residues—all types of waste—were dumped into the river." He didn't want to say that Bruce Davis and other executives were lying when they denied any inappropriate behavior. But, the man explained, "Mr. Bruce Davis is not aware of many things that go on in the plant." The former employee was aware of the illegal dumping, he said, because he had personally overseen it. "And I am willing to take a lie detector test anytime to prove that I did it."

They heard from multiple employees, who testified that by 1970 Hooker knew it had serious landfill problems at Love Canal, Hyde Park, and a third dump located at 102nd Street and the river and yet did nothing to alert the public to potential hazards. Congress produced memos documenting the company's detailed knowledge of odors, fires, small explosions, and chemicals leaching into streams and ditches around their landfills—problems dating back to the 1960s. And one longtime Hooker employee—now working for its parent company, Occidental Petroleum, as director of health and environment—acknowledged that problems at Love Canal dated back even further. The man, Jerome Wilkenfeld, couldn't have denied it, even if he wanted. Al Gore held in his hand a memo that Wilkenfeld himself had written twenty-one years earlier—in June 1958—when he served as superintendent over industrial waste operations. The memo informed top executives at Hooker of two important developments. Four children had been burned, Wilkenfeld wrote, while playing on the old canal, and drums containing residues of thionyl chloride—the chemical Hooker used to make poison gas—had surfaced just north of the new school near Colvin Boulevard.

"Do you believe that children should be allowed to play in an area where they are going to be exposed to hazardous chemicals that have the potential to burn them?" Gore asked Wilkenfeld after sharing the old memo with him.

"No," Wilkenfeld replied. "Of course not."

"Apparently, some of your colleagues didn't share that view," Gore said. "Because in the same memo, you state that they suggested—and I quote—'We should not do anything unless requested by the school board.' "

Gore looked at him and kept talking.

"My question is this: If 20 years ago this company had information that children were using Love Canal as a playground and had, in fact, probably been burned there, why didn't you take some action to inform the school board that this was a hazard and to inform local residents that their children shouldn't be playing around these hazardous chemicals?"

Wilkenfeld explained that Hooker's corporate counsel did ultimately share information with the school board's attorney. The board knew, he said. And Wilkenfeld also believed that at least some residents knew, too. At times, he testified, injured parties skipped calling authorities and phoned Hooker's dispensary directly, looking to speak with a corporate nurse.

But that didn't satisfy Gore.

"Did you ask for or conduct an investigation into the extent of the problem?" he asked.

No, Wilkenfeld admitted.

"Did you continue to monitor the site after the contact with the school board was made?"

No, he said again.

Gore recapped everything just to make sure he understood: Hooker had been aware since 1958 that children were being burned while playing on an old company landfill teeming with twenty thousand tons of chemical waste—waste that only engineers at Hooker could truly understand. The company was further aware that these problems weren't isolated, Gore said, but persistent, surfacing again and again over the course of years. And yet, Gore said, Hooker made no efforts to inform the public or even explain what chemicals were buried in the canal?

"No," Wilkenfeld said. "We did not."

"Why not?" Gore asked.

"We did not feel we could do this without incurring substantial liabilities for implying that the current owners of the property were doing an inadequate care on the property."

"Wait a minute," Gore said. "Let me back up and get this clear in my mind. You had evidence available to you that children were using it as a playground and had been burned, probably by the chemicals there . . . Yet you were reluctant to tell them that there was a hazard and tell them what the chemicals were because you were afraid that you would expose the school board to some legal liability?"

"Yes," Wilkenfeld said.

A corporate lawyer, sitting next to Wilkenfeld, interjected a moment later to make a clarification. He wanted the subcommittee to know that the witness—Wilkenfeld—was not qualified to discuss liability.

"He was only speaking for himself," the lawyer said, "as a person."

"The record will reflect who he is speaking for," the subcommittee chairman acknowledged.

"And the record will also reflect," Gore said, "the position of responsibility that he held within the company."

Bruce Davis could continue to deny that Hooker's landfills posed any health hazards to people in Niagara Falls, and Armand Hammer, the chief executive, at Occidental Petroleum, could argue that authorities were exaggerating the costs involved, as Hammer did in public statements that spring. But Wilkenfeld's testimony made clear, Gore said, that the costs and hazards had been known from the start and ignored by the people in power until it was too late.

"This whole incident," Gore said, "could have been completely avoided."

In Niagara Falls, residents trapped around the canal cheered Gore from afar. Within just a few weeks of his visit to the city, the young congressman from Tennessee had become the residents' loudest advocate, calling out both company executives and state officials, Bruce Davis and David Axelrod, the EPA and the federal government, for all the ways they had failed people in Niagara Falls.

A quieter act of bureaucratic resistance, however, would finally push the EPA's superfund proposal over the edge, into the papers, and into the hands of Congress. On the first Thursday of June 1979—the same day that the bird died in the Kennys' backyard in Niagara Falls and one day before Luella met with Axelrod at Roswell Park—Jorling and Costle reported to the White House around mid-morning for a budget meeting inside the Cabinet Room with a handful of others: Eliot Cutler; Cutler's boss at OMB; half a dozen other budget officers; four domestic policy advisers; one White House science expert; the president's confidant Jack Watson; and the president himself, Jimmy Carter.

As usual, Carter had had a busy morning. He was up at 5:00 a.m. and in the Oval Office less than thirty minutes later, sitting at his desk even before the sun crested over the Potomac, chatting briefly with his wife, Rosalynn, on the phone, and then diving into his schedule for the day. By the time the president walked into his meeting with Jorling and Costle just after 10:30 that morning, Carter had received his daily security briefing, hosted a breakfast in the State Dining Room, hobnobbed with Republican congressional leaders, discussed concerns facing the steel industry, met with his inflation fighter Robert Strauss—the Texas millionaire looking to trim costs everywhere—and sat through a forty-five-minute meeting with his inner circle, including Vice President Walter Mondale.

Carter wasn't much on chitchat, a fact that Jorling knew from a fairly reliable secondhand source. His daughter Julia attended school with Amy Carter, the president's daughter, and the two sixth-grade girls had become friendly enough that Julia had flown on Marine One with the Carters, spent weekends at Camp David, and even enjoyed meals with the president, though "enjoyed" was maybe not the best way to describe it. Julia reported to her father that Carter often spent the family meals in silence, reading governmental reports inside thick binders instead of making conversation.

Now, in the Cabinet Room, the president got down to business in a similar no-nonsense fashion, delving into the details of the EPA's stalled superfund proposal. It didn't take long for Cutler to speak up. In defiance of his own boss sitting right there in the room, Cutler informed the president that he disagreed with OMB's resistance to the legislation. This proposal was too important to fail before even making it to Congress, Cutler believed, and it absolutely needed the president's support because it was bigger than Love Canal. It was about all the Love Canals—thousands of them, maybe—that authorities hadn't discovered yet. This fund—the superfund—was meant to protect people in the future.

Jorling looked at Cutler from across the table. The young bureaucrat was taking a risk, crossing his own bosses to put himself on the line for Jorling and the EPA.

It worked. Carter agreed with Cutler. Within the week, the president sent the legislation to Congress with his personal approval. Jorling unveiled it to reporters in the White House briefing room and then holed up in his office, preparing to appear before Gore's subcommittee to explain the massive bill in greater detail.

There were questions to answer and a new battle to fight. Bruce Davis, Hooker Chemical, and lobbyists working for the petrochemical industry were opposed to the bill, promising opposition for Jorling—"all-out opposition," they said. The superfund would be an administrative nightmare, they argued, an economic liability, an unconstitutional act quite possibly, and an unnecessary one, too.

After all, Davis explained, "there is no major health problem in Niagara Falls."

41

NOT MANY WHISTLEBLOWERS SURVIVE

On the same day that President Carter sent the superfund legislation to Congress—and Jorling briefed reporters about the bill at the White House—Gibbs reported to the homeowners' new office inside a dilapidated home at the corner of One Hundredth Street and Colvin Boulevard. The state had recently relocated Gibbs and the other women to the house in order to clear out the 99th Street School in preparation for the second phase of remediation set to begin that summer. While the accommodations were fine, the prominent location of the new office on a major city street seemed to attract all kinds of crazy, starting that very afternoon.

A homeowner barged in to announce that he'd found his own way to solve the canal problem. He told Gibbs he was going to get some dynamite, build a bomb, and blow up the site. Gibbs tried to explain to the man why he should do no such thing, and an argument broke out. But by the very next morning, she was almost longing for the quaint absurdity of fighting with people over why they shouldn't detonate bombs. The homeowners' office was under attack. The former Hooker employee who had leaked the 1975 pollution report to the press that spring kicked in the door for reasons unknown, shattered glass across the floor, shoved and threatened the woman working inside, tracked down Gibbs at her house on 101st Street minutes later to shout at her too, and then led police on a high-speed chase through Wheatfield and North Tonawanda that only ended after he drove his pickup truck onto the sidewalk, cut across several lawns, and plowed into a squad car at seventy miles per hour.

He was upset, he said later, about a story in one of the Buffalo newspapers that reported that the superfund bill wouldn't help the residents of the neighborhood. But why he had chosen to take out his frustration on the residents themselves—or run from police, putting pedestrians and motorists in danger across the greater Niagara Falls area—was harder to explain. The man's mother speculated that her son needed psychiatric help. The man himself wondered aloud if exposure to pesticides, chlorine, or mercury at Hooker over the years had damaged him in some way, and there was also, perhaps, a third explanation that was harder for people to discuss. It sometimes felt as though just being close to the issue, just being involved at Love Canal, could drive one to madness.

The FBI took notice and started collecting reports on residents that summer, logging their activities under the subject heading "Civil Unrest." Informants told the FBI about comments Gibbs made in meetings or threats that state officials received. They noted that, according to Gibbs, "people are starting to turn to violence" or "people are talking about blowing up the canal," and they also noted that these threats appeared to be serious at times. On one occasion, an individual tracked down a state official at the hotel where he was staying in Niagara Falls to deliver a simple message: "I'm going to blow your head off." On other occasions, they went straight for the top, sending anonymous and menacing hate mail to David Axelrod.

In one such letter, a woman from the neighborhood clipped words out of the newspaper—serial killer style—pasted a photo of a seven-week-old fetus to the cover page, informed Axelrod that she had recently miscarried a child slightly younger than the fetus in the photo, and then blamed him for the child's death because she had not been evacuated earlier.

"It is for these reasons I lay my miscarriage on your Shoulders," she wrote. "How many more Babies must be lost? . . . STOP putting a price on our heads!

"Sleep well tonight Doctor Axelrod. If you can!!!!"

At his office on the Empire State Plaza in Albany, Axelrod had no choice but to take the threats seriously—if not for his own safety, then out of concerns for the people who worked for him. But in truth, he had a bigger problem that summer: his long-simmering scientific spat with Beverly Paigen had now gone public.

Paigen felt as if she had played by the state's rules since being chastised in the late summer of 1978. Despite the inherent difficulties involved—and, in her opinion, the unreasonable nature of her bosses' many requests—Paigen had spent months filing regular reports that documented her activities and listing her interactions with reporters. She had informed her bosses about her interviews with *Redbook* and *Look* magazines, CBS and ABC News. She had explained that she spoke on a weekly basis with several local reporters. She had apologized for not documenting these conversations in greater detail—it simply wasn't possible given the volume of calls she received—and she had also made clear that whenever she gave interviews, she was speaking only for herself. Not for the state and not for David Axelrod. She was just a woman doing her job.

"I would never consider speaking for Roswell Park or the Department of Health unless my role as a spokesman had been cleared with the administration," Paigen said. "I always mention when I have contact with the media that I am speaking as an individual scientist."

But, of course, such clarifications didn't really take the sting out of her comments. The stories quoting Paigen always listed her Roswell Park credentials, pitting her against Axelrod whether that was her intention or not. And Paigen's decisions that spring to testify before Congress—and then argue with Axelrod at the meeting with the governor at the Hilton in Niagara Falls—seemed to only inflame whatever tensions already existed between the two. As one health official in Albany put it later, she was the foot soldier and Axelrod was the commanding officer, and Paigen had violated the chain of command. She had gone AWOL. Only, instead of being punished for her insubordination, she had convinced others that she was possibly right. People were listening to her—people like Al Gore and John LaFalce.

That spring, LaFalce asked federal experts at the EPA and the National Institute of Environmental Health Sciences to review Paigen's Love Canal data. And about a month after Paigen testified before Congress, a committee of eight scientists from the two agencies summoned Paigen and Axelrod for separate meetings—

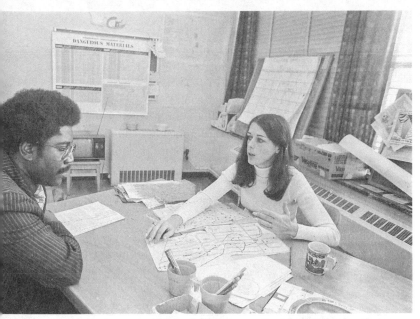

Gibbs and other mothers in LaSalle conducted surveys of health problems along these swales and then plotted them on maps to help make their case. (*Courtesy of Mickey H. Osterreicher*)

avid Axelrod—Governor Carey's appointed health commissioner—ed Gibbs and Paigen's swale theory he start, creating tension in both y and Niagara Falls and a toxic lace for Beverly Paigen. (*Courtesy* nocrat and Chronicle/USA Today *k*)

Around this time, Armand Hammer, the chief executive at Occidental Petroleum (Hooker Chemical's parent company), visited the area, flying in on his pri ate jet. He refused to take any responsibility for the chemicals in the old canal. (*Courtesy of Getty Images*)

Meanwhile, Bruce Davis, Hooker's top executive on the ground in Niagara Falls, went on the offensi e, taking out full-pag advertisements in the local newspapers th argued that the company was doing every it could for the people of the city. (*Courte* Buffalo Courier-Express)

The discovery of dioxin, a dangerous chemical, in both the streams and the soil in the neighborhood only intensified fears in iagara Falls. (*Courtesy of the University Archives, University at Buffal*)

In February 1979, Dr. Axelrod urged that children under the age of two, as well as pregnant mothers, should move out of LaSalle—a decision that served only to incite more panic. (center: *Courtesy of the University Archives, University at Buffalo;* bottom: *Courtesy of* The Buffalo ews)

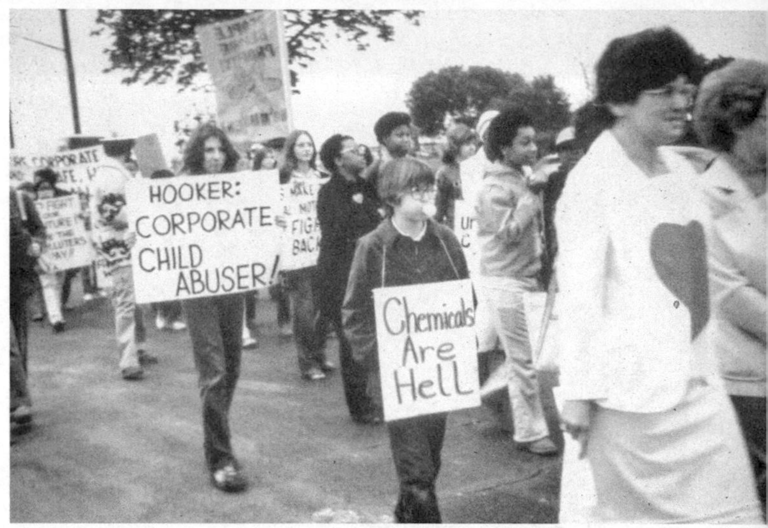

Hundreds of residents still trapped inside their homes and apartments in the neighborhood took to the streets, marching in hopes of mobilizing politicians in both Albany and Washington. (*Courtesy of the University Archives, University at Buffal*)

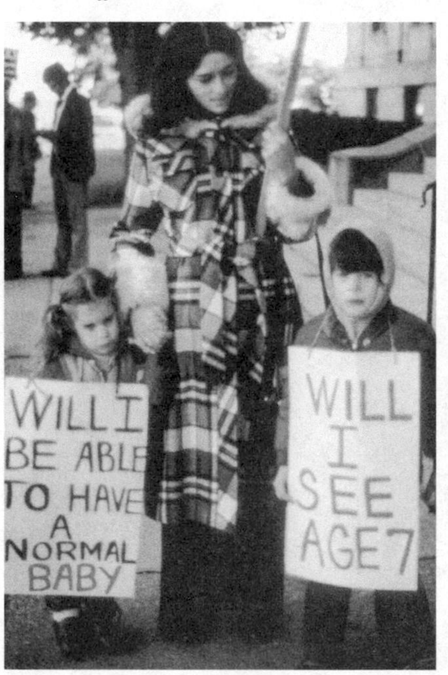

Gibbs at a march with her children, Michael and Missy. (*Courtesy of Lois Gibbs*)

The marches and protests made Lois Gibb something of a media darling; they also he get the attention of two important people Washington. (*Courtesy of Getty Images*)

President Jimmy Carter, in peril of losing the White House in 1980, recognized that the Love Canal problem wasn't going away. (*Courtesy of Mickey H. Osterreicher*)

A young congressman from Tennessee traveled to Niagara Falls to see it all for himself. Al Gore was worried about the residents and soon invited both Gibbs and Paigen to testify before Congress. (*Courtesy of Getty Images*)

Gibbs's fame and notoriety also took their toll. At home, her marriage was falling apart. (*Courtesy of Mickey H. Osterreicher*)

By early 1980, residents couldn wait any longer, Gibbs staged he biggest, most br protest yet, forci politicians to fin take sweeping ac in the neighborh (*Courtesy of Mic Osterreicher*)

At the same time, Luella Kenny (*left*) fl w to Los Angeles with Sister Joan Malone (*right*) to confront the corporate face of the problem: Armand Hammer, the CEO of Occidental Petroleum. (*Courtesy of Luella Kenny Collection*)

President Carter, Governor Carey, and Congressman LaFalce personally thanked Gibbs for her work in shining a light on the chemical time bombs buried in her neighborhood and around the country. (*Courtesy of Mickey H. Osterreicher*)

Paigen soon left Buffalo and her job with the state of ew York. But she continued working for decades, publishing nearly 250 scientific papers, often f om her home in Maine. (*Courtesy of Paigen Family Collection*)

In 1983, authorities finally demolished the school in the heart of LaSalle. (*Courtesy of* The Buffalo ews)

A few years late also began teari down homes an the public housi development. (*Courtesy of* Th Buffalo ews)

While official ultimately opened parts of the neighborhood for resettlement, most people never returned to the place known as Love Canal. (*Courtesy of* The Buffalo ews)

meetings that ultimately led to two notable conclusions. First, residents were justified to question the impartiality of scientists at the state Department of Health. "Although they are highly competent and held in high esteem by their peers," the committee concluded, "the public may perceive a conflict of interest." Therefore, the committee determined, third-party scientists needed to stay involved. Second, the committee ruled, Paigen couldn't be ignored. Even though her data had been collected by housewives with no scientific training and obvious biases, she was potentially onto something. "The concerns and questions raised by Dr. Paigen," the committee declared, "are important and merit attention."

Paigen had won her biggest victory yet: scientific validation from her peers. But it seemed to come at a cost. In June—just as everything else was seemingly imploding in Niagara Falls, with talk of dynamite, and dying birds, and doors being kicked in—Paigen's boss, Dr. David Pressman, called Beverly to discuss a new policy for her. In addition to filing monthly reports and disclosing her contacts with the media, Paigen was now required to tell Pressman everything she was working on—or even contemplating—so that he might determine if the projects were consistent with the institute's objectives.

Pressman explained that the new policy was a benefit to her, really. If she shared her ideas early—say, "at the moment of conception," Pressman said—she wouldn't waste her time chasing experiments that the administration would later reject. But Paigen believed it was retribution for her positions on Love Canal, payback for having crossed Axelrod in such a public manner, and yet another way to control her.

Less than two weeks later, Paigen officially submitted the final draft of the proposal that her bosses had leaked to Whalen and Axelrod the previous fall—a project studying hazardous waste sites in Erie County, in Buffalo. At the time, Whalen had dismissed the project as, essentially, trash science. But this ostensibly flawed plan now had funding from the EPA, backing from the state Department of Environmental Conservation, and the support of the state's highest-ranking official overseeing toxic substances at the DEC: Bob Collin. Put simply, the project was happening now, with or without Paigen, though, ideally, with her. As Collin explained to Axelrod, "The loss of Dr. Paigen's technical and scientific skills and her knowledge of Erie County and its environment will be impossible to replace completely."

Axelrod didn't agree, and he was clearly paying attention, monitoring Paigen's activities. Just one day after she submitted her proposal, Axelrod wrote a memo to another top doctor in Albany with the subject heading "Attached Status Report—Dr. Beverly Paigen." The note was brief, to the point. Axelrod dismissed Paigen's plan as "a poorly conceived witch hunt," science without "rhyme or reason."

Permission for her participation was denied.

The rejection from Albany came almost exactly one year after Paigen first became involved at Love Canal, one year after first visiting the neighborhood and meeting with Lois Gibbs. In that time, she believed she had been questioned, restricted, and insulted, and as a result Paigen had become paranoid. She worried that she was being followed or watched—maybe even wiretapped. Sometimes, she made calls from a phone booth on the street, unwilling to speak freely in her office, and more than once she stashed important files in hiding places inside her house in Buffalo, fearful that the documents weren't safe at Roswell Park.

Now that her latest proposal had been denied, she believed she had proof that she was being targeted, and others that summer agreed, sending angry letters to Albany. Paigen's colleagues at Roswell Park called Axelrod's actions disturbing and potentially dangerous. The institute's independent Council of Scientists said it appeared to them that Paigen was being singled out—"singled out," the council said, "for special review"—and the chairman of Beverly's department, her husband, Ken, finally weighed in as well.

Ken had kept his silence about Beverly's problems for months, hesitating to criticize the administration for obvious reasons. He didn't want it to seem as if he were fighting his wife's battles. "I was concerned," he told Axelrod, "that my actions might be construed in a personal sense." But Ken could no longer abide what he was seeing. "What has overcome my hesitation," he said, "is the realization that if a similar censorship were applied to any other member of this department, or indeed the institute altogether, I would have reacted even more strongly and more immediately."

He called on Axelrod to reverse his decision and asked the health commissioner to get back to him right away. But Axelrod, a prolific letter writer, was slow to reply to Ken and the Council of Scientists. Perhaps he was too busy with other matters. In August 1979, when the news of Paigen's denied proposal finally made it into the press, Axelrod wrote to the reporter who broke the story to complain about the coverage. The next month, he doubled down on his criticism of Paigen, reiterating to Congress that her findings regarding Love Canal were incomplete, biased, and not scientific, and into October, Axelrod challenged Paigen on matters large and small. At one point, he even criticized her for using Roswell Park postage to mail him a letter related to their ongoing dispute about the Love Canal data.

"Your use of Departmental funds and facilities for the forwarding of your request is not only inappropriate," Axelrod informed her by letter, "but conveys the impression that the request is being made in connection with officially assigned duties and responsibilities."

The message to her was clear: find other work to do. But, of course, she'd already gotten that message. That August, amid the growing acrimony between the two scientists, Paigen received a notice from the state tax commissioner that she was being audited. The tax commissioner explained that a computer had flagged her case that July for potential erroneous reporting. Hers was case No. 757 out of 1,500 new audits. Just normal business, according to the tax commissioner. "We do not select taxpayers for audit," he said, "on the basis of their public positions or politics or any such thing."

Yet Paigen was understandably skeptical, especially after she appeared before the auditor for the first time. As the man opened her file, Paigen noticed it was filled with news clippings related to her involvement at Love Canal. She was furious, but there was no way she was quitting now. They could audit her. Deny her proposals. Make it hard for her to work. They could even make it difficult for her to send a letter or fire her, if they wanted. It didn't matter, because she'd made up her mind. She was willing to sacrifice her career for Love Canal, and for what she believed was right. She was willing to give the residents everything she had.

"Not many whistleblowers survive, anyway," she said.

42

STILL HERE, CHEMICALLY TREATED

Lois Gibbs knew how to handle the Paigen controversy: she sat down at the typewriter in her new office, in the vacant house on Colvin Boulevard, and started writing angry letters to newspapers calling for Axelrod's immediate resignation.

"Dear editor," one of the letters read. "In my opinion David Axelrod should not continue as head of the New York State Health Department!"

Gibbs then proceeded to list her reasons:

1. He admits an above average chance of miscarriages and birth defects in the Love Canal neighborhood, but does nothing for families who desire more children.
2. He admits there is no safe level of exposure to dioxin, but allows families to live a matter of feet from the area it was found.
3. He claims there are no abnormal anemia, liver, urinary problems etc. in Love Canal, but cannot or will not provide data to back up his statements.
4. He admits our storm sewers are significantly contaminated and empty in our waterways, but does nothing to alleviate the problems.
5. He also does not seem to be able to separate the politics in Love Canal, from the science.

Gibbs sent the letter to all the usual places. But littered with exclamation points and underlined passages, it sounded a little desperate, almost unhinged, and for once Gibbs struggled to get the attention she wanted. She failed to persuade editors to print her letters attacking Axelrod, and she failed in court that summer, too. A judge denied her legal efforts to stop the second phase of remediation at the canal site, clearing the way for the diggers to continue excavating their trenches, past the school and into the northern reaches of the old landfill, up toward Colvin Boulevard, not far from the Kennys' house. The only way that people still living in the neighborhood could escape, the court ruled, was if they met a series of escalating criteria, each one harder than the last.

First, they had to develop an acute illness. Then a doctor had to determine that the illness—whatever it was—had been triggered by the workers stirring up the chemicals in the ground. At that point, the doctor would have to put the official diagnosis in writing so that it could be reviewed by the state Department of Health. And if the state agreed that the criteria had been met, the people in question would be permitted to relocate to a paid hotel room, but only for a limited period of time. As soon as their symptoms had subsided or the excavation had ended—"whichever comes first," one state official made clear—the relocated families would have to return to their homes or their apartments at Griffon Manor. Bottom line: as usual, it was nearly impossible for residents to escape, forcing Gibbs to send out reminders that summer that nothing had changed. "We are still here," she said at one point, "chemically treated!"

Still, residents refused to surrender themselves to the idea that they would never get out. And ironically, it was more bad luck—yet another string of mishaps and blunders—that began to swing circumstances in their favor. That summer, heavy rains moved across the city, making it difficult for the crews working on the canal. Trenches caved in, thick with mud. Chemical leachate pooled on the surface in large puddles, and the heat of July and August created additional complications that the state had avoided during remediation efforts over the winter. The thick, humid air held the odors right there in the neighborhood. Even state officials had to agree: the place stank. It was so bad, at times, that workers were forced to don masks, a measure that they typically resisted. And still, the crews kept digging, plunging into old swales and finding, inside them, the most unusual, porous fill. Backhoes churned up garbage, toys, bottles and cans, tree trunks and stumps, auto parts covered in chemical slime, rear bumpers from old cars, a chunk of a drinking fountain, two newspapers from January 1954—so perfectly preserved that it was as if they had been deposited in the swale the day before—and, of course, rusted drums, belching rivers of black oily sludge.

Upon seeing the problems with his own eyes, Stephen Lester informed Gibbs there was only one way to describe the situation. He called it "gross contamination"—it looked as if chemicals had been dumped right into the swales themselves, at times—and these newly excavated streambeds were hardly the only places of concern. On his regular visits to the canal, Lester carefully checked the air monitors, spiking with varying levels of benzene and toluene gases, and on Ninety-Sixth Street, Luella Kenny was making observations of her own. Around mid-August, she started keeping a written log of what she saw—and smelled—in the waterway cutting through her backyard: Black Creek.

Crouching at the water's edge at a sewer outfall pipe just upstream from her house—day after day, morning, noon, and night—Kenny noted that the creek at the pipe was often the color of burned tangerines, deep orange and coated with oil slicks. The slicks varied in size, depending on the day. Sometimes, they were small and glassy. Other times, they stretched the full length of her yard, like a layer of coarse skin dotted with brown globules. And on still other days, the water ran almost totally clear, as Kenny remembered it—or thought she remembered it—when she used to allow Jon Allen and his brothers to play in the backyard unattended, sloshing through the water of the creek. But one thing remained consistent in Kenny's log, her daily chronicle jotted into the pages of a notebook. On almost every trip to the water, she noted the sickly sweet smell of chemicals, petroleum, gas—that "Love Canal odor," she called it—and some days late that summer she didn't even have to walk that far to find it.

The stench started at the midpoint of her backyard. It covered her entire lot. It was knocking at the door of her house or had slipped inside while she was making dinner.

It was everywhere.

"In fact," Kenny wrote one day in her log, "I was able to smell it in the kitchen from about 1 p.m. to the present."

"Love Canal type odor . . .

"Evident in the air by our home . . .

"Strong odors all day."

43

LOOKS LIKE YOU'VE BECOME THE ENEMY

By the third week of August 1979, Luella Kenny wasn't the only one concerned about the stench in the air over the creeks on the north end of the neighborhood. Parents of children attending the 93rd Street School—the last public school still open in the neighborhood, on the shores of the creek, just a short walk from the Kennys' house—announced that they'd sooner go to jail for delinquency than send their kids to classes there after Labor Day.

The school board, under fire for mistakes both past and present, had no choice in the matter. To protect kids, they were shutting down that school, too, and then, the morning after the school board meeting, the odors got even worse. Crews struck a swale at the north end of the canal, releasing a buried seam of black chemical leachate into a trench that they were digging. The leachate splashed into the water trapped in the trench with such fury that the foreman on-site ordered the workers to strap on their face shields. He didn't want them getting burned. But there was nothing he could do to mitigate the smell coming from the swale or the piles of newly excavated dirt that the workers called "spoils." These contaminated mounds baked in the sun while crews kept working—running into other problems. Half a mile away at the southern end of the canal, diggers hit a trench that smelled so bad the workers had to breathe with the help of oxygen tanks in order to keep going. Meanwhile, a group of hired contractors spawned yet another malodorous cloud, by washing dirty equipment with steam cleaners—an ill-advised and unauthorized mistake. The result: a storm of odors, a wave of complaints, and fourteen official pleas for immediate evacuation.

At lunchtime, Lois Gibbs showed up to find out what was going on.

"It's just been unbearable today," she complained. "There's no other word for it."

The state's top-ranking official on-site agreed that the smell was worse than usual and then tried to explain the situation to her, discussing the issues that morning with the swales, and the spoils, and the steam cleaning. But Gibbs wasn't having it. She had been looking for a way to get people out—and now, with the remediation problems, she had found it. All they needed were some doctors' notes to satisfy the court ruling—doctors' notes suggesting the odors were causing "acute illnesses" in the neighborhood—and people could leave.

On the last day of August—about a week later—Gibbs informed the state that she and other residents demanded a full stop to all remediation work at the canal. "No further work," she said, "until you figure out 'how' to do it properly."

Then, with their doctors' notes in hand and their suitcases on the curb, people began to move, scattering across the city to the Howard Johnson's and the Rodeway Inn, the Hotel Niagara and the Castle Court Motel. By early September, dozens of families had escaped. Some were so eager to join the ranks of the exiled that they were willing to do almost anything to get out. One woman claimed she fainted from the fumes and struck her head on the floor. Two others cited the stress of the relocation itself as a reason for hospitalization. And in an inspired gambit that was organized by the nuns and religious activists working out of the Methodist church on Colvin Boulevard, 119 families, more than 400 people, went to see the same doctor—a psychiatrist—over a span of forty-eight hours in early September. His written diagnosis: depression.

The psychiatrist didn't charge for the work. As one nun explained, he saw the patients and signed the notes out of a strong sense of social conscience and also because he knew that other doctors didn't want to get involved. Many of them had only a passing knowledge of toxicology and a limited understanding of what was even in the canal. How could they say with definitive medical knowledge what was causing a mother's headaches or a child's asthma? They likely couldn't, and at least some were fearful of wading into a fight that had become both political and public. For every mother who waved a white doctor's note in the air—"I've got it!" one rejoiced—there were three others who had nothing. No note. No exit ticket. No way out.

Still, Axelrod—a medical doctor in his own right—was upset. He believed the psychiatrist and the nuns had violated the spirit of the judge's ruling, allowing for temporary evacuations in local hotels. This wasn't good science or sound medicine, and it wasn't smart economics, either. The state was on the hook to pay the hotel bills for every evacuated family. Just one day after receiving the doctor's 119 cases, the Department of Health dismissed all but 7 of them.

"We reject," Axelrod said, "his certification of a virtual epidemic of acute depression."

But his decision did nothing to change how people actually felt. Whether they had notes or not, hotel rooms or not, many denied families refused to return home. Bedraggled and lost, with their station wagons crammed full of clothes, toys, and schoolbooks—the worldly possessions they needed to live—they protested outside the Rodeway Inn and then drove across town together in an angry motorcade to a different Methodist church downtown. Here, about a mile from the crowds queuing up to board the Maid of the Mist and sail off toward the waterfalls, people slept on cots, homeless by choice, while others—the lucky ones—filled local hotels.

Twenty-nine families escaped from Griffon Manor. Twenty-six families left homes north of Colvin Boulevard, the Kennys' end of the neighborhood, and almost everybody on 101st and 102nd Streets—some fifty-three families—managed to find an excuse to leave. But the temporary relocations came at a cost—both financial and political. With the state spending $7,500 a day to house people in hotels, taxpayers began to complain, forcing Gibbs into the spotlight again. That fall, she stood on the steps of the Howard Johnson's, defending their temporary evacuation and trying to make New Yorkers understand this was no state-funded vacation. People didn't want to be living in hotels. They just didn't have a choice.

"We can't eat out of our gardens," Gibbs complained. "We can't go in our basements. Our kids can't go to the schools in their neighborhood because they're contaminated. We have to be in a motel

Monday through Friday or we can't breathe. We can't get pregnant. We can't sell our house and our kids are all sick.

"What are we supposed to do?"

In early October, Gibbs got some support from an unlikely source. Jane Fonda—the Hollywood film star and known liberal activist—visited the neighborhood for a tour. Fonda wanted to see everything—the Hooker plant, the fence around the canal, the canal itself, and the homes people had left behind. A thousand people came out to see her stand on Ninety-Ninth Street in a green pantsuit, brushing back her flowing hair and telling people they were right.

They were right to want to leave.

"It's unbelievable that this could happen in America today," Fonda told the massive crowd as she stood in front of the fence. "I've never talked to so many people at one time about a disaster—and it's just a bitter irony that the same chemicals we used in Vietnam are buried here and destroying you. It looks like you've become the enemy."

The crowd that day was Black and white and celebratory. Jane Fonda was listening, Jane Fonda cared, and Gibbs took her by the arm before she left town, making sure to get her mailing address and phone number in Beverly Hills. She wanted to stay in touch, and Fonda promised to keep pushing to help everyone find permanent relocation.

"Perhaps I can be of help on some level," Fonda told Gibbs. "I'd like to."

But Governor Carey was quick to temper any enthusiasm people might have felt after seeing Fonda speak in the neighborhood, articulate and beautiful, with her Hollywood shine. She hadn't even left western New York that day—or the late-afternoon cocktail party thrown in her honor in Cheektowaga—when the governor informed the press that there would be no permanent relocation. Jane Fonda could say whatever she wanted. "We don't have the money," Carey said. He was spending too much keeping people in the hotels, which was, truthfully, both increasingly miserable for the residents and a terrible investment for the state. At the rate he was going, Carey could have bought a house in the neighborhood every four to five days. Instead, he was cutting checks to the hotels, where the rooms were small, the quarters cramped, and the tensions fraying quickly.

With no kitchens, meals were whatever people could afford on their $13 daily food stipends or whip up on the hot plates and toaster ovens they smuggled into their rooms. But the small appliances were hard to find sometimes, buried beneath piles of laundry, a task that was hardly getting done anymore. Under pressure, spouses were arguing. Anxious children struggled to sleep, forced to share beds with their siblings, and everyone wondered how it would end. Residents living in the hotels were informed that when the diggers were finished working at the canal—probably by early November 1979—they would have to pack up and move out.

"Temporary Relocation," one state notice declared, "will no longer be provided."

People would have to go back to the neighborhood or find somewhere else to live.

44

VERY BEST WISHES FOR THE NEW YEAR

From her room at the Rodeway Inn, Kenny was furious about the notice that residents would soon be evicted from the hotels, and, frankly, she was a little worried about it.

She had tried to make the best of life in exile that fall. She had relocated to the Rodeway, and while there she continued to work with both Gibbs and the nuns, homeowners and residents of Griffon Manor, trying to find a way out of the situation. She attended so many different meetings with various citizen groups that fall that Gibbs, at one point, asked Kenny to serve as a spy for her, and Kenny had tried. But in a meeting that Gibbs had asked her to monitor, Kenny quickly realized that she wasn't cut out for a life undercover. She confessed her secret mission to the nuns running the meeting. She was too honest to lie—especially to others who were struggling to get out—and she felt she had to be honest with David Axelrod, too. In mid-October, with the hotel evictions looming, she informed Axelrod that he couldn't ask people to go back to the neighborhood.

"My concern for my family grows each day as the time draws near for the end of our hotel stay," she told him in a letter. "What are we supposed to do?" she added. "Can you really expect us to go home?"

Kenny believed everyone in her family was healthier since they had vacated their house in early September, and new reports were about to confirm that she had been right to worry about the water in the creeks. Testing showed high levels of dioxin—"significant levels," Axelrod conceded—in the creek behind the Kennys' house.

Sediment at the outfall pipe where Luella kept her daily log tested positive for dioxin at levels thirty-one times higher than what authorities would later consider acceptable. And there was evidence that the pervasive chemical had gotten into the animals in the creek, too. A crawfish just downstream from the outfall pipe was found to have dioxin in its body at levels sixty times higher than what authorities deemed safe for human consumption. "And now they want us to move back?" Luella thought. She couldn't understand that, and there were other problems in the neighborhood—new problems—that any mother also had to consider.

Back on Ninety-Ninth Street, state officials were more concerned than ever about security. Over the summer, the state had sought bids to fortify its office there, replacing doors, installing motion detectors, rigging up an alarm system, and asking security guards to step up patrols in the area. Now, with the streets empty, homes abandoned, and the neighborhood quiet—a modern ghost town on the edge of one of America's most touristed cities—state officials asked the guards to be more vigilant. They wanted them to watch for protesters during daylight hours and bandits after dark. As it turned out, the bandits posed the bigger problem.

That fall, thieves used crowbars to pry open doors and get inside houses, gutted kitchens of their cabinets and counters, carted away any valuables that people left behind, or just taunted the security guards by breaking into homes and then disappearing into the darkness, undetected. One night, arsonists used kerosene to set fire to a garage on Ninety-Ninth Street. On several occasions, vandals cut holes in the fence around the canal for reasons unknown, and it was only a matter of time perhaps before they returned to the scene of a previous crime: the Kennys' house on Ninety-Sixth Street. Burglars slipped into the house that fall, and this time they hit the kids' rooms, stealing the boys' birthday presents: brand-new portable Sony cassette players and the headphones that came with them.

Luella didn't need a reply from Axelrod to know what she was going to do. As her boys, Christopher and Stephen, cried that night in the hotel room, grieving for everything they had lost, she knew one way or another they were never going home again.

—

In Albany, Axelrod couldn't say what Kenny should do, and he declined to answer her specific questions. But by the time he received her letter, he was troubled about the state of the neighborhood, too. He was worried about the remediation problems at the canal—and the dioxin in the creek—and he was starting to push the governor for more definitive measures, real action. If the goal was saving the neighborhood, Axelrod said, then both state and federal officials needed to be working faster and with greater urgency. They needed a better plan, and they needed to consider a solution that Governor Carey—and Axelrod himself—had been dismissing for more than a year and as recently as just a few weeks earlier when Jane Fonda visited Niagara Falls. They needed to buy more homes.

"We have previously outlined several of the alternatives which could be pursued by the governor's office," Axelrod told Carey's top aides that month. The choice, at this point, was the governor's to make. But Axelrod wanted him to know one thing for sure. "I believe it is imperative that we immediately define a course of action to deal with the problems."

In early November, state lawmakers in Albany finally cobbled together the framework for this new plan. They budgeted $5 million to help purchase more homes over the next two years and relocate people who wanted to leave Griffon Manor in hopes of setting the neighborhood up for future success. The key words were "stabilization" and "revitalization." The state would finish remediating the site, buy houses from people who wanted to leave, flip these homes to interested buyers after cleanup operations were complete, and then maybe rebrand the entire neighborhood by giving it a new name, like Sunrise Park or Black Creek Village.

But the excitement around this new plan faded before the first snows of winter. While Gibbs and most homeowners wanted to leave, they didn't think it safe for the state to sell their houses to anyone else, and many residents at Griffon Manor didn't want to move at all. Either way, it quickly became clear to everyone, no matter where they stood on moving, that the $5 million wasn't materializing anytime soon. It could be a year or more before any homes were purchased under the new state measure; no agencies wanted to assume the liability of Love Canal. And President Carter's proposed superfund legislation, introduced in the House in Washington six months earlier, was equally unhelpful. It had stalled out in committee. People in the neighborhood had run out of time.

Just one day after Governor Carey signed the $5 million legislation in New York, residents faced an 11:00 a.m. deadline to leave their hotel rooms, forcing them to make a choice: go home or go to court to contest the evictions. Gibbs, Kenny, and nearly two dozen other residents tried the latter approach first. But when it became clear that they had no legal standing—that authorities could evict them from their hotels and might do just that, placing their belongings on the street—the residents backed down. People packed up their things and scattered across the city to wherever they could find shelter. The Kennys moved in with Norman's mother that November, while the Gibbs family sought alternative arrangements of their own.

After nearly a year and a half of arguing, silence, and tension over how their lives had changed, Lois and Harry had secretly decided to get divorced. They agreed to stick it out through the holidays for the kids. Then Harry would return to the house on 101st Street, while Lois would move to a low-rent, redbrick condominium complex on the edge of the neighborhood with the children. The condo was a little sad, and her divorce was juicy gossip, of course. The item couldn't escape the newspapers for long. But for Lois, it was better than moving home again. Her son, Michael, still suffered from seizures, and her daughter, Missy, was showing signs of illness now, too. Lois wasn't bringing them back to a neighborhood marked by deserted streets, empty houses, and new sounds ringing out in the night: quick pops of random gunfire.

Thanksgiving came and went, and people across Niagara Falls got ready for the holidays: Christmas 1979. Children flooded the post office below John LaFalce's office with handwritten letters to Santa Claus. Shoppers flocked to the local malls and revelers prepared to ring in the new year, closing the book on the seventies. But Gibbs was working so hard she hardly noticed. She was only paying attention to the news about Love Canal.

Five days before Christmas, federal prosecutors filed suit against Hooker Chemical, seeking $124 million in damages to clean up the company's many dumps in Niagara Falls, including Love Canal. The litigation was deemed so important that Barbara Blum personally announced the news from EPA headquarters in Washington. She wanted to inform Hooker that federal prosecutors were coming. "The problem of unsafe waste is a serious one," Blum said that day. And, she added, "We're serious about attacking it."

Hooker was suddenly on the defensive like never before, and David Axelrod was, too. In recent days, Beverly Paigen had hired a lawyer and filed a complaint at Roswell Park, asking the institute for a public hearing to review the treatment she had endured since first speaking out about Love Canal sixteen months earlier. The board agreed to consider it; Paigen would get her hearing after the holidays. Then, on the same day that the government filed its suit against Hooker, both Buffalo newspapers finally published Gibbs's letter calling for Axelrod to resign. One of the papers printed it—exclamation points and all—almost exactly as Gibbs had written it, and more letters soon followed as people rushed to defend Paigen: "this excellent, caring scientist . . . dedicated to making our world a better place."

"Commissioner Axelrod," one resident wrote, "if you can no longer make an objective decision because of political pressures, please step down."

Yet if the goal was to rattle Axelrod—or force him to resign—the campaign failed. As usual, the health commissioner worked hard through the holidays. On Christmas Eve, he asked the EPA to help him address the hazards in Niagara Falls—"perceived or real." Three days after Christmas, he advised Governor Carey about the status of his ongoing squabbles with Paigen and assured the governor that everything was fine. He could defend the state's positions to board members investigating Paigen's treatment at Roswell Park whenever they took up the matter. Then, in one of his last acts of the year, Axelrod sat down on New Year's Eve and wrote a letter to Bruce Davis at Hooker Chemical. He wanted to thank Davis for his cooperation during a challenging time—"in light of our adversary position"—and he wanted to extend the Hooker vice president his warmest regards for 1980. "With very best wishes for the New Year," he wrote, signing off. "Sincerely, David Axelrod."

PART IV

JANUARY — MAY 1980

45

PRAY FOR THE DEAD

The nun picked her out of the crowd at the Methodist church on Colvin Boulevard and approached her after the New Year with a proposition. Sister Joan Malone wanted Luella Kenny's help. She wanted Kenny to fly with her to Los Angeles and confront top executives at Hooker Chemical in one of the places that mattered to them most of all: a shareholders' meeting. Forget about Bruce Davis, David Axelrod, Governor Carey—or any other official in New York. Malone was aiming higher. The goal, she told Kenny, was to stand up to the man at the top of Hooker's corporate food chain, the multimillionaire executive who oversaw the whole operation and who had been dodging the Niagara Falls issue for months. Malone wanted to go after Armand Hammer, the CEO of Occidental Petroleum—on his birthday.

Kenny studied the nun as she laid out her plan. Like the other religious activists working out of the church, Malone didn't live in the neighborhood or have a personal stake in the fight against the state, the EPA, or Hooker. Malone lived among a dozen other nuns in a dormitory on the top floor of an all-girls Catholic high school about twenty miles away. Malone was the librarian at the school, and she was a good one, too. Just a few months earlier, the University at Buffalo had named her the local librarian of the year, honoring her for the work she had done to increase budgets for books, develop library skills classes for girls at each grade, and create a welcoming atmosphere for both students and staff. In short, on the face of it, Sister Joan Malone, with her dormitory digs and sensible shoes, hardly seemed like someone ready to stare down one of America's best-known corporate executives. She hardly appeared to be a radical at all.

Kenny liked Malone right away, in part because she reminded her of the nuns from her youth, and in part because Malone wasn't anything like those women at all. For starters, she was Luella's age—in her early forties. She was a modern nun, wearing street clothes, no habit, and Luella quickly realized that Malone was bolder than she looked. She was opposed to the Catholic Church's positions on homosexuality and women's equality. She was increasingly unwilling to be told by men—bishops, say—what she could or could not do. And while she considered the sisterhood a calling—she had been called by the Lord to serve—Malone was willing to admit that her choice to become a nun was also a bit more complicated than that. As a child, she had been abused by her father on Buffalo's hardscrabble east side. The convent, for her, was something of an escape, a way out. She joined at age seventeen, right after graduating from high school, and set her mind on two things: healing herself and making a difference in the world.

She taught high school English while also protesting nuclear weapons, the war in Vietnam, and discriminatory hiring practices in Buffalo. She ran the school library and marched down local streets with Black union workers, carrying a sign that said, "We Want Jobs—Not Welfare." She was fully aware that these kinds of positions made some Catholics uncomfortable; they wanted her to teach their children and stay quiet. Yet Malone could not look away from what she believed to be failings—great cultural failings—and in late 1979, just months after she was named librarian of the year, the convent finally gave her a second job that better suited her interests. In addition to running the library at the school, Malone would work, part time, at the Center for Justice. The group, with an office on Main Street in downtown Buffalo, was funded by five different religious orders, and the sign above Sister Joan's desk there told visitors just about everything they needed to know about her.

"Pray for the dead," it said. "But work like hell for the living."

Her plan, she explained to Kenny, was simple. She and other religious activists based in New York City had started purchasing stock in major corporations—not to make money, but to make trouble. With the stock holdings, they were shareholders. And as shareholders, they had a right to attend the companies' annual meetings, address the boards, speak to the other shareholders from microphones set up amid the crowd, and even present resolutions for a vote. The fact that these resolutions almost always failed didn't dissuade the activists from returning to the annual meetings again and again. "Because there are other things that enter into it," explained one of the lead activists at the time. Namely: press attention. They could lose the votes on these resolutions, yet still win public opinion and push their issues into the headlines.

To distract from dissident factions in the room, executives started to use annual meetings as a forum for unveiling shiny new products, announcing positive news, or airing well-produced movies—polished commercials, really—about the company's many achievements in the past year. The longer the movie, the better, because if people had to wait, the crowd might get bored and thin out. The activists would have a smaller audience whenever they got their chance to speak. Still, they kept coming. In 1979 alone, Malone and her colleagues had exposed insurance companies for redlining urban neighborhoods and making it hard for Black families to buy homes; U.S. banks for lending money to the racist government of South Africa; car manufacturers for selling vehicles to foreign countries with questionable rulers; cereal companies for advertisements enticing children to eat unhealthy breakfast products; and defense contractors for building weapons of war. Now, angry about Love Canal, they were coming after Occidental Petroleum—the biggest company Malone had ever faced.

"As you know, I'm new to this," Malone confessed that winter to her colleagues, the other religious activists. She wanted to be honest with them: she didn't really know what she was doing. Also, Malone was still busy with her day job running the library at the all-girls Catholic school—a job she wanted to quit but couldn't, at least until June, the end of the academic year. In order to craft a shareholders' resolution, prepare for the meeting, and ready herself for a confrontation with Armand Hammer, Malone would have to work nights and weekends. But she didn't fear Hammer; Malone was never one to cower. On the contrary, in January 1980, shortly after meeting with Luella Kenny at the church in Niagara Falls, Malone personally informed Occidental's CEO that she was coming.

"I represent the Sisters of St. Francis," she wrote, introducing herself to Hammer in a letter. She wanted him to know that they owned ten shares of Occidental Petroleum stock and they were angry. "The members of my congregation join me in expressing our profound concern and indeed, dissatisfaction, with the actions of our Company regarding corporate responsibility in the area of toxic waste disposal." As a result, Malone was sending him a document—a document that Hammer and his lawyers needed to read: the shareholders' resolution. "I am authorized to inform you of our intention to present the attached proposal for consideration and action by shareholders at the next annual meeting," Malone told Hammer.

The resolution cited Hooker's history of dumping in Niagara Falls and in other cities across the country. It outlined the potential long-term health problems that people now faced. It called out the company's seeming indifference to these issues—"alarming indifference," the resolution said, quoting an editorial from *The New York Times*—and then it asked Occidental to establish safeguards and policies to prevent future environmental hazards, if not for the good of the earth, then at least for the shareholders' bottom line. As the resolution noted in an effort to get shareholders' attention, Hooker's profits had plummeted in the second quarter of 1979 due to its past toxic waste failures, and future expenses were almost guaranteed to grow with legal cases mounting against the company in court.

For a standard resolution that had been introduced by a nun no one had ever heard of and that was guaranteed to fail before the shareholders that spring in an easy up-and-down vote, it sure got Hammer's attention. Corporate lawyers reviewed it, and then they turned to a different lawyer—America's most famous trial lawyer—for help.

Occidental was calling in Louis Nizer.

According to the *Guinness Book of World Records,* Nizer was the highest-paid lawyer in the world in the 1970s. His book *My Life in Court* was a *New York Times* best seller. His life had been portrayed both on Broadway and in made-for-TV movies. His client list included the likes of the basketball star Julius Erving, the

Tonight Show host Johnny Carson, Hollywood movie executives, and anyone rich, and famous, and mired in a bitter divorce battle. Both the Astors and the Rockefellers kept Nizer on speed dial, and Armand Hammer did, too. When he faced criminal charges in the mid-1970s for making $54,000 in illegal campaign contributions to Richard Nixon—and attempting to conceal the donations by making them in the names of other people—Hammer made sure Nizer was standing next to him in court.

The well-known lawyer helped keep Hammer out of prison. Noting Hammer's advanced age and declining health, a federal judge sentenced him to probation for his illegal donations and ordered him to pay a mere $3,000 fine—the Armand Hammer equivalent of loose change found between the seats of the family car. Now the wealthy oilman was apparently hoping that Nizer could pull off a similar trick with Joan Malone and Luella Kenny. The goal: negotiating a truce before the shareholders' meeting. Occidental didn't want them to come.

In mid-February 1980, Nizer invited the group to New York City for a chat. The meeting was to be held in his law office—located in a modern glass tower on West Fifty-Seventh Street with views of Central Park—and it came with a few important rules that Nizer wanted the group to agree to in advance. The discussion would be entirely off the record—secret, even. No one would publicly comment on it, unless a statement could be drafted after the fact on which both sides could mutually agree, and it would take place on a Saturday afternoon, when the streets of midtown Manhattan were quiet. No one would see the group coming and going.

Malone and the others agreed to the terms of the meeting, flew into New York on a Saturday late that winter, and walked into Nizer's law office, taking in their surroundings with a touch of awe. Malone, for one, had never seen anything like it. The posh Manhattan suite was impeccably decorated—even the secretary's outfit matched the decor, she noted, right down to the color of her shoes—and Nizer was as impressive in person as he had appeared in portrayals on Broadway and on television over the years.

He and two other Occidental men wanted to assuage the group's concerns. Why talk about the past, they suggested, when the company was doing so much good in the present? And why fight, they argued, when they could write a joint statement together? Armand Hammer could read the statement himself at the shareholders' meeting that spring, committing Occidental not to harm current or future generations with its waste disposal practices. The lawyers had even drafted something for Malone's group to review.

"Chemicals are vital to this country's health, food, and general welfare," the written statement began. "Their uses enhance our lives, our homes, and our industry. However, chemical manufacturing processes, like other manufacturing processes, often produce waste as a byproduct. Proper waste disposal practices, therefore, must be a significant industry concern."

It was all typed up and prepared; all the group needed to do was approve it. But Malone, Kenny, and the others weren't inclined to let Hammer and Nizer off so easily. They also weren't fooled by the million-dollar sparkle and the corporate savvy on display that Saturday. Over dinner that night in New York, after three hours of meeting with Nizer in his office, Malone's group discussed everything that had happened that day and came to the following conclusion about Hammer, Nizer, and the other Occidental men.

"Debriefing: they are cunning and clever; maintain resolution."

They weren't agreeing to any statement from Hammer. They were going to speak for themselves at the shareholders' meeting that spring.

Rejected, Occidental's lawyers now turned to a second strategy: they would fight. On the same day of the meeting in Nizer's office in New York City, an Occidental executive penned a long and detailed letter to the Securities and Exchange Commission, announcing that the company planned to dismiss the resolution and omit it from the annual meeting for several reasons. Executives wouldn't hear it, because it was "misleading," "highly contentious," and "damaging." It was filled with unproven allegations, they argued, and it was moot. Occidental had already implemented procedures designed to safeguard the environment, the company informed the SEC, and it wanted the government's assurance that it wouldn't face consequences for refusing to entertain the resolution. Then, in early

March, while Occidental awaited the government's reply, one of Hammer's men decided to apply a little pressure.

Charles Diebold—a well-known lawyer and banker in Buffalo, with local roots dating back to the days of Elon Hooker himself—called a meeting with the Catholic bishop of western New York, Edward Head, to discuss the activities of a woman who, heretofore, had received no attention from either of them: Joan Malone.

Diebold wanted Bishop Head to know what the nun was up to, what she was planning with Luella Kenny, and that she seemed to be walking away from a good deal. The written statement that had been offered at the meeting in New York City was a better approach than the resolution that Malone was pushing, Diebold explained to the bishop, and he urged the holy leader to pass along the message to Malone, if possible.

The fact that Diebold managed to get a meeting with the bishop was telling. The fact that the bishop listened to Diebold—and then took action—was even more revealing. Shortly after the meeting, Bishop Head contacted Malone's superiors at the convent to explain Diebold's position and to encourage Malone to at least think about Hooker's proposal.

"Give it due consideration," the bishop said.

Malone and other nuns at the convent saw it as a threat, a veiled threat, if not from the bishop himself, then perhaps from Occidental's lawyers. The message, to the nuns, was clear: Hammer and his men had connections. They could meet with the bishop, and they could find Malone. They could track her down and potentially make life difficult for her at work if she didn't play by their rules. It was as if Armand Hammer were watching.

"He has a lot of people at his bidding," one nun said, "and he can pay for it."

But in the end, none of it mattered. In mid-April, the Securities and Exchange Commission informed Occidental that the company was legally compelled to take up the resolution that spring, and both Malone and Kenny were not going to be dissuaded from bringing it forward, despite any implicit threats.

The two women made plans to fly to Los Angeles, where the shareholders' meeting was set to take place, and Kenny began writing a speech to deliver to Armand Hammer. It was going to be the biggest speech of her life. Sketching it out in longhand inside her mother-in-law's house, she decided it would be best if she started at the beginning.

"My name," she wrote, "is Luella Kenny."

46

A KANGAROO COURT

In Washington that January, President Carter was preparing for a big moment of his own. He was up for reelection amid a tornado of political difficulties: a stagnant economy; a Soviet invasion of Afghanistan; a growing debate about whether the United States should boycott the 1980 Summer Olympics in Moscow; waning support from within his own party; a primary challenge from Democratic royalty, Senator Ted Kennedy from Massachusetts; and a stunning international crisis that would not go away. Iranian militants had taken dozens of U.S. citizens hostage at the embassy in Tehran in November 1979, and months later the Iranians were still refusing to release their American prisoners.

Carter's reward—if he managed to overcome these obstacles and win his party's nomination again—was a presidential race in the fall against a formidable foe. He was likely to face either the former governor of California, Ronald Reagan, or the former CIA director, George H. W. Bush, who in that moment were glad-handing their way across Iowa and New Hampshire, bashing Carter and courting voters. And it was all so vexing to the president that Carter refused to be distracted. He wasn't going to participate in the biggest event unfolding at the time. In New York, Governor Carey, David Axelrod, and other top officials were about to host the 1980 Winter Olympics in Lake Placid—a remote outpost 350 miles from Niagara Falls, on the other side of the state in the Adirondack Mountains near the Vermont border.

It was going to be an unforgettable fortnight, a time for miracles. But Carter was going to be watching from afar, declining to attend the opening ceremonies, and the residents of the neighborhood in Niagara Falls would watch from afar, too. For them, it was just another cold, dark winter, filled with more of the same: medical tests.

One researcher wanted to examine people in the neighborhood who suffered from headaches. Another wanted to test their metabolism. Beverly Paigen was personally looking for volunteers for a nerve study—a study that, she said, would be simple and painless but potentially revealing—and federal officials were asking for Paigen's help recruiting volunteers for one other trial. The government was looking for chromosome damage.

Chromosomes—the microscopic, threadlike bodies in the nucleus of every cell—are known to mutate slowly over time, leading to evolutionary advantages in humans, animals, and plants. But in the 1940s, a pair of scientists in Scotland discovered that mustard gas could cause genetic mutations, too, breaking chromosomes apart. And by the 1970s, scientists now believed that at least two hundred other chemical agents could cause chromosome damage in humans—damage that might go undetected for a lifetime or even generations but could quietly poison the gene pool.

Paigen was well aware of these risks. Since 1978, she had personally identified many of the chemicals in the canal as "mutagenic." Now the Department of Justice wanted proof of that, or at least a scientific snapshot that showed it *could* have happened, it *might* be possible. Federal prosecutors believed that if chromosome damage existed among people who lived in the neighborhood, they could use it as leverage against Hooker in the $124 million case they were bringing against the company. The EPA was sending in a scientist from Houston who had done this sort of work in the past, identifying chromosomal abnormalities in chemical plant workers in Texas, and they wanted Paigen to help connect him with residents. She agreed, bringing the idea to Gibbs and finally to a public meeting inside the Methodist church in the neighborhood that January. The two women wanted to introduce the study to the people and explain the scientist's plans.

He was looking for a specific kind of subject to give blood for this study. He wanted people who had lived along the swales; people who had lived in homes with high levels of chemicals in the air;

people who were still living inside these homes right now; people who had not yet moved away; and people who had struggled to have normal pregnancies, healthy births, or thriving children. A history of miscarriages was a plus, while a job at a chemical plant was not. The goal was to show that by just living in this neighborhood, just being there, people were exposed to toxins that might have altered their DNA, and both Paigen and Gibbs recognized right away that the results could be explosive.

"These tests," Gibbs explained, "are important to all of us."

Twenty people at the church that night raised their hands, volunteering to give blood. And in the days ahead, Paigen and Gibbs called around until they found sixteen others willing to take part. The total number of residents who agreed to participate, three dozen in all, was slightly fewer than what the EPA's scientist had hoped he might get. But it was the best that Paigen and Gibbs could do, given the distractions in their lives at the time.

In late January 1980, as residents lined up at the church on Colvin Boulevard to give blood and scientists began analyzing the samples—first in Buffalo and then back in Houston—Paigen was still battling David Axelrod and others at the state Department of Health. The fight was playing out in the pages of the local newspapers, and it was starting to attract national media attention, too. A producer from *60 Minutes* planned to attend Paigen's next hearing at Roswell Park—a meeting initially scheduled for January and then delayed until early March after a seemingly inexplicable oversight. Paigen hadn't received an invitation to the January hearing, learning of it only when a reporter called her for comment.

It seemed like an improbable mistake, but Paigen didn't dwell on it, and she didn't whip up furor in the press over the mix-up as she might have. Instead, she set her mind on preparing for March. She filed a Freedom of Information request to obtain any memos and letters that her bosses had written about her since August 1978. She compiled these documents, along with her replies to them, into a thick binder that documented, in chronological order, the problems that she and her husband, Ken, had faced at work in the past two years. She sent this binder to board members and Axelrod before the hearing, and then, just like Luella Kenny, Paigen began crafting a speech.

In it, she had no plans to attack Axelrod or call for his removal. For Paigen, this wasn't about him or even about her. "At issue in this controversy," she wrote in an early draft of her speech, "is whether the research of a state scientist must meet a test of political acceptability and whether scientists at Roswell Park will be protected from administrative or political reprisal when their research findings become relevant to questions of public policy." In short, as Paigen saw it, she was fighting for scientific freedom.

On the first Friday of March—with winter still raging outside and flurries blowing through the air—she finally sat before the board, looking up at them from behind her round glasses. It had all started so innocently, she said, that it was hard to imagine how they had ended up here—in a formal dispute, with so much on the line, including, almost surely, her career. In the beginning, she said, she thought she was doing her job. She was helping residents identify patterns of disease amid an unprecedented public health crisis. She was passing on everything she knew to Axelrod and others in Albany, and she had expected no problems—no controversy.

"After all," she told the board, "what I had done is exactly what happens in science all the time. The essence of science is that others question, challenge and repeat findings. Scientists do not take another person's conclusions as truth; they always want to see the data or to repeat experiments. However, even my first phone call indicated clearly to me that trouble lay ahead, that this was not an ordinary scientific relationship. I realized that what I found had enormous political consequences."

From that point on, she testified, life for her only got harder, and she asked the board to read the documents in the binder—nearly a hundred pages of documents—to understand exactly what she had faced. It was all in there: the reporting requirements; the directives that she seek permission before speaking to the press or starting new research; Axelrod's personal intervention, denying her funds and proposals; and other slights that, while seemingly petty, Paigen said, revealed a pattern—"a pattern of harassment."

If board members read these documents and agreed that she had been mistreated, she was asking for just two simple things in return: she wanted the board to draft a statement in support of scientific inquiry, and she wanted a promise.

"That I shall be treated like any other scientist," she said, "no more and no less."

Lois Gibbs had been hoping for a moment like this one for months. But as exciting as it was to watch Paigen stand up to Axelrod—and the board at Roswell Park—Gibbs and other residents knew that cheering was premature.

For one thing, Axelrod sat with the board during the hearing and left with the board when it was over, and whatever testimony he might have offered that day behind closed doors would remain a mystery. No one was permitted to hear it, including, most notably, Paigen herself. This omission alone made the hearing something of a joke, according to one state senator. "A kangaroo court," he called it, rushing to Paigen's defense. The senator didn't understand how Axelrod could serve as both accuser and judge, and Paigen agreed. It only seemed right, she argued, that she be given the chance to answer, or refute, her superiors' claims. Yet Paigen was even more worried about another development. In the aftermath of the hearing, state officials were maligning her in the press, she believed, depicting her as a disgruntled employee—"a chronic troublemaker."

"I truly regret that the issue of my harassment has become a major media event," Paigen informed the board in a follow-up letter that spring as the panel continued to weigh the merits of her case. It was never her intention, she added, to adjudicate her case in the press, and she didn't relish the idea of writing to the board again now—with yet another complaint. But these allegations painting her as a troublemaker had to stop, she said, because they were taking a toll. "A scientist's life depends on their reputation," she said. And every day, she was losing a little bit more of hers. "Unjustified personal attacks," she said, "jeopardize my ability to carry on research."

Gibbs wanted to help, rallying residents to Paigen's defense yet again—by mobilizing the press, calling for letters to the editor, or perhaps organizing a protest, a skill she had honed and polished in the last two years. But as a single mother now, separated from Harry and raising two children in a condo on the edge of the neighborhood, she was overwhelmed with media problems of her own.

On the same day that Paigen testified before the board, the press learned that Lois and Harry were living apart and asked Lois to comment on the new arrangement. She explained that Harry was staying in the house for security reasons while she and the kids had moved into the little redbrick condo to make sure they weren't going to be exposed to chemicals anymore. It was a plausible excuse, and reporters bought it. They knew that her son, Michael, now seven, continued to suffer from seizures and other neurological problems. Lois routinely discussed them in interviews, and she did so again that weekend, telling reporters that she was bringing Michael back to Children's Hospital the following week for yet another battery of tests to help her understand his latest symptoms. The boy was fatigued and struggled at times to use the limbs on the left side of his body.

Michael was older now, and he knew enough to be worried. He knew what he had lived through, and what others had not. He knew what had happened to Jon Allen Kenny, for example, and Michael thought about Jon Allen a lot. Probably too much. But that spring, while Lois was fixated on Michael's ailments—and his worries—her daughter, Missy, aged four, suddenly started bruising. Tiny bruises, smaller than a penny, began cropping up all over her little body, like a rash beneath her skin.

Lois called the family pediatrician, and he quickly sent the girl to Children's Hospital in Buffalo. When blood tests came back, showing that Missy's platelet count was shockingly low, doctors then moved in to conduct a test that Elene Thornton's young son, Gregory, had endured nearly twenty years earlier. They wanted to draw a sample of bone marrow from Missy Gibbs and test her for leukemia.

The word itself nearly brought Gibbs to her knees inside the hospital. Already exhausted and alone, she was barely holding it together as it was. Now doctors were asking her to stop Missy from screaming—to please help them calm her down—while they inserted a large needle into the girl's hip and extracted the sample they needed to run their tests. Lois just looked at them and began to cry—a hard and angry cry emanating from somewhere deep inside her.

"Calm her down?" she thought. "How about calming me down?"

She stayed for the procedure and then slipped away. Mentally spent to the point of being physically ill, Lois found a bathroom and vomited.

Later, there would be good news. Doctors couldn't say why Missy's platelet count was low, or if it would return to normal, or if living near the canal had caused the problem. The condition, they explained, was "idiopathic"—it had no known cause. All they could say for sure was that the test for leukemia came back negative. With proper medication, doctors expected Missy's platelet count would rise again, and they planned to release her that Friday, after three nights in the hospital. The girl was going home—or at least back to her mother's new condo—for the weekend.

But on the afternoon of the test that week, alone in the hospital with her daughter, Lois broke down. After crying in the room and vomiting down the hall and watching her daughter fall asleep in her hospital bed, wondering if the girl had leukemia, Lois made her way to a bank of pay phones near the elevators, dumped out a pile of coins, and started pumping them into the phone, calling everyone she knew: state officials, Axelrod, her mother, her friends, Beverly, reporters, and the other housewives in the office back in the neighborhood.

Lois needed to tell them what was happening. She wanted them to know where she was. She needed them to know that Missy was sick and that she was scared.

She was a mother in a phone booth, and she was sobbing.

47

A SIGNIFICANT POLITICAL PROBLEM

The scientist in Houston finished his chromosome study in early May. He then invited EPA agents to visit his lab to receive the results in person and sent them home with a two-page summary to deliver to one of the most powerful—and feared—liberal attorneys in Washington: Assistant Attorney General Jim Moorman.

Moorman was forty-two that spring, with all the trappings of power. He had a corner office at the Department of Justice, a view of the National Mall out his window, a résumé that included a Duke University law degree and a stint at a top Wall Street law firm, a staff of nearly two hundred attorneys reporting to him every day, and a direct line to top environmental activists across the country and the White House, just five blocks away. Before Carter appointed him to his position at the DOJ in 1977, Moorman had spent years as an attorney at the Sierra Club Legal Defense Fund. He had waged battles against oil companies, coal mines, ski resorts, amusement parks, and any other corporation that threatened to contaminate oceans, rivers, and forests. And for this reason, some Republican senators opposed his appointment. As one senator put it during Moorman's confirmation hearings, "I can just hear the cries of alarm if the president of General Motors was made Secretary of Transportation."

But Moorman also exhibited a quality that was hard to find in Washington, even during the Jimmy Carter era. He possessed a certain backwoods charm that could disarm his opponents—right before he gutted them with his searing legal arguments. Part of the trick of it was the way he looked and how he talked. Moorman wore a thick, bristly beard—flecked with shades of red—and spoke with a southern twang acquired while growing up in rural North Carolina. The combination of the two made him stand out at the Department of Justice or just about anywhere else in Washington. He looked more like a thru-hiker on the Appalachian Trail who'd gotten lost and popped out on Pennsylvania Avenue, wearing a suit and tie—than a high-powered lawyer with White House connections. Yet Moorman was no drifter in flannel. The man was an Eagle Scout, driven and prepared, quickly winning confirmation to his post in 1977, despite the Republican opposition he faced. And now he was going to help build the government's lawsuit against Hooker Chemical.

Moorman saw it as a test case—a chance to prove that corporations couldn't insulate themselves from liability, just because the alleged misbehavior happened some decades past or because the company in question had bequeathed the problem to another party, say, by selling the land to someone else for a dollar. As with any test case, his argument would be difficult to prove in court. Moorman needed every possible report, memo, and study that he could find, and he was especially interested to learn what the chromosome study might reveal. If damage existed, it would bolster his case. But everyone in Washington—Moorman included—knew that findings of broken chromosomes could also create a problem. "A significant political problem for us," one White House staffer admitted in a meeting that spring.

The rumor in Niagara Falls was that Lois Gibbs was planning more protests: a massive relief concert with the folk singer Pete Seeger; a boat parade down the Potomac River in Washington, meant to call to mind the Cuban refugees who were drifting across the Straits of Florida that spring in record numbers; and at least one other potentially explosive plan. According to one report, she and other residents were going to attempt to occupy vacant military housing in western New York, claiming the empty homes for themselves and daring the government to stop them.

Whether true or not, the rumors alarmed officials in Washington—even inside the White House. The last thing President Carter needed—amid his other well-documented political difficulties—was a riot in Niagara Falls led by a bunch of women living on the edge of an old chemical landfill, and, according to one White House staffer, that's exactly what they were risking by ignoring the rumors out of New York.

In one briefing that spring, the staffer said he had no reason to doubt that the reports of potential protests were true. Gibbs had personally shared many of the plans herself, he explained, scripting exactly what might happen if federal officials—or someone else—didn't intervene soon. In news reports in the previous week alone, Gibbs had confirmed that residents intended to demonstrate along the Potomac River—or block the doors of governmental offices in Niagara Falls—until lawmakers found the $5 million they had promised to buy their homes. And that was just the situation today, the staffer added. He couldn't say what might happen in Niagara Falls if the chromosome study came back suggesting long-term health damage.

Jim Moorman couldn't, either, which is why he proceeded with caution when the scientist's two-page summary finally crossed his desk on a hot, humid Tuesday that May. Moorman studied the report and then picked up the phone. He was calling the White House and asking for an emergency meeting that afternoon. No, it couldn't wait, he explained. And no, White House staffers couldn't see the chromosome report in advance, or even take a copy of it with them when the meeting was over. He didn't want the document walking out of his office and leaking to the press.

They just needed to see it, Moorman explained. Right away, if possible.

48

EMOTIONAL FIRES

Three White House staffers hustled over to Moorman's office straightaway: an attorney; a young aide working for Carter; and Robert Harris, one of Carter's top environmental advisers with experience investigating chemical landfills.

Harris was in his late thirties, Harvard trained, and new to both Washington and the White House. He had been appointed to his position just six months earlier, after years of working as a staff scientist for the Environmental Defense Fund studying the impact of chemical agents. In both his research and his fieldwork, Harris had seen firsthand how hazardous waste sites could harm people, and since coming to the White House the previous winter, he had personally met with both Paigen and Gibbs to discuss Love Canal.

Harris had immediately liked both women, in part because he understood their enemy. He was familiar with Hooker Chemical, too—its dumping practices and its products. He understood the composition of chlorinated hydrocarbons—the pesticides that Hooker produced—and he knew what happened when they ended up being thrown away without proper safeguards. Harris had personally analyzed reports documenting how Hooker had tainted the groundwater near its plant in Northern California, and he was well aware of the chromosome study being conducted in Niagara Falls. In fact, few people in Washington were more informed on the subject than Harris was that spring. He was Carter's new expert, highly educated and ready to assist in any way he could, but perhaps one way most of all. Harris was there to give advice. "The best, most objective, most scientific, and most technically sound advice that I can," he promised.

Still, even Harris wasn't truly prepared when he got the call that Tuesday to report to Jim Moorman's office at the Department of Justice. The White House had to track him down at a luncheon at George Washington University, and Harris had to scramble, rushing over in the heat of the afternoon, to connect with the other two White House staffers—everyone hurrying across town to meet with Moorman.

Once in the room together, the bearded assistant attorney general asked them all to take a seat. He pledged them to secrecy. He didn't want them discussing what he was about to say with anyone—outside Carter's inner circle—and then, when they agreed to those terms, Moorman gave them the news.

The chromosome study identified abnormalities in eleven out of the thirty-six people who had given blood in Niagara Falls back in January, Moorman said, and eight of those eleven people had aberrations recorded as "long acentric fragments"—essentially, extra genetic material—which were known to be linked to cancer, birth defects, miscarriages, and other problems. It was Moorman's understanding that such mutations were not only rare; they were hard to find even among factory workers who had been exposed to chemical agents in spills, mishaps—"notorious episodes."

As alarming as it sounded, the scientist in Houston urged officials to be cautious when considering his report. He didn't have a control population with which to compare these numbers, he explained. Also, the sample size—just thirty-six people—was relatively small, and it was biased toward finding problems, based on how the volunteers had been recruited and the format of the study itself. For these reasons, the scientist argued, the results of the study had to be viewed as preliminary—a start. Still, he had to admit, the findings were worrisome, given what he knew about the rarity of this sort of chromosome damage in the wider population. If the study was just a snapshot, he indicated, then it was a disturbing one.

Back at the White house later that day, Harris asked for a meeting with the special assistant to the president—Carter's friend Jack Watson.

The two men, Harris and Watson, hadn't been working together long, and on paper they didn't have much in common. Harris was a scientist; Watson an attorney. While Harris had essentially just arrived in Washington, Watson had been with Carter since their days in Atlanta. But Harris thought Watson to be the smartest man in the White House. Perhaps just as important, Watson had the ear of the president, and Harris wanted him to know everything about his meeting that afternoon in Moorman's office.

Harris told Watson about the chromosome study and its potential implications—for both the residents of Niagara Falls and the president. In the coming days or weeks, they would have to publicly disclose the results of the study. And when they did, Harris said, they needed to expect serious questions from residents about chemical exposure, and also outcry. Harris anticipated people living in the neighborhood would be angry. Fires were already burning in Niagara Falls—"emotional fires," Harris told Watson—and this study would further fuel them. In fact, Harris looked upon it as gasoline, and top officials at the EPA agreed. "When this gets out," one said, "people are going to go crazy."

The good news was, they had a little time, or at least Harris thought they did. The EPA wanted to send in a team of scientists to review the study, confirm the results, and Moorman needed a few days, maybe a week, to use the chromosome findings as negotiating leverage with Hooker Chemical. He wanted to share the study with Hooker's lead counsel and then give the company an ultimatum: pay to at least temporarily relocate the remaining seven hundred families in the neighborhood, or federal prosecutors would file an injunction in court seeking that money, over and above the $124 million they already wanted. On Thursday that week—two days after his meeting with Harris—Moorman finally sat down with the lawyer for the chemical giant, and he made his demands clear. "I want Hooker's answer by Monday," he said.

But by then, some inside the White House were wondering if they even had that much time. On the same day that Moorman met with Hooker, a young woman in Watson's office named Jane Hansen argued that President Carter couldn't afford to wait any longer. He needed to go on the offensive right away, Hansen said. Declare another emergency. Relocate any resident who wanted to move. Get in front of the story now. And even though Moorman was negotiating with Hooker at that very moment, he was inclined to agree with Hansen. After some reflection that day, he decided they didn't need to wait, and probably shouldn't. The president could declare an emergency and begin relocating people now, and Moorman could collect the money from Hooker after the fact. Then he boldly offered his own boss—Attorney General Benjamin Civiletti—some advice. In a detailed memo, Moorman asked the attorney general to communicate this plan directly to President Carter.

If Carter received the message, however, he didn't act on it, and by the next day it was too late. The study had leaked. The press had learned about the chromosome damage and reporters in Niagara Falls, Buffalo, and New York City—*The New York Times*—were calling Barbara Blum for comment at the EPA while copy editors sat at their desks in a swirl of cigarette smoke tinkering with banner headlines for the front pages of the Saturday newspapers.

"Chromosome Damage Found," said one.

"Residents Not Yet Informed," said another.

"Genetic Harm Tied to Canal."

49

TELL US HOW YOU FEEL

The telephone rang inside Lois Gibbs's condo late that Friday afternoon while she was taking a moment to do something unusual. She was trying to relax.

Gibbs was taking a bath.

It was almost five o'clock, the weekend, and despite all the rumors in Washington about the many protests that she was planning, Gibbs had every intention of taking the night off or at least claiming this one hour for herself. Her mother had taken the kids to Burger King for an early dinner, and relieved of any motherly duties for now, Gibbs had seized this rare opportunity. For once, she was ready to think about absolutely nothing, lounging in the water inside the quiet condo, with a glass of wine in her hand.

But just in case, she strung the phone into the bathroom at the top of the stairs and left it sitting next to the tub, and now, of course, it was ringing—as usual—and Gibbs was clambering over the edge of the tub, dripping water everywhere, to grab it.

She took a moment to dry her arm with a towel and then picked up the phone.

"Hello?" she said.

It could have been just about anyone calling: Paigen, Kenny, a lawmaker, a reporter, Missy's doctor, checking in on the girl, or one of the other housewives down at the office. In Niagara Falls that week, the women were fundraising. They were selling $5 T-shirts emblazoned with a simple logo—"Love Canal: Another Product of Hooker Chemical"—and $10 tickets to a buffet dinner at the end of May. They hoped the T-shirts and the dinner might help raise enough money to cover basic office expenses—the phone bills and postage—and defray the costs of whatever revolt Gibbs was planning next.

As it turned out, the intel at the White House was right. Gibbs was, indeed, considering a demonstration involving boats on the Potomac River in Washington, and she had several other plans in the works, too. Maybe residents could peacefully block the doors of local governmental offices in Niagara Falls, Gibbs suggested. Or maybe they would stage a sit-in and just refuse to leave. All she knew for sure was that they needed to do something to force politicians to find the money—or the courage—to buy their houses and relocate everyone now.

"We realize it's been a long, emotional, tiring two years," she told residents that month in her regular typewritten newsletter, shortly after returning home from the hospital with Missy. Yet this was no time to quit. Whatever they did, they needed to keep showing up. "We need to show up en masse," Gibbs said. "If you don't have a babysitter, bring the kids."

Yet the most imminent protest at the moment had nothing to do with crowds, boats, or even Gibbs, for that matter. That weekend, after months of planning, Luella Kenny and Sister Joan Malone were flying to Los Angeles to appear at Occidental Petroleum's annual shareholders' meeting. While officials in Washington worried over the chromosome study, and how to handle it, the two women were practicing their speeches inside the church on Colvin Boulevard—the speeches they would deliver to Armand Hammer, the speeches that Occidental Petroleum had tried to stop.

Kenny wasn't sure she was ready. Aside from interviews with reporters and comments made at public hearings, she had given only one big talk. It was to a group of students at Niagara University that spring, and the crowd that night had been both small and sympathetic. The students, about three dozen in all, had wanted to hear from her. They had invited her to come, and they had cheered her when she urged them to get off the sidelines and get involved. "Don't wait," Kenny said that night, "until barrels come leaking out of the ground."

At the shareholders' meeting in Los Angeles, she knew it would be different. Kenny was sure to receive an icy reception there. At the very least, she would be ignored. But Malone made it clear that they could also be heckled, hissed at, or booed—yes, even Luella Kenny, the mother of a dead boy. She needed to understand, Malone said, that once they stood up to speak, the only thing they could truly control was their own reaction. The rest was out of their hands. And now the phone call in Gibbs's condo was about to inflame the entire situation.

The man on the phone identified himself as an official from the EPA, and he quickly got to the point. He informed Gibbs about the results of the chromosome study. He explained that these results were leaking to the newspapers as he spoke, and he asked if Gibbs could help him track down the thirty-six people who had donated blood for the study back in January. The EPA didn't want them waking up the next morning to panicked headlines in the newspapers about their own health. He wanted to contact each of them now and invite them to meet with EPA scientists the next morning in Niagara Falls—a Saturday—and receive their results in person.

Gibbs was still sitting in the bath as the man began to rattle off a list of names.

Bates.

Foy.

Sandonato.

Whiteknight.

Wait a second, Gibbs told him. She needed a minute. She jumped out of the bath, wrapped a towel around her, and went in search of a pen and paper to take down all the names. Then she got off the phone and started tracking down all thirty-six people—a thankless task that took her, Marie Pozniak, and the other women half the night. Some people insisted that Gibbs knew their personal test results and wasn't telling them everything—that she was lying. Others kept Gibbs on the phone for half an hour, asking reasonable questions. Either way, the people were angry and confused about what Gibbs was telling them. Did it mean their kids would get sick? Did it mean that they would, too? Did it mean that they were broken on the inside forever?

At some point that night, Beverly Paigen started getting these questions, too. And she was honest with the people: She didn't know what it meant for them, individually. But if the results were true, she knew what it meant for the neighborhood.

"It would show that people should not be living there," Paigen said that night. "It would show that women should not be getting pregnant there."

At the very least, it could be their golden ticket out.

In Washington the next morning, Barbara Blum stood before a wall of reporters, prepared to tell them everything she knew, while teams of EPA scientists flew to western New York to deliver the news on the ground in Niagara Falls. The plan was to hold a press conference at LaFalce's office downtown and then privately meet with each of the thirty-six people from the study at the homeowners' office on Colvin Boulevard, to explain the results in detail.

Carter's top environmental adviser, Robert Harris, understood the rationale behind the plan: the government had to say something. But he personally thought it was ridiculous to hold press conferences in two cities announcing the results of the study while asking people not to draw any conclusions, to sit tight and wait for further scientific review, and then put off a decision about relocations until after the review was completed in the days to come. Residents of the neighborhood wouldn't want to wait, Harris thought, when officials were going to make it sound like they were in danger. And the fact that all of this was happening on a Saturday—a slow news day, the weekend—seemed to suggest that maybe people were at risk. If officials couldn't wait until Monday to announce the results, then how were people expected to wait even longer than that to get some clarity on their situation? It seemed bound to go badly, Harris thought, and it did.

At LaFalce's office that Saturday morning, the congressman sat in front of a bank of television cameras with a doctor and a regional administrator from the EPA. The agency was working to review the results, the officials explained. If they were found to be accurate, the EPA would have to conclude that chemical agents were involved. And once they made that conclusion, the officials promised to relocate everyone between Ninety-Third and 103rd Streets—the entire neighborhood, homeowners and residents of Griffon Manor alike. They just needed folks to wait a little longer, the officials said. They were asking for patience until maybe the following Wednesday.

"Why Wednesday?" Gibbs shouted inside LaFalce's office, finding the soft spot in the government's plan right away.

"We don't want to wait for Wednesday," another resident agreed.

They felt as though they had been here before.

"We've been dealing with 'next Wednesdays' for two years," Gibbs said. "Why not today? My daughter got sick within the space of 48 hours recently. Next time, it will be somebody else. There is no reason for residents to be there one more night."

The EPA administrator tried to reason with Gibbs. They were working on it, he said. He just needed a little more time. But as he spoke, he admitted that he'd been unable to reach both local and state officials, including David Axelrod. He didn't know if they were ready to act or not, and Hooker Chemical certainly wasn't helping the EPA administrator in his quest for consensus. As residents shouted inside LaFalce's office that morning, an executive from Hooker's parent company, Occidental Petroleum, moved about the room, handing out a press release contradicting almost everything the EPA was saying—in that very moment.

The man refused to identify himself, when asked. He just wanted to deliver the written statement dismissing the study as inconclusive, not properly understood, and sure to cause anxieties—"unnecessary anxieties," the press release said. The man wasn't taking questions, and he also wasn't coming anywhere close to the homeowners' office in the neighborhood that day as people lined up to get the results of their chromosome tests.

Some wept at the news—out of fear or relief. Others shook with anger, and then, no matter which way it went, whether they had received good news or bad, they stepped out of the office into a sea of reporters gathered in the yard—with their television trucks and their satellite dishes, their microphones and their questions.

"Tell us how you feel."

"Are you bitter, at this point?"

"What is going to happen? What do you think about, when you think about tomorrow? Next month? Next year?"

"My kids dying," one woman replied without even skipping a beat.

—

That afternoon, Gibbs sent a telegram to the White House demanding a full evacuation of the neighborhood. "Please act immediately," she told the president. "Please save our suffering babies. Please let my people go."

Privately, Gibbs was beginning to worry about what might happen if Carter didn't take action. She was concerned about violence, and potentially even bloodshed. And for once, Gibbs and Axelrod were in agreement. Axelrod was concerned, too. On Sunday, the day after the EPA held the press conferences, the health commissioner warned of trouble, and not just in the neighborhood, he said, but in the city of Niagara Falls at large. He saw no way to appease the residents in the neighborhood short of immediately relocating everyone, and more than most he knew Gibbs's tactics. He could imagine what she might try to do.

Yet for the moment, it was quiet. That Sunday, the women opened the office on Colvin Boulevard as usual, serving coffee and doughnuts to anyone who stopped by. Reporters milled around, waiting for news that did not come, and the federal officials who had flown in for the Saturday press conference left town, decamping for Washington or New York City. The EPA was content to leave a small staff on the ground in Niagara Falls to manage whatever announcements were coming that week, and the two agents assigned to the job—a public relations man and a doctor—were confident that they could handle the situation. They even gave interviews that day during which they revealed where they were staying: John's Flaming Hearth Motor Inn, a kitschy tourist lodge on Main Street downtown, a short walk from the waterfalls.

Gibbs noted the location and tucked it away in the back of her mind. The two men might prove useful to her, she thought. But she didn't mention anything about it to the other women in the office or to Luella Kenny, who was on a plane that Sunday, flying west with Sister Joan Malone for the shareholders' meeting in Los Angeles.

As it turned out, Kenny took off just in time. In the state of Washington that morning, Mount St. Helens erupted, blowing thirteen hundred feet of solid rock off its jagged mountain peak, spewing a column of volcanic ash more than ten miles into the air, and unspooling a vast and menacing cloud that grounded flights across the country that week, closed schools and highways throughout the West, blotted out the sun in Montana, and rained dusty grit as far east as Maine, forcing people to rush to buy face masks so they could breathe.

Americans stopped what they were doing and stared at the sky—suddenly black, gray, white, brown, roiling, and hazy—marveling at nature's wrath and wondering how the tiny particles of volcanic dust floating in the wind might be harming their health, their lungs, their kids, the earth. The cloud—hundreds of miles long and four to ten miles high—moved like a storm across the continent, a weather system with its own forecast and rules.

But Kenny put it out of her mind, unable to bear another calamity. As she settled into a cousin's house in Los Angeles that Sunday, she was thinking only about the week ahead and also about what she had left behind in Niagara Falls: Norman, the boys, her family, their home, and everyone back in the neighborhood.

"Help Us, for God's Sake," said a new sign inside the office on Colvin Boulevard.

No one knew what Gibbs might do. Not even Gibbs herself.

50

THAT CROWD WILL RIP YOU APART

Gibbs got dressed that Monday morning in an outfit suitable for the television cameras that were sure to be coming: a short-sleeved navy blue blouse and a matching blue-and-white-striped skirt. She affixed a red carnation near the left lapel—the new symbol of their movement—pegged back her long black hair with a pair of bobby pins, and then hurried Michael and Missy out the door for school.

Gibbs wanted to get down to the office as soon as possible. She needed to check in with the EPA in Washington, circle back to reporters who had been there all weekend, see if the White House had responded to her telegram—she was hoping for a response—and scan the morning papers in search of any headlines that might give them hope.

But she quickly realized that hope was hard to find. Governor Carey wasn't taking action, and President Carter wasn't, either. The eruption at Mount St. Helens—leaving devastation across the Northwest—was about to move Love Canal off the front pages. Carter would be going to Mount St. Helens by the end of the week—not to Niagara Falls. And when the *Buffalo Evening News* published its afternoon edition that day with still nothing—no announcement about relocating the people in the neighborhood—a restless crowd of about fifty residents spilled out of the office in anger, looking for a target.

They stood in the street and stopped cars, yelling at drivers who were just passing through—on their way to the Summit Park Mall or the grocery store. They were offended that others had the audacity to lead normal lives while they were stuck in chemical purgatory, staying with relatives, renting sad apartments to escape their homes, or still living inside their houses near the canal because they simply had no other option. It wasn't long before the police showed up, threatening to arrest anyone who dared interrupt the flow of traffic. Still, people didn't care. They continued to stop cars on Colvin Boulevard. It was as if they wanted to get arrested, and Gibbs knew she had a problem when she saw that it was Marie Pozniak—of all people, the typist from the office—leading the charge. Before Gibbs could stop her or even knew what she was doing, Pozniak grabbed a gasoline can, carefully poured out its contents on the ground across the street, put a match to her creation, and then stood back to see what she had made. Pozniak had used the gas to scrawl three letters in the ground, and now those letters were burning as the crowd roared.

"E. P. A."

Gibbs looked at the faces of the people in the crowd—her neighbors and friends, now wild-eyed and desperate—and realized she needed to do something. Accosting innocent passersby, stopping traffic, taunting police officers, and setting fires—committing arson—wasn't going to win them any friends or any political sympathy, Gibbs thought, and it wasn't even three o'clock in the afternoon. She worried how they would ever survive the day unless she found a way to refocus their rage, and that's when she had an idea.

She went back inside the homeowners' office, picked up the phone, and called the kitschy lodge on Main Street: John's Flaming Hearth Motor Inn. She wanted to speak with the two EPA agents who were staying there—the public relations man and the doctor—and extend them an invitation.

She wanted them to come pay her a visit in the neighborhood.

The public relations man was the first to arrive, walking into the homeowners' office at around 3:30 that afternoon. Frank Napal was young, just thirty-three, and one of the newest hires in the EPA's New York City office. He was a former Democratic campaign manager and college instructor who had taught courses about how to motivate the public. He lived on the Upper West Side of New York, and he was happy to meet with Gibbs. Napal was even a little sympathetic to her cause. But if he was looking for a warm welcome on Colvin Boulevard, he didn't get it. Gibbs took one look at him in his snug-fitting pants and plaid shirt, unbuttoned at the collar, with the sleeves rolled up, and asked him what he thought he was doing, showing up alone, without his colleague.

"The residents want a doctor, not a public relations person," Gibbs snapped. "Get the doctor down here."

Napal eyed Gibbs, taking in his surroundings and mindful of his marching orders from New York. He had been told to maintain a presence in Niagara Falls, field press inquiries on the ground, and handle the situation—"the crisis situation"—until Washington made some kind of final decision, hopefully soon. Given the crowd outside and the wild look on Gibbs's face, Napal tried to play dumb.

"How can I call him," Napal asked, "when no one knows where he is?"

Gibbs refused to accept that answer. Nodding to the crowd in the street, she suggested that it would be in his best interest to find the doctor, and Napal, as if by some miracle, quickly remembered where his colleague was. He picked up the phone inside the office and dialed the hotel, asking for the room of Dr. James Lucas.

The two men hardly knew each other, and together they were a bit of an odd couple. Lucas was from rural Ohio, and though he was only in his mid-forties, he looked as if he could have been Napal's father—a rumpled scientist in square glasses and a tie. Yet if expertise is what Gibbs wanted, Lucas could provide it. He was a career public health servant, a longtime medical doctor, and the deputy director of the EPA's Health Effects Laboratory in Cincinnati. Lucas knew all about toxins, and what they did to people. He had been studying chemical agents for years, and now, Napal informed Gibbs, he was on his way. Lucas would be there shortly.

Outside the homeowners' office, the crowd continued to grow as factory workers finished their shifts and children returned home from school. Everyone was drifting over, it seemed, to find out what was happening, and Gibbs moved about the crowd, informing everyone that she had a plan.

"We're not going to do anything violent," she said.

They were just going to hold the two EPA agents for a while.

"Body barricade the door," she told people in the crowd. "Okay?"

Only Barbara Quimby and Debbie Cerrillo, two mothers from the neighborhood, remained in the office with Gibbs. Most people didn't want to risk getting arrested. Then Gibbs informed Napal that he was a hostage, and when Lucas arrived, she gave him the unsettling news, too.

The men heard a two-by-four click into place outside the door of the house.

"It shouldn't be more than two days," Gibbs said. "Would you like a seat?"

Gibbs wasn't thinking straight anymore. For the first time in a long time, she didn't have a plan. She wasn't sure how they had gotten to this point—with the two EPA agents locked inside the office with her. She definitely wasn't sure how she was going to get out of it, and she was already losing control of the volatile situation. Despite the attempts to keep the front door closed, people were coming and going all the time—in and out of the house—reporters most of all. They had fallen into a major breaking national news story: housewives were holding federal agents hostage in Niagara Falls. They were now inside the room, chronicling the crisis moment by moment—part reporter, part eyewitness to a crime scene. By the time it was over, their stories alone could send Gibbs to prison, and the reporters wanted to know how she felt about that. How did she feel about being locked up?

Gibbs wasn't sure how to answer the question. Also, she was busy. Around four o'clock, she called the White House and the EPA's regional headquarters in New York City to let them know what was happening. Gibbs wanted to alert officials in both places that they were holding Napal and Lucas hostage—until the president did what she described as the "proper thing." She wanted Carter to issue a new emergency declaration, pledge to buy their homes, and move everyone from the neighborhood today, no matter where they lived.

At the White House, Jack Watson's secretary put Gibbs on a long hold, giving Gibbs little choice but to hang up the phone in frustration. "Excuse me," she said, "but it's a little stupid to place somebody on 'hold' when they are holding somebody hostage." At the

EPA's offices in New York, Gibbs managed to get a little further. She spoke with the chief of staff for the top regional administrator, Chuck Warren, and once Warren had been informed of the call, he knew what he needed to do. Warren immediately phoned the homeowners' association office and asked to speak with Napal.

One of the women handed the phone to the young public relations man, and Napal briefly described the situation. They were indeed being held hostage, he explained. The crowd outside was a little concerning to him, and there was the whole issue of the two-by-four blocking the door. But to Napal, this seemed like a stunt—nothing more. There were no weapons. There were no threats. He noted the reporters who were coming and going, and it seemed as if the two EPA agents could leave, too, if they wanted. The question was, should they try?

Napal agreed to sit tight while Warren consulted with others. Within the hour, the news was all over Washington. Barbara Blum summoned LaFalce to her office. LaFalce, looking agitated, went alone, but then quickly called for Bonnie Casper to join him. They were all worried about how the FBI and local police might react and how, if they stormed the house, guns drawn, it could make matters worse for everyone involved. At the same time, they had no choice but to inform the Department of Justice about the situation because it was almost surely a violation of the law.

At 4:40 that afternoon—about forty minutes after Gibbs made her initial calls from the office—a top lawyer at the EPA informed Jim Moorman about what was happening in Niagara Falls. Moorman quickly called federal authorities in western New York, and exactly fifteen minutes later FBI agents mobilized to investigate two potential federal crimes—kidnapping and extortion—on Colvin Boulevard. They put the house under surveillance from a discreet distance, set up a command post at a nearby restaurant—the Perkins Cake & Steak, half a mile away—established telephone communications with the house, and then decided to test the will of the women inside. On the phone with Napal, an EPA supervisor asked him to just walk out the door.

Napal set down the phone and made his move. But Gibbs and Quimby jumped up and blocked his path, standing between Napal and the door, the office and the crowd outside.

"I've been told to leave," he explained.

"If you leave, honey, you're dead," Gibbs said. "That crowd will rip you apart."

Napal wasn't sure what to do. He knew he could push his way out. But Gibbs knew it, too, and she just glared at him.

"Try it," she said.

Napal returned to the phone and explained to his supervisor that the attempt had failed. They couldn't just walk out, and he didn't think it wise that he force his way out and escalate the situation, even if FBI agents and the Niagara Falls police officers were standing by outside. He was cool and calm, winking at the reporters in the room. He could wait.

But Lucas didn't like the idea that they were just going to sit there, potentially for hours—or, if they were to believe Gibbs, two more days. She was asking the crowd to supply them with blankets and pillows, bedding for the long haul—an indication that maybe she was serious. And even though Lucas had no problems with the women—they were warm and polite, telling him stories about their lives in Love Canal and serving him oatmeal cookies—he believed it was reasonable to be concerned about the crowd outside. He wanted to call his family, and he wanted his superiors at the EPA to go ahead and clear the FBI to come on in.

"You're damn right I fear for my safety," Lucas said.

On the phone, he began to describe the dimensions of the room where they were being held, what he and Napal were wearing just in case agents broke down the door, and who was holding them there.

Suspect No. 1—Gibbs—was five feet three, he guessed, with blue eyes and a dark blue blouse. Suspect No. 2—Quimby—was built about the same, he estimated, with blond hair, khaki pants, and a white shirt, and Suspect No. 3—Cerrillo—was standing at the door, in blue pants. The apparent muscle of the operation. He could go on, but he was apparently out of time. With a quick flick of her wrist, Gibbs disconnected the phone from the wall and just looked at him.

"Relax," she said. "I don't think you'll be here long enough to damage *your* chromosomes."

—

At home in Buffalo, Beverly Paigen was horrified to learn what Gibbs was doing. Already under fire at work, awaiting a decision from the board at Roswell Park, and still hopeful—deep down—that she might be able to win her case, salvage her reputation, and keep her job with the state of New York, Paigen worried that Gibbs's hostage stunt threatened to hurt the residents and maybe even Paigen herself.

She didn't want to be associated with this kind of behavior, and neither did John LaFalce. Around six o'clock that night, he called to inform Gibbs that he was having dinner with President Carter at the White House in a few minutes and that he would be pressing her case directly. But LaFalce worried that her actions that day had made his job harder. The White House wasn't going to bow to threats of violence or negotiate with women holding federal officials against their will—even if the women were serving them cookies or claiming they were protecting them from the crowd outside. She needed to let them go, and she needed to do it soon, before things got worse. Innocent plans, LaFalce said, have a way of ending in disaster.

Gibbs hung up the phone and peered out the window at the crowd assembled in the yard—two hundred people, Black and white, and growing by the hour. Children played on the porch. Parents cheered behind them. Dinners would be late tonight, and no one seemed to care.

"We are sick!" they chanted. "We want out!"

Even Napal was amazed at the sight of them. He had never seen a crowd like this one. But Gibbs knew LaFalce was right. The White House wasn't calling back. No one was meeting her demands. At some point, she would have to be willing to go to prison, or she would have to disappoint the crowd and release the EPA agents—with nothing to show for it, after hours of holding them—and who knew what would happen then? Already, someone had punched out a window, and others had thrown bottles at the house. Gibbs needed an exit strategy.

Around 6:40 that night, her attorney, Richard Lippes, informed the FBI that he was going in. He left his office in Buffalo, arrived at the house about half an hour later, parked his Audi in the street, and cut through the crowd, stepping inside to inform Napal and Lucas that they would be released soon. Lippes then got on the phone with an FBI agent assigned to headquarters in Washington and began to negotiate the terms of their release.

It was 7:30 by then, and the agent on the phone made it clear that the clock was ticking. The FBI wanted Napal and Lucas out of there before sunset—8:35—and ideally even sooner than that. The agent liked that there were still women and children in the crowd—a population that, for him, seemed to diminish the chances of violence. If Lippes could get Gibbs to agree to release the men under these parameters, then the FBI would promise not to barge in.

It sounded good to Lippes, who was concerned about his client. He didn't even want Gibbs uttering the word "hostage" anymore. But Gibbs wanted to delay any surrender until the last possible moment. She was hoping Bonnie Casper might call with good news from LaFalce's dinner with President Carter or that Robert Harris, Carter's environmental adviser, might come through for them instead. Throughout the evening, Gibbs's friends—Stephen Lester, the state-hired toxicologist, and a second man, who was a national environmental activist—repeatedly called Harris at his home in Washington trying to broker a deal on Gibbs's behalf. Anything seemed possible—until, around 8:20, when it wasn't anymore.

The FBI was moving in. A long line of dark, unmarked sedans began to creep down Colvin Boulevard, and Gibbs hurried to write—in her head—some kind of statement that would achieve several things at once. She needed to calm the crowd, conceal the fact that she had gained nothing from the standoff, frame the moment to help prevent her from going to prison, and still somehow win the next day's headlines—all at the same time.

Amid the rush, she missed the 8:35 deadline, and she was still inside ten minutes later, too. The FBI agent on the phone was losing his patience. The sun had set and the glow on the horizon was fading fast; it was almost dark. These were not the terms to which they had agreed, and he informed Lippes that agents would be at the doors momentarily.

"You have two minutes," he said.

Finally, at 8:49, almost six hours after the crisis began, Gibbs emerged from the house to tell the people two things. First, she wanted everyone to know that she had asked federal officials to meet with every faction of the neighborhood—the homeowners, the Griffon Manor residents, the church group, and a fourth splinter organization. Then she wanted them to know that—for now—she had agreed to end the standoff.

"I have told the White House—and this is upon your approval—that we will allow the two EPA representatives to leave," Gibbs said on the front steps, awash in the lights of the television cameras, making it up as she went. "But if we do not have a disaster declaration Wednesday by noon, then what they have seen here today is just a *Sesame Street* picnic."

The crowd roared, in part because Gibbs had planned it that way. In the final, frantic minutes, before making her statement, she had strategically asked allies to stand in the yard among the crowd. They would cheer Gibbs's announcement and, in doing so, encourage others to do the same. She wanted to do everything she could to make sure the day didn't end with violence, which made some residents question Gibbs's dedication. Right away that night, critics complained that she should have held the agents by force, refused to let them go, taken more hostages if possible, and gone to prison to save them all if necessary. "It looks like she's working for the state," one woman said, shortly after the FBI hustled the hostages out of the house and into the back of a waiting squad car. "If she had any backbone, we'd be out of here."

But Gibbs, as usual, ignored the chatter. If they wanted to take more hostages, she said, her critics could grab them tomorrow, or the next day, or the day after that. Federal officials were going to be in the neighborhood for years, she promised. In the meantime, she believed, she had proven her point.

"We've demonstrated we mean business," she said.

Then she cleaned out the file cabinets in the office, worried that law enforcement might raid the building that night. She collected the kids from Harry at her old house on 101st Street and went home to her condo, exhausted and, in her mind, a horrible mother once again. It was a school night, and it was way past everyone's bedtime. But Gibbs wasn't going to sleep. After she got the kids off to bed, she washed up and lay down on the couch, fully dressed.

She was ready to be arrested.

51

TODAY WE HAVE TO BE MEEK

Norman called Luella the next morning on the West Coast to give her the news: Lois had imploded. She had taken *hostages.* Luella had been gone for all of forty-eight hours, and the neighborhood was even crazier than usual—a mess.

But Luella didn't need a report from Norman to know what was happening back home. She had seen it on the national news and read about it in that morning's paper, in the *Los Angeles Times.* She could feel it—something was about to break their way—and the national press could feel it, too. That morning, *CBS Evening News* was flying Dan Rather into Niagara Falls, and the network was also queuing up its long-awaited Love Canal feature for the weekend. The story—which included interviews with Gibbs, Paigen, and Axelrod—was set to air on America's most popular television show, *60 Minutes,* that Sunday night.

Kenny hopped in a car and headed across town, fighting Los Angeles traffic to meet up with Sister Joan Malone at the site of the next day's shareholders' meeting: the Beverly Wilshire Hotel. It was a rare cloudy day in Southern California, jacket weather for locals, and as she stared out the window of the car inching west on the 10, Kenny couldn't help but note the irony of her destination. The Beverly Wilshire—at the foot of Rodeo Drive, in the heart of Beverly Hills—was one of the nation's most opulent establishments, with a rooftop veranda, coveted poolside cabanas, a private cobblestone street dotted with jet-black limousines, and a lobby dripping with the scent of Chanel and the sparkle of diamond-studded Rolexes. Foreign dignitaries stayed there. Some Hollywood movie stars *lived* there, and kings and queens—true royalty—had been feted in the grand ballroom, where Armand Hammer would be presiding over Occidental's shareholders' meeting with his usual millionaire charm.

Inside the lobby, Kenny tried not to be intimidated by the glittering scenery and beautiful people around her. She and Malone needed to make a final plan for tomorrow, and Malone needed to introduce Kenny to the two others who would be joining them for the ambush: an Irish priest from Baltimore and a young former Peace Corps volunteer now making a living as a professional activist—Bob Morris. It was Morris's job to attend shareholders' meetings, to point out to corporate executives their many failures, and to make noise about them, trying to effect change by wielding what could be a powerful tool: public shame.

The plan for tomorrow, Morris explained, was for three of them to speak. The Irish priest would go first, setting up the resolution for the board. Malone would go second, explaining the problems at Love Canal in detail, and they would finish with Kenny. They wanted to leave the audience, and Armand Hammer, with the emotional, heart-wrenching story of the mother from Niagara Falls whose son had died and a picture of her vacant house on the banks of the dioxin-laced creek at the edge of the old Hooker landfill.

Kenny was nervous—out of her element, twenty-five hundred miles from home, underdressed compared with the guests inside the hotel, and not ready for the spotlight. Despite all the practicing she had done with Malone at the church back in Niagara Falls, she couldn't help but feel a little unprepared. But Morris assured her that she would be fine. He had presented shareholder resolutions at countless corporate meetings in the past. They had every right to be there. Occidental knew they were coming, and these presentations typically went the same way. The presenters spoke. The CEO and board of directors sat there in steely silence. The shareholders voted, many of them annoyed. The resolution would fail, and then you hoped for a few headlines—media coverage. It would probably go that way again tomorrow, Morris expected. Kenny had a powerful story to tell, and she was exactly the right person to tell it. She was going to be great.

Kenny and Malone checked in at a nearby hotel, walkable to the Wilshire, but also cheaper, a significant step down. The two women—bankrolled by churches and convents—weren't exactly

Wilshire material, and even here, at the lesser hotel, they'd have to share a room, crammed in together for the night. But neither was complaining about the accommodations. They were going to dinner and then straight to bed, hoping to be rested for the next day. It was going to be a long one. After the shareholders' meeting, Kenny and Malone were heading straight to LAX and taking the red-eye home.

Until then, Malone had some advice for Kenny—a little tip she had picked up after years of protesting and one that Morris, being a man, probably couldn't fully appreciate. In the morning, Malone said, it was best for Kenny to limit her water intake, and maybe skip the coffee, too. She didn't want to end up in a holding cell, a squad car, or a hotel manager's office, surrounded by beefy security guards, and realize in that moment that she needed to use the ladies' room.

Back in Niagara Falls that night, there was a "Vacancy" sign blinking outside the kitschy lodge on Main Street—John's Flaming Hearth Motor Inn—due to a couple of surprise early checkouts. The EPA had told Napal and Lucas to pack and go home, to leave immediately.

At best, the agency believed, the two men would be a distraction to the important work that needed to get done. Gibbs's stunt the day before had made the men famous, or at least notorious. They were the hostages held by the housewives, and that label was going to make it hard for them to be useful, the EPA believed. But there was perhaps another reason to get Napal and Lucas out of town. Because everyone knew who they were and what they looked like, they were easy targets for someone who was more violent than Gibbs, someone who might be looking to finish what she had started.

On his way home that day, Napal, at least, was laughing it off. The public relations man understood that he was a pawn in a play for national headlines. He was okay with that, and he wanted everyone to know that he had been treated well during the six hours he had spent inside the house on Colvin Boulevard. "In a way," Napal said, "it was amusing." But others took a less humorous view of the previous day's events.

At the EPA, Blum accused the women of taking the wrong

guys—"the wrong prisoners," she said—and at Hooker, executives believed they knew what Blum meant. They thought she was implying that Gibbs should have taken them hostage instead. As a result, Bruce Davis requested a security detail. He wanted protection in Niagara Falls, and many people hoped Gibbs would face legal consequences for her actions. But on Tuesday, the day after the hostage crisis, the U.S. attorney's office in western New York announced that it wanted a little more time to sort everything out. While federal prosecutors weren't charging Gibbs and the other women with a crime just yet, they reserved the right to change their minds, they declared, if the women didn't behave going forward.

Barbara Quimby, for one, agreed to stand down. As the mother of two little girls, including one with serious birth defects and mental disabilities, she couldn't afford to go to federal prison, even if the chances of that were small. Also, she was scarred from the night with the hostages. In the chaos getting Napal and Lucas out of the house and through the teeming crowd, FBI agents had accidentally pushed Quimby into the back of the waiting squad car, too, driving her away with the two men. It was blocks before they realized their mistake, stopped the car, and let her out, and by then Quimby had made up her mind.

"I just want to be a housewife," she said. "Today," she added, "we have to be meek."

Gibbs, on the other hand, was as loud as ever that Tuesday, defiant in the face of the U.S. attorney's directive that she avoid causing what he described as further aggravation. As Missy played on the floor of the office, coloring the flattened side of a cardboard box, Lois gave interviews almost daring authorities to come back and arrest her. She was going to say whatever she wanted, and she was going to protest again that night, too. Along with about a hundred other residents, she showed up at a meeting of the Niagara County Legislature. And when these local legislators voted 16–15 not to join the state's long-delayed effort to buy homes in the neighborhood, Gibbs commandeered a folding chair, stood up on it, and shouted at the legislators for minutes.

Twice, sheriff's deputies took Gibbs by the arms and threw her out of the chamber, and twice she marched right back in to shout some more. By the next day, she predicted, these small-time legislators were going to look like fools—"damn fools," Gibbs said. She predicted that the White House would declare its emergency—the emergency she had demanded—just hours after local legislators sat there, doing nothing. But in truth, Gibbs didn't know what the White House was going to do. Washington and Albany, Carter and Carey, were still working out the details behind the scenes, and for the moment Carter hadn't said a word.

In a memo that day, Jack Watson explained the president's options in detail, describing the chromosome study, the previous day's hostage situation, Paigen's research showing other health problems in the neighborhood, the state's long resistance to doing much of anything for the seven hundred families still there, and their own complicity, too.

"The federal government," Watson said, "has provided no assistance to helping these low and middle income families move."

He argued that it was time to change that—based on the science, the clear evidence of health damage, the mental anguish that people were suffering, the obvious urgency of the situation, and one more element. Watson described it as human need. They had to respond to the needs in Love Canal, he said, and he thought they should do it by tomorrow.

But the choice was the president's to make.

52

WE'RE FROM NIAGARA FALLS

The crowd cheered inside the grand ballroom at the Wilshire the next day and then rose to its feet, twenty-two hundred people, smiling and applauding and giving Armand Hammer what he deserved: a standing ovation.

Hammer acknowledged the applause and led his board of directors onstage, clearly relishing the moment. The Wilshire, for starters, was his kind of place. Occidental Petroleum had been holding the annual shareholders' meeting at the hotel in Beverly Hills for years, and it was company tradition to schedule the meeting as close to Hammer's birthday as possible. But today lined up perfectly—in a way that even a multimillionaire had to appreciate. It was his actual birthday.

Hammer awoke that morning to find himself eighty-two years old, defying the odds, and defying the press, too. For years, reporters had been predicting his demise—either figuratively or literally—writing stories about how the oilman was losing control of his company, how he was physically ailing or growing weak, how he sounded tired or looked unsteady. And to be fair, it was hard to blame the press. At times in the 1970s, Hammer made public appearances in a wheelchair or while hooked up to heart monitors. He looked shriveled and small, dwarfed by the large, square glasses on his face. He looked like a man who was slipping away.

But not anymore, not today. The narrative had flipped. The press was writing the story of the rally—a man in full control of his company and his faculties, jetting across the globe in his twenty-passenger Gulfstream, negotiating billion-dollar deals with Russian dictators who wouldn't even deign to meet with President Carter, and acting as a quasi-diplomat for the country through these deals. According to some press tributes, Hammer was helping to secure dividends for his shareholders and world peace for us all. The story was in *Forbes, Fortune,* and even that morning's *Los Angeles Times.* As Hammer stepped onstage in the grand ballroom, guests in the hotel lobby couldn't help but notice the *Times*'s above-the-fold, front-page profile of Hammer, splayed out across three additional pages inside and running under the flattering headline "Oil, Art, Peace: Hammer at 82 Sets Pace of Defiance."

Sitting squarely in the middle of the ballroom, a couple hundred feet from the stage and right on the aisle, Luella Kenny could not believe what she was up against. She stayed firmly planted in her seat during the standing ovation and she declined to participate in the ceremonial presentation of Hammer's birthday cake. As a little girl appeared onstage with the cake in hand—and the crowd regaled Hammer, singing him "Happy Birthday"—Kenny said nothing. Instead, she quivered with a potent cocktail of anger and anxiety coursing through her body and wondered how she'd ever stand up in front of this crowd.

It was clear that Hammer didn't want to consider resolutions from combative shareholders; he wanted to revel in the good news, and for roughly two and a half hours he and other executives did just that, enjoying the festivities, the warmth in the room, and moving through the agenda at a leisurely pace. They announced record sales for the previous year—$9.6 billion—and record earnings, too. With the company pocketing $562 million in 1979, and already off to a healthy start in 1980, Hammer said he wanted to pass these earnings on to shareholders. In the ballroom, he announced a quarterly dividend of fifty cents a share, payable on July 15. He projected another record year for 1980, equal to or exceeding the success of 1979. Executives thanked him for his instinct and his foresight, his modesty and his touch—"a very sure touch," one executive said, "that even Midas would have envied"—and then everyone settled in for a movie documenting the company's many achievements.

In the dim light of the ballroom, Kenny knew her moment was coming, and she steeled herself for it, clutching her typewritten speech in her hands, trying to stop herself from shaking, and eyeing the microphone in the aisle where she knew she was to stand. But when it came time for shareholder resolutions, Hammer tried to rush through them.

He had no patience for a resolution questioning his relationship with communist leaders, cutting off a presenter and batting his arguments away, and when it was finally Kenny's turn to go, Hammer seemed inclined to skip through the comments and get to the vote already. As the priest, Joan Malone, Bob Morris, and Kenny moved to different microphones in the room, Occidental's chief executive wondered aloud if the crowd really needed to hear from them all.

Morris was stunned.

"Dr. Hammer," he protested, "we were assured by management that we would have sufficient time to present this proposal."

At her microphone, Kenny froze. Maybe she had come to Beverly Hills for nothing.

Back in Niagara Falls that morning, Gibbs stood at her desk inside the homeowners' office on Colvin Boulevard, waiting for a call from Washington to meet the arbitrary noon deadline that she had made up in front of the angry crowd two days before. She was exhausted, and for once it showed. Her face appeared pale. Her hair was flat, matted down, and she had dark circles beneath her eyes, as if she hadn't slept in days. In truth, she hadn't really.

Between the hostage situation, her fears of being arrested, sleeping on the couch fully clothed, and shouting at the county legislators' meeting the night before, Gibbs had barely stopped all week. What she needed was rest, several hours of sleep, and some food, a good meal. But there was no time for any of that. The night before, Gibbs hadn't gotten home until after midnight. Then, amped up from all the shouting, she hadn't fallen asleep until around 1:30, and less than four hours after that the phone in her condo was ringing, waking the whole house at 5:00 a.m. Morning shows, reporters, television, and radio—everyone wanted to know the plan for the day.

Gibbs didn't have one. They were going to sit at the office, she said, hope for good news, and try not to think of anything else. She was worried what might happen if the White House chose to do nothing, and the FBI seemed worried, too. Federal agents took seriously Gibbs's remark that the hostage situation would end up looking like a "*Sesame Street* picnic" if the White House didn't take action by noon. They didn't appreciate her pointing out, after the fact, that people in the neighborhood could take hostages anytime, and federal authorities also had to have been aware of the comments Gibbs had made at the county legislators' meeting the night before—because these comments were on the front page of that morning's *Buffalo Courier-Express.* In between getting thrown out of the meeting twice, Gibbs blamed government officials for whatever people did next. "It's their fault," she said. "If they burn down the neighborhood now, it's all their fault."

Outside the office, the street was turning into a parking lot. Television trucks jockeyed for space on the curb. All three national networks were represented. ABC, NBC, and CBS would all be carrying Love Canal stories on their national broadcasts that night, and both ABC and NBC planned to lead with the news out of Niagara Falls.

But the early morning came and went with no word out of Washington. No call. At ten o'clock that morning, Gibbs still had nothing. Finally, about an hour later, she learned that Barbara Blum would be holding a press conference at the EPA's headquarters in Washington at noon, but the agency's press officer refused to reveal what Blum was going to say, and Blum wasn't calling Gibbs in advance to tell her anything. As it was, Blum was running late. She was still waiting for the go-ahead from Jack Watson at the White House—official word about whether Carter had declared an emergency—and she was apologizing to the horde of national beat writers crammed into the briefing room at the EPA.

By the time Blum walked into the room a few minutes after noon and stood behind the lectern filled with almost two dozen microphones, the EPA's deputy director was almost out of breath. She needed a moment to gather herself before delivering the verdict on the biggest, most expensive, most destructive man-made environmental problem she would ever face. Meanwhile, at the office on Colvin Boulevard, Gibbs needed a moment, too. The press there had coaxed her to string the office phone through the window and take the call outside the house, allowing the swarm of cameras to move in around her and capture everything. The only problem was,

Gibbs couldn't watch Blum's announcement live on television, and she couldn't hear it on the radio, either. In a final act of harried negotiation, Gibbs had to persuade an EPA press officer to dictate Blum's statements to her over the phone live—so that she could relay these statements to the crowd on Colvin Boulevard—as Blum herself was speaking in the press room.

At around 12:05, in both Niagara Falls and Washington, cameras finally rolled. Photographers snapped pictures, and Blum began to speak.

She got straight to the point.

"Today," Blum said, "the federal government and the state of New York are setting in motion an action plan to temporarily relocate over 700 families in the Love Canal area of Niagara Falls."

These relocations were necessary, Blum explained, in order to protect the health and welfare of people in the community and in order to respond to what she described as "cumulative evidence of exposure"—exposure to Hooker's toxic wastes. "The health effects studies performed by others so far are preliminary," Blum explained, "and none of these examined in isolation would warrant the action I am announcing today. But in the aggregate, they do suggest very significant health risks."

As a result, President Carter was issuing an emergency order.

"He just signed it," Blum said.

The order would pave the way to clear out the entire neighborhood: from Ninety-Third to 103rd Street, Black Creek to the river. Griffon Manor residents and homeowners, Black and white, everyone would be allowed to leave—and leave immediately—if they wanted, living rent-free for up to a year in another place of their choosing. In the days ahead, Blum expected these places to include hotels, motels, and local homes typically occupied by military families; the EPA was opening a relocation office in Niagara Falls that afternoon to handle all requests. But ultimately, she believed these people, who had endured so much, would transition into new apartments and permanent homes, paid for by the state or perhaps another party.

"My expectation," Blum said, "is that Hooker Chemical will pay."

In Niagara Falls, Gibbs hadn't even hung up the phone when people began to celebrate. Residents cheered, wept, honked horns, poured cheap pink champagne on each other's heads, and asked for recommendations for a hotel. A good place, if possible. Near the waterfalls, perhaps. Maybe one of those places where the tourists liked to stay.

Gibbs just smiled.

"Get your family packed," she said, "and get ready to move."

For a long moment inside the grand ballroom, Armand Hammer and Bob Morris stared each other down, while Kenny, Malone, and more than two thousand other people looked on. They had come for a birthday party—for their cake and their dividends—but the singing at the Wilshire was over now. The mood in the room had changed.

Morris demanded that his group be allowed to deliver their three statements—statements that together would last no more than ten to fifteen minutes. But Hammer pressed for something shorter. "We have other business to transact," he noted. He then allowed the priest to begin his presentation, graciously inviting him to speak, but cut him off, interrupting his talk after less than ninety seconds.

The priest and Hammer now began to squabble.

"May I finish?" the priest asked.

Given all the time they had dedicated that day to corporate movies, birthday wishes, and long speeches from executives, the priest didn't think he was asking for much, and standing at his microphone, he wanted Hammer to know that he objected.

"I respectfully object," the priest said, "to the way we are being dealt with."

"We have no objection to your objection," Hammer said as laughter rippled through the crowd. He was just moving on.

"Next speaker, please," he said.

Inside the ballroom, Kenny and Malone stood at least a hundred feet apart, positioned behind two different microphones in the crowd. And from across the room, Malone shot her a glance. It had been Malone's turn to go next; that had been the plan. But she recognized in that moment that the plan didn't matter anymore. Hammer was driving the train off the rails, and they were all just hanging on now. If Malone spoke next, it seemed possible to her that Kenny might never get her chance, and making a swift decision, the nun backed away from the microphone. Malone was ceding the floor to the woman from Niagara Falls.

Kenny looked down at her speech, remembering who she was: a mother to boys, a singer of songs, a woman who did not curse, but also one who did not suffer fools, the Italian girl from Seventeenth Street in Niagara Falls who, through a stroke of bad luck, had ended up living on the edge of an old landfill and then lost everything. She remembered these details, and then she introduced herself to the crowd, starting with the line she had written back home.

"My name," she said, "is Luella Kenny."

She explained that she used to live just a tenth of a mile from the northern edge of Love Canal. She described the creek that ran through her backyard there, and she explained how her sons had played in the waters of that creek—at least before she learned the truth about her neighborhood and before one of those sons, her youngest, Jon Allen, had gotten sick.

"Initially," she told the crowd, "his illness had been diagnosed as an allergy."

But doctors quickly realized they were wrong about that, she said. What he really had was something called nephrosis—a chronic problem that was supposed to get better in time, but didn't, and he was dead now, the boy. "Jon's death," Kenny told the crowd, "was caused by a cardiac arrest brought on by the exertion of trying to breathe."

As a mother, she had to live with that—every single day. And for a time, she was even willing to entertain the idea that Jon Allen's illness had nothing to do with the location of their home in Niagara Falls. But then, she told the crowd, she started reading medical journals. She learned that nephrosis, Jon Allen's disease, was often linked to chemical exposure, and she learned, too, that she was not alone. Other families in her neighborhood had their own medical problems—their own quiet tragedies—and suddenly, Kenny said, it was all much harder to accept.

As shareholders, she suggested, they should feel the same way. They needed to know that they were worrying about the wrong things. Instead of discussing inflation, or communism, or even Armand Hammer's cozy relationships with Soviet leaders, they should be focused on the danger in their midst—the danger all around them, perhaps.

"Why worry about an enemy who will destroy us when we are self-destructing?" Kenny said. "All we need are the multitude of dumps strategically placed all over the country that will insidiously destroy everything—and everyone—in its path."

They could all stand by and watch it happen. Or as shareholders, Kenny said, they could push Occidental and its subsidiaries to change their ways—"before it's too late."

"Now is the time," Kenny said, "to publicly exhibit what a giant we are and magnanimously lead the way in insuring a world for our grandchildren and future generations."

The crowd applauded Kenny when she was finished, and Hammer thanked her for coming. Her speech had been short, as Morris had promised, to the point, and not overly dramatic, and Hammer wanted her to know that he appreciated that, and her.

"We sympathize greatly with your predicament," he said.

He could have left it at that and pushed on with the meeting. But Hammer couldn't help himself. For the next few minutes, he explained in wandering detail all of the reasons why Kenny was misinformed on this topic. For one thing, he said, Occidental didn't own Hooker Chemical back when the company had dumped in the canal; Hammer had inherited this problem when he acquired Hooker in 1968. But even if Occidental had owned the land back in the 1950s, he said, it still wouldn't be the company's fault, because the deed absolved it of any liability. He then seemed to question the seriousness of the problem—as though only a few houses were affected, or only a few kids had been burned on a playground. He attacked the chromosome study for all its known flaws. He repeatedly blamed officials in Buffalo—the school board and the road builders in Buffalo—apparently mistaking one blue-collar city in western New York for another, and he told Kenny if she really had a problem, she should take it up with local officials there in Buffalo, or just be thankful that President Carter had gotten involved today. Hammer informed Kenny about the emergency declaration handed down in Washington that morning.

"I think the actions of our president in doing what he has done," Hammer said, "ought to satisfy you and your neighbors."

With that, Hammer declared, he was finished with this discussion. He wasn't going to recognize Sister Joan Malone. He wasn't going to allow any more debate on this topic, and he didn't care what Bob Morris had to say about it. The shareholders voted to end the comments with a show of hands. They struck Kenny's resolution down, and then they turned on the group, cheering when Hammer asked the sergeant at arms to remove Morris from the meeting for continuing to ask questions.

"Would you please eject this gentleman?" Hammer said.

At that point, Malone tried to jump in several times. But she got nowhere, too.

"I don't care what your opinion is right now," Hammer told Malone, and he seemingly didn't want to hear Kenny's opinions anymore, either. Just minutes after thanking her for coming and extending her his sympathies, Hammer now cut Kenny off, too.

"We are not going to listen to you," he said.

"You haven't listened to us," Kenny shot back.

"Why do you come here?" he asked. "Why don't you go to Buffalo?"

"We're from Niagara Falls," Kenny said, correcting him.

She was glad to have that on the record. But the correction seemed to only frustrate Hammer more. He didn't know why they were still talking about this or why she was even there—unless it was just about making headlines.

"Is that your purpose in coming here?" he asked.

No, Kenny replied.

"We're determined to see that no other child dies in this world because of corporate irresponsibility."

Hammer then threatened to throw her out of the ballroom, too. She could join Morris on the sidewalk outside the hotel if she wanted. But the company, heading off a possible public relations disaster, found a better way.

It cut Kenny's microphone and quickly brought the meeting to a close.

—

On the red-eye home that night, Kenny could not know the impact that she'd had. She was isolated from the world, tucked away deep in coach, and flying east in the darkness, filled with old questions and new doubts about the future.

Back in Niagara Falls, people were already shouting again. The poorest residents of the neighborhood were rightly frustrated that they didn't have the money to just pick up and relocate—unless someone was going to front them the cash now. Homeowners were still demanding that officials buy their houses outright—a demand that would go unmet until the fall—and Governor Carey was complaining that the president hadn't done enough for the people, just as White House staffers predicted he would. This fight, everyone knew, was far from over.

Yet, without question, something had shifted—both in Niagara Falls and inside Luella Kenny herself. While she was in the air that night, the *Los Angeles Times* and *The Wall Street Journal* were printing their dispatches from the Occidental shareholders' meeting. The wire services picked up their stories, telling the tale of the nun and the mother from Niagara Falls who had stared down the multimillionaire capitalist, and Malone made sure to alert local reporters back home that the news was coming. From a pay phone at the airport before takeoff, she called newsrooms across western New York to explain what had happened at the meeting, shaking with anger as she recounted the details.

By the time Luella's plane landed in Buffalo the next morning and Norman picked her up at the airport, the news of her confrontation was everywhere. Networks were trying to find Luella Kenny, and at least one was already waiting on the curb outside her mother-in-law's house in Niagara Falls, hoping to interview her as soon as she got home.

Jet-lagged and exhausted, Kenny agreed to sit for the cameras, while outside, on the street, the city bustled with the sounds of change. Roughly seventy families had already moved out of the neighborhood since the relocation order, and dozens more were packing at that moment, throwing their belongings in boxes and walking out the door. It was the start of an exodus that would nearly empty the neighborhood in the months to come, and this time there were signs that it was for good. In a meeting at the Howard Johnson's Motor Lodge that day, officials told residents they should forget about booking hotel rooms and go get apartments instead, something more like home.

No one was ever going to have to spend another night living on the edge of Hooker's old landfill, wondering if chemicals were harming their children. They could leave right now if they wanted, reporting to the relocation office to file their paperwork and learn their options. Officials would be working straight through the upcoming holiday weekend, Memorial Day weekend, to find people a place to live, and Lois Gibbs would be working, too. Everyone knew where to find her: in the office, in the neighborhood, toiling day and night to make sure politicians didn't forget about the people in Love Canal.

But not Luella Kenny. Not that weekend at least. If they wanted to reach her, she said, they'd have to call her in New York City. For weeks, Norman had been planning to attend a convention there for Polish choirs, and Luella had not only agreed to go with him and sing; she had promised to take the boys. It was a promise she intended to keep. The Kenny family was going away.

That weekend, Luella and Norman sang Polish ballads with old friends. The boys, Christopher and Stephen, scampered through the halls of their Manhattan hotel. The whole family attended a show at Radio City Music Hall—the Kennys were tourists on the town, doing touristy things—and then on Monday, Luella surprised the kids. A state senator had given Luella four tickets to the New York Yankees game that afternoon. They were going to be sitting right behind home plate.

Later, much later, none of them would be able to remember the score of the game that day, if the Yankees won, or whom they even played. But each of them would recall with crystal clarity the feeling they had that afternoon—Luella, perhaps, most of all. The sun was shining; spring had come to New York. She was sitting in the finest seats at Yankee Stadium, and her children were smiling, amazed at their good fortune.

Someone ordered popcorn. Luella and Norman shared a beer, and at some point it dawned on her why she felt so different. In the crowd at the stadium, no one knew who they were. No one could find them, even if they wanted to, and no one was going to remind them about where they lived or what they had lost.

For the first time in years, they were just like everybody else. They were a family at a ball game, and they were happy.

EPILOGUE

President Carter finally visited Niagara Falls four months later, touching down on Air Force One just a couple miles from William T. Love's old canal on the first day of October 1980. He then climbed into a black limousine bearing the presidential seal and streamed to the convention center downtown in an impressive thirty-vehicle motorcade that stopped traffic across the city and brought crowds of people to the edge of the road.

Carter was the first president to set foot in Niagara Falls in almost two decades, but he was going to be there for only a few hours, and he had no time to stop at the city's two most famous sites. He skipped the falls altogether, and if he saw the canal itself, it was only out the windows of his moving limousine. On its way to and from the airport, the motorcade skirted the edge of the neighborhood on the east side of town, rolling right past Griffon Manor, the sad streets lined with empty bungalows, and the old Hooker landfill. But there would be no photo of the president in this place known far and wide as Love Canal.

With just a month to go until Election Day 1980, Carter was in danger of losing both the White House and the state of New York to Ronald Reagan, and Carter's press team couldn't have the president strolling through a contaminated neighborhood that one reporter described as "a monument to despair," a neighborhood where agitated residents had taken federal agents hostage that spring. The event that evening in Niagara Falls was to be controlled, invite only, and the news would be strictly positive: Carter was there to join Governor Carey and John LaFalce in signing an agreement that would allot $20 million in federal and state money to finally begin purchasing hundreds of homes in the neighborhood and start relocating people for good.

For residents, it was about time. From the moment Carter had issued his emergency declaration that spring allowing people to temporarily relocate, residents had called upon state and federal officials to end years of fighting with them—and each other—and buy their homes already. At a public meeting in late May, just days after the presidential order, Arthur Tracy, a resident of 102nd Street for some thirty-five years, might have said it best.

"If somebody was going to say to me, 'What do you want, Mr. Tracy, after thirty-five years in this Love Canal?' I'll tell you what I want," he said. "Just give me the $28,500 you appraised my house for—boy, you sure are good to me. I loved every minute of it," he noted with sarcasm. "You give me my $28,500," he said again, and then he turned to the crowd with a question.

"What time is it now?"

"Seven thirty-seven," someone said.

"Seven thirty-seven," Tracy said, nodding, "and I'll be out of here at 10:37. And you won't have to worry about a motel and you won't have to worry about anything."

The people howled in agreement that night because they understood how Tracy felt. In the end, as in the beginning, residents just wanted out, and they felt that they had earned that. If Hooker couldn't definitively say what the buried contents in the canal might do to them—and state and federal scientists couldn't say, either—then most people wanted the chance to leave and start over somewhere else. But even after Carter's emergency declaration in May, it took the entire summer and most of the fall of 1980 to sort out the details about who would pay for what. Meanwhile, critics, including top Hooker executives, continued to question the science—namely, the all-important chromosome study—looking for reasons not to clear out the neighborhood and raising questions, some of them legitimate, until most people didn't know what to believe anymore, except maybe one thing. "A whole neighborhood is stigmatized to the point that the property there is literally valueless," LaFalce told President Carter that July, "and the people who live there frightened beyond belief."

One U.S. senator presciently pointed out that the entire affair proved just how unprepared the nation was at every level to face an unexpected public health crisis, and he called upon authorities to heed the lessons of Love Canal—a case study in mistakes, miscommunication, finger-pointing, secrets, the limitations of science, and the dangers of half-truths, and an expensive case study, at that. The state of New York would ultimately spend $74 million on cleanup and evacuation costs at the canal. The federal government would have to chip in an additional $101 million, and Hooker Chemical would, effectively, cease to exist. In the wake of the scandal and the stigma, Occidental dropped the Hooker name altogether, erasing the legacy of Elon Hooker's men and going with the name Occidental Chemical instead. The company set aside an estimated $750 million to cover what one industry analyst called its "environmental liabilities"—its legal costs—and then, throughout the 1980s and 1990s, it settled one massive Love Canal lawsuit after another until the company paid out almost a quarter of a billion dollars to the state, the U.S. government, and the residents themselves.

But during his brief appearance in Niagara Falls in October 1980, President Carter mentioned none of these looming problems. Instead, he basked in the spotlight with Carey and LaFalce, promising that America would never again endure another Love Canal, standing atop his limousine at one point to wave to the crowd, and even inviting Gibbs to join him onstage to share in this moment—a moment that, Carter said, Gibbs had helped create.

Gibbs, of course, understood what the purpose of the event was.

"He needs New York for votes," she remarked. "It's going to be a close election."

Yet even she couldn't criticize Carter after he squeezed her hand onstage and congratulated her for everything she had done for her neighborhood and was still doing for him, in fact, at that very moment.

The president was about to lose to Reagan in a landslide, the likes of which are hard to imagine today. In November 1980, liberal strongholds including New York, Oregon, Washington, Reagan's home state of California, and every state in New England except Rhode Island all voted Republican—for Reagan—sending Carter back to Georgia in a humiliating and historic defeat. But in the lame-duck congressional session that fall—in the brief amount of time that Carter had left in the White House—another thing happened that's just as hard to imagine these days: Democrats and Republicans, working together in the House and Senate, passed sweeping bipartisan legislation that forever changed U.S. environmental policy.

It didn't matter that Carter had lost. It didn't matter that powerful corporate lobbyists, including the Chemical Manufacturers Association, opposed the legislation, and it also didn't matter that senators and representatives knew that the president-elect, Reagan, would likely oppose what they were doing at that very moment. As Reagan said on the campaign trail in language that was easy to decode, "There is a difference between environmentalism and environmental extremism."

In the final weeks of Carter's administration, Congress passed what we know today as the Superfund Act—a $1.6 billion fund, at the time, financed almost exclusively with fees on the polluters themselves and designed to hold companies accountable for burying poison in the ground, dumping chemicals in lakes and streams, emitting foul gases into the air, and generally polluting the environment.

The legislation, two years in the making, was flawed when it finally reached Carter's desk in early December, watered down with compromises, and it remains an imperfect solution today, weakened even further over time by industry lobbyists and conservative politicians. In 1995, Newt Gingrich's Republican-controlled Congress let lapse the corporate tax at the heart of the Superfund legislation—the idea that the polluter pays. People interested in protecting the environment were furious. "There is no reason to destroy a law that makes most polluters pay for the mess they have made," the *St. Louis Post-Dispatch* declared in an editorial at the time. "If we cannot find some responsible party to pay for the cleanup," one policymaker explained, "the states could get stuck with the bill and the polluters will get away."

But Democrats were powerless to preserve the tax, and without it, there have been new problems: slower cleanups, languishing sites, and more suffering for ordinary Americans. Decades after Carter signed the original legislation, working-class families and people of color are far more likely to live near a Superfund site than anyone else.

Still, despite these shortcomings, the Superfund Act has altered the American landscape for the better in the last four decades, giving federal authorities the power to begin remediating nearly two thousand sites since 1980, turning contaminated textile mills into soccer fields, converting toxic landfills into wind farms, transforming piles of incinerator ash into public tennis courts for children, and remaking old asbestos plants into lush green riverfront parks.

Even more important, studies have shown that Superfund interventions help reduce the chances of childhood lead poisoning and the risks of babies being born with birth defects. By this measure, the legislation—sparked by Love Canal, developed by EPA administrators, supported by elected officials across the political spectrum in a lost era of bipartisanship, and signed by Carter in one of his final acts as president—has saved or improved countless American lives. And though it was undoubtedly a collective effort, only one person found fame as a result.

They called her the "Mother of the Superfund"—Lois Gibbs.

Like a rock star, Gibbs went on tour in the summer of 1980. She returned to Washington with reporters in tow. She made appearances on *Good Morning America* and the nation's most popular daytime television talk show hosted by Phil Donahue. And then, at the invitation of Jane Fonda, Gibbs flew to California to visit a handful of toxic waste sites on the West Coast. Fonda and her husband, the civil rights activist Tom Hayden, were starting a movement called the Campaign for Economic Democracy, and there was no one better suited to help bring attention to their cause than America's most famous citizen activist: Lois Gibbs.

Her hostage stunt that May had been roundly criticized by her allies and her enemies alike. The local press, Hooker executives, legal authorities, other residents of the neighborhood, and the Black residents in particular couldn't believe what she had done. If Gibbs were Black, one resident of Griffon Manor said at the time, "she'd still be in jail now." These days, Gibbs conceded, that would surely be true. An activist, even a young mother of two, could never hold federal agents against their will today, she believes, without facing some sort of criminal charge, some sort of consequence. But in 1980, the FBI chose to let it go, and the legend of Lois Gibbs only grew.

A producer at *60 Minutes* at the time called Gibbs a "most clever tactician" and one of the smartest media manipulators in America. In television interviews, Gibbs knew to keep her answers short, honing the art and science of the sound bite. At public meetings, she realized she had to speak in the first fifteen minutes—even if it meant interrupting officials—in order to make newspaper deadlines. And when reporters asked her a question she didn't want to address, Gibbs had a proven strategy for that, too. "Just drag out your answer," she said. "They'll never use it."

According to one profile written about her that summer, she had gone in the span of just two years from being "mama, maker of peanut butter sandwiches, housewife, doer of laundry, and scrubber of kitchen floors" to "an unlikely badgerer of bigwigs, corraller of politicians, and, in May, taker of hostages." One of those hostages—the EPA's public relations man, Frank Napal—even wrote Gibbs a telegram after the fact, congratulating her for her success and wishing her all the best. "I miss your oatmeal cookies," Napal wrote, before signing off, "Your Happy Hostage, Frank." And in the summer of 1980, Jane Fonda helped Gibbs sell the film rights to her story, paving the way for a made-for-TV movie called *Lois Gibbs and Love Canal* that aired on CBS two years later in February 1982.

By then, Gibbs was in her early thirties and had started a new chapter in her life. Not only had she and Harry officially divorced, but Lois and the kids had left Niagara Falls altogether, moving from their condo on the edge of the old neighborhood to live with a certain scientist in Arlington, Virginia: the homeowners' state-hired toxicologist, Stephen Lester. The couple married in 1983. The bride kept her name, and together Gibbs and Lester began running an organization called the Center for Health, Environment & Justice. The goal, Gibbs explained at the time, was simple. She wanted to help other people learn how to organize against major corporations and big government, powerful forces that seem beyond the control of little people—people like Gibbs had once been and, in her mind, still was.

But between the new job, which kept her in the spotlight and in the press all the time, hopping from one man-made disaster to another, and the movie treatment, which dramatized her story for millions of viewers, Gibbs wasn't so little anymore, and her fame came with a certain cost, if not for her, then at least for others. "At some point," one Buffalo columnist wrote, "Lois Gibbs *became* Love Canal." Everyone else faded into the shadows.

Bonnie Casper's role in exposing the problems in Niagara Falls as a young, unheralded congressional aide in John LaFalce's office went unrecognized and completely forgotten. Hollywood producers never called Luella Kenny, despite everything she had survived, and with the spotlight fixed on Gibbs from the start, the press was quick to ignore every other citizen leader who emerged in the neighborhood in the late 1970s—especially perhaps those who emerged in Griffon Manor. Still, it was impossible not to appreciate what Gibbs had managed to accomplish. Homeowners praised her—"Thank you, Lois Gibbs," one person spray-painted on his house, before abandoning it forever—and residents of Griffon Manor complimented Gibbs, too. In 1980, shortly after President Carter's emergency declaration making possible the relocation of both homeowners and residents of Griffon Manor, Sarah Herbert, the newest tenant leader in the public housing development, gave Gibbs credit for getting them all out. "I believe Lois has done good for all of us," Herbert said. "In this neighborhood, Black and white doesn't matter because we're all in the same boat."

It was a theme that Gibbs herself would sound in the decades to come, and still sounds today, at seventy years old, as she goes from town to town, helping people organize by explaining what she did once long ago, when she was young and scared, in a place called Love Canal. She especially enjoys telling ordinary folks that they are more powerful than they think.

"The American people," she likes to say, "don't know the power that they have."

Then Lois climbs into her car to go home, back to Stephen in Virginia. She's a grandmother now, but still the same woman she used to be. The letters stamped on the license plate of her car make that perfectly clear.

The plate reads, "TOXIC 2."

Beverly Paigen didn't take long to decide that she was also leaving western New York. From the earliest days of the Love Canal crisis, Paigen had predicted that it probably wouldn't end well for her at Roswell Park, and it didn't. In the spring of 1980, just two weeks after President Carter signed the emergency declaration, the board at Roswell Park denied Paigen's harassment claims, finding no evidence that Axelrod or her direct superiors had engaged in "political interference" as a result of Paigen's activities in Niagara Falls.

The local press and at least one prominent state lawmaker immediately dismissed the decision as "bunk," "unsatisfactory," and "suspect"—"a suspect review," the *Buffalo Courier-Express* called it. The newspaper's editorial board believed there was no way Paigen could have received a fair hearing, given the influence that Axelrod held over the people assigned to rule on her case, and it demanded an investigation. The newspaper called on Governor Carey to form an independent commission to review everything about his handling of Love Canal, "including, as one major aspect of that, the handling of the Paigen case."

Carey listened—sort of. In June 1980, he appointed a five-member panel to examine two years of scientific findings from the neighborhood. But the panel didn't reconsider any aspect of Paigen's harassment claims—her case was closed—and by the time the panel released its report that fall, finding no evidence of any acute health effects in the neighborhood and rejecting the housewife surveys as "literally impossible to interpret," Paigen knew her days at Roswell Park were numbered.

She had long believed that she was being watched, and as it turned out, she was. In 2021, responding to a Freedom of Information request filed for this book, the state of New York released three hundred pages of previously shielded memos, letters, and reports detailing the level of concern—obsession, even—that top state health officials had about Paigen. These documents, though heavily redacted at times, reveal that her bosses, including Axelrod, wanted to know whom she was speaking to and when; what she had said and how; if she had mentioned her Roswell Park credentials in the interview; and if she had been cleared to make these contacts in advance. If she was appearing with Gibbs or Kenny, they wanted to know about it. If she was talking to Channel 4 or Channel 7 in Buffalo, they wanted to know that, too. And when she began discussing her story with producers at *60 Minutes* in early 1980, the Department of Health's top public relations man, Marvin Nailor, informed Axelrod right away. "We should discuss the scenario," Nailor said.

But with the board's rejection of her harassment claims in June that year, Paigen's experiences at work reached a new low. Someone was now opening her mail before she could get to it, she alleged, and the unauthorized reader, whom Paigen believed to be a top administrator, wasn't even trying to hide the transgression. She reported that the opened letters were resealed with tape and placed in her mailbox. It was time for her to go.

In the summer of 1981, while on their annual vacation to Mount Desert Island in Maine, Beverly and Ken laid out their options to their two youngest children, now fourteen and ten years old. The couple had employment opportunities in North Carolina, Utah, and California, they said, and they wanted the kids to help them choose a new home. Later, Beverly's son, David, would come to realize it was something of a parenting ruse. Beverly and Ken knew they were moving to California, where she had a research job waiting for her at Children's Hospital in Oakland and Ken was going to be running the genetics department at the University of California in Berkeley—a bit of an upgrade over Roswell Park. But because the move was going to be disruptive to the kids—especially David, who was in high school—Beverly and Ken wanted their buy-in. Needed it, really. And inside the house in Maine, the couple guided the kids to the only reasonable choice.

Months later, in statements made just before the Paigens' official departure in the spring of 1982, Axelrod denied that he had ever participated in any kind of harassment against Beverly. "I've never harassed any employee in the health department," he said, "and I've never sanctioned such a process." But he also wasn't inclined to compliment Beverly on her way out the door, citing what he called their "major disagreements." While thanking Ken for his "outstanding contribution" to scientific knowledge during his twenty-seven years at Roswell Park, Axelrod would say only that Beverly had "fulfilled a role."

In the years to come, Axelrod and Paigen never fully resolved their personal or scientific differences. As the Pulitzer Prize–winning environmental writer Dan Fagin noted in 2013, the neighborhood was—and is—a Rorschach test "in which people see what they wish to see" and no one is right and no one is wrong. In time, scientists even reversed themselves on the chromosome report. In a 1984 study performed on forty-six former Love Canal residents—including seventeen people from the original chromosome experiment—the Centers for Disease Control reported no significant chromosome damage whatsoever.

But in the 1980s, a few events unfolded allowing Paigen to claim at least a partial victory. In 1983, she published a comprehensive study of 523 children, both Black and white, who had grown up in the Love Canal neighborhood and then compared their health problems with a control population of 440 similar children living elsewhere in Niagara Falls. Paigen made sure the controls matched her study population as closely as possible—both racially and socioeconomically—and then announced the first of several findings. Children born and raised in Love Canal, she said, were physically smaller than their cohorts outside the neighborhood. "The simple truth," Paigen announced, "is that children who grew up near the canal show evidence of retarded growth patterns."

Two years later, analyzing the same study group, Paigen identified seven maladies that children from Love Canal suffered at rates far exceeding the control: seizures, learning disabilities, hyperactivity, abdominal pain, rashes, eye irritation, and kidney problems. Six of these seven conditions were found to be elevated in the "wet" areas of the neighborhood—along the old swales. And while Paigen couldn't say if chemical agents had caused the problems, she couldn't rule it out, either—especially given what she knew about dioxin, neurotoxins, and other chemicals known to be buried in the old canal. Either way, Paigen said, the elevated rates of these seven health problems were unlikely to be caused by stress or biased reporting from people who wanted to get out of the neighborhood. Most people by then were already gone. By the mid-1980s, only sixty-two families remained, and about a dozen of these stubborn holdouts were about to move, because they had no choice in the matter. They lived in Griffon Manor, and the development was finally being torn down.

But Paigen's greatest vindication was perhaps the announcement that Axelrod himself made in Niagara Falls in September 1988. After ten long years studying the troubled neighborhood from every possible angle, Axelrod declared that the state was going to permit the resettlement of 220 homes north and west of the canal—the Kennys' side of the neighborhood—under some limitations and conditions. Axelrod wanted authorities to finish removing twelve thousand cubic yards of dioxin-contaminated sediment from the creeks where Jon Allen had once played. The land east of the canal, however—everything from Ninety-Ninth to 103rd Street—was uninhabitable, Axelrod announced, due to slightly elevated levels of several chemicals in the soil that might have migrated there along buried utility lines, in tainted dirt dumped there as fill during home construction in the 1950s, in the dust on the wind, or in one other possible way—as "surface runoff of leachate along swales."

Axelrod had finally granted some validity to Gibbs and Paigen's swale theory, but there was little cheering in Niagara Falls. The people still living in homes near the old canal were furious that Axelrod had labeled their neighborhood poisoned, while those who had escaped long ago—Gibbs and others—couldn't believe the state was going to resettle the area and sell their old homes to new residents at prices estimated at anywhere between $35,000 and $100,000.

Everyone was still arguing about the plan three years later in 1991, when Axelrod suffered a massive stroke at the age of fifty-six and slipped into a coma from which he would never truly recover. His wife had to resign his position for him two months later, notifying the state that he would no longer be serving as health commissioner. He died in 1994 in a rehab facility north of Albany. Paigen, on the other hand, lived into her eighties—just long enough to retire to the house in Maine where she liked to spend her summers, take her lunches with Ken in the dining room enjoying the view of the ocean out the windows, and tell her story one last time before both she and Ken died in the span of four months in 2020.

Her memory in that final year wasn't what it once was, and she would apologize whenever she had to stop and circle back to collect a thought or detail she had forgotten.

"But it'll come," she promised, sitting at that table near the windows.

In the meantime, there were some documents in the small office down the hall.

"We're talking about a file cabinet," she said. "Four drawers."

Maybe more, she added, considering the boxes she had in storage. Beverly Paigen, always neat and meticulous, had saved everything, as if she were just waiting for someone to come to Maine, drive up the gravel road to her house, and ask her about that time in Niagara Falls all those years ago when she chose to risk everything for what she believed.

"Well," she said, opening the file cabinet, "what are you looking for?"

In the end, only one woman would remain in western New York.

Like the others, she had left the neighborhood long ago. And like the others, she could have gone just about anywhere. But Luella Kenny was never leaving the area. She and Norman, and the boys, went only as far as Grand Island—about ten miles from their old house on Ninety-Sixth Street. They bought a new home near the banks of the Niagara River, rushing north toward the falls, and here Luella would stay.

She wanted to remain close to Niagara Falls to be able to visit Jon Allen in the cemetery, and later Norman, when he died, too. She wanted to serve on the Love Canal Medical Fund—a nonprofit set up with Hooker settlement money—disseminating awards to people suffering from health problems today that might possibly be related to the time when they lived in the neighborhood in the 1970s or 1980s. She wanted to help.

As the years went by, Kenny realized that she was good at the work, and she also realized that she could do more. She could give speeches and visit classrooms. She could tell young students about what had happened at Love Canal, because every once in a while young students want to know. Then, if there's time or the teacher will allow, Kenny takes people out to the old neighborhood and gives them a tour.

"I give good tours," she boasted at age eighty-two. "You don't know how many tours I give."

On her trips out there, she moves west to east, starting downtown, on the side of the canal where Griffon Manor once stood, and then turns north toward her end of the neighborhood. She cuts along the edge of the canal itself—still fenced off from the world around it—and eases into the resettled parts of the neighborhood, where, Kenny notes, some families claim to have new problems and have filed new lawsuits. They're worried about the odd smells in their kitchens or the illnesses they can't explain. They're worried because of where they chose to live: in a little house on the east side of Niagara Falls.

"Turn right over here," Kenny says. "We're going into Love Canal . . . They call it Black Creek Village now . . . The school was right here . . . And my house is right back there . . . Right at the end of the street . . . See that kind of redbrick house with the small windows? That was my house . . . Mrs. Schultz lived next door here. The Kolanos lived over here and—I'm trying to think of his name, Ted? . . . They're pretty nice houses and people didn't want to move from there. But eventually some of them did . . .

"Turn left . . . See the fence? Turn left here . . . I want to show you the other side of the neighborhood that was declared not habitable . . . This was a residential street—Lois's street . . . It's not too bad today, but usually this is like the dumping ground—you find old couches, you find everything dumped here . . . Nobody lives here . . . Totally abandoned . . . This looks abandoned . . .

"When I was eighty, I thought, you know, I should retire from this . . . But I made up my mind—like I made up my mind that I have to talk about Jon . . . I have to tell people about him because I couldn't live with myself if I didn't . . . Is it helping? I don't know . . . Let's go straight and I'll take you down Buffalo Avenue . . . That was part of the evacuation . . . I'll show you . . . I don't know if you want to get close—or stop . . . You could turn here, if you want to get another look . . . Did you get a good picture of it? Of Love Canal?"

ACKNOWLEDGMENTS

Every word of this book—from the first to the last—was written in the thick of the pandemic and in the face of some sort of quarantine lockdown. If you lived through it, as I did, you can appreciate the challenges of that endeavor.

As I wrote, my two children were remote learning in the house. My wife, at least early on, was hardly working, her office shuttered. One close friend died of COVID; loved ones got sick and recovered. We doomscrolled. We panic purchased canned goods. We were more fortunate than many, and yet we still struggled in all the usual ways. And then, amid it all, there was this book to write—with the archives closed and my last two research trips scrapped—as my kids Zoomed in the next room and sometimes in this room, my office. It was a long year.

To get through a time like this, we all needed a crew, and I was lucky to have mine: my parents and my brother and sister, whom I almost never saw but talked to all the time; the good friends who checked in and kept reaching out to make sure I hadn't fallen into the abyss—David Abel, Jim and Alissa Bartkus, Chris Blagg, Brett Clanton, Dan Crow, Jeff Goldscher, Tom and Julie Haines, Eric Heinberg, Chris Hitler, John Lilly, Ian McNulty, Sam Patel, Mark Price, Jennifer and Steven Serio, Ed and Cheryl Thompson, Scott Voegele, Dan Wenner, and Dave Yu; our enduring and beautiful bubble, the Carlson and Moriarty families, who made the act of writing possible; and my friend, the wonderful author James Tobin, who assured me at my lowest point that I wasn't lost. I would find my way, he said, out of the dark, deep forest. He was right.

As usual, librarians and archivists also saved the day, helping me on the ground before the pandemic and then remotely, after COVID sent everyone home for months, gathering important historical documents at my request and sharing them with me digitally and by mail. I couldn't have finished this book without the kindness, generosity, knowledge, and assistance of Cynthia Van Ness at the Buffalo History Museum; Youlanda Logan at the Jimmy Carter Presidential Library and Museum; Jim Folts and Bill Gorman at the New York State Archives; Pam Hopkins at the Tufts University Archives; Linda Webster at Buffalo State College; Courtney Geerhart in the Local History Department at the Niagara Falls Public Library; Jessica Hollister and William Offhaus at the University at Buffalo; Wanda Calderon, Stephen McBay, and Elias Rodríguez at the EPA; Jess Ross, my local librarian near my home in New Hampshire, who handled my many interlibrary loan requests; Yana Dushko at the New York State Department of Health, who processed the massive Freedom of Information requests for this book under less-than-ideal circumstances; Kristina Curtis, who tracked down the Love Canal legal case files in boxes in storage at the National Archives in Missouri; and the deputy clerk of court at the federal courthouse in Buffalo, "Miss Betty," who ordered those boxes for me and allowed me to camp out in her office for days, requesting hundreds of photocopies.

I also couldn't have made it without others who assisted along the way: Will Battersby and Tamara Jones, who introduced me to Lois Gibbs and Luella Kenny; my trusted research assistant Michelle Betters, who due to the pandemic didn't get to travel as much as she had hoped; the authors who tackled this subject before me, including most importantly the late Adeline Levine and the former *Niagara Gazette* reporter Michael Brown; Sadie Garland, who scrolled through days of microfilm for me; John Pasquale, who taught me about the science of chemical exposure; Dr. Caroline Straatmann, the pediatric nephrologist who helped me understand Jon Allen Kenny's illness; and Melinda Miller, a former reporter for *The Buffalo News,* who gathered material for me in western New York, when I myself could not travel there, and allowed me to double my efforts there in late 2019 and early 2020—time that, as it turned out, I would need. Without Melinda's work, toiling beside me in the weeks before the lockdown, I wouldn't have been able to collect everything necessary to write this book.

But *Paradise Falls* wasn't created with just records and documents. I also conducted interviews with people who lived through this time, meeting them in person before the pandemic and speaking to them by phone after it changed our lives. There are too many to thank here, yet a few must be mentioned: Lois Gibbs; Luella Kenny; Elene Thornton's family—Jackie Nix, Howard Nix, Kathryn Thornton, and Audrey Thornton; Agnes Jones's daughter Carol; Sarah Rich, a former resident and leader in Griffon Manor, who met with me twice in her nursing home in Niagara Falls, shortly before her death in the spring of 2020; the White House and EPA staffers Jack Watson, Tom Jorling, Chuck Warren, Larry Snowhite, Eliot Cutler, and Bruce Kirschenbaum; the Hugh Carey staffers Robert Morgado and Robert Schiffer; the former U.S. representative John LaFalce and his aide Rich Lee. These sources not only gave generously of their time, taking my calls again and again; they welcomed me into their homes, before the pandemic, and dug through their attics, garages, and storage units in search of Love Canal documents they had saved in boxes for decades—documents that, until now, had never seen the light of day.

I will not soon forget having lunch with the former EPA deputy director Barbara Blum inside her townhome in Washington, D.C., and then retiring to her basement for hours to go through the boxes she kept in a storage unit there—a storage unit packed from the floor to the ceiling. I am forever indebted to Bonnie Casper, who not only took my call and agreed to meet with me in early 2020 but then scoured her Maryland home for the Love Canal boxes she had kept, sharing these invaluable records with me. And I must also mention Beverly Paigen, Paigen's caregiver Amy Picard, and the entire Paigen family, including most notably her children, David, Jennifer, and Gina, and her granddaughter Cassia Roth. In what turned out to be the final months of Paigen's life, Beverly graciously met with me over two long days in her home in Maine, recalled for me the road she had traveled one last time, and then opened up her records, too. I never thought I would be scanning hundreds of documents outside a storage shed, with a view of the water in Maine. But thanks to Beverly—and her children—that happened, too.

Of course, I must thank my agent, the amazing Richard Abate; Reagan Arthur, the publisher at Knopf, who recognized the power of this story from the start; Lisa Lucas, my publisher at Pantheon, whose love for great books inspires me to be better; and my editor, the talented Maria Goldverg, who, just like me, was working from home throughout this entire process and wouldn't allow me to use my work-from-home situation or my general pandemic angst as an excuse not to meet my deadlines. Maria made this book stronger with her insightful edits every step of the way—as did three other people who read the manuscript over my shoulder. My friend and former editor, James O'Byrne, helped me shape this narrative, as if it were his job. It wasn't. But without James's support I'm not sure I would have finished. My lifelong pal Andrew Bauer improved the book every time he read it, just as he has improved every book I have ever written; Andrew remains the best editor *not* to be working in publishing. And then there's my wife, Eva. She not only edited the manuscript along the way; she lived it with me. Without Eva, none of this happens.

Finally, a note about the dedication: In the summer of 2020, staring down a full academic year of remote learning, one of our sons announced that he couldn't do it; he preferred to be homeschooled. As working parents, my wife and I weren't in a position to make that happen, but as our son talked about the challenges he had faced after a spring of Zooms, we realized we couldn't say no, either. Scrambling, we connected with two other families in our small community who were interested in homeschooling to get through the year and then began creating a curriculum for our kids. We all took a job, and suddenly, among other things, I was a part-time English teacher, too.

It was every bit as hard as it sounds, and we were far from perfect. We failed all the time, as parents and as teachers. But the children—including both of my sons—gave me purpose in a dark time. They made me laugh. They reminded me that we were still alive. On their best days, they energized me with their love for words. On their worst days, they at least forced me to get out of bed and shower. And at some point, as the fog of the year lifted, I realized something.

The kids had saved me.

NOTES

ABBREVIATIONS USED IN NOTES

Newspapers

BCE	*Buffalo Courier-Express*
BEN	*Buffalo Evening News*
LAT	*Los Angeles Times*
NG	*Niagara Gazette/Niagara Falls Gazette*
NYDN	*New York Daily News*
NYT	*New York Times*
RDC	*Rochester (N.Y.) Democrat and Chronicle*

Collections

CC	Bonnie Casper Personal Collection
LGLC	Lois Gibbs Love Canal Papers, Tufts University
PC	Beverly Paigen Personal Collection

Book

LW Michael H. Brown, *Laying Waste: The Poisoning of America by Toxic Chemicals* (New York: Pantheon Books, 1980)

INTRODUCTION

3 **sixteen acres:** "Love Canal: Public Health Time Bomb—a Special Report to the Governor and Legislature," New York State Department of Health, Sept. 1978.

3 **Parents sometimes wondered:** Former residents, interviews with author, including Lois Gibbs, Nov. 25, 2019, and Luella Kenny, Nov. 25, 2019.

3 **Debbie Gallo—eleven years old:** The details of the incident involving Deb-

bie Gallo and other children on the playground in May 1972 come primarily from these sources: Debbie Gallo, interview with author, April 1, 2020; Karen Gallo (Debbie's mother), interview with author, March 12, 2021; Bruno Primerano, interview with author, March 23, 2020; and two detailed reports, Record Group 412, Love Canal Docket Hazardous Waste Enforcement Files, box 4, National Archives, College Park, Md. One of these is the company report filed by Hooker's safety supervisor on May 15, 1972, after his visit to the site: G. F. Brierley (safety supervisor) to J. D. Sweeney (insurance department), "Re: Eye and Skin Irritation Complaint on May 15, 1972, by 99th Street School Students." The other is a Niagara County Department of Health report, three pages long, filed one day later on May 16, 1972, under the heading "Check Old Hooker Disposal Site—99th—97th St."

5 **Hooker Chemical:** The name of the company changed slightly over the decades. At times, it was Hooker Electro-Chemical, Hooker Electrochemical, Hooker Chemicals and Plastics Corp., or Hooker Chemical Corp. For simplicity, the author chose to refer to it as locals did: Hooker Chemical.

5 **a one-page report:** This report, filed by Hooker Chemical's safety supervisor George F. Brierley on May 15, 1972, documents what happened to Gallo, Primerano, and a third child over the course of twenty-four hours at the playground.

6 **"rust-colored material":** Niagara County Department of Health report, May 16, 1972.

6 **litany of curious plights:** Hooker Chemical subject files, *Buffalo Courier-Express* Newspaper Collections, E. H. Butler Library, SUNY Buffalo State University Archives & Special Collections, multiple stories, including "Manhole Covers 'Pop' Near Hooker," Jan. 19, 1963; "Fumes Sicken 37 as Valve Breaks," Jan. 6, 1965; "Hooker Gas Sickens Many," Feb. 18, 1966; "Hooker Plant Gas Escapes; Many Ill," Feb. 18, 1966; "Residents of Falls Alerted to Hazard," March 24, 1966; "Manhole Covers Fly; Probe Due," Dec. 12, 1967; "Traffic Normal After Gas Leak," Oct. 12, 1968; "Hooker Gas Causes Two Sewer Blasts," Aug. 1, 1970; "Tank Car Fire Blocks Falls Traffic," Dec. 31, 1971.

6 **believed he knew:** Brierley to Sweeney, "Re: Eye and Skin Irritation Complaint on May 15, 1972, by 99th Street School Students."

6 **an odd flavor:** Newspaper accounts described the BHC taste as an "off-flavor" or "musty odor and taste." Rachel Carson, "Washed-in Poisons Peril Life-Giving Soil," *Minneapolis Star,* Jan. 28, 1963; "Corn Insects in N.C. and How to Kill Them," *Charlotte Observer,* Feb. 19, 1951; "Ant Habits Should Be Known for Most Effective Control," *Sacramento Bee,* Aug. 26, 1950; "Warns on Use of Benzene Hexachloride," *Benton Harbor (Mich.) News-Palladium,* April 9, 1948.

6 **burst into flames:** "Residents of Falls Alerted to Hazard."

6 **found the call to be notable:** Niagara County Department of Health report, May 16, 1972.

1. LOIS

11 **Christmas decorations:** Gibbs, interview with author, Feb. 18, 2020.

12 **died going over the edge:** In the *Buffalo Courier-Express* Newspaper Collections in the SUNY Buffalo State University Archives & Special Collections at the E. H. Butler Library, there are two clip files that contain decades of news coverage of people who died going over the falls—either on purpose or by accident. These two files are titled "Persons Swept Over the Falls or Rapids to Their Deaths" and "Suicides and Rescues." All details in these passages are pulled directly from these news stories.

13 **the impossible tale of Roger Woodward:** Woodward's epic fall and seemingly impossible survival were chronicled in all the local papers and elsewhere. See, among others, "Falls Plunge Spares Boy; Sister Plucked from Rim," *BCE,* July 10, 1960; "Falls Boat Captain Disbelieved Eyes," *BCE,* July 10, 1960; and a ten-year-anniversary story written in Woodward's new hometown newspaper, "Roger Fell over Niagara Falls," *Lakeland (Fla.) Ledger,* July 5, 1970.

13 **beer-fueled rages:** Both Lois Gibbs and her sister Kathy Hadley recounted their difficult childhood and their father's problems. Gibbs, interview with author, Nov. 25, 2019; Hadley, interview with author, Feb. 4, 2020.

13 **spoke with a stutter:** Gibbs, interview with author, Nov. 25, 2019.

14 **improper young lady:** Hadley, interview with author, Feb. 4, 2020.

15 **his own residue:** Gibbs, interview with author, Nov. 25, 2019.

2. LUELLA

16 **they juggled two worlds:** Kenny, interviews with author, Nov. 25 and 27, 2019, and April 24, 2020.

17 **one-girl revolt:** Kenny, interview with author, Nov. 25, 2019.

17 **had come to America by ship:** According to the ship's manifest, Luella's father, Giuseppe, arrived in New York on July 24, 1909, aboard a French steamer called the SS *Lorraine.*

17 **first husband died:** According to death records and news reports, Jennie's first husband, Emil Baccelli, died in Jan. 1928, two weeks after the chemical plant accident.

17 **scrubbed floors, and cleaned bathrooms:** Kenny, interview with author, Nov. 25, 2019.

18 **married in June 1964:** Kenny, interview with author, April 24, 2020.

19 **didn't want her to get sick:** Kenny, interview with author, Nov. 25, 2019.

20 **The weather was brutal:** "Decembr-r Coldest Here in 16 Years," *NG,* Jan. 3, 1977.

20 **The day after Christmas:** Details of the storm that hit western New York after Christmas 1976 can be found in the following stories: "Seven Inches

of Snow Covers City," *RDC,* Dec. 27, 1976; "Storm Skirts City—for Now," *RDC,* Dec. 30, 1976; "Snow Jobs Buffalo Again," *NYDN,* Dec. 30, 1976; "Buffalo Hit Again; Winter Total at 91 Inches," *NYDN,* Dec. 31, 1976.

20 **ferocious blizzard:** "Heavy Snows, Wind Paralyze Niagara County" and "Snowmobile Set for the Pregnant," *NG,* Jan. 10, 1977; "Blizzard Conditions Subside in Niagara County," "'A Good Old Storm,'" and "'Downright Rotten Night,' Police Moan," *NG,* Jan. 11, 1977.

20 **Local weather stations:** Details of the deep freeze that hit the region in mid-Jan. come from the following sources: "Frigid Air to Stay All Week; Schools Shut, Gas Cuts Asked," *NG,* Jan. 17, 1977; "Cold Wave? It's Simply a 'Lack of Variation Fluctuation,'" *NYT,* Jan. 17, 1977; "Area's 'Ice Box' Reading Plunges to Minus 11" and "Cold Snap Keeps Schools, Firms Closed," *NG,* Jan. 18, 1977.

20 **crippled the city:** Details about the Blizzard of 1977 in Niagara Falls can be found in the coverage of the *Niagara Gazette* between Jan. 27 and 30, 1977, including the following stories: "Gas Emergency, Arctic Winds Close Schools, Businesses Again," Jan. 27, 1977; "Snow, Winds Hold County in Icy Grip," Jan. 28, 1977; "Niagara County Frozen by Blizzard," "Harrison Workers Stuck; Towns Snowed Under," and "Storms Maroon 900 Students in Schools," Jan. 29, 1977; "Niagara County Declared Disaster Area," Jan. 30, 1977.

20 **almost seventeen feet:** National Weather Service data, Record Group 412, Love Canal Docket Hazardous Waste Enforcement Files, box 4, National Archives, College Park, Md.

20 **by May 1, 1977:** "Dump Seepage Tested; City Needs Plan," *NG,* May 1, 1977.

3. ENERGETIC, EFFECTIVE, EXPERIENCED—LAFALCE!

21 **The telephone rang:** For decades, Bonnie Casper kept the original memos, letters, and other correspondence related to the Love Canal issue, starting with a memo she sent to LaFalce about her lunch meeting with Joseph McDougall and Richard Leonard on June 30, 1977. She graciously dug all of these files out of storage in her Maryland home and shared them with the author for this book. They were an invaluable resource that allowed many scenes to be reconstructed in detail. Hereafter, they will be referred to as CC.

21 **a stressful year:** Casper, interview with author, Feb. 13, 2020.

22 **called him Clark Kent:** Becky Muscoreil, interview with author, June 4, 2020.

22 **"Meet the maximum":** LaFalce, interview with author, Nov. 27, 2019.

22 **Casper—short and petite:** At the time these events began unfolding in the late 1970s, Bonnie was separated from her husband, though still going by the name Bonnie Alderfer. She soon divorced, returned to her maiden name, and

requested that the author use that name in this book. The author honored that request.

23 **a student of politics:** Casper, interview with author, Feb. 7, 2020.

23 **"Energetic . . . Effective . . . Experienced!":** LaFalce subject files, Nov. 3, 1976, *Buffalo Courier-Express* Newspaper Collections, E. H. Butler Library, SUNY Buffalo State University Archives & Special Collections.

23 **Casper was a natural:** Casper, LaFalce, and Rich Lee, interviews with author.

24 **"the subcommittee will come":** U.S. House of Representatives Subcommittee on Capital, Investment, and Business Opportunities, congressional transcript, May 18, 1977.

24 **by the teaspoon:** "Fire Ant Poison Offered at Cost to Parish Residents," *Tensas Gazette,* Feb. 26, 1965.

24 **B-17s and B-25s:** "Finishing Up," *Shreveport Journal,* March 22, 1967; "B25s Will Bomb Fire Ants with Insecticides Next Week," *Atlanta Constitution,* March 5, 1963.

24 **got into everything:** "Air War on Fire Ants Ready to Start as Scientists Protest," *Atlanta Journal,* March 19, 1963; "Stung by Critics in Fire Ant Fuss," *Atlanta Constitution,* June 17, 1963; "South Suncoast Outdoors," *Tampa Bay Times,* May 9, 1968; "Doctors Back Louisiana Mirex Fire Ant Ban Plea," *Opelousas (La.) Daily World,* Dec. 3, 1970; "Scientists Question Use of DDT Cousin in Fire Ant Eradication Program," *Orlando Sentinel,* Jan. 10, 1971; "Mirex Spraying Angers Landowner," *Anniston Star,* May 29, 1973; "Scientists Still Fishing for Mirex Answers," *RDC,* Oct. 3, 1976; "Human Population Exposures to Mirex and Kepone," U.S. Environmental Protection Agency, Office of Research and Development, June 1978; David Axelrod, "Mirex—Toxicological Considerations," March 24, 1977, Department of Health Commissioner's Office Files, Record Series 13307-83, box 14, Mirex 1977–78, New York State Archives.

24 **leaching into the river:** "Hooker Held Dumping Mirex," *NG,* Sept. 3, 1976; "Chemical Flowing Illegally into Niagara," *NYT,* Sept. 3, 1976.

25 **beautiful day:** Weather, *Baltimore Sun,* June 30–July 1, 1977.

25 **sour mood:** McDougall, interview with author, May 22, 2020; Leonard, interview with author, June 6, 2020.

25 **The agents running the hearing:** Transcript, "Public Meeting on the Proposed Revisions to the EPA Grant Regulations for Implementation of Resource Conservation and Recovery Act of 1976," June 30, 1977.

25 **At lunch with Casper:** Details of this lunch come from interviews with all three participants—Casper, Leonard, and McDougall—and the June 30, 1977, memo sent from Casper to LaFalce, CC.

26 **"We have a real problem":** Transcript, "Public Meeting on the Proposed Revisions to the EPA Grant Regulations for Implementation of Resource Conservation and Recovery Act of 1976," June 30, 1977.

4. A MODEL CITY

27 **first laid eyes:** Previous histories on Love Canal written in newspapers, magazines, and books have described William T. Love as an "enigmatic" man "hailing from parts unknown." These histories either repeated the falsehoods that Love himself had claimed about his past or declared that Love's background was not known. Through genealogical research utilizing U.S. Census records, passport applications, and archival newspapers published in Iowa, South Dakota, Tennessee, and elsewhere in the 1880s and 1890s, the author unraveled this mystery and tells the real story of William T. Love here for the first time.

27 **spring of 1892:** Love first visited the area on May 22, 1892, according to two stories: "Love's Utopia," *Buffalo Courier,* Aug. 25, 1893; "The Cataract City," *Buffalo Courier,* May 24, 1894.

27 **unequaled in beauty:** Details about Love's plan can be found in "The Substitute," *Buffalo Enquirer,* March 29, 1893; "A Model Town," *Buffalo Enquirer,* March 17, 1893; "Who Wants a Fortune? Speak Out Now," *Buffalo Enquirer,* Aug. 11, 1893; and "Model City Plans," *Buffalo Morning Express,* March 29, 1896.

27 **thirty-six years old:** Love's age, like most of his past, was never known or printed in any news coverage. But his birth date can be found in his 1917 U.S. passport application. According to the application, and affidavits filed with it, he was born on May 26, 1856, in Keokuk, Iowa. U.S. Passport Applications, Jan. 2, 1906–March 31, 1925, roll 0420, certificate 70615.

27 **done his research:** David Parry, "William T. Love and the Development of Model City," SUNY Buffalo, Dec. 1976.

28 **"the greatest water power":** "Love's Utopia."

28 **had been talking about:** "The Model Town Project," *Buffalo Courier,* April 9, 1893.

28 **"We are going to succeed":** "Who Wants a Fortune?"

28 **work was backbreaking:** "Niagara County," *Buffalo Courier,* May 9, 1893; "Who Wants a Fortune?"

28 **$2.5 million:** "Building a City," *Buffalo Weekly Express,* Aug. 2, 1894.

28 **eighty feet wide:** Ibid.

28 **even a song:** Ibid.; "Love Canal: Public Health Time Bomb—a Special Report to the Governor and Legislature," New York State Department of Health, 1978.

29 **a mighty town builder:** Advertisement, *Chicago Tribune,* Sept. 6, 1889.

29 **an important railroad man:** Details about his railroad can be found in the *Daily Plainsman* in Huron, South Dakota: "City Council," July 26, 1886; "Street Railway Location," Aug. 27, 1886; "Huronitems," Sept. 21, 1887.

29 **"One of the greatest enterprises":** "Gigantic Scheme," *Chattanooga Times,* March 23, 1891.

29 **"Love has had a very checkered career":** "Knoxville Men in It," *Knoxville Journal,* June 4, 1893.

29 **"Mr. Love might pay":** "In a Bad Way," *Buffalo Morning Express,* July 24, 1896.

29 **nowhere to be found:** As the canal project began to struggle, and people claimed that Love owed them money, the local newspapers tracked Love's movements in stories, including "Love Sails Away," *BEN,* April 19, 1897, and "Gold Fields in the Northwest," *Buffalo Courier,* Feb. 8, 1897.

30 **He was on the move:** "Western New York in Brief," *Buffalo Times,* Feb. 8, 1897.

30 **"The big ditch":** "Anxious Farmers," *Buffalo Express,* Nov. 13, 1896.

30 **connected in all the places:** Features written about Hooker executives over the years in the local papers regularly mentioned their memberships in civic clubs; genealogical research conducted by the author revealed their ancestries.

30 **a religious dissident:** A fawning biography of Hooker and his company—called *Salt & Water, Power & People: A Short History of Hooker Electrochemical Company*—was written by Robert E. Thomas and published by Hooker in 1955. While it is no doubt a piece of corporate storytelling, it is also a valuable historical document, offering insight into how the company thought about itself and how it grew, and details on Hooker himself.

30 **friendship with Teddy Roosevelt:** Hooker was so close with the former president and governor of New York that upon Roosevelt's death in 1919 Hooker was one of the first to visit the family at Roosevelt's famed Long Island home, Sagamore Hill.

30 **"Poison Gas King":** "Who's News Today?," *Oakland Tribune,* Oct. 29, 1932.

30 **what they needed:** This list of chemicals, and their uses, comes directly from Hooker's company documents. Hooker list of chemicals, n.d., Publications and Other Reports folder, Hooker Electrochemical Collection, Local History Department, Niagara Falls Public Library.

31 **more than $600,000:** "Hooker Leaves $604,078 Estate," *RDC,* June 10, 1938.

31 **a hundred different chemicals:** *Hooker Gas,* Dec. 1943, 10–11, Publications and Other Reports folder, Hooker Electrochemical Collection.

31 **"Arsenal for Democracy":** *Hooker Gas* company newsletter, Dec. 24, 1941, Publications and Other Reports folder, Hooker Electrochemical Collection.

31 **known irritants:** According to the EPA, exposure to benzyl chloride can cause "severe irritation of the upper respiratory tract, skin, eyes, and mucous membranes, and lung damage." At "high concentrations," the EPA says, exposure "also causes effects on the central nervous system." According to the National Library of Medicine, exposure to thionyl chloride "may cause severe injuries, burns, or death." These are just two of the many chemicals dumped into the canal. Additionally, as stories of mishaps regularly made it into the local newspaper, and inside the *Hooker Gas* company newsletter, executives implored employees to be mindful of the dangers in the workplace.

31 **the new Hooker man:** The executive's name was Edwin "Ned" Bartlett. Details about his lineage come from George Norbury Mackenzie and Nelson Osgood Rhoades, editors, *Colonial Families of the United States* (Baltimore: Genealogical Publishing Co., Inc., 1966), 6:72–87.

31 **about half a mile long:** The description of the canal comes from "The Lesson of Love Canal," a state report written by C. Stephen Kim in 1980 and obtained in 2021 in a Freedom of Information request from the New York Department of Health.

31 **"as a waste disposal area":** Hooker internal memo, written by Bartlett to his brother and one other executive about exploring the purchase of the canal, Sept. 16, 1941, Record Group 412, Love Canal Docket Hazardous Waste Enforcement Files, box 4, National Archives, College Park, Md.

32 **"A mixture of all kinds of things":** Deposition of Leonard Bryant (former Hooker vice president), taken on May 6, 1986, 246–47, federal case file, CIV-79-990, National Archives, Lee's Summit, Mo.

32 **posted a guard:** Details of the precautions the company took come from company memos in the court record at the National Archives, including Ainsley Wilcox (corporate counsel) to Bartlett, Aug. 16, 1946, Record Group 412, Love Canal Docket Hazardous Waste Enforcement Files, box 4, National Archives, College Park, Md.

32 **it could explode:** On at least one occasion, a drum of thionyl chloride did indeed explode. Hooker internal memo, Sept. 6, 1961, titled "Investigation of Exposed Residue at Love Canal Property Formerly Owned by Hooker," Record Group 412, Love Canal Docket Hazardous Waste Enforcement Files, box 4, National Archives, College Park, Md.

32 **three hundred drums:** The details about the process of puncturing the drums, the number of drums, and the time when executives brought coffee and doughnuts to the site come from affidavit of Stephen Witkowski (former Hooker employee), May 1, 1985, 1–2, Record Group 412, Love Canal Docket Hazardous Waste Enforcement Files, box 3, National Archives, College Park, Md.

32 **"serious damage":** Wilcox to Bartlett, Aug. 16, 1946, Record Group 412, Love Canal Docket Hazardous Waste Enforcement Files, box 4, National Archives, College Park, Md.

33 **He wanted to build:** Letter from Bjarne Klaussen to Bartlett and others titled "Love Canal," March 27, 1952, federal case file, CIV-79-990, National Archives, Lee's Summit, Mo.

33 **$36 million:** Exhibit 2823, Hooker Chemical annual sales, net income, and payroll, 1940–1953, federal case file, CIV-79-990, National Archives, Lee's Summit, Mo.

33 **"It's not like a city garbage dump":** Deposition of Bryant, taken on May 6, 1986, 251.

33 **"The Love Canal property":** Letter from Klaussen titled "Love Canal,"

April 25, 1952, Record Group 412, Love Canal Docket Hazardous Waste Enforcement Files, box 4, National Archives, College Park, Md.

33 **"in whole or in part":** Deed for the land, April 28, 1953, box 2, LGLC.

5. WE SHOULD AT LEAST VISIT THE PLACE

34 **The first time:** McDougall, interview with author, May 22, 2020.

35 **"I invite both you":** McDougall to Casper, July 5, 1977, CC.

35 **"According to these gentlemen":** Casper to LaFalce, memo, June 30, 1977, CC.

36 **"When you have a chance":** Casper to LaFalce, memo, July 20, 1977, CC.

36 **"It is imperative and urgent":** Casper to LaFalce, memo, Sept. 6, 1977, CC.

36 ***"McDougall upset":*** Phone message received by Casper, Sept. 2, 1977, CC.

37 **"I'm not sure":** Casper to LaFalce, memo, Sept. 6, 1977, CC.

37 **Muscoreil agreed with Casper:** Lee, interview with author, Jan. 24, 2020; Muscoreil, interview with author, June 4, 2020.

6. KIDS SHOULD BE WARNED

38 **The following morning:** Lee, interview with author, Jan. 24, 2020.

38 **Before he became the first:** LaFalce, interview with author, Nov. 26, 2019.

39 **The owners had been complaining:** The *Niagara Gazette,* led by the reporters David Pollak and Michael Brown, chronicled the early complaints in many places, including "Hooker Faces Dump Crisis," Sept. 12, 1969; "Love Canal, a Landfill of Hell, That's a Cesspool of Death and Disease," Oct. 1978; Adeline Levine, *Love Canal: Science, Politics, and People* (Lexington, Mass.: Lexington Books, 1982), 11; and Brown's book, *LW,* 4, 16, 17.

39 **"Hooker dump":** Details about the so-called Hooker Dump and the fires that broke out there can be found in many places, including "Family Recalls Fires at Hooker Dump," *NG,* June 5, 1977; "Garage Fire Here Does $500 Damage," *NG,* Feb. 19, 1949; "Hooker Checking Pollution Report," *NG,* Aug. 14, 1961; and Record Group 412, Love Canal Docket Hazardous Waste Enforcement Files, box 5, National Archives, College Park, Md.

40 **"disagreeable problems":** Arch to Niagara Falls city manager, Sept. 9, 1954, Record Group 412, Love Canal Docket Hazardous Waste Enforcement Files, box 5, National Archives, College Park, Md.

40 **pulled away in silence:** Lee, interview with author, Jan. 24, 2020.

40 **John S. Coey II:** Details about Coey come from multiple places, including the Amherst College yearbook, *The Olio,* 1937, 51, 156, 164–66; "Coey Gets Hooker Sales Promotion," *NG,* Nov. 1, 1950; "Bank Aide Is Appointed," *NG,* June 6, 1960; "New Chest President Is Named," *NG,* March 1, 1962; and "John Coey 2d, 71," *Boston Globe* obituary, Nov. 9, 1985.

41 **"As you may know":** LaFalce to Coey, Sept. 14, 1977, CC.

41 **"I would like to sit down":** Casper to LaFalce, memo, recounting her conversation with Hooker Chemical's public relations chief Charles Cain, Sept. 23, 1977, CC.

41 **the rains came down:** The *Niagara Gazette* ran multiple stories about the heavy rains in the city that fall. These can be found, among other places, in Record Group 412, Love Canal Docket Hazardous Waste Enforcement Files, box 4, National Archives, College Park, Md.

42 **the folly of their choices:** Outwater died in 2014. However, he recounted the story of his ruined shoes to others, including his EPA colleague Dick Dewling and to Casper. Dewling, interview with author, April 9, 2020; Casper, interview with author, Feb. 19, 2020.

42 **Leonard was worried, too:** Leonard, interview with author, June 6, 2020.

42 **"the extreme danger":** Casper to LaFalce, memo, recounting Leonard's fears, Sept. 23, 1977, CC.

42 **standing in right field:** Details about Leonard's run-in with the chemical drum in right field come from interviews with Leonard and Casper and Casper's memo to LaFalce, recounting the story, Sept. 23, 1977.

43 **completely safe:** "Toxic Waste: It's Seeping from Niagara Falls Landfill," *Louisville Courier-Journal,* May 16, 1977.

43 **"The material can be quite odorous":** "Seepage Health Threat Slight," *NG,* May 3, 1977.

44 **slip into the Communion line:** Sister Denise Cona, interview with author, March 10, 2020.

45 **Gibbs had missed something:** Gibbs, interview with author, June 10, 2020.

45 **"There's no history":** Lois Marie Gibbs, *Love Canal: My Story* (Albany: State University of New York Press, 1982), 10.

7. CONTAINERS OF DUBIOUS CONDITION

49 **Brown's ordinary background:** Brown, interview with author, Dec. 11, 2019.

49 **allegedly clairvoyant teacher:** The story of this teacher can be found in news clippings from the time, including "ESP Topic Brings Various Opinions at Spencer Meet" and "Haven't Talked with Devil, Says Jordan," *Elmira Star-Gazette,* March 30, 1973; "Students, Teachers React to Spencer ESP Lecture," *Elmira Star-Gazette,* April 1, 1973; "ESP Classes to Be Resumed," *Elmira Star-Gazette,* April 11, 1973; and "His Career Field Is Not Crowded," *Binghamton Press and Sun-Bulletin,* July 15, 1973.

49 **book deal:** The book, titled *PK: A Report on the Power of Psychokinesis, the Mental Energy to Move Matter,* was published by Steinerbooks in 1976.

50 **no best seller:** "Author Rides Roller Coaster from Rags to Riches," *Binghamton Press and Sun-Bulletin,* Aug. 24, 1980.

50 **He filed stories:** Brown, interview with author, Dec. 11, 2019.

50 **a company called Chem-Trol:** Details about Chem-Trol's dumping operation can be found in "Porter Chemical Graveyard Seen Possible Time Bomb," *BCE,* July 10, 1977, and "Expert Proposes 'Remedies' to Chem-Trol Opponents," *BCE,* July 16, 1977, Chem-Trol subject file, *Buffalo Courier-Express* Newspaper Collections, E. H. Butler Library, SUNY Buffalo State University Archives & Special Collections.

50 **"repeated spills":** Thomas Tower (chairman of the Porter Environmental Commission) to the Lewiston Town Board, May 19, 1977, Chem-Trol folder, CC.

50 **a woman stepped to the microphone:** *LW,* xii.

51 **collecting comments:** Question cards from Nov. 12, 1977, public hearing, Chem-Trol folder, CC.

51 **"green acidy gook":** LaFalce to William Friedman at the New York State Department of Environmental Conservation, Feb. 22, 1978, Chem-Trol folder, CC.

51 **"It actually burns":** Mrs. Don Jackson, in Ransomville, N.Y., to LaFalce, July 28, 1978, Chem-Trol folder, CC.

51 **a short editorial:** "Seal Off Love Canal," *NG,* Aug. 15, 1977.

52 **The engineer in question:** Descriptions of Lawrence Moriarty come from his World War II draft card, serial No. 208, order No. 2716.

52 **collected stamps:** "Lawrence Moriarty Dies at 78," *RDC,* Feb. 8, 1995.

52 **In walking the old canal:** Moriarty's memo summarizing his findings on his visit, dated Oct. 18, 1977, can be found in multiple locations, including the Task Force on Hazardous Waste Commissioner's Files, Record Series 22574-13, box 2, folder 23, New York State Archives, and CC. According to Casper's notes at the time, LaFalce's office received Moriarty's report just before Thanksgiving 1977, about one month after he wrote it up.

53 **trying to diminish:** Rich Lee to Casper and LaFalce, memo, Oct. 3, 1977, CC.

53 **at least fourteen homes:** Documents revealing the data for early air and water testing can be found in multiple locations, including the CC; LGLC; the federal case file, CIV-79-990, National Archives, Lee's Summit, Mo.; and the New York State Archives. Key reports include several found in the Task Force on Hazardous Waste Commissioner's Files, Record Series 22574-13, box 2, folder titled "Hooker Chemical & Plastics Corporation Disposal Sites Memos and Correspondence, 1978–1979," New York State Archives. These reports are "Epidemiologic Investigation of the Potential Health Hazard from Toxic Chemical Among Residents near the Love Canal Chemical Waste Landfill in Niagara Falls, New York" and "Report of Air Sampling at the Love Canal Site, Niagara, New York," June 1978. Other key reports, found in the federal court record, include "Suspect Carcinogens in Air of Household Basements," EPA data, April 18, 1978, and Robert G. Lewis, "Summary Report on the Occurrence of Specific Chemicals

Found in the Indoor Air of Love Canal Residences in Several Studies by New York State and the US Government," CIV-79-990, National Archives, Lee's Summit, Mo.

54 **"Sealed within ice":** "First Phase Analysis: Groundwater Contamination Incident in Niagara Falls, New York," Record Group 412, Love Canal Docket Hazardous Waste Enforcement Files, box 4, National Archives, College Park, Md.

54 **modern-day standards:** Today, according to federal standards set by the National Institute for Occupational Therapy & Health, factory workers should not be exposed to more than 100 ppm toluene, 50 ppm chlorotoluene, or 1 ppm benzene over the course of their shifts. Readings inside homes in Niagara Falls varied, but many basements exceeded these standards by wide margins. Table 1 (Ninety-Seventh Street readings) and Table 2 (Ninety-Ninth Street readings), n.d., CC; Drs. Bush and Richards (state Department of Health) to Dr. Kaminsky (state Department of Health), "Interim Report—The Voorhees' Residence," June 30, 1978, and Dr. A. Carlson (state Department of Health) to Dr. W. Stasiuk (state Department of Health), "Discussion of Love Canal Soil Sampling: CONFIDENTIAL—PREPARED FOR LITIGATION," Oct. 2, 1979, Task Force on Hazardous Waste Commissioner's Files, Record Series 22574-13, box 2, New York State Archives.

54 **"There is growing evidence":** "Epidemiologic Investigation of the Potential Health Hazard from Toxic Chemical Among Residents near the Love Canal Chemical Waste Landfill in Niagara Falls, New York."

54 **"I think if I lived there":** George Randels (staffer) to LaFalce, memo, April 24, 1978, CC.

55 **From the start:** Casper to LaFalce, memo, subject heading "Meetings at EPA/Region II on 3/23/78," CC. In the memo, Casper recounts all of the problems she had at the EPA during her visit.

8. A SEA OF RED TAPE

56 **He started by digging:** *LW,* xii; Brown, interview with author, Dec. 11, 2019.

56 **The *Gazette* building:** "Gazette's Storied Past at 310 Niagara St.," *NG,* Oct. 18, 2015.

56 **In the library:** Brown, interview with author, Dec. 11, 2019.

56 **a chance encounter:** Details about this encounter were gathered from three different sources: *LW,* 11; "$400,00 Project Is Asked to Seal Off Love Canal Dump," *NG,* Aug. 18, 1977; Brown, interview with author, Dec. 11, 2019. The quoted conversation is pulled directly from Brown's accounts both in his book and in his newspaper story written at the time.

56 **Pilié was from New Orleans:** Details about Pilié come from multiple sources, including the 1930 U.S. Census; Pilié's draft card for World War II, serial No. w-180-a, order No. 11784-a; and *The Wolf,* Loyola University yearbook, class of 1949.

57 **In the late winter of 1978:** "Red Tape Stalls Dump Solution," *NG,* Feb. 5, 1978.

9. CERTAIN DEFINITIVE ACTION

60 **a towering mound:** Former colleagues of Axelrod's all noted his organizational style—or lack thereof. Interviews with Martha Harvey, Glen Haughie, Leo Hetling, Stephen Kim, Peter Millock, and Peter Slocum were helpful in this regard.

60 **for personal medical advice:** Leo Hetling, interview with author, May 11, 2020.

60 **happy to weigh in:** Details about Axelrod's youth and his upbringing in Great Barrington, Massachusetts, come from multiple stories printed in his hometown newspaper, *The Berkshire Eagle,* including "Axelrod Wins Second Time," Feb. 6, 1952; "David Axelrod Wins Harvard Scholarship," May 15, 1952; "David Axelrod Appointed to Annapolis," Sept. 17, 1952; "Rabbi for 60 Years Retiring," Sept. 21, 1984; and "Rabbi Jacob Axelrod Dies," Jan. 10, 1986.

61 **The man had read:** Stephen Kim, interview with author, May 11, 2020.

61 **defer to him:** Whalen to Peter Berle, Dec. 22, 1976, Task Force on Hazardous Waste Commissioner's Files, Record Series 22574-13, New York State Archives.

61 **already grooming him:** Robert Morgado (executive secretary to Governor Hugh Carey) and Robert Schiffer (head of health and human services for Governor Carey), interviews with author, June 2 and June 9, 2020, respectively.

61 **$200,000:** Axelrod to Whalen, memo, Nov. 3, 1977, Department of Health Commissioner's Office Files, Record Series 13307-83, box 14, Mirex 1977–78, New York State Archives.

61 **"a purposeful effort":** Axelrod to Whalen, memo, Feb. 17, 1978, Department of Health Commissioner's Office Files, Record Series 13307-83, box 14, Mirex 1977–78, New York State Archives.

61 **In a phone call late one evening:** Axelrod to Whalen, memo, Jan. 24, 1978, Department of Health Commissioner's Office Files, Record Series 13307-83, box 14, Mirex 1977–78, New York State Archives.

61 **sent a top aide:** Attendance list for a Feb. 1, 1978, meeting between state officials and Hooker executives, Department of Health Commissioner's Office Files, Record Series 13307-83, box 14, Mirex 1977–78, New York State Archives.

63 **A dentist's son:** U.S. Census records, 1920.

63 **the nickname Doc:** *The Forum,* Lockport High School yearbook, 1930.

63 **for two decades:** "Dr. Francis J. Clifford Dies; Physician Served as Niagara County Health Chief," *Buffalo News,* May 18, 1999.

63 **"I look at the EPA's record":** *LW,* 20.

63 **"There's a high rate":** Ibid.

63 **"When are you going to go back":** Ibid., 21.

63 **"the deplorable conditions":** Letter from Whalen to Clifford, "RE: Love Canal Chemical Waste Landfill," April 25, 1978, CC.

63 **nine state doctors:** Minutes from the state Department of Health toxicology committee meeting, April 18, 1978, CC.

64 **there to give a speech:** "New Hooker Energy Plant Pleases Carey," *BCE,* April 21, 1978.

64 **black-tie dinner:** Details of Armand Hammer's visit, his art exhibit, and his schedule for the day come from multiple sources, including Presidential Daily Diary, April 20, 1978, Jimmy Carter Presidential Library and Museum; "Carey May Be Seeking New Image," Gannett News Service, April 23, 1978; and "Hammer Exhibit a Pure Delight" and "Magnate Hammer Escorts His 'Priceless' Rembrandt to Buffalo," *BCE,* April 21, 1978.

65 **finally issued a decision:** "State Orders Love Canal Site Cleanup," *NG,* April 28, 1978.

65 **tersely worded letter:** Whalen to Axelrod, April 25, 1978, CC.

65 **"In view of the ready access":** Whalen to Clifford, April 28, 1978, CC.

66 **"Is it feasible":** Memo from Axelrod, May 12, 1978, Task Force on Hazardous Waste Commissioner's Files, Record Series 22574-13, New York State Archives.

10. THIS IS OUR ANSWER

67 **see if Casper knew:** Phone message, April 7, 1978, CC.

68 **"Vapors from Love Canal":** *NG,* May 15, 1978.

68 **Gibbs read Brown's stories:** Gibbs, *Love Canal: My Story,* 10; Gibbs, interview with author, Dec. 11, 2019.

68 **Osage bloodlines:** Wayne Hadley, interview with author, Feb. 6, 2020.

69 **"Do you think this could be":** Gibbs, interview with author, Dec. 11, 2019; Wayne Hadley, interviews with author Feb. 6 and 20, 2020; Kathy Hadley, interview with author, Feb. 4, 2020.

69 **hysterical mother:** Gibbs, interview with author, Dec. 11, 2019.

69 **The day of the meeting:** Both Gibbs and Brown recalled their original meeting in the newsroom and discussed it in interviews with the author. Gibbs, interview with author, Dec. 11, 2019; Brown, interview with author, Dec. 11, 2019.

70 **"viscous sludge":** R. P. Leonard, P. H. Werthman, and R. P. Ziegler, "Characterization and Abatement of Groundwater Pollution from Love Canal Chemical Landfill, Niagara Falls, N.Y.," Calspan Technical Report, Aug. 1977.

70 **"I think this is our answer":** Gibbs, interview with author, Dec. 11, 2019.

11. A FULL AND FRANK DISCUSSION

71 **"a full and frank discussion":** Whalen to LaFalce, May 4, 1978, CC.

71 **"How long":** List of questions, spring 1978, n.d., CC.

72 **a letter from a young mother:** Letter from Judy Freiermuth, received by LaFalce's office on May 9, 1978, CC.

72 **"non-project":** "Falls Authority Signs 'Non-project' Contracts," *BCE,* Nov. 22, 1969; "Housing for Niagara's Community," *NG,* March 19, 1972.

72 **Griffon Manor was integrated:** "Griffon Manor Not a Typical Project," *NG,* August 1963, and Elizabeth D. Blum, *Love Canal Revisited: Race, Class and Gender in Environmental Activism* (Lawrence, Kan.: University of Kansas Press), 161.

73 **three hundred families:** Beverly Paigen and Lynn R. Goldman, "Lessons from Love Canal: The Role of the Public and the Use of Birth Weight, Growth, and Indigenous Wildlife to Evaluate Health Risk," in *Health Effects from Hazardous Waste Sites,* ed. Julian B. Andelman and Dwight W. Underhill (Chelsea, Mich.: Lewis, 1987).

73 **curious problems:** Details about the drainage problems at Griffon Manor can be found in multiple places, including "City Crew Seeks to Drain 'Lake' at Griffon Manor," *NG,* March 27, 1953; "Board of Education meeting notes," *NG,* Jan. 5, 1955; "Corporation Proceedings," *NG,* April 7, 1962; and "Housing Project Tenants Protest," *BCE,* Aug. 11, 1968.

73 **rocks would light up**: Kathryn Thornton, interview with author, June 26, 2020.

73 **"Canal Hill":** "Old-Time School Bell Is Advised to Call Pupils," *NG,* Feb. 4, 1957.

73 **pushing for a bailout plan:** LaFalce to Eckhardt C. Beck (EPA regional director), April 28, 1978, CC.

73 **"WHO WILL BE LIABLE":** List of questions, spring 1978, n.d., CC.

74 **room 1432:** Whalen to LaFalce, May 4, 1978, CC.

74 **the only woman:** Attendance list for May 11, 1978, meeting, CC.

74 **Whalen started:** Upon returning to Washington after this meeting, Casper wrote a detailed, five-page summary of what happened that day for LaFalce—an invaluable historical resource documenting the discussion in Albany. Casper to LaFalce, memo, May 15, 1978, CC.

75 **"Because the Health Dept.":** Ibid.

76 **a public notice:** Meeting announcement from the Niagara County Health Department, May 15, 1979, CC.

76 **"the interested parties?":** Casper to LaFalce, memos, May 16 and 18, 1978, CC.

77 **At the meeting that Friday night:** The details from the Friday night meeting come from three sources: Brown's news coverage, "Love Canal Residents' Evacuation Mulled," *NG,* May 20, 1978; Casper's three-page summary to

LaFalce, recapping the events of the meeting, CC; Stephen Kim to David Axelrod, memo, May 22, 1978, Task Force on Hazardous Waste Commissioner's Files, Record Series 22574-13, box 2, New York State Archives. The memos from both Kim and Casper line up, recounting the events of the meeting in a similar fashion.

77 **"Aren't there emergency funds":** "Love Canal Residents' Evacuation Mulled."

78 **"From a public relations viewpoint":** William Friedman to Peter Berle, memo, May 23, 1978, Task Force on Hazardous Waste Commissioner's Files, Record Series 22574-13, New York State Archives.

78 **to get a drink:** Casper, interview with author, Feb. 19, 2020.

78 **"If we find a high rate of cancer":** "State to Study Love Canal Health Ills," *NG,* May 21, 1978.

79 **"We don't even know":** Ibid.

12. THE BOY AT THE CONCERT

81 **threatened to break:** "In the Chips with Pat and Debby," *LAT,* May 1, 1978.

81 **If the song came on:** Luella Kenny, interview with author, Feb. 21, 2020.

81 **wasn't feeling like himself:** The details of the onset of Jon Allen's sickness come from testimony that Luella Kenny submitted to the House Subcommittee on Oversight and Investigations on April 2, 1979; notes that Luella made in 1979, kept in her own personal collection for decades, and shared with the author in Jan. 2020; and multiple interviews with the author in 2019 and 2020.

13. PLAN C

83 **She was calling the superintendent:** Gibbs, *Love Canal: My Story,* 11.

83 **Utter had been on the job:** "Utter to Take Upstate Post," *White Plains (N.Y.) Journal News,* Nov. 27, 1977.

84 **Utter was denying her request:** Gibbs, *Love Canal: My Story,* 12.

84 **maybe there was a third option:** Details of the conversation between Kathy Hadley, Wayne Hadley, and Lois Gibbs come from interviews with all three of them: Kathy Hadley, interview with author, Feb. 4, 2020; Wayne Hadley, interview with author, Feb. 20, 2020; Lois Gibbs, interview with author, Dec. 11, 2019.

85 **"set speech":** Gibbs, *Love Canal: My Story,* 15.

85 **clipboard:** Grenzy, interview with author, Feb. 14, 2020.

85 **people she knew:** Gibbs, *Love Canal: My Story,* 13.

85 **Gibbs met Debbie Cerrillo:** Cerrillo, interview with author, Feb. 14, 2020.

85 **Gibbs met Liz Retton:** Retton, interview with author, March 10, 2020.

86 **Patti Grenzy saw Gibbs coming:** Grenzy, interview with author, Feb. 14, 2020.

14. PRESUMED NEPHROTIC SYNDROME

88 **Luella Kenny refused to delay any longer:** Details about Jon Allen Kenny's hospital stay in July 1978 come from three sources: Luella Kenny, multiple interviews with author; Dr. Maria Crea, interview with author, Sept. 9, 2020; more than two hundred pages of Jon Allen's medical records that Luella Kenny saved and shared with the author in Jan. 2020. Between the interviews and the medical records chronicling Jon Allen's condition in granular detail, from day to day and hour to hour, the author was able to rebuild this moment in time. All material in quotation marks comes directly from the medical records. And if not otherwise noted, the material in this chapter comes from one of these three sources.

88 **lone female physician:** Dr. Maria Crea was such a pioneer and so beloved in western New York that in 2010 when the Health Association of Niagara County Inc. opened its new community services center, it named the facility after Crea. "Dedicated Physician Hailed by New Center," *Buffalo News,* June 6, 2010.

89 **tested the urine:** Details about how to run the protein test and the implications of the condition come from three sources: Dr. Timothy S. Larson, "Evaluation of Proteinuria," *Mayo Clinic Proceedings* 69 (1994): 1154–58; Melvin I. Marks, Peter N. McLaine, and Keith N. Drummond, "Proteinuria in Children with Febrile Illnesses," *Archives of Disease in Childhood* 45, no. 240 (1970): 250–53; Dr. Caroline Straatmann, interview with author, Dec. 7, 2020.

92 **perfect midsummer morning:** Weather report, *RDC,* July 25, 1978.

15. THE TRUE BELIEVER

93 **That same day:** Gibbs to LaFalce, July 25, 1978, CC.

93 **161 signatures:** Gibbs, *Love Canal: My Story,* 29.

93 **plenty of residents who disagreed:** Ibid., 24.

94 **"periphery":** Announcement received by Axelrod on June 16, 1978, discussing the second round of public meetings to be held in Niagara Falls on June 19–20, Task Force on Hazardous Waste Commissioner's Files, Record Series 22574-13, box 2, New York State Archives.

94 **"You are their mother":** Gibbs, *Love Canal: My Story,* 19.

94 **"The board didn't put any chemicals":** "Schools Dropping Role in Dump Remedy," *NG,* June 20, 1978.

95 **First, he introduced her:** Hadley, interview with author, Feb. 20, 2020; Paigen, interview with author, Jan. 17, 2020; Lippes, interview with author, Jan. 31, 2020.

95 **waged legal fights:** Lippes, interview with author, Jan. 31, 2020.

95 **"true believer":** Ibid.

96 **stayed on best-seller lists:** "Rachel Carson Fights Nature's Enemies," Associated Press, Sept. 28, 1962.

96 **"Only once or twice":** "Two Best Sellers," *NYT,* April 27, 1952.

96 **"poisonous and biologically potent":** "Rachel Carson Fights Nature's Enemies."

96 **"It's ironic to think":** "'Silent Spring' Is Now Noisy Summer," *NYT,* July 22, 1962.

96 **"fanatic defender":** Ibid.

97 **"the immensely useful":** "House Unit Criticizes Carson Book," *Boston Globe,* April 20, 1965.

97 **"I call them cultists":** "A Real but Cruel Tradeoff," *NYT,* April 5, 1977.

98 **"The list we published was accurate":** "Sierra Club Revises List of County's Top Polluters," *BEN,* n.d., PC.

98 **as a girl growing up:** The author spent two days interviewing Beverly Paigen in person in Jan. and Feb. 2020, and both she and her family shared with the author several boxes of her personal papers related to her time investigating Love Canal in the 1970s and 1980s. These papers, and interviews, were critical to building out Beverly's story.

98 **garbage collector:** According to the World War II draft card for Beverly's father, Bernard Vander Molen, serial No. 643, order No. 1111, the official name of his company was the Vander Molen Refuse Disposal Company.

98 **At Wheaton Academy:** Details of Paigen's time at Wheaton Academy come from two sources: Paigen, interviews with author; the Wheaton Academy yearbook from 1956, *The Compass.*

98 **one that changed her life:** Paigen, interview with author, Jan. 17, 2020.

99 **But life didn't work out:** Ibid.

99 **"Ours is a truly modern household":** "Air Pollution Cited as One of the Major Causes of Cancer," *BEN,* May 30, 1976.

100 **most days, Beverly drove alone:** David Paigen, interview with author, Jan. 29, 2021.

100 **half a million dollars:** "Dr. Beverly Paigen—Present Grant Support," spring 1980, PC.

100 **They liked that she was a visible presence:** Later, after Paigen became a problem for state officials, they claimed she was a disgruntled employee with a history of problems. But in Oct. 1977—less than a year before the controversies around Love Canal—top administrators privately praised Paigen for a recent promotion and for being such a public figure for Roswell Park. Dr. Gerald Murphy to Dr. Edwin Mirand, memo, Oct. 6, 1977, Beverly Paigen files, 13307-86A, obtained by author via a Freedom of Information request, New York State Archives.

100 **"It is important":** Mirand to Paigen, memo, Oct. 21, 1977, Beverly Paigen files, 13307-86A, obtained by author via a Freedom of Information request, New York State Archives.

100 **"Academic scientists tend not":** "Beverly Paigen," *Buffalo Spree* (Fall 1979), PC.

100 **spent weeks in the hospital:** David Paigen, interview with author, Jan. 29, 2021.

101 **"I am a homeowner":** Gibbs to LaFalce, July 25, 1978, CC.

16. WHITEWASH

102 **"The County, City, Bd. of Ed.":** Casper to LaFalce, memo, May 15, 1978, CC.

103 **stoked panic:** Gibbs, testimony to U.S. Congress Subcommittee on Oversight and Investigations, March 21, 1979, 91.

103 **"I'm not God":** "Tests Outlined for Love Canal Area Residents," *NG,* June 20, 1978.

103 **water would gather:** Kim to Axelrod, memo, June 30, 1978, Task Force on Hazardous Waste Commissioner's Files, Record Series 22574-13, box 2, New York State Archives.

103 **"The net result":** Vianna to Whalen, n.d., Task Force on Hazardous Waste Commissioner's Files, Record Series 22574-13, box 2, New York State Archives.

104 **wasn't sure whom to believe:** Casper to LaFalce, memo, May 15, 1978, CC.

104 **"Twenty-five years ago":** Transcript of NBC *Today Show* story about Love Canal that aired on June 21, 1978, CC.

104 **"They came in with special drums":** All quotations from Frank Ventry in this section, unless otherwise noted, come from his deposition in the federal case file, CIV-79-990, 44 and 51, National Archives, Lee's Summit, Mo.

104 **the son of Italian immigrants:** U.S. Census records for Ventry's parents, Rosario and Frances Ventry, 1920.

105 **"Immediate and thorough action":** "LaFalce Decries Canal Inquiry," *NG,* June 26, 1978.

105 **nearly forty interviews:** "Report on Army Investigation into Alleged Dumping of Toxic Substances in Love Canal Area, Niagara Falls, New York," Department of the Army, Aug. 14, 1978, List of Interviews Appendix, 1–4, box 4, folder 11, LGLC.

105 **"no evidence":** Ibid., 18.

105 **"Love Canal—an Overview":** All quotations in this section come directly from Casper and Randels's memo, "Love Canal—an Overview," July 5, 1978, CC.

107 **State officials complained:** Casper to LaFalce, memo, under the subject heading, "Love Canal—June 12, 1978 . . . Meeting and Call from Mike Brown/Gazette," CC.

107 **Hooker wanted a word:** *LW,* 25.

17. THE WITCHES' END OF FAIRYLAND

108 **On the first day of August:** *LW,* 25.

108 **"the witches' end of fairyland":** "Reporter's Notebook: Niagara Olfactory Impact," *NYT,* Aug. 9, 1978.

108 **Brown walked through the doors:** Details of the meeting between Brown and the Hooker executives come from three places: *LW;* Brown, interviews with author; "Reporter's Notebook: Niagara Olfactory Impact."

108 **was ushered into a luxurious boardroom:** *LW,* 25.

110 **"Did Hooker really believe":** Ibid., 26.

110 **living in a foreign place:** Ibid., 27.

110 **"there should be some very explicit statements":** "Evacuation Mulled at Dump Side," *NG,* Aug. 1, 1978.

110 **laughed at the absurdity:** *LW,* 27.

110 **front-page news:** "Upstate Waste Site May Endanger Lives," *NYT,* Aug. 2, 1978.

111 **prepared for a massive crowd:** Levine, *Love Canal: Science, Politics, and People,* 28.

111 **Only 26 people:** Original attendance list, handwritten by the attendees themselves, Aug. 2, 1978, box 24, New York State Department of Health documents, Adeline Levine Love Canal Collection, Buffalo History Museum.

112 **"I do hereby find":** "Order of Robert P. Whalen in the Matter of the Love Canal Chemical Waste Landfill Site," Aug. 2, 1978, box 3, LGLC.

112 **Gibbs couldn't believe:** Gibbs, interview with author, Dec. 12, 2019. Also, Gibbs, *Love Canal: My Story,* 30.

113 **"You're murdering us!":** Multiple sources confirm Gibbs's statement that day, including Brown; Gibbs herself; Gibbs's memoir, *Love Canal: My Story,* 29; and Levine in her book *Love Canal: Science, Politics, and People,* 29.

113 **overdoing it:** Brown, interview with author, Dec. 11, 2019.

113 **97 families:** "Order of Robert P. Whalen in the Matter of the Love Canal Chemical Waste Landfill Site," Aug. 2, 1978.

113 **only sound in the car:** Gibbs, *Love Canal: My Story,* 32. Also, Gibbs and Cerrillo, interviews with author, Dec. 12, 2019, and Feb. 14, 2020, respectively.

113 **taken to the streets:** Details of the spontaneous protest the night of Aug. 2, 1978, come from multiple sources, including Gibbs, *Love Canal: My Story,* 33; "Waste Site's District Grim as Fear, Anger Visit 99th Street Homes," *BCE,* Aug. 3, 1978; and "Canal Residents Vow a Tax Strike," *NG,* Aug. 3, 1978.

113 **"There's a big ugly monster":** "Waste Site's District Grim as Fear, Anger Visit 99th Street Homes."

114 **"Oh, God":** Levine, *Love Canal: Science, Politics, and People,* 29.

114 **found the microphone:** Gibbs, interview with author, Dec. 12, 2019;

Wayne Hadley, interview with author, Feb. 20, 2020; Gibbs, *Love Canal: My Story,* 33.

18. IF ANYONE SHOULD COMPLAIN

115 **Blum was perfectly suited:** In the early winter of 2020, Blum opened her storage unit for the author and shared several bound scrapbooks filled with newspaper articles, memos, and other documents—hereafter labeled BB scrapbooks. The details about her life and the quotations contained here all come from stories in these scrapbooks, including "Barbara at Ease—the View from Here" *Hutchinson (Kan.) News,* Dec. 12, 1977; "This Former Lobbyist Not Harmless Anymore," *Atlanta Constitution,* May 6, 1977; "Capable Women Hurt by 'Old Boy' System," *Citizen-Journal,* March 10, 1977; and "A Carter Conservationist Rocks the Boat," *California Living, the Magazine of the San Francisco Sunday Examiner,* Sept. 17, 1978.

116 **"She moves carefully":** "How Blum Rose to Become a Top Carter Aide," *Washington Star,* n.d., 1977, BB scrapbooks.

116 **canoeing with just any lobbyist:** Ibid.

116 **commute to Washington:** Blum, interview with author, Feb. 21, 2020.

116 **"We are determined":** "Nixon Pledges War Against Pollution," *LAT,* Jan. 2, 1970.

117 **"the lifeblood of America's economic":** "Now, Second Thoughts About Cleaning Up the Environment," *U.S. News & World Report,* Jan. 19, 1976.

117 **seven hundred new pesticides:** "The Dilemma of Pesticides," *U.S. News & World Report,* Nov. 3, 1977.

117 **"run amok":** Richard M. Nixon, *Beyond Peace* (New York: Random House, 1994), 201–2.

118 **"esoteric upper-class movement":** Congressional transcripts, Hearing before the Committee on Environment and Public Works, Nominations of Doug Costle and Barbara Blum, Blum testimony, 25.

118 **Texas millionaire:** "All Quotas on Imports Opposed by Strauss," *Pittsburgh Post-Gazette,* April 19, 1978.

118 **Strauss said he had identified:** "Strauss Picks 3 Inflation Targets," *Boston Globe,* April 20, 1978.

118 **"inflation fight":** Ibid.

118 **Carter directed all federal agencies:** "Carter Bids All Agencies Trim Costs," *NYT,* May 19, 1978.

118 **"The lowest cost means":** Congressional transcripts, Hearing before the House Subcommittee on Economic Stabilization, Blum testimony, July 26, 1978, 140.

119 **"parallel investigations":** Congressional transcripts, Hearing before the House Subcommittee on Oversight and Investigations, Oct. 30, 1978, John Lehman to Hugh Kaufman, EPA memo regarding Toone contamination, Aug. 14, 1978, 349.

119 **fifty-seven million metric tons:** "Hazardous Waste Information," EPA, Office of Public Awareness, Feb. 1980.

119 **no budget, one employee:** Two whistleblowers, Hugh Kaufman and William Sanjour, alerted the press and Congress to alleged EPA shortcomings, and Kaufman testified before Congress in the fall of 1978. Congressional transcripts, Hearing before the House Subcommittee on Oversight and Investigations, Oct. 30, 1978, 306.

119 **"It's the largest commercial transaction":** "First Ship Filled with Ammonia from Russia Docks in Tampa," *Tampa Bay Times,* Jan. 22, 1978.

119 **"Where there is understanding":** "U.S. Firm Opens Ammonia Terminal on Black Sea," *Tampa Tribune,* Aug. 23, 1978.

119 **$8 million in damages:** The details of the charges against Hooker in Florida, Michigan, California, and New York can be found in multiple sources, including a detailed legal summary in the Securities and Exchange Commission Docket, May 27, 1980, 569–72.

120 **"the most serious and deliberate":** "State May Press Charges Against Phosphate Firm," *Tallahassee Democrat,* Oct. 25, 1978.

120 **gone sterile:** "DBCP Exposure," *Modesto Bee,* March 11, 1979.

120 **"If anyone should complain":** This quotation about the problems in Lathrop, California, can be found in internal memos in the congressional record, such as the memo from Robert Edson (corporate environmental coordinator), June 25, 1976, Hearings Before the Subcommittee on Oversight and Investigations, Serial No. 96-49.

120 **"First, shocked innocence":** Bennett's explanation for why the paper wouldn't be printing any more negative stories about the Hooker pollution problem in Montague can be found in "A Public Apology for Not Printing All the News," *The White Laker Observer,* April 20, 1977.

120 **began to feel threatened:** "The Poisoning of Montague, Michigan," *Detroit Free Press,* July 26, 1981.

121 **"I'm ashamed to admit":** "Public Apology for Not Printing All the News."

121 **"There are probably thousands":** "Poison Plague at Love Canal Unearthed a National Scandal," *Philadelphia Inquirer,* Sept. 26, 1979.

121 **"Who's going to pay":** "Upstate Waste Site May Endanger Lives," *NYT,* Aug. 2, 1978.

122 **"Everyone knows me":** Levine, *Love Canal: Science, Politics, and People,* 36.

19. A LONG, STRANGE DREAM

123 **Gibbs was nervous:** Gibbs, *Love Canal: My Story,* 33; Gibbs, interview with author, Dec. 12, 2019.

123 **raised a finger:** Gibbs and Kathy and Wayne Hadley, interviews with author.

123 **thought Gibbs was perfect:** Lippes, interview with author, Jan. 31, 2020.

123 **"I'll make sure":** Gibbs, *Love Canal: My Story,* 31.

123 **"Meeting: Thursday, 7 p.m.":** Box 17, LGLC.

124 **roughly five hundred people:** "Angry Crowd Greets Officials," *NG,* Aug. 4, 1978.

124 **"We've already heard":** Gibbs, *Love Canal: My Story,* 36.

124 **"My wife is eight months pregnant":** This quotation, and others in this section, come from the *Niagara Gazette*'s coverage on Aug. 4, 1978.

125 **nearly fifteen families:** "Several Families Are Sent Away from Niagara Falls Landfill Site," *NYT,* Aug. 7, 1978.

125 **"Wanted: Safe Home":** "First Families Leaving Upstate Contamination Site," *NYT,* Aug. 5, 1978.

125 **officials assured tourists:** "Publicity Isn't Killing Tourism, McLeod Says," *NG,* Aug. 4, 1978.

126 **"I'm thinking about putting a toll booth":** "Reporter's Notebook: Niagara Olfactory Impact."

126 **"Why am I here?":** Gibbs, *Love Canal: My Story,* 38.

126 **"A long, strange dream":** Ibid.

126 **Brown got the sense:** Brown, interview with author, Dec. 11, 2019.

20. MANY ABUSIVE PHONE CALLS

128 **Gibbs barely got a chance:** Gibbs, interview with author, Dec. 12, 2019; LaFalce, interview with author, Dec. 13, 2019; Gibbs, *Love Canal: My Story,* 39; "Canal Residents' Fright Fades; LaFalce Cheered," *BCE,* Aug. 5, 1978.

128 **people wouldn't soon forget:** The sociologist Adeline Levine and her team did scores of interviews with residents in the fall of 1978, asking dozens of questions "for teaching and research purposes." These views of LaFalce come directly from interviews 103, 106, 111, and 125, archived in the Adeline Levine Love Canal Collection, Buffalo History Museum.

128 **"LaFalce line":** Robert Morgado (former executive secretary to Governor Hugh Carey), interview with author, May 27, 2020.

129 **the latest polls:** "Carey Passes Krupsak, Bloom Under Blizzard of TV Ads," *NYDN,* Aug. 6, 1978.

129 **state agencies had been aware:** "Krupsak Blasts Carey on Love Canal Aid," *RDC,* Aug. 12, 1978.

129 **done nothing:** "Carey vs. Krupsak," *Ithaca Journal,* Aug. 25, 1978.

129 **"Love Creek":** Associated Press, Aug. 27, 1978.

130 **couldn't stop thinking:** Paigen, interview with author, Jan. 17, 2020.

130 **thirty-one different locations:** The details about the tests Paigen ran—and her findings—were no secret to her superiors at Roswell Park. She noted them twice—once in her July 1978 monthly report, even before the canal problem became a big news story, and again in a more detailed memo in Sept. 1978. Monthly report from Paigen to Dr. Gerald Murphy, Aug. 1, 1978, and Paigen to Murphy, memo, Sept. 15, 1978, Beverly Paigen files, 13307-86A, obtained by author via a Freedom of Information request, New York State Archives.

130 **"The laboratory smelled":** Paigen to Murphy, memo, Sept. 15, 1978, Beverly Paigen files, 13307-86A, obtained by author via a Freedom of Information request, New York State Archives.

130 **most of the chemicals in the ground:** "Cancer Researcher Urges Relocation of 50 Families near Toxic Dump Site," *BEN,* Aug. 3, 1978.

131 **everyone in the room faced risks:** "Canal Residents' Fright Fades; LaFalce Cheered."

131 **"If it were my home":** "Researcher Says Canal Is Harmful," *BCE,* Aug. 4, 1978.

131 **"I don't think the neighborhood is safe":** "Long Buried Poisons Ooze out of the Ground," *Washington Post,* Aug. 5, 1978.

131 **Paigen and Gibbs walked home:** Details of the walk home that night come from three sources: Gibbs, *Love Canal: My Story,* 40; Gibbs, interview with author, Dec. 12, 2019; Paigen, interview with author, Jan. 17, 2020.

133 **"You would have to be a walking encyclopedia":** "Experts Find Carcinogen at Love Site," *BCE,* Aug. 5, 1978.

133 **Murphy sent Whalen's public relations man:** Murphy to Whalen, memo, Aug. 4, 1978, Beverly Paigen files, 13307-86A, obtained by author via a Freedom of Information request, New York State Archives.

133 **dictatorial zeal:** "Roswell Park's Director Too Authoritarian but Effective, Report Says," *BEN,* Nov. 11, 1977.

134 **"I'd like to know":** Ibid.

134 **"Dr. Whalen feels":** All of these details about the comments made by Paigen's bosses come from interoffice memos that they sent to each other between Sunday, Aug. 6, and Friday, Aug. 11, 1978, the week that Paigen was in Maine. These memos, later obtained by Paigen and saved for decades, are archived in two locations: Levine's collection at the Buffalo History Museum and Beverly Paigen's personal collection, opened to the author by Paigen.

135 **"Many abusive phone calls":** This detail comes from the official complaint that Paigen ultimately filed against her bosses in 1980. The author obtained the complete binder from Paigen herself, before her death in June 2020, and via a Freedom of Information request filed with the New York State Archives. Materials from this Roswell Park Board of Visitors binder will hereafter be cited with the abbreviation RPBOV.

21. MOMMY'S GOING TO STAY

136 **The doctors had given:** Details about Jon Allen's medical condition in July, Aug., and Sept. 1978 come from interviews that Luella Kenny gave to the author and the boy's medical records that Kenny saved for decades and shared with the author in Jan. 2020.

22. GIVE MY REGARDS TO BROADWAY

140 **For the first time in U.S. history:** "The Love Canal Tragedy," *EPA Journal,* Jan. 1979.

140 **"save lives":** "Carter Approves Emergency Help in Niagara Area," *NYT,* Aug. 8, 1978.

141 **Carey's aides informed LaFalce:** LaFalce, interview with author, Feb. 3, 2020.

141 **began making promises:** *LW,* 37; Gibbs, *Love Canal: My Story,* 44.

141 **"Leave it behind":** "State to Assume Canal Mortgages," *NG,* Aug. 8, 1978.

141 **"Oh, my God":** Gibbs, *Love Canal: My Story,* 45; LaFalce, interview with author, Feb. 3, 2020.

142 **The event that Tuesday:** Details of Carter's event in New York City come from four sources: Presidential Daily Diary, Aug. 8, 1978, Jimmy Carter Presidential Library and Museum; Jack Watson, interview with author, April 29, 2020; and local news coverage, including "Carter Signs Aid Bill for New York at Gala Celebration at City Hall," *NYT,* Aug. 9, 1978, and "Carter Gives City a $1.65B Bill," *NYDN,* Aug. 9, 1978.

143 **"I would greatly appreciate":** Francis M. Williams to Carey, telegram, Aug. 7, 1978, Records of the Governor's Office, Hugh Carey correspondence, Environmental Conservation, reel 53, New York State Archives.

143 **had been advised to discuss Love Canal:** Morgado, interview with author, June 1, 2020.

143 **Gibbs got a phone call:** Gibbs, *Love Canal: My Story,* 48.

144 **The next day, for Gibbs:** "All 310 Canal Families to Get Aid," *BCE,* Aug. 10, 1978; Gibbs, interview with author, Feb. 5, 2020.

144 **$7 million:** "U.S. Aide Says Homes Might Be Made Safe," *BCE,* Aug. 11, 1978.

145 **Gibbs boarded her flight home:** Gibbs, *Love Canal: My Story,* 51; Gibbs, interview with author, Feb. 5, 2020.

23. LET OUR PEOPLE SPEAK

146 **starting to worry about it:** Details in this chapter about Elene Thornton, Agnes Jones, and other residents of Griffon Manor come from multiple sources including interviews conducted with former Griffon Manor residents. Key interviewees include several members of Thornton's family, including two of her children and two of her siblings; Lester Sconiers, a Black attorney hired by Thornton to represent the renters; Sarah Rich, a Griffon Manor resident who would later become one of the leaders in the housing development; and Carol Jones, the daughter of Agnes Jones.

147 **"They forget us":** "Project Families Feel 'Ignored' in Canal Plan," *BEN,* Aug. 29, 1978.

147 **"I knew it was":** Interview 117, Adeline Levine Love Canal Collection, Buffalo History Museum, shared with the author by Dorothy Atkinson's daughter, Susan, and utilized here with her permission.
148 **"You're afraid":** Interview 114, Levine Love Canal Collection.
148 **they all had problems:** Rich, interview with author, Jan. 30, 2020.
149 **outsider in Griffon Manor:** Carol Jones, interview with author, Oct. 24, 2020.
149 **fiercely independent:** Sconiers, interview with author, Sept. 2, 2020.
149 **needed to be focusing:** Rich, interview with author, Jan. 30, 2020.
149 **"It is extremely important":** Association newsletters, Aug. 9, 1978, box 1, LGLC.
149 **"property owners":** Certificate of Incorporation of The Love Canal Homeowners Association Inc., Aug, 21, 1978, Record No. A511803, New York State Department of State.
149 **failed to catch:** In an interview with the author on Nov. 12, 2020, Lippes explained that creating a homeowners' association was a standard legal procedure. He had not intended to slight anyone.
149 **splinter organization:** "Security of Area Belies Turmoil of Love Canal," *BCE,* Aug. 12, 1978.
150 **"Forget it":** This quotation, and those that follow complaining about the renters, come from interviews that Levine's sociology team conducted in the late 1970s. Interviews 124, 125, 135, and 138, Levine Love Canal Collection.
150 **"It's the minorities":** Interview 125, Levine Love Canal Collection.
151 **"This meeting":** "Love Canal Issue Splits Community," *BCE,* Sept. 7, 1978.

24. THE BOY IN BED 11

152 **The nun called:** Details in this chapter come directly from Jon Allen Kenny's medical records, given to the author in Jan. 2020, and from the following sources: Denise Cona, interview with author, March 10, 2020; Luella Kenny, interviews with author, Dec. 10, 2019, and Sept. 10, 2020; Stephen Kenny, interview with author, April 10, 2020.

25. TWO SIDES OF THE SQUARE

156 **"I blame the city":** "Waste Site's District Grim as Fear, Anger Visit 99th Street Homes," *BCE,* Aug. 3, 1978.
157 **a new media strategy:** C. Y. Cain, "Our HCPC Corporate Image," *Hooker Pipeline,* summer 1977, Love Canal Collection, Local History Department, Niagara Falls Public Library.
158 **directed any employee:** Hooker interoffice memo stamped "CONFIDENTIAL" from Hooker president Donald Baeder to all Hooker employees, Aug. 10, 1978, under the subject heading, "LOVE CANAL PROBLEM," box 24.4, Adeline Levine Love Canal Collection, Buffalo History Museum.

158 **"we are sure as hell":** "Canal Landfill Techniques Were Highly Advanced, Hooker Official Says," *BEN,* Aug. 11, 1988.

158 **"We believe":** Ibid.

158 **"like a shotgun":** Incident report stamped "CONFIDENTIAL" under the subject heading "Injuries of Two Youths Alleged to Have Occurred at 102nd Street Hooker Dump Area," July 27, 1967, collection 13307-94, box 10, New York State Archives.

158 **thirty-eight thousand discarded drums:** This total comes directly from Hooker's own inventory list compiled in the late 1970s for the EPA. "Inventory of Materials Located at Hyde Park Landfill," n.d., circa late 1970s, collection 13307-94, box 10, New York State Archives.

159 **"emotionalism":** "Possible Love Canal Backlash Worries Area Industrial Firms," *BCE,* Aug. 20, 1978.

26. CAN I GO HOME SOON?

160 **The seizures for the boy:** All details in this chapter—including the comments in quotation marks—come directly from Jon Allen Kenny's medical records.

27. MARKED HOUSES

164 **150 families had fled:** "154 Families Moved Out from Love Canal Homes," *BCE,* Sept. 29, 1978.

164 **state started erecting a chain-link fence:** "Love Canal Fence Work Set Today," *BCE,* Aug. 22, 1978.

164 **$5 million purchasing homes:** "154 Families Moved Out from Love Canal Homes."

165 **"like monkeys in a cage":** "Love Canal Families Face Eviction from Hotel as Charity Funds Ebb," *BCE,* Sept. 28, 1978.

165 **"People hear of a home":** "Love Canal Disaster Sends Home Values into Nose Dive," *BCE,* Oct. 23, 1978.

165 **Under the plan:** Conestoga-Rovers & Associates, "Love Canal Remedial Action Project," Aug. 1978.

166 **sixty hulking vehicles:** "Engineers Eye Love Canal Pit as 'Chemical Soup' Seeps In," *BCE,* Oct. 18, 1978.

166 **"There doesn't seem to be":** "Little Protest Expected on Canal Remedial Work," *NG,* Oct. 2, 1978.

166 **"immediate action":** Letter from Thornton to the city's public housing director, Henry Wrobel, Sept. 18, 1978, Niagara Falls Housing Authority archive.

167 **NAACP took notice:** "Love Canal Issue Splits Community," *BCE,* Sept. 6, 1978.

167 **William Abrams, the chapter's president:** "Griffon Manor Residents Form Group to Learn of Love Canal Dangers," *BCE,* Sept. 27, 1978.

167 **less than a hundred feet:** "Love Canal Investigators Overlooking Black Residents, Falls NAACP Claims," *BCE,* Sept. 10, 1978.

167 **"Many Black people":** Ibid.

167 **a small law office:** At the time, Lester Sconiers's office was located at 8711 Buffalo Avenue—so close to Griffon Manor that Thornton could have walked there.

168 **tree shaker:** Sconiers, interview with author, April 7, 2020.

168 **"Water just moves":** Sconiers, interview with author, Sept. 2, 2020.

168 **"The administration":** Pressman to Paigen, memo, Sept. 21, 1978, PC.

169 **Late at night:** Paigen, interview with author, Feb. 12, 2020.

169 **"When I make public statements":** Paigen to Pressman, memo, Sept. 12, 1978, PC.

170 **aerial photographs:** "Air Photos, Maps Show New Site," *BCE,* Aug. 12, 1978.

170 **streambeds offered natural drainage:** "Comments on the Love Canal Pollution Abatement Plan," box 2, LGLC.

171 **pulled out a street map:** Gibbs, *Love Canal: My Story,* 67.

172 **"a systematic phone survey":** Paigen, testimony to U.S. Congress Subcommittee on Oversight and Investigations, March 21, 1979, 61.

172 **swales were everywhere:** Swale maps, box 4, LGLC.

172 **Paigen and Gibbs logged the address:** Handwritten list of homes built on swales and the families who lived at each location, box 5, LGLC.

28. GOD ONLY KNOWS

173 **the entire Kenny family:** Luella Kenny, interviews with author, Feb. 21 and Sept. 9, 2020.

173 **another difficult day:** After Jon Allen's discharge on Sept. 29, 1978, Luella took detailed notes about his condition throughout the weekend. The details about his decline come directly from these notes.

174 **five different medications:** Jon Allen Kenny medical records, Children's Hospital of Buffalo, summary of admission, Oct. 4, 1978.

175 **busy weekend:** "Javits: Canal 'an Inheritance of the Past,'" "Senator Tours Site," "Javits Visits, Hears Gripes," *NG,* Oct. 1, 1978; "Javits Visits Canal, Calls Problem 'Grave,'" *BCE,* Oct. 1, 1978.

176 **be prepared to leave:** "Little Protest Expected on Canal Remedial Work," *NG,* Oct. 2, 1978.

176 **"Respond to public address system":** Love Canal Task Force Information Bulletin, Sept. 15, 1978, box 5, state bulletins, LGLC.

177 **"Breathing heavy, labored":** Luella's handwritten notes, Oct. 1, 1978.

177 **affixed suspenders:** Luella Kenny, interview with author, Sept. 9, 2020.

178 **"Jon is very sick":** Jon Allen Kenny medical records.
178 **seventy-six breaths:** This—and all other details of Jon Allen's hospital stay—come directly out of his medical records, unless otherwise noted.
178 **"He can't go on like this":** Luella Kenny, interview with author, Nov. 25, 2019.
179 **in the hospital cafeteria:** Ibid.; Luella Kenny, interview with author, Sept. 9, 2020.
180 **"I want an autopsy!":** Luella Kenny, interview with author, Nov. 25, 2019.
180 **scrubbed the linoleum floor:** Luella Kenny, interview with author, Dec. 10, 2019.
180 **sheet cake:** Luella Kenny, interview with author, Nov. 25, 2019.
181 **first frost:** "Rough Weather Stirs Season's 1st Visions of Snow," *BCE,* Oct. 7, 1978.

29. WE'VE DONE EVERYTHING WE CAN

185 **In the final days of the campaign:** "Krupsak Competes for 'Little People' Votes," Gannett News Service, Sept. 7, 1978; "Carey, Krupsak Enter Final, Frantic Hours of Campaigning," *Poughkeepsie Journal,* Sept. 11, 1978.
186 **"There are reams of paper":** "A Tardy Carey Hustles to Make Political Time," Gannett News Service, Sept. 7, 1978.
186 **"If you waited around":** "Carey, Krupsak Battle up to Last Minute of Campaign," *Poughkeepsie Journal,* Sept. 12, 1978.
186 **never lost:** "Dems See All Roads Leading to Victory," *NYDN,* Nov. 8, 1979.
186 **The latest state budget:** "Pressing Business Halts Legislators' Electioneering," *White Plains (N.Y.) Journal News,* Sept. 27, 1978.
187 **"Oh, lady":** "Lois Gibbs of Love Canal: She's Getting Herself Involved," *BEN,* Aug. 26, 1978.
187 **opened the homeowners' association office:** Quimby, interview with author, Dec. 16, 2019.
187 **painted the protest signs:** Cerrillo, interview with author, March 1, 2020.
188 **filled in the gaps:** McCoulf, interview with author, Jan. 22, 2020.
188 **Carey greeted the president:** Details of Carter and Carey's campaign stop in Buffalo in late Oct. 1978 come from multiple sources, including "President Offers Prayers, No Aid for Love Canal," *BEN,* Oct. 29, 1978; "Carter Tells Local Crowd Carey Is 'Man of Courage,'" *BCE,* Oct. 29, 1978; McCoulf, interview with author, Jan. 22, 2020; Cerrillo, interview with author, March 1, 2020.
189 **down by twenty points:** "Another Success Story in the Carey Success Story," *NYT,* Nov. 8, 1978.
189 **seven times:** "State Turns Cool on Canal Action After Campaign," *BEN,* Feb. 17, 1979.

30. USELESS HOUSEWIFE DATA

191 **The morning after Election Day:** "From the Pits to the Pinnacle—How Carey Did It" and "Carey Romps to Reelection Win," *NYDN,* Nov. 8, 1978.

192 **less scientific terms:** As part of his job, consultant Stephen Lester kept a daily log of what he did and saw at the canal. "Steve Lester's Daily Reports," box 5, LGLC.

192 **wasn't the same:** Details about Lois and Harry's marriage come from Lois Gibbs, interviews with author, Dec. 12, 2019, and Feb. 18, 2020, and Interview 126, Adeline Levine Love Canal Collection, Buffalo History Museum, shared with the author by Lois Gibbs and utilized with her permission.

193 **"Poor Harry":** Interview 125, Levine Love Canal Collection.

193 **worried about Lois:** Kathy Hadley, interview with author, Feb. 4, 2020.

193 **"Who made you pretty today?":** Interview 126, Levine Love Canal Collection.

193 **"Now that I've gotten into this":** "Lois Gibbs of Love Canal: She's Getting Herself Involved," *BEN,* Aug. 26, 1978.

193 **instructions had been simple:** Paigen, interview with author, Feb. 12, 2020.

194 **"A structured questionnaire":** Paigen, interview with Bill Sanjour, Jan. 16, 2004, Bill Sanjour Tape Collection.

194 **"Go laterally":** Undated interview transcript with Lois Gibbs from the fall of 1978, box 15, LGLC.

194 **hung up on them:** Gibbs, *Love Canal: My Story,* 68.

194 **"totally, absolutely, and emphatically incorrect":** Gibbs first publicly aired her swale theory in mid-Oct., and the state quickly dismissed it. "Wider Pattern of Canal Illness Found," *BEN,* Oct. 18, 1978.

195 **"useless housewife data":** Congressional transcripts, House Subcommittee on Oversight and Investigations of the Committee on Interstate and Foreign Commerce, can be found at the Library of Congress. Gibbs testimony, March 21, 1979, 80.

195 **By Election Day 1978:** Paigen to Love Canal Homeowners Association, memo, Oct. 31, 1978.

195 **aware of the scientific limitations:** Paigen, interview with author, Feb. 12, 2020; Paigen to Love Canal Homeowners Association, memo, Oct. 31, 1978, PC; congressional testimony, March 1979, 61.

195 **"Definite illnesses":** Undated interview transcript with Lois Gibbs from the fall of 1978.

195 **"It appears likely":** Paigen's monthly report for Oct. 1978, filed to Dr. Murphy, Nov. 9, 1978, Beverly Paigen files, 13307-86A, obtained by author via a Freedom of Information request, New York State Archives.

195 **about to explode:** Paigen, interview with Sanjour, Jan. 16, 2004.

31. CLUSTERS

196 **She had expected:** Gibbs, interview with author, Feb. 19, 2020.

196 **didn't think it appropriate:** "Session Set Today on Differences in Claims on Taxing," *BCE,* Nov. 1, 1978.

196 **beautiful morning to fly:** The author interviewed everyone who attended this Nov. 1978 meeting who is still alive. Details come from several sources, including interviews that Stephen Lester and Beverly Paigen gave to the author in 2020; an interview that Paigen gave to Bill Sanjour on Jan. 14, 2004; news accounts in the *NG, BCE,* and *BEN;* and perhaps most important the notes that Lester wrote in his daily log that very day and filed to the state at the time: "Steve Lester's Daily Reports," Nov. 1, 1978, box 5, LGLC.

197 **The governor's top aides:** Morgado, interview with author, May 19, 2020; Robert Schiffer, interview with author, June 9, 2020.

197 **how to win the Jewish vote:** Schiffer, interview with author, June 9, 2020.

197 **"The buried stream theory":** "Official Can't Tie Illness to Stream Beds," *BCE,* Oct. 21, 1978.

198 **"Not a toxicologic one":** Memo from Axelrod, May 12, 1978, Task Force on Hazardous Waste Commissioner's Files, Record Series 22574-13, New York State Archives.

198 **the Merril Eisenbud philosophy:** "Environmentalist Disputes Priorities," *NYT,* May 12, 1978.

199 **"since the position you take":** Axelrod to Eisenbud, June 13, 1979, Task Force on Hazardous Waste Commissioner's Files, Record Series 22574-13, New York State Archives.

200 **"Miscarriages":** Paigen to the Homeowners Association, memo, Oct. 31, 1978, PC.

200 **a compelling scientific case:** Paigen, interview with author, Feb. 12, 2020; Paigen, interview with Sanjour, Jan. 14, 2004; Lester, interview with author, Feb. 20, 2020; Lester's notes, Nov. 1, 1978.

201 **"How do you separate":** "State Disputes Claims of Love Canal Assn.," *BCE,* Nov. 2, 1978.

201 **couldn't believe what they were reading:** Paigen, interview with author, Feb. 12, 2020; Paigen, interview with Sanjour, Jan. 14, 2004; Lester, interview with author, Feb. 20, 2020.

202 **"It is the opinion":** A series of memos between Nov. 2 and 14, 1978, detail the dispute that Paigen had with her supervisors over her travel expenses being denied. This quotation comes from a memo from Michael DeLellis to Paigen on Nov. 14, 1978, PC.

202 **a tanker truck:** "Tank Trailer Tips, Spills Love Canal Liquids," *BCE,* Nov. 2, 1978.

32. WHITE MICE

203 **A growing number of people:** Rich, interview with author, Jan. 30, 2020.
203 **Gibbs hated the idea:** Gibbs, interview with author.
203 **"Do *not* try to stop":** Charles Ebert (University at Buffalo professor and soil expert) to Gibbs, handwritten note, Dec. 5, 1978, box 2, LGLC.
204 **in trace amounts:** Hooker Chemical internal memo, "Toxicology Brief on Tetrachlorodibenzo-p-dioxin," Dec. 11, 1978, Record Group 412, Love Canal Docket Hazardous Waste Enforcement Files, box 4, National Archives, College Park, Md.
204 **cautionary tale of Seveso:** "The Seveso Case," *EPA Journal,* Sept. 1976.
204 **Brown asked Hooker about it:** The details about Brown's investigation into Hooker come from three sources: *LW,* 52; Michael H. Brown, "Love Canal and the Poisoning of America," *Atlantic,* Dec. 1979; Brown, interview with author, Dec. 11, 2019.
205 **According to one expert:** "Talk of the Town," *New Yorker,* Dec. 18, 1978.
205 **"organic curiosities":** "200 Chemicals Found in Canal," *NG,* Nov. 22, 1978.
205 **Privately, Axelrod admitted:** Letter from Axelrod, Nov. 29, 1978, Task Force on Hazardous Waste Commissioner's Files, Record Series 22574-13, New York State Archives.
205 **"In the event that we find it":** "200 Chemicals Found in Canal."
205 **"It's a cover-up!":** Rich Lee to Casper and LaFalce, memo, Nov. 21, 1978, CC.
206 **"I've lost control":** "Canal Group Threatens to Stall Cleanup," *BEN,* Nov. 22, 1978.
206 **almost became physical:** "Love Canal Residents, in Fight over Evacuation, Vote to Disrupt Cleanup," *BCE,* Dec. 6, 1978.
206 **Community leaders met:** Dec. 4, 1978, meeting, attendance list, and agenda, Governor's Love Canal Inter-Agency Task Force Chairman's Files, Record Series 13430, box 8, New York State Archives.
206 **Recent inspections:** Letter concerning conditions at Griffon Manor, Oct. 10, 1978, Governor's Love Canal Inter-Agency Task Force Chairman's Files, Record Series 13430, box 2, New York State Archives.
206 **Thornton didn't think:** Howard Nix, interview with author, June 18, 2020; Jackie Nix, interview with author, June 25, 2020.
206 **Her list included:** Letter from the Homeowners Association to William Hennessey, regarding "health disorders of area residents," Nov. 30, 1978, Governor's Love Canal Inter-Agency Task Force Chairman's Files, Record Series 13430, box 2, New York State Archives.
206 **Rats had now moved into the neighborhood:** Internal state memo regarding "Rodent Control Program in the Love Canal Area," Dec. 21, 1978, box 1, LGLC.

206 **"I have a 10-year-old son":** "Love Canal Residents Expected to Vote on Shutting Down Work," *BCE,* Dec. 5, 1978.
207 **"The last thing":** "Canal Residents Calmer as Fear Yields to Reason," *BEN,* Aug. 16, 1978.
207 **"what are you doing to me?":** Gibbs, interview with author, Nov. 24, 2020.
207 **a miserable morning:** "Love Canal Pickets to Resume," *BCE,* Dec. 9, 1978.
208 **The next morning:** "Nasty," *BCE,* Dec. 10, 1978.
208 **"We found it":** *LW,* 53; Brown, "Love Canal and the Poisoning of America"; Brown, interview with author, Dec. 11, 2019.
208 **"we know the answer":** "Dioxin Found in New Canal Drain Trench," *BCE,* Dec. 10, 1978.
208 **sixteen times the amount:** Task Force on Hazardous Waste Commissioner's Files, Record Series 22574-13, box 2, New York State Archives.
209 **Executives could explain:** Paul O. Nees (Hooker toxicologist) to upper management, memo, Dec. 11, 1978, Record Group 412, Love Canal Docket Hazardous Waste Enforcement Files, National Archives, College Park, Md.
209 **everyone was calling:** Gibbs, interview with author, Nov. 24, 2020; Paigen, interview with author, Feb. 12, 2020.
209 **"Dioxin is the most toxic":** Gibbs to homeowners, Dec. 20, 1978, LGLC.
209 **Before dawn that Monday:** Details about the protests and arrests that Monday and Tuesday come from multiple sources, including "Canal Protesters Arrested," *NG,* Dec. 11, 1978; "Six Picketers at Canal Site Are Arrested," *BEN,* Dec. 11, 1978; "State to Seek Picket Halt at Love Canal to Avoid Worse Confrontations," *BCE,* Dec. 12, 1978; "Eight More Love Canal Pickets Arrested at Cleanup Site," *BEN,* Dec. 12, 1978; "Gibbs, 7 Other Pickets Arrested at Canal Site," *NG,* Dec. 12, 1978; Gibbs, interview with author, Dec. 16, 2019; Lippes, interview with author, Jan. 31, 2020; McCoulf, interview with author, Jan. 22, 2020; Paigen, interview with author, Feb. 12, 2020.

33. UNCOMFORTABLE FEELINGS

211 **didn't put up Christmas lights:** Luella Kenny, interview with author, Nov. 27, 2020.
211 **amber of memories:** Norman to his late son, Jon Allen, letter, n.d., Luella Kenny personal collection.
211 **stopped eating:** Luella Kenny, interview with author, Nov. 27, 2019.
211 **"Dear Jon":** Norman to his late son, Jon Allen, letter, n.d., Luella Kenny personal collection.
212 **Luella began to question:** Luella Kenny, interview with author, Nov. 27, 2020.
212 **the press had announced:** "State Probing Love Canal Area Boy's Death at 7," *BCE,* Oct. 7, 1978.
212 **burglarized for the first time:** Luella Kenny, interview with author, Dec. 10, 2019.

213 **hit by a car:** Luella Kenny, interview with author, Nov. 25, 2019; Stephen Kenny, interview with author, April 8, 2020.

214 **confirmed these findings:** John W. Harman, "Chronic Glomerulonephritis and the Nephrotic Syndrome Induced in Rats with N,N—Diacetylbenzidine," *Journal of Pathology* 104, no. 2 (June 1971).

214 **detailed case studies:** Gregory J. Beirne and John T. Brennan, "Glomerulonephritis Associated with Hydrocarbon Solvents," *Archives of Environmental Health* 25, no. 5 (1972).

214 **repeated these findings:** Stephen W. Zimmerman, Ken Groehler, and Gregory J. Beirne, "Hydrocarbon Exposure and Chronic Glomerulonephritis," *The Lancet,* Aug. 2, 1975.

214 **the case of a healthy fifty-nine-year-old:** Christian von Schéele et al., "Nephrotic Syndrome due to Subacute Glomerulonephritis—Association with Hydrocarbon Exposure?," *Acta Medica Scandinavica* 200, no. 5 (1976).

215 **at risk of dying:** Robert A. Parrish, R. Brooks Scurry, and Alex F. Robertson III, "Recurrent Arterial Thrombosis in Nephrosis," *American Journal of Diseases of Children* 130, no. 4 (1976).

215 **"It has to be done":** Luella Kenny, interview with author, Nov. 27, 2019.

34. THE PAIGEN PROBLEM

216 **hand on a Bible:** "Carey, at Inauguration of 2d Term, Pledges a 'New Era of Opportunity,'" *NYT,* Jan. 4, 1979.

216 **packing conditions:** "Wind, Snow Rip Through WNY," *BCE,* Jan. 4, 1978; "Cold Front Holds East in Icy Grip," *Albany Times-Union,* Jan. 4, 1979.

217 **breaking in:** Martha Harvey, interview with author, April 20, 2020.

217 **"At that time":** Axelrod to top staffers, memo, Jan. 2, 1979, Department of Health Commissioner's Office Files, Record Series 13307-95, box 1, New York State Archives.

217 **On any given day:** A sampling of the problems that Axelrod faced can be found in his correspondence files at the New York State Archives. See above for reference.

217 **"The formidable pile":** Memo from Axelrod, Jan. 22, 1979, Department of Health Commissioner's Office Files, Record Series 13307-95, box 1, New York State Archives.

218 **Roswell Park denied Ken:** Pressman to Ken Paigen, memo, Nov. 10, 1978, RPBOV.

218 **"You have requested":** Beverly Paigen to her supervisors, memo, Nov. 28, 1978, RPBOV.

218 **excited about Paigen's involvement:** Multiple memos, including letter from Henry Nowak (U.S. representative) to Ned Regan (Erie County executive), Dec. 28, 1978; letter from Edward Rutkowski (Erie County executive) to Governor Hugh Carey, Aug. 10, 1979; and memo from Robert Collin (assis-

tant director of the state Department of Environmental Conservation's office of toxic substances), July 5, 1979, RPBOV.

218 **"The major difficulty":** Whalen to Beverly Paigen's supervisors, memo, Nov. 28, 1978, RPBOV.

219 **the state had failed to notice:** Paigen lists all her problems with the state's miscarriage data in a memo to Gibbs and Thornton, Dec. 19, 1978, PC.

219 **the Montreal study:** Dorothy Warburton and F. Clarke Fraser, "Spontaneous Abortion Risks in Man: Data from Reproductive Histories Collected in a Medical Genetics Unit," *American Journal of Human Genetics* 16, no. 1 (March 1964).

35. RELOCATION BY IMPREGNATION

221 **"I truly believe that":** "Axelrod Meets with Canal Pickets," *NG,* Jan. 12, 1979.

221 **"We may never be":** Axelrod to Patricia Sandonato, Feb. 2, 1979, Department of Health Commissioner's Office Files, Record Series 13307-95, box 1, New York State Archives.

221 **four thousand medical questionnaires:** Details about the volumes of information that the state had can be found in Axelrod's Feb. 8, 1979, supplemental health order. Box 4, LGLC.

222 **on the last day of January:** Axelrod reveals what he knows and what he's thinking in two important internal memos found in his correspondence file—Department of Health Commissioner's Office Files, Record Series 13307-95, box 1, New York State Archives. The first is a memo from Axelrod to Michael Del Giudice, a member of Governor Carey's cabinet, on Jan. 31, 1979, and the second is a memo to the state commissioners William Hennessey and Robert Flacke on Feb. 2, 1979.

224 **Freedom of Information request:** James Clark to Axelrod, Feb. 5, 1979, box 4, Axelrod memos, LGLC.

224 **Option one:** Axelrod laid out all the options in detail in his Feb. 2, 1979, memo.

225 **"Expert on Useless Housewife Data":** Gibbs, *Love Canal: My Story,* 94.

225 **the state had considered everything:** Axelrod supplemental order, Feb. 8, 1979.

226 **"You're going to kill us!":** "Residents Attack State Actions," *NG,* Feb. 9, 1979.

226 **"Bravo":** James Clark to Axelrod, Feb. 11, 1979, box 4, Axelrod memos, LGLC.

227 **"By the time a woman":** "State Will Push for U.S. Help on Latest Canal Relocations," *BEN,* Feb. 10, 1979.

227 **"We're going to leave it":** "Canal Homeowners Take Coffin to Carey's Office," *BEN,* Feb. 15, 1979.

227 **"The health statistics in Harlem":** "State Turns Cool on Canal Action After Campaign," *BEN,* Feb. 17, 1979.

227 **"What he was attempting":** Axelrod to LaFalce, Feb. 22, 1979, Department of Health Commissioner's Office Files, Record Series 13307-95, box 1, New York State Archives.

228 **"Do you know what it's like":** Transcript of the television documentary "A Love Canal Family," *U.S. Chronicle,* Luella Kenny personal collection.

36. NOW AND FOREVERMORE

229 **Gibbs watched Kenny:** Gibbs, interview with author, Dec. 16, 2019.

229 **didn't need to be convinced:** Kenny, interview with author, Nov. 25, 2019.

229 **wouldn't have had much in common:** Gibbs, interview with author, Dec. 12, 2019; Kenny, interview with author, Nov. 27, 2019.

230 **"How many more children":** "Canal Parents Recall Helpless Feeling as Death Claimed Child," *BEN,* April 22, 1979.

230 **$20 million:** Love Canal Task Force status report to state legislature, "Love Canal Toxic Waste Dump Site," March 7, 1979.

230 **shaky legal ground:** "State Will Push for U.S. Help on Latest Canal Relocations," *BEN,* Feb. 10, 1979.

230 **"We are not purchasing":** "Love Canal Aid Could 'Snowball,' Carey Says," *BCE,* Feb. 23, 1979.

231 **"they bought it":** "EPA Official Under Fire for Canal Cost Remarks," *NG,* Feb. 22, 1979.

231 **"Let's be honest":** "U.S. Spurns Bulk of Love Canal Costs," *BEN,* Jan. 27, 1979.

231 **hoped to be part:** Casper, interview with author, Dec. 7, 2020.

231 **new legislation:** "LaFalce Seeks Toxin Curbs, Aid for Victims," *BEN,* Jan. 18, 1979.

231 **going nowhere:** Casper, interview with author, Dec. 7, 2020.

231 **a unique combination:** Nomination of Thomas Cash Jorling, Hearing Before the Committee of Environment and Public Works, U.S. Senate, 95th Cong., June 13, 1977; Jorling, interview with author, April 8, 2020.

232 **thirty-two thousand forgotten landfills:** "Pollution Crisis of the '80s: Industrial, Chemical Wastes," *Boston Globe,* Dec. 11, 1978.

232 **"The one who pays":** "Oozing Earth," *Washington Post,* Sept. 4, 1978.

232 **What the government needed:** The author conducted interviews with multiple EPA administrators who were part of the legislative talks that winter, including Jorling, interview with author, April 8, 2020; Larry Snowhite, interview with author, April 9, 2020; and Chuck Warren, interview with author, April 23, 2020.

232 **hit the road:** Details about Jorling's tour of the Valley of the Drums and the site itself come from multiple sources including interviews with Jorling, interviews with others on the trip, and two key news sources: "Tour of Ille-

gal Dumping Grounds Leaves Federal Official Shocked," *Louisville Courier-Journal,* Feb. 3, 1979; "Kentucky's Valley of Drums," *San Francisco Examiner,* Feb. 25, 1979.

233 **one of the EPA's loudest critics:** Gore had been critical of the EPA since the fall of 1978, when some agents testified before his House committee that budgetary cutbacks and concerns about inflation were limiting the agency's ability to stop polluters.

37. LISTEN TO THE PEOPLE WHO KNOW

234 **"I have no idea":** In March 1979, Lois Gibbs began keeping a handwritten journal in a composition notebook, which she shared with the author in Jan. 2020. Many details in this chapter—and the chapters to follow—come from these journals. Gibbs journal, March 14, 1979.

234 **early dress rehearsal:** Ibid., March 9, 1979.

235 **laughed in his face:** Paigen, interview with author, Jan. 17, 2020.

235 **nearly $3 billion:** "Canal Residents Plan Push for Full Evacuation," *BEN,* Jan. 29, 1979.

235 **the best way to recoup:** "State May Sue Hooker for Canal Cost," *NG,* March 13, 1979.

235 **By the state's count:** Dump inventory list, Task Force on Hazardous Waste Commissioner's Files, Record Series 22574-13, box 2, New York State Archives.

236 **summoned the press:** Details of the press conference can be found in the news coverage of March 15, 1979, as well as the first full-page ad that Hooker placed in the newspapers four days later on March 19.

236 **"Bruce knows":** *BCE,* May 29, 1979.

237 **bum a ride:** Gibbs journal, April 4, 1979.

237 **begging for money:** Fundraising letters, winter and spring 1979, box 2, LGLC.

237 **"I don't know how":** Gibbs journal, March 14, 1979.

238 **"Harry will have a fit":** Ibid., March 19, 1979.

38. NO JOB IS WORTH YOUR LIFE

239 **"Do you solemnly swear":** Details in this chapter come from these sources: interviews with Gibbs, Paigen, LaFalce, and Casper; Gibbs's hand-written journal recorded at the time; and the transcript of the Hazardous Waste Disposal hearings from March, April, May, and June 1979, before the House Subcommittee on Oversight and Investigations of the Committee on Interstate and Foreign Commerce. Testimony transcript, March 21, 1979, 60.

239 **a whirlwind of events:** Gibbs journal, March 20, 1979.

239 **knew what he really wanted:** Gibbs, interview with author, Feb. 3, 2021.

240 **"The subcommittee will come to order":** House Subcommittee on Oversight and Investigations, testimony transcript, March 21, 1979, 1.

240 **"populist shinkicker":** "Grazing the Tall Grass in Retirement," *Washington Post,* Jan. 18, 1980.

241 **"There is scum":** House Subcommittee on Oversight and Investigations, testimony transcript, March 21, 1979, 24.

241 **"are more dangerous than nitroglycerin":** Ibid., 20.

241 **Casper watched:** Casper, interview with author, Dec. 7, 2020.

241 **"It pinpointed":** House Subcommittee on Oversight and Investigations, testimony transcript, March 21, 1979, 25.

242 **"This little boy":** Ibid., 26.

242 **"Complaints got so bad":** Ibid., 33.

242 **"Have any of the three of you":** Ibid., 52.

242 **"As Congressman Gore said":** Ibid., 35.

243 **thought the union workers disorganized:** Gibbs journal, March 20, 1979.

243 **"No job is worth your life":** House Subcommittee on Oversight and Investigations, testimony transcript, March 21, 1979, 51.

243 **"I will present information":** Ibid., 60.

244 **"What you are telling us":** Ibid., 78.

244 **"I think you can immediately see":** Ibid., 63.

244 **"When did you present":** Ibid., 80.

244 **"There were several comments":** Ibid.

245 **"Their chemicals will not melt away":** Ibid., 69.

245 **"This is a boy":** Ibid., 67.

245 **tried to track down advance copies:** Gibbs journal, March 22, 1979.

246 **"I just wanted to make it clear":** House Subcommittee on Oversight and Investigations, testimony transcript, March 21, 1979, 140.

246 **"I ask that you do what you can":** Ibid., 92.

246 **"I do not question":** Ibid., March 22, 1979, 306.

247 **An embarrassing mess:** Gibbs journal, March 22, 1979.

247 **"Who cares?":** Ibid., March 23, 1979.

247 **more commotion:** Ibid., April 11, 1979.

248 **would soon be leaving:** The Niagara Falls Housing Authority did not keep records noting the exact date of their moves. But according to interviews with Thornton's family, Elene moved sometime in 1979. The city directory notes Elene's forwarding address as an apartment on Cherry Walk. And according to the *Buffalo Courier-Express,* Agnes Jones moved by that fall. The *Courier-Express* records the Joneses' next address on Fifty-Ninth Street.

248 **Agnes Jones stabbed:** Details of this event come from two places: "Girl, 15, Stabbed; Mother Charged," *BCE,* Oct. 20, 1979; Carol Jones, interview with author, Oct. 24, 2020.

248 **Gibbs would face criticism:** Elizabeth D. Blum's 2008 book, *Love Canal Revisited,* is a deeply researched academic review of how race, class, and gen-

der played important roles bringing people together—and also, at times, tearing them apart—during the crisis in the late 1970s.

248 **two key mistakes:** Handwritten notes, box 5, folder 17, LGLC.

248 **Had the two groups come together:** Gibbs, interview with author, Feb. 5, 2020.

249 **green chemical leachate:** "More Leachate Spills on Canal Area Road," *BCE,* April 13, 1979.

39. THE BIRD IN BLACK CREEK

250 **thinking she saw something:** "A Love Canal Family," *U.S. Chronicle,* Luella Kenny personal collection.

251 **many arguments:** Testimony of Eileen Matsulavage, April 5, 1979, Love Canal Collections, Ecumenical Task Force of the Niagara Frontier Records, University at Buffalo.

251 **$3,600 in annual bills:** Eileen Matsulavage to President Carter, Nov. 15, 1978, Ibid.

251 **would have been considered unacceptable:** New York State Department of Health, chemical report for the house at 9714 Greenwald Avenue, Task Force on Hazardous Waste Commissioner's Files, Record Series 22574-13, box 2, folder 32, New York State Archives. The state recorded benzene at 27 ppm inside the house and toluene at 48 ppm. According to federal standards at the time, workers were not to be exposed to more than 25 ppm of benzene over the course of an eight-hour shift or 100 ppm of toluene over a ten-hour shift. But acceptable levels of benzene were later significantly reduced. Today, employers are required by law to ensure that workers aren't exposed to more than 1 ppm of benzene over the course of an eight-hour shift.

251 **"I recommend that you move":** Paigen to Eileen Matsulavage, Feb. 16, 1979, Task Force on Hazardous Waste Commissioner's Files, Record Series 22574-13, box 2, folder 32, New York State Archives.

251 **refused to even list it:** Eileen Matsulavage to Kane Brokerage, Jan. 29, 1979, Ibid.

251 **an enthusiastic classified ad:** Prozeller appraisal report, Ibid.

251 **"And who knows what else?":** Matsulavage to Carter, Nov. 15, 1978, Ibid.

252 **twenty times higher:** "Higher Dioxin Levels at Love Canal," *BCE,* April 14, 1979; "Dioxin Facts: Answers to Commonly Asked Questions," EPA, Office of Public Affairs, July 1984.

252 **"troublesome" and "long-term":** The leaked internal report, called "Operation Bootstrap," can be found in its entirety in the congressional records of the hearings before the Subcommittee on Oversight and Investigations of the Committee on Interstate and Foreign Commerce, 96th Cong., Serial No. 96-49, 1704.

252 **"I know that two out of every three":** "Tale Unfolds Hazards at Niagara Chemical Plant," *Camden (N.J.) Courier-Post,* April 19, 1979.

253 **honor student:** "NTHS Honor Society Initiates 22 Members," *Tonawanda News,* May 25, 1964.

253 **didn't particularly like:** Gibbs journal, April 20, 1979.

253 **interview while shaving:** "Releasing Hooker Report Brought Peace of Mind," *BEN,* April 18, 1979.

253 **whirlpool bathtub:** "Employees Tell Federal Investigators About Hooker 'Chamber of Horrors,'" *BEN,* April 19, 1979.

253 **"He's a little crazy":** Gibbs journal, April 20, 1979.

253 **cold to her:** Ibid., April 14, 1979.

253 **"We welcome each and all!":** Ecumenical Task Force flyer, n.d., Niagara Falls Housing Authority archive.

254 **"I just found out":** Ibid., March 12, 1979.

254 **Gibbs led a group of residents:** The residents burned Carey and Axelrod in effigy on April 16, 1979.

254 **That night:** Gibbs journal, April 16, 1979.

254 **"The time is still not set":** Love Canal Homeowners Association newsletter, April 20, 1979.

255 **"We Voted You In":** Details of the protests around Carey's visit come from "Carey Encounters Boos, Applause in Falls Visit," *BEN,* April 27, 1979, and "Gov. Carey to Restudy Position on Love Canal," *BCE,* April 27, 1979.

255 **"Expect demonstrators":** "Briefing Material—Love Canal—Governor's Trip to Niag. Falls—April 26, 1979," Governor's Love Canal Inter-Agency Task Force Chairman's Files, Record Series 13430, box 8, New York State Archives.

255 **Inside the hotel:** Gibbs journal, April 26, 1979.

256 **tried to put a positive spin:** "Gov. Carey to Restudy Position on Love Canal."

256 **glare at him:** Gibbs journal, April 26, 1979.

257 **"But even after a couple of reminders":** Luella Kenny to Stephen Kim (state scientist), March 23, 1979, Kenny personal collection.

257 **The day before the meeting:** Kenny initially informed the author about the bird dying in the creek in her backyard in an interview on Nov. 27, 2019. Skeptical that such a fantastic story could be true, the author then confirmed it with interviews with the other two people who were there that day: Stephen Lester and the state scientist Stephen Kim. But the key document confirming this anecdote comes from Lester's daily logs, written in the moment, at that time, in order to document his work for the state. In his daily log on June 7, 1979, Lester chronicles his visit to the Kennys' house and writes in detail about the dead bird. Lester dailies, box 5, LGLC.

258 **In a small room at Roswell Park:** Kenny to an independent doctor investigating Jon Allen's death, Nov. 30, 1979, Kenny personal collection.

40. ALL-OUT OPPOSITION

259 **Jorling was beginning to fear:** Jorling, interview with author, April 8, 2020.

259 **"Something must be done":** "Federal Officials Shocked by Tour of Illegal Dumping Grounds," *Louisville Courier-Journal,* Feb. 3, 1979.

259 **resistance at every turn:** Jorling, interview with author, April 8, 2020; Eliot Cutler, interview with author, April 20, 2020.

259 **One evening late that spring:** Three people were party to this phone call: Costle, Cutler, and Jorling. The author rebuilt this scene from interviews with the two surviving people in the room: Cutler and Jorling.

261 **"Up until the time":** Statement of Robert Powers, May 18, 1979, in testimony before the Subcommittee on Environmental Pollution and Resource Protection of the Committee on Environment and Public Works, U.S. Senate, 96th Cong., Serial No. 96-H9, 60.

261 **a memo that Wilkenfeld himself had written:** The memo from 1958 can be found in the congressional records of the hearings before the Subcommittee on Oversight and Investigations of the Committee on Interstate and Foreign Commerce, 96th Cong., Serial No. 96-49, 651.

261 **"Do you believe that children":** Congressional transcript, Hearing Before the Subcommittee on Oversight and Investigations, 651.

262 **"Did you ask for":** Ibid., 653.

262 **"Did you continue to monitor":** Ibid., 654.

262 **"No," Wilkenfeld said. "We did not":** Ibid., 665–66.

263 **"He was only speaking":** Ibid., 667.

263 **"This whole incident":** Ibid.

263 **quieter act of bureaucratic resistance:** Details of the meeting with President Carter in the Cabinet Room come from three sources: Tom Jorling, interview with author, April 8, 2020; Eliot Cutler, interview with author, April 20, 2020; and Presidential Daily Diary, Appendix "C," June 7, 1979, Jimmy Carter Presidential Library and Museum.

264 **busy morning:** Presidential Daily Diary, June 7, 1979, Carter Presidential Library and Museum.

265 **"all-out opposition":** "CMA Blasts Superfund Plan on Dump Cleanups," *Chemical Week,* Sept. 5, 1979.

265 **administrative nightmare:** "Chemical Industry Group Hits 'Superfund' Proposal," *BEN,* July 13, 1979.

265 **"there is no major":** "Hooker Aide Defends Firm on Love Canal," *BEN,* Sept. 13, 1979.

41. NOT MANY WHISTLEBLOWERS SURVIVE

266 **On the same day:** Gibbs journal, June 13, 1979.

266 **get some dynamite:** Ibid.; FBI report filed in Buffalo on Aug. 30, 1979, and obtained via a Freedom of Information request in 2019.

266 **kicked in the door:** Details of the incident involving the former Hooker employee come from Gibbs's journal, June 14, 1979, and multiple news stories, including "Chase, Violence in Love Canal Office Leads to Arrest of Man," *BCE,* June 15, 1979; "'I've Been Hounded,' Claims Jailed Bayliss," *BCE,* June 17, 1979; "Bayliss Held for Jury," *Tonawanda News,* June 21, 1979; "Bayliss Now Faces Life's Bitter Ashes," *BCE,* June 24, 1979; and coverage of his guilty plea in the *Tonawanda News,* Jan. 28, 1981.

267 **"Civil Unrest":** Complaint, Aug. 30, 1979, FBI records.

267 **appeared to be serious:** Congressional transcripts, Subcommittee on Oversight and Investigations of the Committee on Interstate and Foreign Commerce, 96th Cong., Serial No. 96-49, testimony of David Axelrod, 307.

267 **"It is for these reasons":** Anonymous letter, n.d., box 1, Axelrod memos sent out, LGLC.

268 **about her interviews:** Paigen to Charles Pokrandt in the Communications Department, memo, Feb. 16, 1979, RPBOV, PC.

268 **"I would never consider":** Ibid.

268 **she was the foot soldier:** Glen Haughie, interview with author, April 6, 2020.

268 **That spring, LaFalce asked:** According to Gibbs's journals, LaFalce first mentioned that he would ask the EPA and NIEHS to review Paigen's data at a meeting with Paigen and Gibbs on March 9, 1979. These meetings ultimately took place on April 12, with Paigen, and April 26, with Axelrod, according to the committee's own report.

269 **two notable conclusions:** Dr. David Rall, director of NIEHS, "Report of Meetings Between Scientists from HEW and EPA, and Dr. Beverly Paigen and Scientists of the State of New York Department of Health Concerning Love Canal," July 26, 1979. Box 3, folder 35, Rall, David—NIEHS, LGLC.

269 **called Beverly to discuss a new policy:** Pressman to Paigen, memo, June 8, 1979, RPBOV.

269 **was a benefit to her:** Paigen written explanation, 73, RPBOV.

269 **Less than two weeks later:** Ibid., 2.

269 **"The loss of Dr. Paigen's technical":** Collin to Eugene Seebald (director of the Division of Water for the DEC), memo, July 5, 1979, RPBOV.

270 **"a poorly conceived witch hunt":** Axelrod to Dr. Robert Huffaker (on-site safety officer in Niagara Falls), memo, June 19, 1979, Department of Health Commissioner's Office Files, Record Series 13307-95, box 1, New York State Archives.

270 **being followed or watched:** Paigen, interview with author, Feb. 12, 2020.

270 **"singled out":** Council of Scientists to Axelrod, memo, Sept. 19, 1979, RPBOV.

270 **"I was concerned":** Ken Paigen to Axelrod, memo, Sept. 17, 1979, RPBOV.

271 **slow to reply:** In her documentation in the Roswell Park Board of Visitors Binder, Paigen says Axelrod never replied, and a review of his correspondence confirms that. The Department of Health Commissioner's Office Files, Record Series 13307-95, at the New York State Archives contains a record of Axelrod's outgoing mail. There are no letters to either Ken Paigen or the Council of Scientists.

271 **to complain about the coverage:** Axelrod to Paul MacClennan (reporter for the *Buffalo Evening News*), memo, Aug. 27, 1979, Department of Health Commissioner's Office Files, Record Series 13307-95, box 1, New York State Archives.

271 **findings regarding Love Canal were incomplete:** Axelrod to Clare Whitney, memo replying to follow-up questions submitted by Congressman Al Gore's subcommittee in Washington, Sept. 26, 1979, Department of Health Commissioner's Office Files, Record Series 13307-95, box 1, New York State Archives.

271 **"Your use of Departmental funds":** Axelrod to Paigen, memo, Oct. 16, 1979, Department of Health Commissioner's Office Files, Record Series 13307-95, box 1, New York State Archives.

271 **received a notice:** Paigen, interview with author, Feb. 12, 2020; James Tully (state tax commissioner) to Paigen, letter, May 25, 1980, PC; "State Denies Audit Tied to Canal Role," *BCE,* July 26, 1980; "Paigen Gets Apology on Audit of Taxes; Canal Link Is Denied," *BEN,* July 25, 1980.

271 **"We do not select":** James Tully (state tax commissioner) to Beverly Paigen, May 25, 1980, PC.

271 **filled with news clippings:** Paigen, interview with author, Feb. 12, 2020; *BCE; BEN.*

271 **"Not many whistleblowers":** This quotation appeared in a profile of Paigen in *Buffalo Spree* (Fall 1979). The issue was saved by Paigen and given to the author as part of her personal collection.

42. STILL HERE, CHEMICALLY TREATED

272 **"Dear editor":** Letter to the editor, n.d., box 3, folder 11, LGLC.

273 **a series of escalating criteria:** Dr. Laverne Campbell to William Hartenstein (on-site Love Canal coordinator), memo, June 21, 1979, Task Force on Hazardous Waste Commissioner's Files, Record Series 22574-13, box 2, New York State Archives.

273 **"We are still here":** Gibbs to Axelrod, July 12, 1979, Task Force on Hazardous Waste Commissioner's Files, Record Series 22574-13, box 2, New York State Archives.

273 **That summer, heavy rains:** Stephen Lester dailies, July 31 and Aug. 1, 10, 13, and 20, 1979, box 5, LGLC.

274 **Crouching at the water's edge:** Outfall pipe log for Black Creek at Ninety-Sixth Street and Greenwald Avenue, Aug. 1979, Kenny personal collection. Kenny kept the log for roughly two weeks, before making a copy of her findings and sharing it with the state.

43. LOOKS LIKE YOU'VE BECOME THE ENEMY

276 **sooner go to jail:** "Would Go to Jail, Parents Vow in Canal-School Rift," *BCE,* Aug. 24, 1979.

276 **Crews struck a swale:** Stephen Lester dailies, Aug. 24, 1979, box 5, LGLC.

277 **"It's just been unbearable":** "Residents Flee Fumes in Love Canal Area," *BCE,* Aug. 25, 1979.

277 **"No further work":** Gibbs to William Hartenstein (on-site coordinator), Aug. 31, 1979, Task Force on Hazardous Waste Commissioner's Files, Record Series 22574-13, box 2, New York State Archives.

277 **claimed she fainted:** "Felled by Love Canal Area Fumes, Woman with Head Injury Claims," *BCE,* Aug. 29, 1979.

277 **strong sense of social conscience:** "Hundreds of Canal Residents Face Eviction," *BCE,* Sept. 12, 1979.

277 **didn't want to get involved:** "Love Canal 'Refugees' 'at Home' in Church," *BCE,* Sept. 13, 1979.

278 **"I've got it!":** Ibid.

278 **"We reject":** Axelrod statement, Sept. 11, 1979, Task Force on Hazardous Waste Commissioner's Files, Record Series 22574-13, box 3, New York State Archives.

278 **protested outside the Rodeway Inn:** "35 Win Canal Tiff; Scores Wait," *BCE,* Sept. 13, 1979.

278 **Twenty-nine families escaped:** Dr. Laverne Campbell to Dr. Glen Haughie, memo, Oct. 25, 1979, includes a chart breaking down where the evacuated residents lived in the neighborhood, Task Force on Hazardous Waste Commissioner's Files, Record Series 22574-13, box 3, New York State Archives.

278 **"We can't eat":** "Mrs. Gibbs Plans Trip to Washington to Seek Assistance," *BCE,* Nov. 1, 1979.

279 **"It's unbelievable":** "Fonda Calls Love Canal 'Immense Tragedy,'" *BCE,* Oct. 5, 1979.

279 **Black and white and celebratory:** Sarah Rich, interview with author, Jan. 30, 2020.

279 **"Perhaps I can be of help":** Fonda to Gibbs, Feb. 21, 1980, box 2, folder 25, Fonda and Hayden, LGLC.

279 **late-afternoon cocktail party:** Advertising flyer for the fundraising event, "Conversations with Jane Fonda/Tom Hayden," 3:30–5:00 p.m., Oct. 4, 1979, box 2, folder 25, Fonda and Hayden, LGLC.

279 **"We don't have the money":** "Carey Rejects Canal Appeals," *BCE,* Oct. 5, 1979.

279 **At the rate he was going:** According to weekly expense reports in the Task Force on Hazardous Waste Commissioner's Files, Record Series 22574-13, box 3, New York State Archives, the state was spending at least $50,000 a week on hotel rooms throughout the fall.

280 **With no kitchens:** Kenny, interview with author, Jan. 28, 2020; Gibbs, interview with author, Feb. 18, 2020.

280 **"Temporary Relocation":** "Notice to Temporarily Relocated Love Canal Residents," Task Force on Hazardous Waste Commissioner's Files, Record Series 22574-13, box 3, New York State Archives.

44. VERY BEST WISHES FOR THE NEW YEAR

281 **furious about the notice:** Kenny to Axelrod, Oct. 12, 1979, Kenny personal collection.

281 **spy for her:** Gibbs, interview with author, Feb. 6, 2020; Kenny, interview with author, Jan. 28, 2020.

281 **"My concern for my family":** Kenny to Axelrod, Oct. 12, 1979.

281 **high levels of dioxin:** "Dioxin Found in Black Creek," *BCE,* Nov. 10, 1979.

281 **"significant levels":** Axelrod to Robert Flacke, Nov. 7, 1979, Department of Health Commissioner's Office Files, Record Series 13307-95, box 1, New York State Archives.

282 **thirty-one times higher:** "Dioxin Facts: Answers to Commonly Asked Questions."

282 **sixty times higher:** Officials recorded the crawfish with levels of dioxin at three parts per billion. The Food and Drug Administration recommends not eating fish with levels greater than .05 parts per billion.

282 **sought bids:** Cataract Security Systems proposal, June 14, 1979, Task Force on Hazardous Waste Commissioner's Files, Record Series 22574-13, box 3, security reports folder, New York State Archives.

282 **be more vigilant:** Harvey Albond (city manager) to Hartenstein (on-site coordinator), Oct. 4, 1979; Hartenstein to Joseph Slack (project manager), memo, Oct. 17, 1979; Slack to SCA Waste Services, Oct. 31, 1979; and Hartenstein to Cataract Security, Nov. 5, 1979, all in Task Force on Hazardous Waste Commissioner's Files, Record Series 22574-13, box 3, security reports folder, New York State Archives.

282 **thieves used crowbars:** Multiple patrol reports, fall and winter 1979, Task Force on Hazardous Waste Commissioner's Files, Record Series 22574-13, box 3, security reports folder, New York State Archives.

282 **stealing the boys' birthday presents:** Luella Kenny, interview with author, Jan. 28, 2020; Stephen Kenny, interview with author, April 9, 2020.

283 **couldn't say what Kenny should do:** Axelrod to Kenny, Oct. 16, 1979,

Department of Health Commissioner's Office Files, Record Series 13307-95, New York State Archives.

283 **real action:** Axelrod to Flacke, Nov. 7, 1979, and Axelrod to Michael Del Giudice (member of Governor Carey's cabinet), memo, "Subject: Niagara Falls," Oct. 12, 1979, Department of Health Commissioner's Office Files, Record Series 13307-95, box 1, New York State Archives.

283 **needed to buy more homes:** In a letter to the governor dated Oct. 17, 1979, William Hennessey, chair of the Love Canal Task Force, tells the governor that he and Axelrod have discussed "a program whereby we would purchase the properties." Task Force on Hazardous Waste Commissioner's Files, Record Series 22574-13, box 3, New York State Archives.

283 **"We have previously outlined":** Axelrod to Michael Del Giudice (member of Governor Carey's cabinet), memo, "Subject: Niagara Falls," Oct. 12, 1979.

283 **framework for this new plan:** "Assembly OKs Aid for Canal Residents," *BCE,* Nov. 2, 1979; "Love Canal Aid Boosted by $5 Million," *BCE,* Nov. 3, 1979; "Carey Signs Purchase Bill for Canal Homes," *BCE,* Nov. 6, 1979; "Love Canal Home-Buying Bill Clarified," *BCE,* Nov. 9, 1979.

284 **tried the latter approach:** "Motel Takes Families to Court," *BCE,* Nov. 8, 1979.

284 **Norman's mother:** Kenny, interview with author, Jan. 28, 2020.

284 **get divorced:** Gibbs, interview with author, Feb. 18, 2020.

284 **quick pops of random gunfire:** Task Force on Hazardous Waste Commissioner's Files, Record Series 22574-13, box 3, security reports folder, New York State Archives. Details referenced here come from the patrols on Oct. 20, Nov. 1, and Nov. 11, 1979.

284 **hardly noticed:** Gibbs, interview with author, Feb. 18, 2020.

284 **Five days before Christmas:** "U.S. Files Suit for $124 Million on Love Canal," *NYT,* Dec. 21, 1980.

285 **"serious about attacking it":** "U.S. Sues Chemical Dumpers," *Washington Post,* Dec. 21, 1979.

285 **agreed to consider it:** "Dr. Paigen's Open Hearing Bid Denied," *BCE,* Dec. 15, 1979.

285 **finally published Gibbs's letter:** "Axelrod Ouster Urged by Gibbs," *BCE,* Dec. 21, 1979; "State Harassing Love Canal Angel," *BEN,* Dec. 21, 1979.

285 **to defend Paigen:** These quotations come from multiple letters written to newspapers in 1980, including *BCE,* Jan. 21, 1980; *NG,* Jan. 28, 1980; and *NG,* Feb. 13, 1980.

285 **"perceived or real":** Axelrod to Dick Dewling (acting EPA administrator), Dec. 24, 1979, Department of Health Commissioner's Office Files, Record Series 13307-95, box 1, New York State Archives.

285 **squabbles with Paigen:** Axelrod to Carey, memo, Dec. 28, 1979, Department of Health Commissioner's Office Files, Record Series 13307-95, box 1, New York State Archives.

285 **"With very best wishes":** Axelrod to Davis, Dec. 31, 1979, Department of

Health Commissioner's Office Files, Record Series 13307-95, box 1, New York State Archives.

45. PRAY FOR THE DEAD

289 **picked her out of the crowd:** Joan Malone, interview with author, March 9, 2020.

289 **librarian of the year:** "Sr. Malone Honored for Library Work," *BCE,* June 6, 1979.

290 **liked Malone right away:** Kenny, interview with author, Jan. 28, 2020.

290 **bolder than she looked:** Malone, interview with author, March 9, 2020.

290 **abused by her father:** Malone broke her silence about the abuse after her father's death in 1981. "Seeking Justice in a Crime of Everlasting Pain," *Buffalo News,* April 27, 1992.

290 **"We Want Jobs":** Joan Malone scrapbook, Joan Malone personal collection.

290 **made some Catholics uncomfortable:** Malone, interview with author, March 9, 2020.

290 **"Pray for the dead":** "The Religious Life," *Buffalo News,* June 10, 1983.

291 **"Because there are other things":** "For Activists, Some Victories from Defeats," *Chicago Tribune,* May 21, 1979.

291 **To distract from dissident factions:** "The Metamorphosis of the Shareholders' Meeting," *NYT,* April 9, 1978.

291 **In 1979 alone:** "Churches Resume Long Battle over S. Africa with GM, Ford," *Detroit Free Press,* Jan. 31, 1979; "Directors Gird for Activists' Siege," *Chicago Tribune,* Feb. 26, 1979; "Sweet Victory for Cereal Maker," *Detroit Free Press,* April 22, 1979; "For Activists, Some Victories from Defeats"; "G.M. Backed on S. Africa," *Detroit Free Press,* May 26, 1979.

291 **"As you know":** Malone to Bob Morris (Interfaith Center on Corporate Responsibility representative), Feb. 7, 1980, Interfaith Center on Corporate Responsibility records, 1966–2011 (hereafter referred to as ICCR), Rare Book & Manuscript Library, Columbia University.

292 **"I represent the Sisters of St. Francis":** Malone to Hammer, Jan. 8, 1980, ICCR.

292 **The resolution cited:** This resolution can be found in at least two places: ICCR and Luella Kenny's personal records.

292 **"alarming indifference":** "Trying to Be Fair About Poison," *NYT,* Aug. 9, 1979.

292 **highest-paid lawyer:** "World Records," *Detroit Free Press,* Oct. 23, 1972.

292 **client list:** "Erving Sues to Break Squires' Pact," *NYDN,* June 14, 1972; "Johnny Carson Will Return to 'Tonight' Monday," *NYT,* April 21, 1967; "J.J. Has Never Been Through Such Hell," *NYDN,* Oct. 2, 1954; "Lawyers 'Setting Fire' Under Stubborn Bobo," *Miami News,* June 30, 1953.

293 **faced criminal charges:** "Hammer Pleads Guilty to Illegal '72 Campaign Gifts," *LAT,* Oct. 2, 1975; "Prosecutors to Seek Felony Charges Against

Hammer," *LAT,* Jan. 20, 1976; "Hammer Fined, Gets Probation," *LAT,* March 24, 1976.

293 **Nizer invited the group:** Dick Ullrich to Malone and Morris, memo, Feb. 14, 1980, ICCR.

293 **touch of awe:** Details of this meeting come from multiple sources, including Malone, interview with author, March 9, 2020; Roger Cook (activist), interview with author, Aug. 31, 2020; Bishop Edward Head to Sister Paula Fox, March 11, 1980, Malone personal collection; "Power, Wealth Tools for Occidental's Boss," *St. Catharines Standard* (Ontario, Can.), Oct. 18, 1986; "Activist Nun Makes Point of Keeping Firms Honest," *BCE,* Sept. 7, 1981; and a detailed memo in ICCR, documenting what happened at the meeting: Dick Ullrich to Filers of Occidental Resolution, March 6, 1980.

294 **"Chemicals are vital":** Proposed Occidental statement, March 1, 1980, Kenny personal collection.

294 **weren't inclined to let:** Malone, interview with author, March 9, 2020; Cook, interview with author, Aug. 31, 2020.

294 **"Debriefing":** ICCR minutes from the post-meeting dinner, compiled by Dick Ullrich and sent to Filers of Occidental Resolution, March 6, 1980.

294 **On the same day:** Paul Hebner (vice president at Occidental) to William E. Morley (special counsel in the division of corporation finance at the Securities and Exchange Commission), March 1, 1980, Kenny personal collection.

295 **called a meeting:** Bishop Head to Sister Fox, March 11, 1980, Malone personal collection.

295 **"He has a lot of people":** *St. Catharines Standard* (Ontario, Can.), Oct. 18, 1986.

295 **In mid-April:** William E. Morley (special counsel in the division of corporation finance at the Securities and Exchange Commission) to Paul Hebner (vice president at Occidental), April 16, 1980, Kenny personal collection.

296 **Sketching it out in longhand:** Kenny, interview with author, Jan. 15, 2021.

296 **"My name":** Luella Kenny, "Statement to the Annual Meeting of Occidental Petroleum Shareholders—Corporate Responsibility Resolution," May 21, 1980, Love Canal Collections, Ecumenical Task Force of the Niagara Frontier Records, University at Buffalo.

46. A KANGAROO COURT

298 **a public meeting inside the Methodist church:** Handwritten announcement of meeting, Jan. 10, 1980, box 1, Association Reports, LGLC.

299 **"These tests":** Newsletter from Jan. 10, 1980, meeting, box 1, Association Reports, LGLC.

299 **Twenty people:** Paigen to Dr. Dante Picciano, May 8, 1980, box 5, LGLC.

299 **hadn't received an invitation:** "Roswell Meeting Set; Dr. Paigen Uninvited," *BCE,* Jan. 7, 1980.

299 **preparing for March:** RPBOV.

300 **"At issue in this controversy":** Statement to the Roswell Park Board of Visitors, March 7, 1980, PC.
300 **with winter still raging:** Weather reports, *BCE,* March 7–8, 1980.
300 **"After all," she told the board:** Statement, March 7, 1980, PC.
301 **hoping for a moment:** Newsletter from Jan. 10, 1980, meeting, box 1, Association Reports, LGLC.
301 **Axelrod sat with the board:** Paigen to the board, May 28, 1980, PC.
301 **"A kangaroo court":** "Lawmaker Scoffs at Roswell Ruling on Dr. Paigen Charge," *BCE,* June 4, 1980.
301 **"a chronic troublemaker":** Paigen to the board, May 28, 1980, PC.
301 **"I truly regret":** Ibid.
302 **On the same day:** "Gibbs Family Kept Apart by Love Canal," *BEN,* March 9, 1980; "Son's Illness Forces Lois Gibbs to Move," *BCE,* March 8, 1980.
302 **Michael was older now:** Michael Gibbs, interview with author, April 29, 2020.
302 **Tiny bruises:** Gibbs, interview with author, April 14, 2020; "Gibbs' Child Illness Not Leukemia," *BCE,* April 17, 1980.
303 **"idiopathic":** "Gibbs' Leukemia Tests Negative, Doctors Report," *BEN,* April 17, 1980.
303 **release her that Friday:** "Gibbs Child Returns Home from Hospital," *BCE,* April 18, 1980.
303 **Lois broke down:** Gibbs, interview with author, April 14, 2020.

47. A SIGNIFICANT POLITICAL PROBLEM

304 **corner office:** Moorman, interview with author, Jan. 25, 2021.
304 **a staff of nearly two hundred attorneys:** "U.S. Sues Chemical Dumpers," *Washington Post,* Dec. 21, 1979.
304 **"I can just hear":** "Environmentalist Now Calls for Unity, Not Confrontation," *St. Louis Post-Dispatch,* Nov. 22, 1977.
305 **saw it as a test case:** "U.S. Sues Chemical Dumpers"; Moorman, interview with author, Jan. 25, 2021.
305 **"A significant political problem":** Robert Harris (adviser on Carter's Council on Environmental Quality) to Barbara Blum, memo, June 2, 1980, Record Group 412, Love Canal Docket Hazardous Waste Enforcement Files, box 5, National Archives, College Park, Md. This two-page memo recounts for Blum the meetings that Harris had throughout the spring concerning the chromosome study. Hereafter cited as Harris to Blum, June 2, 1980.
305 **The rumor in Niagara Falls:** Details about the rumors come from two sources: Robert Harris, interview with author, Jan. 25, 2021; Harris to Blum, June 2, 1980.
306 **In one briefing:** Harris to Blum, June 2, 1980.
306 **picked up the phone:** Details about this day come from three sources: interviews with both Moorman and Harris; Harris to Blum, June 2, 1980.

48. EMOTIONAL FIRES

307 **Three White House staffers:** Harris to Blum, June 2, 1980; Harris, interview with author, Jan. 25, 2021.

307 **"The best, most objective":** Hearing Before the Committee on the Environment and Public Works, U.S. Senate, 96th Cong., Serial No. 96-H31, Nov. 13, 1979, 7.

308 **track him down:** Harris to Blum, June 2, 1980; Harris, interview with author, Jan. 25, 2021.

308 **"long acentric fragments":** Margery Shaw, "Love Canal Chromosome Study," *Science,* Aug. 15, 1980.

308 **extra genetic material:** Letter from a scientific review team at the University of Texas Health Science Center to Dr. Vilma Hunt at the EPA, June 5, 1980, box 1, chromosome study folder, LGLC.

308 **"notorious episodes":** Moorman to Attorney General Benjamin Civiletti, memo, May 15, 1980, Record Group 412, Love Canal Docket Hazardous Waste Enforcement Files, box 13, National Archives, College Park, Md.

308 **urged officials to be cautious:** In his completed study, dated May 14, 1980, and received by the federal government the next day, Dr. Dante Picciano clearly states that the findings were "preliminary" and required more investigation.

309 **"emotional fires":** Harris to Blum, June 2, 1980.

309 **"I want Hooker's answer":** Moorman to Civiletti, May 15, 1980.

309 **go on the offensive:** Hansen to Watson, memo, May 15, 1980, Record 309 412, Love Canal Docket Hazardous Waste Enforcement Files, box 13, National Archives, College Park, Md.

310 **it was too late:** Details about the leak come from multiple sources, including Harris to Blum, June 2, 1980; Harris, interview with author, Jan. 25, 2021; "State Rules Out New Canal Aid," *BCE,* May 19, 1980; and "Love Canal Chromosome Study," a letter written by the EPA's Stephen Gage and published in the journal *Science,* Aug. 1980.

310 **"Chromosome Damage Found":** *NG,* May 17, 1980.

310 **"Residents Not Yet Informed":** *NYT,* May 17, 1980.

310 **"Genetic Harm Tied to Canal":** *BCE,* May 17, 1980.

49. TELL US HOW YOU FEEL

311 **taking a bath:** Gibbs, *Love Canal: My Story,* 142.

311 **glass of wine:** Gibbs, interview with author, Feb. 18, 2020.

311 **dry her arm:** Gibbs, *Love Canal: My Story,* 142.

311 **selling $5 T-shirts:** Newsletter, May 2, 1980, box 1, association reports, LGLC.

312 **demonstration involving boats:** "Love Canal Task Force Moves on Relocation," *BCE,* May 10, 1980.

312 **"We realize":** Newsletter, May 2, 1980, box 1, association reports, LGLC.

312 **two women were practicing:** Malone, interview with author, March 9, 2020; Kenny, interview with author, Jan. 15, 2021.

312 **"Don't wait":** "Real Concern over Canal" (article from unknown publication), March 1980, Beverly Paigen files, 13307-86A, obtained by author via a Freedom of Information request, New York State Archives.

313 **could also be heckled:** Malone, interview with author, March 9, 2020.

313 **The man on the phone:** Gibbs, *Love Canal: My Story,* 142.

313 **list of names:** The names come from multiple news sources, including Fran Lucca, "Channel 17 Reports: Love Canal Special," 1980; *NBC Nightly News,* May 17, 1980; and "Tense Reactions of Those Tested," *BCE,* May 18, 1980.

313 **Wait a second:** Gibbs, *Love Canal: My Story,* 142.

314 **"It would show":** "Genetic Harm Tied to Canal," *BCE,* May 17, 1980.

314 **Blum stood before a wall:** *NBC Nightly News,* May 17, 1980.

314 **thought it was ridiculous:** Harris to Blum, June 2, 1980.

314 **The agency was working:** Lucca, "Channel 17 Reports: Love Canal Special."

315 **"Why Wednesday?":** "790 Canal Families May Evacuate," *BCE,* May 18, 1980.

315 **"We don't want to wait":** "Homeowners Are Bitter and Fearful as Results of Study Are Released," *NYT,* May 18, 1980.

315 **"We've been dealing with":** "790 Canal Families May Evacuate."

315 **unable to reach:** Ibid.

315 **The man refused to identify himself:** "Health Report Adds Fuel to Canal Relocation Push," *NG,* May 18, 1980.

315 **"unnecessary anxieties":** Hooker press release, May 17, 1980, Record Group 412, Love Canal Docket Hazardous Waste Enforcement Files, box 3, National Archives, College Park, Md.

315 **Some wept at the news:** Residents' reactions to their chromosome results come from multiple sources, including "790 Canal Families May Evacuate"; "Homeowners Are Bitter and Fearful as Results of Study Are Released"; "Health Report Adds Fuel to Canal Relocation Push"; Gibbs, interview with author, Feb. 18, 2020; Paigen, interview with author, Feb. 12, 2020; Barbara Quimby, interview with author, Dec. 16, 2019.

315 **their questions:** Lucca, "Channel 17 Reports: Love Canal Special"; *NBC Nightly News,* May 17, 1980.

316 **"Please act immediately":** Gibbs to Carter, telegram, May 17, 1980, box 6, telegrams folder, LGLC.

316 **bloodshed:** "Niagara OK of Authority Forecast," *BCE,* May 19, 1980.

316 **warned of trouble:** "State Rules Out New Canal Aid," *BCE,* May 19, 1980.

316 **coffee and doughnuts:** "Residents Banding Together for Support," *NG,* May 19, 1980.

316 **revealed where they were staying:** "710 Families May Be Evacuated from Canal," *NG,* May 19, 1980.

316 **Gibbs noted the location:** It was hard not to know where the two men were staying. Their location was mentioned in a story stripped across the banner of the *Niagara Gazette* that morning.

316 **In the state of Washington:** Details about the eruption of Mount St. Helens come from multiple sources, including "At Least 8 Dead as Peak Erupts; Worst Blast Yet," *NYT,* May 19, 1980; "Ash Makes Helena Ghostly," *Helena (Mont.) Independent Record,* May 19, 1980; "Mt. St. Helens Pours Its Cloud of Ashes Across Northwest," *NYT,* May 20, 1980; "Eruption Hits Northwest Harder Than Blizzard," *Springfield (Mo.) Leader and Press,* May 20, 1980; and "Volcano Spewing 'Fallout' over U.S.," *Cincinnati Enquirer,* May 20, 1980.

317 **thinking only about:** Kenny, interview with author, Jan. 15, 2021.

317 **"Help Us, for God's Sake":** "Residents Banding Together for Support."

50. THAT CROWD WILL RIP YOU APART

318 **that Monday morning:** The details of the events of this momentous day come from dozens of sources, including interviews with the participants, archival television news footage, and on-the-ground reporting published in five different newspapers the next day, including the *Buffalo Evening News,* the *Buffalo Courier-Express,* the *Niagara Gazette,* the *Rochester Democrat and Chronicle,* and *The New York Times.* But the most important documents are nearly two hundred pages of previously unseen FBI records, documenting blow by blow the events of the day.

318 **a restless crowd:** Gibbs, interview with author, Feb. 18, 2020; Quimby, interview with author, Dec. 16, 2019; Gibbs, *Love Canal: My Story,* 146; "Canal Residents' Fear Turns to Rage as 2 EPA Agents Held for 6 Hours," *NG,* May 20, 1980.

319 **needed to do something:** Gibbs, interview with author, Feb. 18, 2020; Gibbs, *Love Canal: My Story,* 147.

319 **picked up the phone:** According to the FBI records, it appears Gibbs was initially unable to reach Frank Napal and James Lucas at the hotel and made several other calls trying to find them. She subsequently spoke with someone at EPA headquarters in Washington, who seems to have relayed the message to the men to go to the neighborhood.

319 **first to arrive:** Frank Napal's FBI statement, May 19, 1980.

319 **taught courses:** "One Hostage 'Doesn't Mind,'" *BCE,* May 20, 1980.

319 **Upper West Side:** Napal lived at 40 West Seventy-Seventh Street in New York City.

320 **"The residents want a doctor":** Among the news coverage that day, one of the most intimate and detailed stories was reported by the *Rochester Democrat and Chronicle.* According to the note attached to the original story, Michael

Cordts and Jack Jones were the only two reporters inside the house for the entire affair. " 'Leave, Honey, You're Dead,' " *RDC,* May 20, 1980.

320 **marching orders:** Napal's FBI statement, May 19, 1980.

320 **"How can I call him":** Gibbs, *Love Canal: My Story,* 147.

320 **picked up the phone:** Napal's FBI statement, May 19, 1980.

320 **rural Ohio:** U.S. Census records for James Lucas, 1940.

320 **career public health servant:** According to his wedding announcement in *The Cincinnati Enquirer,* on May 7, 1961, Lucas attended medical school at the University of Cincinnati and joined the U.S. Public Health Service shortly thereafter.

320 **studying chemical agents for years:** "EPA Surveys Liver, Kidney Ailments During Peak of Carbon Tet in River," *Cincinnati Enquirer,* July 22, 1977.

320 **"We're not going to do":** Fran Lucca, "Channel 17 Reports: Love Canal Special," 1980.

321 **"Body barricade":** Ibid.

321 **remained in the office:** While people moved in and out of the office for much of the afternoon and evening, FBI records make clear that these three women were the prime "suspects."

321 **two-by-four:** James Lucas's FBI statement, May 19, 1980.

321 **"It shouldn't be":** " 'Leave, Honey, You're Dead.' "

321 **Gibbs wasn't thinking:** Gibbs, interview with author, Feb. 18, 2020.

321 **send Gibbs to prison:** Gibbs, *Love Canal: My Story,* 150.

321 **Around four o'clock:** FBI statements of Jeff Miller (the EPA's acting assistant administrator for enforcement) and Chuck Warren (the EPA's region II administrator), May 19, 1980.

321 **"proper thing":** "EPA Insists Incident Won't Affect Love Canal Decision," *BEN,* May 20, 1980.

321 **"Excuse me":** Ibid.

322 **once Warren had been informed:** Warren's FBI statement, May 19, 1980.

322 **Napal briefly described:** Napal's FBI statement, May 19, 1980.

322 **the news was all over Washington:** Blum, interview with author, Feb. 21, 2020; LaFalce, interview with author, Nov. 27, 2019; Casper, interview with author, Dec. 7, 2020.

322 **They were all worried:** FBI statements, multiple parties, May 19–20, 1980.

322 **informed Jim Moorman:** Jim Moorman's FBI statement, May 20, 1980.

322 **exactly fifteen minutes later:** FBI field report, May 19, 1980.

322 **put the house under surveillance:** Ibid.

322 **Perkins Cake & Steak:** Richard T. Bretzing (FBI's special agent in charge) to the manager of the Perkins Cake & Steak, May 21, 1980, FBI records.

322 **just walk out the door:** Napal's FBI statement, May 19, 1980.

323 **"I've been told":** The dialogue in this scene comes from the reporting of Cordts and Jones in the *RDC,* May 20, 1980. It was also corroborated by the FBI statements of both Napal and Lucas.

323 **didn't think it wise:** Napal's FBI statement, May 19, 1980.

323 **winking at the reporters:** " 'Leave, Honey, You're Dead.' "

323 **But Lucas didn't like:** Lucas's FBI statement, May 19, 1980.

323 **blankets and pillows:** In her memoir—*Love Canal: My Story*, 152—Gibbs noted that this request was strategic. She was trying to give the agitated crowd a job, something to do.

323 **concerned about the crowd:** In his FBI statement, Lucas said he was afraid not of the people inside the house but of the people outside the house.

323 **"You're damn right":** " 'Leave, Honey, You're Dead.' "

323 **describe the dimensions:** FBI notes, taken in the moment, show a detailed drawing of the layout of the house, provided by Napal and Lucas. " 'Leave, Honey, You're Dead.' "

323 **Suspect No. 1:** Handwritten notes of the FBI special agent Henry E. Ragle III, May 19, 1980.

323 **disconnected the phone:** In an interview, Gibbs said she doesn't remember disconnecting the phone. But this detail appears in two stories published the next day—" 'Leave, Honey, You're Dead' " and "EPA Insists Incident Won't Affect Love Canal Decision"—and a third story in the *NYT* on May 21, 1980, "Peaceful Vigil Resumed at Love Canal." The stories disagree about whether it was Napal or Lucas on the phone at that moment. The author went with the version written by the reporters who had the greatest access that day.

323 **"Relax":** " 'Leave, Honey, You're Dead.' "

324 **Paigen was horrified:** Paigen, interview with author, Feb. 12, 2020.

324 **he called to inform:** "LaFalce Prods Carter on Canal Evacuation," *BCE*, May 20, 1980.

324 **in a few minutes:** According to Carter's daily diary from May 19, 1980, the dinner that LaFalce attended began at 6:21 p.m.

324 **The White House wasn't going to bow:** Robert Harris's FBI statement, May 20, 1980.

324 **Innocent plans:** Gibbs, *Love Canal: My Story*, 152.

324 **"We are sick!":** Lucca, "Channel 17 Reports: Love Canal Special."

324 **Even Napal was amazed:** "EPA Insists Incident Won't Affect Love Canal Decision."

324 **Gibbs knew LaFalce was right:** Gibbs, *Love Canal: My Story*, 152; Gibbs, interview with author, Feb. 18, 2020.

324 **Around 6:40:** FBI reports of Special Agent Charles B. Wagner and Special Agent in Charge Richard T. Bretzing, May 20, 1980.

325 **would be released:** Napal's FBI statement, May 19, 1980.

325 **terms of their release:** The FBI agent on the phone with Lippes was Special Agent Henry E. Ragle III. The details of the negotiations between 7:30 p.m. and 8:49 p.m. come from his report, May 19, 1980.

325 **the word "hostage":** Gibbs, *Love Canal: My Story*, 153.

325 **wanted to delay:** Gibbs, interview with author, Feb. 3, 2021.

325 **Throughout the evening:** FBI report, Ragle interview with Robert Harris, May 20, 1980.

325 **A long line of dark, unmarked sedans:** "Peaceful Vigil Resumed at Love Canal."

325 **"You have two minutes":** Gibbs, *Love Canal: My Story,* 154.

326 **"I have told the White House":** Lucca, "Channel 17 Reports: Love Canal Special."

326 **asked allies to stand in the yard:** Ragle's FBI report, May 19, 1980.

326 **"It looks like she's working":** "Canal Residents' Fear Turns to Rage as 2 EPA Agents Held for 6 Hours," *NG,* May 20, 1980.

326 **If they wanted to take more hostages:** "EPA Insists Incident Won't Affect Love Canal Decision."

326 **"We've demonstrated we mean business":** Ibid.

326 **cleaned out the file cabinets:** "Peaceful Vigil Resumed at Love Canal."

326 **collected the kids:** Gibbs, interview with author, Feb. 3, 2021.

327 **lay down on the couch:** Gibbs, interview with author, Feb. 18, 2020.

51. TODAY WE HAVE TO BE MEEK

328 **Norman called Luella:** Kenny, interview with author, Sept. 9, 2020.

328 **Dan Rather:** Brit Hume was on the ground in Niagara Falls for *ABC Nightly News* the day of the hostage situation. CBS sent Rather up the next morning.

328 **set to air:** "WKBW Gets Program Chief from Indy," *BCE,* May 22, 1980.

328 **hopped in a car:** Kenny, interview with author, Feb. 4, 2021.

328 **rare cloudy day:** Weather, *LAT,* May 20–21, 1980.

328 **one of the nation's most opulent establishments:** "Beverly Hills—if You Want to Rub Elbows with Cheryl Ladd or Howard Cosell, Stay at the Wilshire Hotel," *Minneapolis Star,* Jan. 17, 1978.

328 **movie stars *lived* there:** Warren Beatty, Steve McQueen, and Roman Polanski were among the stars who lived at the Wilshire in the late 1970s. "Star-Studded Hotels Are as Different as Their Patrons," *Tampa Bay Times,* Aug. 26, 1979.

329 **Malone needed to introduce:** Malone, interview with author, March 9, 2020.

329 **It was Morris's job:** Morris, interview with author, Jan. 14, 2021.

329 **The plan for tomorrow:** The priest, the Reverend John D. Mulligan, died in 2004. The author interviewed all the other parties who took part in this meeting: Kenny, Malone, and Morris.

329 **typically went the same way:** Morris, interview with author, Jan. 14, 2021.

329 **checked in at a nearby hotel:** Malone, interview with author, March 9, 2020; Kenny, interview with author, Feb. 4, 2021.

330 **some advice for Kenny:** Malone, interview with author, March 9, 2020.

330 **hard for them to be useful:** "EPA Recalls Two Officials Held by Crowd," *BEN,* May 20, 1980.

330 **had been treated well:** Ibid.

330 **"it was amusing":** "Peaceful Vigil Resumed at Love Canal."

331 **"the wrong prisoners":** "EPA Recalls Two Officials Held by Crowd," *BEN,* May 20, 1980.

331 **reserved the right:** " 'Hostage' Prosecution Tied to Future Acts," *BEN,* May 20, 1980.

331 **accidentally pushed Quimby:** "Peaceful Vigil Resumed at Love Canal"; Gibbs, *Love Canal: My Story,* 155; Quimby, interview with author, Dec. 16, 2019.

331 **"I just want to be a housewife":** "Peaceful Vigil Resumed at Love Canal."

331 **As Missy played on the floor:** "Canalers Assail 16 Legislators," *BCE,* May 21, 1980.

331 **almost daring:** "Hope, Rumors, Lois Gibbs Keeps Homeowners Going," *BEN,* May 21, 1978.

331 **shouted at the legislators:** Details of Gibbs's outburst at the county meeting on May 20 come from multiple sources, including "Homeowners Vent Anger at Niagara Legislators," *BEN,* May 21, 1980; "Canalers Assail 16 Legislators" and "Mrs. Gibbs Booted Again and Again," *BCE,* May 21, 1980; Gibbs, *Love Canal: My Story,* 157; Liz Retton, interview with author, March 10, 2020.

332 **In a memo that day:** Watson to Carter, memo, May 20, 1980, Record Group 412, Love Canal Docket Hazardous Waste Enforcement Files, box 13, National Archives, College Park, Md.

52. WE'RE FROM NIAGARA FALLS

333 **The crowd cheered:** Details from the Occidental Petroleum shareholders' meeting held on May 21, 1980, come from multiple sources, including several news accounts: "Hammer Tells Nun to Go Back to Buffalo," *BCE,* May 22, 1980; "Occidental Increases Dividend," *LAT,* May 22, 1980; "Oxy Forum Kills Environmental Plan," *NG,* May 22, 1980; "Meeting Is Mirthful as Armand Hammer Marks His 82nd Year," *Wall Street Journal,* May 22, 1980; "Church Delegation Squelched at Occidental Stock Meeting," Religious News Service, May 19, 1980. Additional quotations and dialogue come from the Interfaith Center on Corporate Responsibility, "Report from the Occidental Petroleum Annual Shareholders' Meeting," May 27, 1980, and meeting transcript (hereafter referred to as ICCR report and transcript); Luella Kenny, "Statement to the Annual Meeting of Occidental Petroleum Shareholders—Corporate Responsibility Resolution"; and interviews with the three surviving speakers at the shareholders' meeting that day: Kenny, Malone, and Morris.

333 **his kind of place:** According to news accounts, Occidental held its shareholders' meeting at the Beverly Wilshire in 1979, 1978, and 1976, among other years.

333 **in a wheelchair:** Hammer appeared in a wheelchair, connected to a heart monitor, in March 1976, when pleading guilty to illegal campaign contributions to President Richard Nixon. But *The New York Times* later suggested that Hammer was just trying to avoid jail time because after receiving probation and a $3,000 fine, he "underwent a miraculous medical recovery."

333 **story of the rally:** "Hammer at 82 Sets Pace of Defiance," *LAT,* May 21, 1980.

334 **Sitting squarely in the middle:** Kenny, interview with author, Jan. 28, 2020; Malone, interview with author, March 9, 2020.

334 **birthday cake:** "Occidental Increases Dividend"; "Meeting Is Mirthful as Armand Hammer Marks His 82nd Year"; ICCR report and transcript.

334 **record sales:** "Occidental Increases Dividend"; "Meeting Is Mirthful as Armand Hammer Marks His 82nd Year."

334 **"a very sure touch":** Occidental Petroleum Annual Shareholders' Meeting 1980, p. 7, ICCR.

335 **He had no patience:** "Occidental Increases Dividend"; "Meeting Is Mirthful as Armand Hammer Marks His 82nd Year"; ICCR report and transcript.

335 **"Dr. Hammer":** ICCR report and transcript.

335 **dark circles:** Fran Lucca, "Channel 17 Reports: Love Canal Special," 1980.

335 **after midnight:** "Homeowners Vent Anger at Niagara Legislators."

335 **until around 1:30:** Gibbs, *Love Canal: My Story,* 158.

335 **agents took seriously:** FBI memo to the Special Agent in Charge, No. 9-1498, May 20, 1980.

336 **"It's their fault":** "Lawmakers Deal 2nd Snub to Love Canal Rescue Plan," *BCE,* May 21, 1980.

336 **parking lot:** Gibbs, *Love Canal: My Story,* 158.

336 **lead with the news:** Vanderbilt Television News Archive, May 21, 1980.

336 **refused to reveal:** Gibbs, *Love Canal: My Story,* 159.

336 **Blum was running late:** EPA Transcript of Proceedings, Press Briefing by Barbara Blum, May 21, 1980, Record Group 412, Love Canal Docket Hazardous Waste Enforcement Files, box 3, National Archives, College Park, Md.

337 **At around 12:05:** Accounts vary on the exact time but are within a few minutes of each other. This figure comes from Gibbs's memoir, *Love Canal: My Story,* 159.

337 **"the federal government":** This quotation, and all of the details about Blum's presentation, come directly from the transcript at the National Archives, referenced above.

337 **began to celebrate:** Details of the reaction come from multiple sources, including "Disaster Status Expected Next at Love Canal," *BEN,* May 21, 1980; "Love Canal Declared a Federal Emergency," *NG,* May 21, 1980; "Residents Hope 'Hoorays' Aren't Premature," *BCE,* May 22, 1980; "Gibbs Expects More Action from White House Soon," *RDC,* May 22, 1980; "President Orders Emergency Help for Love Canal," *NYT,* May 22, 1980; "Love

Canal Families to Be Relocated," *Washington Post,* May 22, 1980; archival television footage from Channel 17; and Gibbs, *Love Canal: My Story,* 160.

338 **"Get your family":** "Disaster Status Expected Next At Love Canal," *NG,* May 21, 1980.

338 **The mood in the room:** "Occidental Increases Dividend"; "Meeting Is Mirthful as Armand Hammer Marks His 82nd Year"; ICCR report and transcript.

338 **Morris demanded:** ICCR report and transcript.

338 **"May I finish?":** Ibid.

338 **stood at least:** Kenny, interview with author, Jan. 28, 2020.

339 **Malone was ceding the floor:** Kenny and Malone, interviews with author.

339 **"My name":** This quotation—and others from Kenny's speech—come from her written remarks. Kenny, "Statement to the Annual Meeting of Occidental Petroleum Shareholders—Corporate Responsibility Resolution."

340 **"We sympathize":** This—and other dialogue between Hammer and Kenny in this section—come from the ICCR report and transcript; "Meeting Is Mirthful as Armand Hammer Marks His 82nd Year"; and interviews with Kenny, Malone, and Morris. Anything in quotation marks comes directly from the transcript.

341 **cut Kenny's microphone:** Interviews with Kenny, Malone, and Morris; ICCR report and transcript.

342 **The poorest residents:** "Renters at Canal Protest Federal Plans," *NG,* May 22, 1980.

342 **still demanding:** Lucca, "Channel 17 Reports: Love Canal Special."

342 **Carey was complaining:** "Carey Pushes Carter on Canal Plan," *BEN,* May 24, 1980.

342 **shaking with anger:** *BCE,* May 22, 1980.

342 **already waiting:** Kenny, interview with author, Jan. 28, 2020.

342 **Roughly seventy families:** "Canal to Cost Another $80 Million," *BEN,* May 23, 1980.

343 **something more like home:** "Canal Families Urged to Seek 'Homes,' Not Motels," *BCE,* May 23, 1980.

343 **Later, much later:** Luella Kenny, interview with author, Jan. 28, 2020; Stephen Kenny, interview with author, April 9, 2020.

343 **score of the game:** The New York Yankees beat the Detroit Tigers, 13–5, May 26, 1980.

343 **The sun was shining:** Weather, *NYDN,* May 26–27, 1980.

EPILOGUE

345 **first day of October:** The details of Carter's visit to Niagara Falls come from multiple stories printed in the *Niagara Gazette, Buffalo Evening News,* and *Buffalo Courier-Express,* on Oct. 1–2, 1980, as well as the Presidential Daily Diary, Oct. 1, 1980, Jimmy Carter Presidential Library and Museum.

346 **"If somebody was":** Fran Lucca, "Channel 17 Reports: Love Canal Special," 1980.

346 **"A whole neighborhood":** LaFalce to Carter, June 20, 1980, Record Group 412, Love Canal Docket Hazardous Waste Enforcement Files, National Weather Service data, box 13, National Archives, College Park, Md.

347 **presciently pointed out:** "LaFalce, Moynihan Laud D.C. Decision," *BEN,* May 22, 1980.

347 **$74 million:** "Occidental Agrees to Pay $98 Million in Love Canal Case," *LAT,* June 22, 1994.

347 **$101 million:** "Occidental to Pay $129 Million in Love Canal Settlement," U.S. Department of Justice official statement, Dec. 21, 1995.

347 **dropped the Hooker name:** Michael H. Brown, "A Toxic Ghost Town," *Atlantic,* July 1989.

347 **"environmental liabilities":** "Occidental Agrees to Pay $98 Million in Love Canal Case."

347 **"He needs New York":** "Happy Falls Crowd Hails Carter," *BCE,* Oct. 2, 1980.

348 **"There is a difference":** "See How They Stand," *Charlotte Observer,* Nov. 2, 1980.

348 **"There is no reason":** "Endangered Superfund," *St. Louis Post-Dispatch,* Aug. 24, 1995.

349 **working-class families and people of color:** "Hazardous Homes," *Intercept,* Jan. 13, 2021; "Poisonous Homes: The Fight for Environmental Justice in Federally Assisted Housing," Shriver Center on Poverty Law, June 2020.

349 **childhood lead poisoning:** Heather Klemick, Henry Mason, and Karen Sullivan, "Superfund Cleanups and Children's Lead Exposure," *Journal of Environmental Economics and Management* 100 (March 2020).

349 **babies being born with birth defects:** "Protecting Taxpayers and Ensuring Accountability: Faster Superfund Cleanups for Healthier Communities," testimony before the U.S. Senate Committee on Environment and Public Works, June 10, 2014; Janet Currie, Michael Greenstone, and Enrico Moretti, "Superfund Cleanups and Infant Health," *American Economic Review* 101, no. 3 (May 2011).

349 **"Mother of the Superfund":** "The Lessons of Love Canal," *LAT,* Aug. 11, 1998.

349 **went on tour:** "Toxic Chemical Dump Foe Tours 'Love Canal West,'" *LAT,* July 16, 1980.

349 **roundly criticized:** "Love Canalers' Poor Tactic," *BCE,* May 21, 1980; "Love Canal Renters No Longer 'Invisible,'" *NG,* May 23, 1980.

349 **"she'd still be in jail now":** "Love Canal Renters No Longer 'Invisible.'"

350 **These days, Gibbs conceded:** Gibbs, interview with author, Feb. 9, 2021.

350 **"most clever tactician":** "WKBW Gets Program Chief from Indy."

350 **In television interviews:** "Crusader for the Love Canal Fights On," *LAT,* June 20, 1980.

350 **"mama, maker of peanut butter":** Ibid.

350 **"I miss your oatmeal cookies":** Napal to Gibbs and Quimby, telegram, May 22, 1980, box 6, telegrams folder, LGLC.

350 **sell the film rights:** "Insider TV," *LAT,* July 22, 1980.

350 **married in 1983:** Gibbs and Lester, interview with author, Feb. 18, 2020.

351 **"At some point":** "The Public, the News Media, and the Cult of Personality," *BCE,* Feb. 28, 1982.

351 **"Thank you, Lois Gibbs":** "Five Years After," *In These Times,* Feb. 23–Mar. 1, 1983, ICCR.

351 **"I believe Lois":** "Griffon Manor's President Feels Firm Stand Vindicated," *BCE,* May 22, 1980.

351 **"The American people":** "A Mother Defending Her Children Becomes the Heroine of Love Canal," *Chicago Tribune,* Feb. 15, 1982.

352 **dismissed the decision:** "Lawmaker Scoffs at Roswell Ruling on Harassment," *BCE,* June 4, 1980; "The Board vs. Dr. Paigen," *BCE,* June 5, 1980.

352 **Freedom of Information request:** In March 2020, the author filed a Freedom of Information request for all records related to Paigen's employment at Roswell Park and the investigation that followed. Nearly a year later, the state released three hundred pages of documents, many of them heavily redacted. New York State Department of Health, FOIL, #20-03-105.

353 **"We should discuss the scenario":** Nailor to Axelrod, memo, Jan. 2, 1980, Beverly Paigen files, 13307-86A, box 9, obtained via Freedom of Information request, New York State Archives.

353 **opening her mail:** Paigen made this allegation in several places over the years, including "Love Canal Researcher Details Harassment Charge," *BCE,* May 25, 1980; "Scientist Escapes Strife at Roswell by Moving to Calif.," *BCE,* April 20, 1982; Levine, *Love Canal: Science, Politics, and People,* 133; and in an interview with the author on Jan. 17, 2020.

353 **laid out their options:** David Paigen, interview with author, Jan. 29, 2021.

353 **"I've never harassed":** "Scientist Escapes Strife at Roswell By Moving to Calif.," *BCE,* April 20, 1982.

354 **"in which people see":** "Love Canal and Its Mixed Legacy," *NYT,* Nov. 25, 2013.

354 **In a 1984 study:** C. W. Heath Jr. et al., "Cytogenetic Findings in Persons Living near the Love Canal," *Journal of the American Medical Association* 251, no. 11 (1984).

354 **In 1983, she published:** "Study Cites Stunted Growth in Children of Love Canal," *St. Louis Post-Dispatch,* July 6, 1983; Beverly Paigen et al., "Growth of Children Living near the Hazardous Waste Site, Love Canal," *Human Biology* 59, no. 3 (June 1987).

354 **Two years later:** Beverly Paigen et al., "Prevalence of Health Problems in Children Living near Love Canal," *Hazardous Waste and Hazardous Materials* 2, no. 1 (Jan. 1985).

355 **sixty-two families:** "62 Families Remain at Love Canal," *Miami Herald,* Nov. 2, 1986.

355 **They lived in Griffon Manor:** By the mid-1980s, there were only about a dozen people still living in the public housing unit, and then the city cleared it out in order to tear it down. The buildings were finally razed in March 1989.

355 **September 1988:** Axelrod released the final decision in a forty-four-page report in late Sept. 1988 and then personally announced the findings in Niagara Falls. "Habitability Decision—Report on Habitability," New York State Department of Health, Sept. 27, 1988.

355 **little cheering:** "Axelrod Says 220 Love Canal Families Can Return," *NYT,* Sept. 28, 1988.

355 **massive stroke:** "Axelrod Hospitalized After Apparent Stroke," *Albany Times-Union,* Feb. 27, 1991.

355 **never truly recover:** "Dr. David Axelrod, Former State Health Chief, Dies at 59," *Albany Times-Union,* July 5, 1994.

355 **His wife had to resign:** "Search to Replace Axelrod Begins," *Albany Times-Union,* April 18, 1991.

355 **He died in 1994:** "David Axelrod, Health Chief Under Cuomo, Is Dead at 59," *NYT,* July 5, 1994.

355 **Her memory in that final year:** The author visited Paigen's house in Maine twice before her death in June 2020. These comments come from those two visits.

356 **"Four drawers":** Paigen, interview with author, Jan. 17, 2020.

356 **"what are you looking for?":** Paigen, interview with author, Feb. 12, 2020.

357 **"I give good tours":** Kenny, interview with author, Nov. 25, 2019.

357 **filed new lawsuits:** Between 2012 and 2014, more than a thousand people signed on to new lawsuits related to alleged Love Canal contamination after new chemicals were found in a sewer at Ninety-Seventh Street and Colvin Boulevard—right on the edge of the old canal. As of late 2020, nineteen of these lawsuits were still pending. "Federal Judge Dismisses a Love Canal Lawsuit, but 19 Others Still Remain," *Buffalo News,* Oct. 1, 2020.

357 **worried about the odd smells:** "Are Love Canal Chemicals Still Making People Sick?," *Buffalo News,* July 1, 2018.

357 **"Turn right over here":** These comments come from a driving tour of the old neighborhood that Kenny gave to the author on Jan. 28, 2020.

INDEX

Page numbers in *italics* refer to maps.
Page numbers followed by "n" indicate notes.